War, Economy and Society

1939–1945

Alan S. Milward

University of California Press
Berkeley and Los Angeles

University of California Press
Berkeley and Los Angeles

First Paperback Printing 1979
ISBN 0-520-03942-4
Library of Congress Catalog Card Number: 76-40823

Printed in the United States of America

5 6 7 8 9

History of the World Economy in the Twentieth Century
General Editor: Wolfram Fischer

Contents

List of Tables

Preface to the English Edition

When Professor Fischer asked me to write this book I decided at first against it because I was not sure that it was as yet possible to write an economic history of the Second World War. Having changed my mind and written it I think my first opinion was probably correct. Very little is known of the economic history of the Soviet Union or of Italy in this period. The history of other combatant powers often has to be culled from 'official' histories which could not be described as frank. Worst of all the Second World War is still the greatest statistical gap in the twentieth century. When considering the history of a long period the fact that for many countries there are four years of blanks in most important series is not crucial. But it means that for a history of the war itself the basic statistical information is missing more often than not. I chose my own way out of this situation by writing at greater length about the subjects which have been explored in more depth. And in those areas where it is still only possible to purvey half-truths because so little scholarly research has been done I have purveyed them as quietly and unobtrusively as permissible.

In surrendering, Germany and Japan bared all their secrets. The victors exposed theirs in a more discreetly titillating way in a great many volumes of official publications. Although the quality of these volumes is occasionally high the more usual style is to combine intellectual blandness with a frenzied interest in the details of civil and military administration. There remains therefore a considerable task of research, for the Second World War was a war over the future nature of the European economy and body politic and perhaps over those of Asia too. We still live in the long shadow cast by these decisions and we ought to try to take its measure. I hope this book will stimulate more research into its darker patches.

If there are any as infuriated as myself by the seemingly countless works on military history in which armies and navies come and go, commanded by greater or lesser figures deciding momentous historical issues, and nothing is said of the real productive forces which alone give such events meaning or, indeed, make them possible, they will surely sympathize with my attempt to simplify history by looking at the war as an economic event. But it has meant that two major combatant powers, the Soviet Union and Italy, get far less than their fair share of the book. There are now, it seems, 15,000 Russian volumes on the Second World War; never were so many questions left unasked and unanswered by so many. But this book, however imperfect, must now take the field against the huge and ponderous armies of all other kinds of histories of the war. Faced with such numerous opposing forces the only sane tactic was to ignore most of them, and this book does that.

The English edition has been considerably altered from the original German edition. Delay in publishing in English has allowed me in several places to incorporate some of the latest research. The last chapter has been almost completely changed, partly to fit in with the suggestions made by the publishers and partly because my own ideas changed.

Most of those whose work I have drawn on are still young enough to see where I have followed their trails. There is no space in such a work for the just number of footnotes and rather than overload the text with references I have simply tried to indicate to the reader firstly the places where I have been most dependent on the work of others and secondly where the themes handled are developed further in other books. I hope that those who recognize their own research will be content with what is often one solitary acknowledgement. That or a large number of footnotes on almost every page were the only fair alternatives.

My wife made the book less pompous and mediocre than the original draft, but the influence of universities on the author was too much to overcome. One other person made the book possible, Mrs Christine Clarke, whose patient humour and qualities of organization meant that it was finished and typed. The final version would have been much less satisfactory without the wise editorial help of Professor Wolfram Fischer. Those who deserve the greatest acknowledgement, however, are those who deserved so much more of me while I was escaping into these abstractions. My warmest thanks go to all my friends who did not write me off as lost, and above all it is to you, Claudine, Ada and Maya, that this book is especially offered, a poor recompense.

Les batailles gagnées où l'on ne tue que des hommes, sans causer d'autres dommages, affaiblissent peu l'ennemi, si le salaire des hommes qu'il a perdu lui reste, et s'il est suffisant pour attirer d'autres hommes. Une armée de cent mille hommes bien payés est un armée d'un million d'hommes; car toute armée où la solde attire des hommes ne peut être détruite: c'est alors aux soldats à se défendre courageusement; ce sont eux qui ont le plus à perdre, car ils ne manqueront pas de successeurs bien déterminés à affronter les dangers de la guerre. C'est donc la richesse qui soutient l'honneur des armes. Le héros qui gagne des batailles, qui prend des villes, qui acquiert de la gloire, et qui est le plus tôt épuisé, n'est pas le conquérant. L'historien, qui se borne au merveilleux dans le récit des exploits militaires, instruit peu la postérité sur les succès des évènements décisifs des guerres, s'il lui laisse ignorer l'état des forces fondamentales et de la politique des nations dont il écrit l'histoire; car c'est dans l'aisance permanente de la partie contribuable des nations et non dans les vertus patriotiques que consiste la puissance permanente des États.

[Those victorious battles in which only men are killed without causing any other damage weaken the enemy little if the pay of the men he has lost remains and is sufficient to attract other men. An army of one hundred thousand well-paid men is an army a million strong, for an army to which men are attracted by pay cannot be destroyed: it is then up to the soldiers to defend themselves bravely; it is they who have most to lose for there will be no lack of replacements determined to face the perils of war. It is therefore wealth which upholds the honour of armies. The hero who wins battles, captures towns, acquires glory and is soonest exhausted is not the conqueror. The historian who limits himself to relating the wonders of military feats does little to inform posterity of the issue of decisive events in wars if he keeps it in ignorance of the state of the fundamental forces and of the politics of the nations the history of which he writes; for it is in the constant affluence of a country's taxpayers, not in patriotic virtues that the permanent power of the state is to be found.]

F. Quesnay, *Maximes générales du gouvernement économique d'un royaume agricole et notes sur ces maximes*, xxvi, 1758

1   War as Policy

> For Warre, consisteth not in Battell onely, or the act of fighting;
> but in a tract of time, wherein the will to contend by Battell is
> sufficiently known: and therefore the notion of Time, is to be
> considered in the nature of Warre; as it is in the nature of
> Weather. For as the nature of Foule weather, lyeth not in a
> showre or two of rain; but in an inclination thereto of many
> days together: So the nature of Warre, consisteth not in actuall
> fighting; but in the known disposition thereto, during all the
> time there is no assurance to the contrary. All other time is
> Peace.
>
> Thomas Hobbes,
> *Leviathan*, 1651

There are two commonly accepted ideas about war which have
little foundation in history. One is that war is an abnormality.
The other is that with the passage of time warfare has become
costlier and deadlier. The first of these ideas established itself in
the eighteenth century, when the theory of natural law was used
to demonstrate that peace was a logical deduction from the
material laws governing the universe or, sometimes, from the
psychological laws governing mankind. The second of these ideas
came to reinforce the first, which might otherwise have been
weakened by the weight of contrary evidence, towards the end of
the nineteenth century. The historical record of that century had
not been such as to substantiate the logical deductions of
eighteenth-century philosophy, for it was a century of unremitting
warfare. But after 1850 a large body of economic literature began
to reconcile agreeable predictions with unpleasant facts by demon-
strating that in spite of the prevalence of warfare it would eventually
cease to be a viable economic policy because it would price itself
out of the market, a process which, it was agreed, had already begun.

Neither of these ideas has ever been completely accepted by
economists but their influence on economic theory has been so
powerful as to focus the operation of a substantial body of that
theory on to the workings of a peacetime economy only. In spite

of the fact that the world has practically never been at peace since the eighteenth century peace has usually been seen as the state of affairs most conducive to the achievement of economic aims and the one which economic theory seeks to analyse and illuminate. In the early nineteenth century, indeed, it was seen as the goal to which economic theory tended.

The frequency of war is in itself the best argument against accepting the idea of its abnormality. The second idea, that war has become more costly, is based less on a refusal to consider history than on a mistaken simplification of it. It was an idea which first gained wide credence with the development of more complicated technologies. War itself was an important stimulus to technological development in many industries in the late nineteenth century such as shipbuilding, the manufacture of steel plate and the development of machine tools. The construction of complex weapons which could only be manufactured by states at a high level of economic development seemed to change the economic possibilities of war. The first heavily armed steel battleships only narrowly preceded the adaptation of the internal combustion engine to military and then to aerial use, and these new armaments coincided with a period of enormous and growing standing armies. The productive capacities which economic development had placed in the hands of developed economies raised prospects of warfare on an absolute scale of cost and deadliness never before conceived. And these prospects in themselves seemed to indicate the economic mechanism by which war would disappear after its rather disappointing persistence in the nineteenth century. These ideas were succinctly expressed by de Molinari, one of the few economists who tried to integrate the existence of war into classical economic theory.

> Can the profits of war still cover its cost? The history of all wars which have occurred between civilized peoples for a number of centuries attests that these costs have progressively grown, and, finally that any war between members of the civilized community today costs the victorious nation more than it can possibly yield it.[1]

In the half century after de Molinari so firmly expressed his opinion there were two world wars, each of a far higher absolute

1. M. G. de Molinari, *Comment se résoudra la question sociale?*, Guillaumin, Paris, 1896, p. 126.

cost and each responsible for greater destruction than any previous war. There is, to say the least, circumstantial evidence that de Molinari's judgement was a superficial one and that nations did not continue to go to war merely because they were ignorant of what had become its real economic consequences. War not only continued to meet the social, political and economic circumstances of states but, furthermore, as an instrument of policy, it remained, in some circumstances, economically viable. War remains a policy and investment decision by the state and there seem to be numerous modern examples of its having been a correct and successful decision. The most destructive of modern technologies have not changed this state of affairs. Their deployment by those states sufficiently highly developed economically to possess them is limited by the rarity of satisfactory strategic opportunity. The strategic synthesis by which the Vietnam war was conducted on the American side, for example, is very like the rational decisions frequently taken by all combatants in the First World War against the use of poison gas. The existence of the most costly and murderous armaments does not mean that they will be appropriate or even usable in any particular war, much less that all combinations of combatants will possess them.

The question of the economic cost of war is not one of absolutes. The cost and the effectiveness of a long-range bomber at the present time must be seen in relation to that of a long-range warship in the eighteenth century and both seen in relation to the growth of national product since the eighteenth century. In each case we are dealing with the summation of many different technological developments, and the armament itself is in each of these cases pre-eminently the expression of an extremely high relative level of economic development. The meaningful question is whether the cost of war has absorbed an increasing proportion of the increasing Gross National Products of the combatants. As an economic choice war, measured in this way, has not shown any discernible long-term trend towards greater costliness. As for its deadliness, the loss of human life is but one element in the estimation of cost. There are no humane wars, and where the economic cost of the war can be lowered by substituting labour for capital on the battlefield such a choice would be a rational one. It has been often made. The size of the Russian armies in the First World War reflected the low cost of obtaining and maintaining a Russian soldier and was intended to remedy the Russian deficiencies in more expensive capital equipment. It may be argued that modern technology changes the analysis because it offers the possibility of near-to-total destruction of the complete human and capital stock of the enemy. But numerous societies were so destroyed in the past by sword, fire and pillage and, more appositely, by primitive guns and gunpowder. The possibility of making a deliberate choice of war as economic policy has existed since the late eighteenth century and exists still.

The origins of the Second World War lay in the deliberate choice of warfare as an instrument of policy by two of the most economically developed states. Far from having economic reservations about warfare as policy, both the German and Japanese governments were influenced in their decisions for war by the conviction that war might be an instrument of economic gain. Although economic considerations were in neither case prime reasons in the decision to fight, both governments held a firmly optimistic conviction that war could be used to solve some of their more long-term economic difficulties. Instead of shouldering the economic burden of war with the leaden and apprehensive reluctance of necessity, like their opponents, both governments kept their eyes firmly fixed on the short-term social and economic benefits which might accrue from a successful war while it was being fought, as well as on the long-term benefits of victory. In making such a choice the ruling élites in both countries were governed by the difference between their own political and economic ideas and those of their opponents. The government of Italy had already made a similar choice when it had attacked Ethiopia.

This difference in economic attitudes to warfare was partly attributable to the influence of fascist political ideas. Because these ideas were also of some importance in the formulation of Axis strategy and in the economic and social policies pursued by the German occupying forces it is necessary briefly to consider some of their aspects here in so far as they relate to the themes considered in this book. Whether the National Socialist government in Germany and the Italian Fascist party are properly to be bracketed together as fascist governments and indeed whether the word fascist itself has any accurate meaning as a definition of a set of precise political and economic attitudes are complicated questions which cannot be discussed here.[2] Although the Japanese government had few hesitations in using war as an instrument of political and economic policy there is no meaningful definition of the word fascist which can include the ruling élites in Japan. There was a small political group in that country whose political ideas resembled those of the Fascists and the National Socialists but they had practically no influence in the Home Islands although they did influence the policy of the Japanese military government in Manchuria.[3] But for the German and Italian rulers war had a deeper and more positive social purpose and this was related to certain shared ideas. Whether the word fascism is a useful description of the affinities of political outlook between the Italian and German governments is less important than the fact that this affinity existed and extended into many areas of political and economic life. The differences between National Socialism in Germany and Fascism in Italy partly consisted, in fact, of the more unhesitating acceptance of the ideas of Italian Fascism by the National Socialist party and the linking of these ideas to conceptions of racial purity.

The basis of Fascist and National Socialist political and economic thought was the rejection of the ideas of the eighteenth-century Enlightenment. In the submergence of the individual will in common instinctive action, which warfare represented, rational doubts and vacillations, which were regarded as a trauma on human society produced by the Enlightenment, could be suppressed. War was seen as an instrument for the healing of this trauma and for the restoration of human society to its pristine state. Both Hitler and Mussolini, whose writings in general not only subscribed to but advanced the political ideas of fascism, referred to war constantly in this vein, seeing it as a powerful instrument for forging a new and more wholesome political society. 'Fascism', wrote Mussolini,

the more it considers and observes the future and the development of humanity, quite apart from the political considerations

2. The reader is referred for a recent, short and relatively unbiased discussion of these issues to W. Wippermann, *Faschismustheorien. Zum Stand der gegenwärtigen Diskussion*, Wissenschaftliche Buchgesellschaft, Darmstadt, 1972.

3. G. M. Wilson, 'A New Look at the Problem of "Japanese Fascism"', in *Comparative Studies in Society and History*, no. 10, 1968.

of the moment, believes neither in the possibility nor the utility of perpetual peace. . . . War alone brings up to its highest tension all human energy and puts the stamp of nobility upon the peoples who have the courage to meet it.[4]

Hitler similarly wrote and spoke of war and preparation for war as an instrument for the spiritual renewal of the German people, a device for eliminating the corrupting egotistical self-seeking which he saw as the concomitant of false ideas of human liberty, progress and democracy. The basis of existence in Hitler's view was a struggle of the strong for mastery and war was thus an inescapable, necessary aspect of the human condition.[5]

What made this not uncommon viewpoint especially dangerous and what gave to the Second World War its unique characteristic of a war for the political and economic destiny of the whole European continent was the way in which the ideas of fascism were developed by Hitler and the theorists of the National Socialist party. The wound that had been inflicted on European civilization could, they argued, only be healed by a process of spiritual regeneration. That process of regeneration must begin from the small surviving still uncorrupted élite. But politics was not a matter of debate and persuasion but of the instinctive recognition of social obligations, community ideas which were held to be carried not in the brain but in the blood. The élite was also a racial élite and the restoration of the lost European civilization was also a search for a lost racial purity. The nationalist conceptions of race had been derived from the rational mainstream of European politics. What now replaced them was an irrational concept of racial purity as the last hope for the salvation of European society.[6]

Within Germany, the National Socialist party from its earliest days had identified those of Jewish race as the source of corrup-

4. Quoted in W. G. Welk, *Fascist Economic Policy. An Analysis of Italy's Economic Experiment* (Harvard Economic Studies, no. 62), Harvard University Press, Cambridge, Mass., 1938, p. 190.

5. The connections between Hitler's political thought and his strategy are developed in an interesting way by E. Jäckel, *Hitlers Weltanschauung. Entwurf einer Herrschaft*, Rainer Wunderlich Verlag Hermann Leins, Tübingen, 1969.

6. The most comprehensive discussion remains A. Kolnai's *The War against the West* (Gollancz, London, 1938), but E. Weber, in *Varieties of Fascism, Doctrines of Revolution in the Twentieth Century* (Van Nostrand, Princeton, 1964), draws out the further implications of these ideas.

tion and racial pollution. But it was scarcely possible that the 'problem' of the German Jews could be solved as an entirely domestic issue. The spiritual regeneration of Germany and, through Germany, the continent, also required a great extension of Germany's territorial area – *Lebensraum*. This area had to be sufficiently large to enable Germany militarily to play the role of a great power and to impose her will on the rest of the continent and perhaps on an even wider front. This expansion could also take the form of the destruction of what was seen as the last and most dangerous of all the European political heresies, communism and the Soviet state. The need to achieve these goals and the messianic urgency of the political programme of National Socialism meant that war was an unavoidable part of Hitler's plans.

But it was not the intellectual antagonism to communism which determined that the ultimate target of Germany's territorial expansion should be the Ukraine. That choice was more determined by economic considerations. The task of materially and spiritually rearming the German people had meant that Germany after 1933 pursued an economic policy radically different from that of other European states. A high level of state expenditure, of which military expenditure, before 1936, was a minor part, had sharply differentiated the behaviour of the German economy from that of the other major powers. The maintenance of high levels of production and full employment in a depressed international environment had necessitated an extensive battery of economic controls which had increasingly isolated the economy. After 1936 when expenditure for military purposes was increased to still higher levels there was no longer any possibility that the German economy might come back, by means of a devaluation, into a more liberal international payments and trading system. Rather, the political decisions of 1936 made it certain that trade, exchange, price and wage controls would become more drastic and more comprehensive, and the German economy more insulated from the influence of the other major economies. This was particularly so because of the large volume of investment allocated in the Four-Year Plan to the production, at prices well above prevailing world prices, of materials of vital strategic importance, such as synthetic fuel, rubber and aluminium.[7]

7. The best account is D. Petzina's *Autarkiepolitik im Dritten Reich. Der*

The National Socialist party did not support the idea of restoring the liberal international order of the gold exchange standard. But neither did they have any clear positive alternative ideas. Economic policy was dictated by political expediency and each successive stage of controls was introduced to cope with crises as they arose. Nevertheless the political ideas of National Socialism favoured an autarkic as opposed to a liberal economic order and it was not difficult to justify the apparatus of economic controls as a necessary and beneficial aspect of the National Socialist state. The international aspects of the controlled economy – exchange controls and bilateral trading treaties – could readily be assimilated to an expansionist foreign policy. Indeed Hitler himself regarded a greater degree of self-sufficiency of the German economy as a necessity if he were to have the liberty of strategic action which he desired, and also as a justification of his policy of territorial expansion. The memory of the effectiveness of the Allied naval blockade during the First World War, when Germany had controlled a much larger resource base than was left to her after the Treaty of Versailles, strengthened this line of thought.

National Socialism elaborated its own theory to justify international economic policies which were in fact only the outcome of a set of domestic economic decisions which had been accorded priority over all international aspects. This was the theory of *Grossraumwirtschaft* (the economics of large areas). Although it was only a rhetorical justification after the event of economic necessities, it also played its part in the formulation of strategy and economic policy. On the basis of these economic ideas, it was hoped that the war would bring tangible economic gain, rather than the more spiritual benefits of a transformation of civilization. At an early stage in his political career, Hitler had come to the conclusion that the Ukraine was economically indispensable to Germany if she was to be, in any worthwhile sense, independent of the international economy and thus free to function as a great power. As the insulation of the German economy from the international economy became more complete in the 1930s the economic relationship of Germany to the whole of the continent came to be reconsidered, and National Socialist writers were

nationalsozialistische Vierjahresplan (Schriftenreihe der *Vj.f.Z.*, no. 16, Deutsche Verlags-Anstalt, Stuttgart, 1968).

advocating not merely a political and racial reconstruction of Europe but an economic reconstruction as well.

National Socialist economists argued that the international depression of 1929 to 1933 had brought the 'liberal' phase of economic development, associated with diminishing tariffs and an increasing volume of international trade, to an end. On the other hand, the extent to which the developed economies of Europe still depended on access to raw materials had not diminished. They argued that the epoch of the economic unit of the national state, itself the creation of liberalism, was past, and must be replaced by the concept of large areas (*Grossräume*) which had a classifiable economic and geographical unity. Such areas provided a larger market at a time of failing demand and could also satisfy that demand from their own production and resources. Improving employment levels and increasing *per capita* incomes depended therefore, not on a recovery in international trade, which could only in any case be temporary and inadequate, but on a re-ordering of the map of the world into larger 'natural' economic areas. The United States and the Soviet Union each represented such an area. Germany too had its own 'larger economic area' which it must claim.[8]

The future economy of this area would be distinguished by its autarkic nature. The international division of labour would be modified into specialization of function within each *Grossraum*. Germany would be the manufacturing heartland of its own area, together with its bordering industrial areas of north-eastern France, Belgium and Bohemia. The peripheral areas would supply raw materials and foodstuffs to the developed industrial core.

There were close links between these economic ideas and the political and racial ones. Such large areas were considered to have a racial unity in the sense that central Europe was developed because of the racial superiority of its inhabitants, the 'Aryans'; the periphery would always be the supplier of raw materials

8. Typical of this line of argument are, F. Fried, *Die Zukunft des Welt-handels*, Knorr und Hirth, Munich, 1941; R. W. Krugmann, *Südosteuropa und Grossdeutschland. Entwicklung und Zukunftsmöligchkeiten der Wirtschafts-beziehungen*, Breslauer Verlag, Breslau, 1939; H. Marschner, ed., *Deutschland in der Wirtschaft der Welt*, Deutscher Verlag für Politik und Wirtschaft, Berlin, 1937; J. Splettstoesser, *Der deutsche Wirtschaftsraum im Osten*, Limpert, Berlin, 1939; H. F. Zeck, *Die deutsche Wirtschaft und Südosteuropa*, Teubner, Leipzig, 1939.

because its population was racially unsuitable for any more
sophisticated economic activity.[9] For a time it seemed that
Germany might create her *Grossraumwirtschaft* and dominate
international economic exchanges in Europe through peaceful
means; a series of trade agreements was signed between Germany
and the underdeveloped countries of south-eastern Europe after
1933. Germany was able to get better terms in bilateral trading
from these lands than from more developed European economies
who were able to threaten, and even, like Britain, to carry out
the threat, to sequestrate German balances in order to force
Germany to pay at once on her own (import) side of the clearing
balance, and German trade with south-eastern Europe increased
in relation to the rest of German and world trade in the thirties.
But German–Russian trade after 1933 became insignificant and
it was clear that a re-ordering of Europe's frontiers to correspond
with Germany's economic ambitions would ultimately have to
involve large areas of Russian territory. South-eastern Europe,
without Russia, could make only a very limited contribution to
emancipating Germany from her worldwide network of imports.
A war against the Soviet Union seemed to be the necessary
vehicle for political and economic gain.

Many scholars, particularly in the Soviet Union and eastern
Europe, maintain that there was a further economic dimension
to German policy and that the Second World War represented an
even more fundamental clash over the economic and social destiny
of the continent. Although the definition of faccism in Marxist
analysis has varied greatly with time and place it has nevertheless
been more consistent than definitions made from other standpoints. The tendency has been to represent it as the political
expression of the control of 'state-monopoly capital' over the
economy. It is seen as a stage of capitalism in decline, when it can
survive only by a brutal and determined imperialism and through
a monopolistic control over domestic and foreign markets by the
bigger capitalist firms backed by the government. The changes in
the German economy after 1933 are explained as following these
lines: the readiness to go to war by the bigger profits it might
bring and also by the ultimate necessity for an imperialist domination of other economies. Warfare, it is argued, had become an

9. W. Daitz, *Der Weg zur völkischen Wirtschaft und zur europäischen
Grossraumwirtschaft*, Meinhold, Dresden, 1938.

economic necessity for Germany and its ultimate purpose was the preservation of state capitalism, for which both territorial expansion and the destruction of the communist state were essential. The argument is succinctly put by Eichholtz:

> Towards the close of the twenties Germany stood once more in the ranks of the most developed and economically advanced of the imperialist powers. The strength and aggression necessary for expansion grew with the development of her economic strength. German imperialism was an imperialism which had been deprived of colonies, an imperialism whose development was limited by the financial burdens stemming from the war and by the limitations and controls, onerous to the monopolies, which the victorious powers had imposed, especially on armaments, finances, etc. On that account extreme nationalism and chauvinism were characteristic of the development of the fascist movement in Germany from the start; once in power fascism maintained from its first days an overweening purposeful imperialistic aggression – which had been obvious for a long time – towards the outside world. With fascism a ruling form of state monopoly capital had been created which aimed at overcoming the crisis of capitalism by domestic terror and, externally, by dividing the world anew.[10]

Such a theory offers not merely a serious economic explanation of the war but also implies that the most fundamental causes of the war were economic. The major German firms, it is argued, had definite plans to gain from a war of aggression and supported the National Socialist government in many of its economic aims.

Thus the results of research on the period immediately preceding the war, although still fragmentary, already show that German monopoly capital was pursuing a large and complex programme of war aims to extend its domination over Europe and over the world. The kernel of this programme was the destruction of the Soviet Union. Two main aims of war and expansion united the Hitler clique and all important monopolies and monopoly groups from the beginning: the 'dismantling of Versailles' and the 'seizure of a new living space (*Lebensraum*) in the east'. By the 'dismantling of Versailles' the monopolies understood, as they often expressed it later, the 'recapture' of all the economic and political positions which had been lost and the 'restitution' of all the damage to the sources of profit and monopoly situations which the Versailles system had inflicted on them. As an immediate step they

10. D. Eichholtz, *Geschichte der deutschen Kriegswirtschaft, 1939–1945,* vol. 1, 1939–1941, Akademie-Verlag, Berlin, 1969, p. 1.

planned to overrun the Soviet Union, to liquidate it and appropriate its immeasurable riches to themselves, and to erect a European 'economy of large areas' (*Grossraumwirtschaft*), if possible in conjunction with a huge African colonial empire.[11]

How the *Grossraumwirtschaft* eventually functioned in practice will be examined later. But as far as pre-war plans were concerned it was a concept which attracted sympathy and support from certain business circles in Germany. Some German firms were able to benefit from the government's drive towards a greater level of autarky and hoped to expand their new interests to the limits of the future frontiers of the Reich. This was true, in spite of its extensive extra-European connections, of the large chemical cartel, I. G. Farben. Its profits increasingly came from the massive state investment in synthetic petrol and synthetic rubber production. Several of its important executives had high rank in the Four-Year Plan Organization which was entrusted with these developments, and the company had plans ready in the event of an expansion of German power over other European states.[12] These plans stemmed in part from the German trade drive into south-eastern Europe after 1933 and the consequent penetration of German capital into that region, but there were also unambiguous proposals, some part of which were later put into effect, to recapture the supremacy of the German dyestuffs industry in France, which had been lost as a result of the First World War.[13] Nor was this the only such firm with similar plans prepared.[14] Other firms regarded the expansionist foreign policy as a possible way of securing supplies of raw materials. Such was the case with the non-ferrous metal company, Mansfeld, and with the aluminium companies, who understandably were able to get a very high level of priority because of the great importance of aluminium for aircraft manufacture and the power which the Air Ministry exercised in the German government.[15]

11. D. Eichholtz, *Geschichte*, p. 63.

12. D. Eichholtz, *Geschichte*, p. 248 ff.; H. Radandt, 'Die I G Farben-industrie und Südosteuropa 1938 bis zum Ende des zweiten Weltkriegs', in *Jahrbuch für Wirtschaftsgeschichte*, no. 1, 1967.

13. A. S. Milward, *The New Order and the French Economy*, Oxford University Press, London, 1970, p. 100 ff.

14. W. Schumann, 'Das Kriegsprogramm des Zeiss-Konzerns', in *Zeitschrift für Geschichtswissenschaft*, no. 11, 1963.

15. H. Radandt, *Kriegsverbrecherkonzern Mansfeld. Die Rolle des Mansfeld-*

However, the support for the National Socialist party came in large measure from a section of the population whose political sympathies were in many ways antipathetic to the world of big business. It drew its support from a protest against the apparently inexorably increasing power both of organized labour and of organized business. Its urban support came mainly from the lower income groups of the middle classes, such as clerical workers, artisans and shopkeepers, and was combined with massive rural support in Protestant areas after 1931. This support was maintained by a persistent anti-capitalist rhetoric but also by a certain amount of legislation which cannot by any shift of argument be explained by a theory which assumes National Socialism to be a stage of state capitalism. Attempts to establish hereditary inalienable peasant tenures, to show favour to artisan enterprises, to restrict the size of retail firms, to restrict the movement of labour out of the agricultural sector, all of which were futile in the face of a massive state investment in reflation which produced a rapid rate of growth of Gross National Product, show the curious ambivalence of National Socialist economic attitudes.[16] On the whole such legislation did little to affect the profits which accrued to the business world in Germany after 1933, some part of which came also from the severe controls on money wages and the destruction of the organized labour movements. But the National Socialist movement kept its inner momentum, which was driving towards a different horizon from that of the business world, a horizon both more distant and more frightening. It was in some ways a movement of protest against modern economic development and became a centre of allegiance for all who were displaced and uprooted by the merciless and seemingly ungovernable swings of the German economy after 1918. National Socialism was as much a yearning for a stable utopia of the past as a close alliance between major capital interests and an authoritarian government.

Konzerns bei der Vorbereitung und während des zweiten Weltkriegs (Geschichte der Fabriken und Werke, vol. 3), Akademie-Verlag, Berlin, 1957; A. S. Milward, *The Fascist Economy in Norway*, Clarendon Press, Oxford, 1972, p. 86.

16. They are well described in D. Schoenbaum's *Hitler's Social Revolution: Class and Status in Nazi Germany 1933–1939* (Weidenfeld & Nicolson, London, 1966).

These fundamental economic contradictions and tensions within the movement could only be exacerbated, not resolved, by a war of expansion. The idea – held in some conservative nationalist German business circles – that Germany must eventually dominate the exchanges of the continent if her economy was to find a lasting equilibrium, had a lineage dating from the 1890s and had found some expression in economic policy during the First World War.[17] The theory of *Grossraumwirtschaft* was only a reformulation of these ideas in terms of National Socialist foreign policy. The much more radical idea of a social and racial reconstruction of European society – accepted by some parts of the National Socialist movement – ran directly counter to it, and raised the possibility of a Europe where the 'business climate' would, to say the least, have been unpropitious.

Although, therefore, the German government in choosing war as an instrument of policy was anticipating an economic gain from that choice, it was by no means clear as to the nature of the anticipated gain. It has been argued that it was the irreconcilable contradictions in the National Socialist economy which finally made a war to acquire more resources (*ein Raubkrieg*) the only way out, and that the invasion of Poland was the last desperate attempt to sustain the Nazi economy.[18] But it is hard to make out a case that the Nazi economy was in a greater state of crisis in the autumn of 1939 than it had been on previous occasions particularly in 1936. Most of the problems which existed in 1939 had existed from the moment full employment had been reached, and some of them, on any calculation, could only be made worse by a war – as indeed they were.

In Italy there were episodes in the 1930s when foreign and economic policy seemed to be directed towards the creation of an Italian *Grossraumwirtschaft* in Europe as a solution to Italy's economic problems. But in the face of the powerful expansion of German trade in the south-east such aspirations were unattainable. In Italy, also, there were attempts at creating by pro-

17. The history is traced by J. Freymond, *Le IIIe Reich et la réorganisation économique de l'Europe 1940–1942: origines et projets* (Institut Universitaire de Hautes Etudes, Geneva, Collection de Relations Internationales, 3), Sithoff, Leiden, 1974.

18. T. W. Mason, 'Innere Krise und Angriffskrieg 1938/1939', in F. Forstmeier and H. E. Volkmann (eds.), *Wirtschaft und Rüstung am Vorabend des zweiten Weltkrieges*, Droste, Düsseldorf, 1975.

tection and subsidy synthetic industries which might prove strategically necessary in war. But there was little resemblance between these tendencies and the full-scale politico-economic ambitions of Germany. If the Italian government viewed war as a desirable instrument of policy it did not contemplate a serious and prolonged European war and made no adequate preparations for one.

In Japan, however, the choice in favour of war was based on economic considerations which had a certain similarity to those of Germany. It lacked the radical social and racial implications but it was assumed that investment in a war which was strategically well-conceived would bring a substantial accretion to Japan's economic strength. The Japanese government hoped to establish a zone of economic domination which, under the influence of German policy, it dignified by the title 'Co-Prosperity Sphere'. As an economic bloc its trading arrangements would be like those of the *Grossraumwirtschaft*, a manufacturing core supplied by a periphery of raw-material suppliers.[19] If the Co-Prosperity Sphere was to be created in the full extent that would guarantee a satisfactory level of economic self-sufficiency, war and conquest would be necessary. Germany's decision for war and early victories over the colonial powers gave Japan the opportunity to establish a zone of domination by military force while her potential opponents were preoccupied with other dangers. After the initial successes the boundaries of the Co-Prosperity Sphere were widened to include a more distant periphery, a decision which had serious strategic consequences, but the original Japanese war aims represented a positive and realistic attempt at the economic reconstruction of her own economic area in her own interests. All the peripheral areas produced raw materials and foodstuffs and semi-manufactures which were imported in large quantities into Japan; rice from Korea, iron ore, coal and foodstuffs from Manchuria, coal and cotton from Jehol, oil and bauxite from the Netherlands East Indies, tin and rubber from Malaya and sugar from Formosa. The variety of commodities and the scope for further developments in the future made the Co-Prosperity

19. F. C. Jones, *Japan's New Order in East Asia; Its Rise and Fall, 1937–45*, Oxford University Press, London, 1954; M. Libal, *Japans Weg in den Krieg. Die Aussenpolitik der Kabinette Konoye 1940–41*, Droste-Verlag, Düsseldorf, 1971.

Sphere potentially more economically viable and more economically realistic than a European *Grossraumwirtschaft* still heavily dependent on certain vital imports.[20] The Japanese decision for war, like the German, was taken under the persuasion that in Japan's situation, given the correct timing and strategy, war would be economically beneficial.

Of course such plans could only have been formulated where a harshly illiberal outlook on the problems of international economic and political relationships prevailed. But in the government circles of Japan proper the ready acceptance of war had no ideological connotations beyond this generally prevailing political attitude of mind. The major influence on the Japanese decision for war was the strategic conjuncture; with German military successes in Europe, the pressure on the European empires in the Pacific became unbearable and this in turn intensified the strategic dilemma of the United States. If Japan's ambitions were to be achieved it seemed that the opportune moment had arrived.

The probable and possible opponents of the Axis powers viewed this bellicosity with dismay. In these countries the First World War and its aftermath were seen as an economic disaster. Consequently the main problem of a future war, if it had to be fought, was thought to be that of avoiding a similar disaster. The components of that disaster were seen as a heavy loss of human beings and capital, acute and prolonged inflation, profound social unrest, and almost insuperable problems, both domestic and international, of economic readjustment once peace was restored. It was almost universally believed that the unavoidable aftermath of a major war would be a short restocking boom followed by worldwide depression and unemployment. When the *American Economic Review* devoted a special issue in 1940 to a consideration of the economic problems of war the problem of post-war readjustment was regarded by all contributors as the most serious and unavoidable. That the major economies after 1945 would experience a most remarkable period of stability and economic growth was an outcome which was quite unforeseen and unpredicted. The western European powers and the United States were as much the prisoners of their resigned pessimism about the unavoidable economic losses of war as Germany and Japan were the

20. J. R. Cohen, *Japan's Economy in War and Reconstruction*, University of Minnesota Press, Minneapolis, 1949, p. 7.

prisoners of their delusions about its possible economic advantages. In fact the economic experience of the First World War had been for all combatants a chequered one. The First World War had not been a cause of unalloyed economic loss; it had on occasions brought economic and social advantages. What is more it had demonstrated to all the combatant powers that it lay in the hands of government to formulate strategic and economic policies which could to some extent determine whether or not a war would be economically a cause of gain or loss; they were not the hopeless prisoners of circumstance. The extreme importance of what governments had learned of their own potential in this way during the 1914-18 war can be observed in almost every aspect of the Second World War. Nevertheless in most countries this learning process had been thought of as an ingenious economic improvisation to meet a state of emergency, having no connection with peacetime economic activity nor with the 'normal' functioning of government. Although the First World War had left massive files of invaluable administrative experience on the shelves of government, which in 1939 had often only to be reached for and dusted, the influence of wartime events on economic attitudes in the inter-war period had been small.

Faced with a decision for war by two important powers the other major powers accepted the fact reluctantly and with much economic foreboding. The reluctance seems to have been greatest in the Soviet Union, which was in the throes of a violent economic and social transformation, and in the United States, which was less immediately threatened by German policy. The strategic initiative lay with the Axis powers; the strategies of the other powers were only responses to the initial decisions of their enemies. This fact, and the difference in economic attitudes towards warfare, operated decisively to shape each combatant power's strategic plans for fighting the war. By shaping strategy at every turn they also shaped economic policy and economic events. For the combatants the national economy had to be accommodated to a strategic plan and had to play its part in that plan. The economic dimension of the strategy was, however, only one part of the whole strategic synthesis, and the variety of the strategic and economic sytheses which were devised by the combatant powers show how complex and varied the economic experience of warfare can be.

2

The Economy in a Strategic Synthesis

Da hier die Mannigfaltigkeit und die unbestimmte Grenze aller Beziehungen eine grosse Menge von Grössen in die Betrachtung bringen, da die meisten dieser Grössen nur nach Wahrscheinlichkeitsgesetzen geschätzt werden können, so würde, wenn der Handelnde dies alles nicht mit dem Blick eines die Wahrheit überall ahnenden Geistes träfe, eine Verwicklung von Betrachtungen und Rücksichten entstehen, aus denen sich das Urteil gar nicht mehr herausfinden könnte. In diesem Sinne hat Bonaparte ganz richtig gesagt, dass viele dem Feldherrn vorliegende Entscheidungen eine Aufgabe mathematischer Kalküls bilden würden, der Kräfte eines Newton und Euler nicht unwürdig.

[Since in this matter the diversity and the undetermined boundaries of all relationships bring a great number of quantities into consideration, since most of these quantities can only be estimated according to the laws of probability unless the true flash of genius discovers in a glance what is correct, a complexity of relationships and hindsights arises from which a judgement can no longer be drawn. In this sense Bonaparte was quite right when he said that many of the decisions which confront a commander-in-chief would constitute problems in mathematical calculus not unworthy of a Newton and an Euler.]

Carl von Clausewitz,
Vom Kriege, 1833

The components of a strategic synthesis

The construction of a correct strategic plan requires a correct assessment of the potentiality of the economy for waging war. But warfare is not simply an economic event and a strategic plan is a synthesis of all the other factors which it is necessary to take into account, political, military, social and psychological. The more factors which are correctly assessed and incorporated into this synthesis the greater its chances of success. Many of these other factors have a direct bearing on the functioning of the economy in the strategic synthesis. Morale, to take but one example, is not exogenous to the working of the economy, because any good strategic plan will further and improve it. The economy does not in wartime function in the vacuum in which it often seems to be considered by economists and strategists alike. It functions in a complicated mesh of social, military, political and psychological considerations which are as much and perhaps more constraining in wartime than in peacetime.

Economists often seem to assume that economic priorities are greatly simplified in wartime because the economic priority is the maximization of production no matter what the cost. But this is quite false. There are very few historical examples where such a simple economic strategy was justifiable, acceptable or attempted. Economic strategy must certainly take into account the ultimate potential of the economy to defeat the enemy by outproducing him in the weapons of combat. But the ultimate economic limitations are very seldom reached. It is rare that an economy reaches the position where there are no more raw materials, or where there is no more manufacturing capacity, or no more labour. It is the general rule that the non-economic factors decide, in the first place, to what extent economic potential needs to be realized and, in the second place, how far it can be realized.

There are accordingly two concepts of economic potential for war which need to be distinguished. The first is the concept of the economy's absolute potential for warfare. Suppose the choice to lie between victory and annihilation, as it did for Poland in 1939 or as it has done in the past for Israel, the only reasonable strategy will be to try to reach the uttermost productive capacity of the economy. In this case the distinction so frequently made by economists between 'the economy' and 'the war economy' will have a logical justification because the only criterion governing economic priorities will be the maximization of production. The second concept of economic potential for war, however, is in most cases a more useful and operative one; it may be defined as the extent to which economic priorities must be re-ordered so as to attain the desired strategic objectives. If annihilation is not the certain outcome of defeat this concept will apply, because the assumption of only one priority, the maximization of war production, would ultimately reduce civilian society to so miserable a level of existence that continued concentration of the economy on so narrow an objective would be politically impossible.

Nevertheless the more absolute concept of economic potential is the only yardstick by which the second and more operative one can be adequately measured. Obviously the availability of factors of production sets finite limits to the volume of production. Given the possibilities of substitution it is unlikely that shortage of raw materials would be the first of these limits to be reached, except in the case of a closed economy. But this exception is an important one because international trade in wartime can be seriously disrupted. The deliberate and calculated restriction of supply to an opponent is one of the oldest of all policies in wartime, and in the Second World War it played a major role in Allied strategy. The other possible limits set by the factors of production may also be extended by substitution. The experience of recent history has been that the substitution of labour by capital is greatly speeded up in periods of warfare. War may be a potent inspiration to technological innovation because the bounds of economic practicability set for inventions are usually set much wider by the removal of many of the constraints imposed in peacetime by the high relative costs of innovation. For example, the constant increases in fire-power per man shown by the development of more complicated automatic rifles and guns and, more strikingly, by that of fighter aircraft and long-range bombers were only achieved by heavy capital investment. In the long run, however, despite substitution, some limit to the inputs either of raw materials or labour will be reached, the curve of production will flatten out and the economy may then be said to have achieved its war potential. In practice, to reach these bounds would require a very cohesive society and a skilled and smoothly working administration. Political difficulties, social resistance, or administrative friction are usually the first effective limits to be reached.

These limits need to be incorporated into the second and operative definition of economic potential for war. Although, for example, the Soviet Union was a much more cohesive society than its invaders and other enemies expected, it had been badly riven by the Stalinist purges and the merciless autocracy of its government, as well as by the continuing disputes over the meaning of the communist revolution. This lack of harmony was especially noticeable in the army. Full military and social cohesion could not be achieved at the start of the war and came only under the pressure of the German invasion. Some inefficiency in administration is inevitable everywhere, but it is much more likely in wartime because of sudden shifts in priorities and the much closer control and supervision of the economy. Some forms of government and administration will cope better with these problems than others. Some states will not have the trained personnel and the level of expertise necessary to cope adequately.

In order to recognize these facts of existence we can admit that administrative friction will prevent the gross product theoretically available for war from being realized and thus, categorizing that gross product as x, we could define the first concept of war potential as

$$x = p + r + s + e - f$$

where p is the national product in a peacetime year, r the reserves available in the economy, s the saving that can be made from not maintaining the peacetime rate of capital replacement, e the volume of resources external to the economy which can be drawn on, and f the reduced efficiency caused by administrative friction.

But although this is a useful measurement of economic potential for war it will only serve as a strategic synthesis in the most extreme case. The correct strategic synthesis will be that which only makes exactly those demands on the economy which are sufficient to achieve the strategic purpose. For example, the strategic aim of defence against an enemy is not served if the demands made on the economy change society and the political system so much that it is no longer the same as the one originally to be defended. This particular dilemma did in fact occur in Germany in 1944, when further production increases could only be achieved by going back on the political changes which the

Nazi movement had introduced. The political system must govern the economy as surely as it governs all other aspects of life, and in the last resort the economy cannot be made to function in such a way as to change fundamentally the social system of the country without raising the most serious political issues. In a correct strategy the level to which civilian consumption is reduced will be no more than what is necessary to achieve the final strategic objective. The extent to which new investment is postponed will be determined in the same way because all strategy must presuppose an ensuing peace which has its proper objectives. Labour will not be diverted into new occupations, especially into the armed forces, except where necessary. In all strategies except the extreme case, therefore, the maximization of production will not be the overriding priority of the economy. A finite level of production will be defined by the global purpose of the strategy and thus the second concept of war potential is more usefully represented as a set of limitations on the first:

$$W = x - c - i - d$$

where W is the second concept of war potential, c is the amount of civilian consumption which it is not necessary to forego, i is the amount of new investment for non-war purposes which it is not necessary to postpone, and d is the amount of disruption of the political and social system which it is not necessary to suffer.

It might be argued that there are also real economic costs of any war, however limited, which must also be a limitation on war potential. But this is an ambiguous point because there might also be real gains from any war which will be realizable while the war is being fought and which will counteract those costs. This was in fact one of the economic assumptions underlying German strategy. It was envisaged by the German government that the cost of the short campaigns could be recouped by the subsequent exploitation of the conquered territories and to a certain extent this was achieved. The costs of war are not therefore necessarily a limitation on war potential. Whether they are or not will be determined by the overall strategic design.

The economy is therefore not merely one component of a strategic plan; it is one of a complicated set of factors whose interactions on each other direct the formulation of a correct strategy. Nevertheless it has also to be emphasized that the first and more absolute concept of economic potential for war is an important governing factor in the second concept and thus a strong determinant of strategy. For example, in the Second World War Japanese strategy was formulated to take account of the narrow raw material base of the economy, whereas in the United States' strategy the limitations on W exercised as much influence as the components of x. The extent to which the strategy will be limited by the availability of labour and raw materials increases as the size of the economy decreases. Were Iceland to wage war on Britain the components of x would be decisive; were the Soviet Union to wage war on Romania they would be relatively unimportant.

German strategy and the economy

The evolution of German strategy was based on a military attempt to avoid the tactical stalemates of the First World War.[1] But the translation of this into a genuine strategic synthesis, the *Blitzkrieg*, seems to have been the result of a set of decisions taken only in part consciousness of their full implications. The leading figure in these decisions was Hitler himself.

There was widespread military opposition to this strategy, most of which stemmed from the failure of the soldiers to conceive strategy in the wider social and political sense in which it has been defined here. Taking only military factors into account there might seem to be no reason for the German government to run the extreme risks which a *Blitzkrieg* strategy entailed and to raise the possibility of the fearful disasters which did in the end ensue. Such were the lines along which this strategy was opposed at the time by military strategists like Beck and Halder; it has been subsequently criticized in the same vein in military memoirs. It is hardly surprising that if the scope of the *Blitzkrieg* strategy was misunderstood in Germany it should have been much more misunderstood outside Germany.

Seen from outside its frontiers National Socialist Germany was a country which had already geared its economy to the more absolute limit of war potential. It was widely assumed that the German state in 1939 had long been fully prepared for a major

1. G. Förster, *Totaler Krieg und Blitzkrieg* (Militärhistorische Studien no. 10, N.F.), Deutscher Militärverlag, Berlin, 1967.

war and that Germany's economic resources were wholly engaged in the purpose of war. All Allied strategic planning started from this assumption, but nothing in fact could have been further from the truth. It is not too difficult to see how such a complete misapprehension came to prevail almost universally. In the first place the achievements of the German economy in the 1930s in eliminating unemployment seemed only explicable on the grounds that investment in rearmament had provided enough jobs to soak up the excess labour. This impression was strengthened by the outward appearance of the state, monolithic, militaristic, nationalistic, bellicose and, apparently, highly efficient. This was the impression which it suited the régime to give abroad. Hitler's meaningless statement, on 1 September 1939, that he had spent 90 billion RM on rearmament was intended to reinforce this impression. That it was so readily believed is indicative of the extent to which German strategy was so wrongly interpreted abroad.

That rearmament was not alone responsible for the recovery of the German economy after 1933 is now well known.[2] It was but one aspect of an extensive programme of public investment.[3] A difficult conceptual problem is raised here which makes it impossible to describe Hitler's statement as a lie. What range of investment in an economy can be said to be investment for war? Was investment in Germany in the national network of fast motor roads, for example, investment for war? Obviously there was a military purpose in such roads and this was acknowledged at the time but the main purpose of their construction was to create employment and to further the plans to develop the car industry in Germany. Yet it is almost impossible to think of any item of social overhead capital which is not as important to the economy in war as in peace and since war was the goal of National Socialist economic policy a very high proportion of all public investment could perhaps be properly considered as investment for war. Even so rearmament expenditure by the definitions which were used in Britain or the United States was until 1938 less important than other forms of investment in Germany's economic recovery.

2. B. H. Klein, *Germany's Economic Preparations for War* (Harvard Economic Studies, no. 109), Harvard University Press, Cambridge, Mass., 1959.
3. R. Erbe, *Die nationalsozialistische Wirtschaftspolitik 1933–39 im Lichte der modernen Theorie*, Polygraphischer Verlag, Zürich, 1958.

But it is also true that the level of military expenditure was very high when compared to that of other powers. Military investment in Germany, excluding the cost of administration and personnel, amounted to 41,800 million RM between 1933 and the end of 1938. The total investment in industry and in transport in the same period was 25,400 million RM and in the rest of the 'civilian' economy 38,700 million RM.[4] The difficulty of establishing any meaningful exchange rates in this period allows only the most general and imprecise comparisons of the level of German 'military' expenditure in these years with that in other states. One attempt at such a comparison is made in Table 1 where Hillmann's calculations for the other powers are compared to the most recent calculations for Germany.[5]

TABLE 1
'MILITARY' EXPENDITURE OF THE COMBATANT POWERS IN THE SECOND WORLD WAR, 1933–8 (in millions of £ sterling)

(Germany)	(£2,868 m.)
Russia	£2,808 m.
Japan	£1,266 m.
United Kingdom	£1,200 m.
U.S.A.	£1,175 m.
France	£1,088 m.
Italy	£930 m.

SOURCE: H. C. Hillman, 'The Comparative Strengths of the Great Powers' in R.I.I.A., *The Economic Structure of Hitler's Europe*, Oxford University Press, 1954.

If this arbitrary division between military and other forms of investment is allowed to be reasonably indicative of the extent of investment for war the German economy can be described as one in which the level of economic preparation for war was high but not one in which war priorities prevailed over all others.

The word *Blitzkrieg* is frequently misunderstood in English as though it had a purely tactical meaning, in the sense of a highly

4. B. A. Carroll, *Design for Total War. Arms and Economics in the Third Reich*, Mouton, The Hague, 1968, p. 188. For other estimates of 'war' investment in Germany see Klein, *Germany's Economic Preparations*, pp. 4–27; K. D. Bracher, W. Sauer and G. Schultz, *Die nationalsozialistische Machtergreifung*, Westdeutscher Verlag, Cologne, 1960, p. 661 ff.

5. At 15 RM to the £.

mechanized and mobile campaign designed to smash the enemy's resistance as soon as possible. But the concept of *Blitzkrieg* was a much wider one. It was a strategic synthesis embracing all the factors considered here and for National Socialist Germany it was the correct synthesis. It involved preparation for a series of short wars which would require no greater degree of commitment of the economy to war than had already existed in 1938. The political objectives, Hitler believed, were most likely to be achieved by not exceeding this level and by aiming at short campaigns with limited objectives. There was no sudden reorientation of the German economy in 1939; the same economic priorities that had been ordered in 1936 by the Second Four-Year Plan served their purpose until the *Blitzkrieg* strategy finally failed to achieve its objectives before Moscow in the winter of 1941–2. The declaration of war in September 1939 had little or no significance for the German economy because the economic strategy remained the same. Compared to all possible opponents Germany was already at a high level of economic preparedness for war. The basic investment for a successful series of short campaigns had been completed and the armaments were to hand. Little or no economic preparation had been made for a long war because the strategic synthesis was formulated to avoid a prolonged struggle.

What led Hitler to this strategy against so much opposition? In the first place it was a reaction against the enormous economic effort, social disruption and blood-letting of the First World War, all of which he had himself experienced most directly. In that sense Hitler was only one of many strategists seeking an alternative to the murderous and apparently useless infantry and artillery campaigns of 1915 to 1918. The experience of these years had been that long wars were self-defeating. In the second place, Germany's situation in Europe since the Versailles settlement no longer required a 'total war' as a means of expansion. Except on the Rhine Germany was surrounded by a ring of weaker powers which could be broken either by the threat of force, as in the case of Czechoslovakia, or by its exercise for only a brief period, as in the case of Poland. In this connection Hitler decided that Russia would also prove a weaker power. Thirdly, Hitler's aims were most consistent; but the method by which he pursued them was opportunistic. It required great flexibility in which each diplomatic threat could be backed up by the ability to strike quickly if necessary, and that required ready armaments. Economic commitment to any one war would only impede this flexibility. A war on Russia would entail different economic priorities from a naval and aerial war against Britain. Too thorough a commitment of the economy to war would have reduced the diplomatic and strategic flexibility which Hitler needed. Fourthly, the *Blitzkrieg* strategy reduced the amount of administrative friction because it suited the working methods of the National Socialist party very well. Fifthly, it suited the domestic political situation and the social policy of the party. Lastly, it corresponded to the economic realities of Germany's position since Versailles.

The last three points need further consideration. The utter rejection of the Weimar Republic as a social system had given the National Socialist party the character of a sect, fiercely suspicious of all administrative machinery not under its own supervision and imbued with its own world-outlook. The new society required new machinery and it became a regular part of National Socialist administrative practice, when important administrative tasks needed to be done, to appoint a new administrative machine to do the job. The party itself was governed on the 'leader-principle' (*Führerprinzip*) and each administrative machine likewise depended on its own leader whose decisions were transmitted as commands down a hierarchical administrative ladder where the leader-principle guaranteed implementation. Usually the responsibility of the head of a new machine was to a very high leader, sometimes only to the Führer himself. The *Organisation Todt* (O.T.), originally created to construct the Autobahn network, was, for example, Fritz Todt's own machine. He himself later became the first Minister of Munitions and the Ministry of Munitions itself was created as an administrative machine quite outside the competence of the surviving Weimar civil service. There are many such instances of this method of government and as in the case of the Ministry of Munitions it was the normal method of overcoming the administrative frictions that arose in wartime. It is far more difficult in such a system to conduct the exhaustive collection and sifting of information and to carry out the detailed day-to-day planning of priorities required in a closely controlled and supervised economy such as that of Britain became in 1940. Committee decisions are hard to make in such a system and are very suspect; planning tends to depend on the decisive powers and initiative of a small number of individuals' perceptions of the social and economic situation.

The political situation of the National Socialist party has to be seen in the light of the extremely divisive political policies it pursued, and the contradictory nature of its economic policies. Although it was the most widely supported political party at the polls in the last days of the Weimar Republic it never obtained the expressed support of half of the voters. After 1933 there were no effective tests of public opinion in Germany but the radical actions of the government did nothing to widen its basis of support. For a much larger section of the population to be converted to active fascist consciousness first required substantial changes in society; while awaiting this mass conversion the revolution was maintained by armed force and savage repression. One part of the body politic – those of Jewish descent – was outlawed. The leading figures of the Social Democratic and Communist parties fled into exile and attacked the régime from foreign capitals. Important groups and members of the National Socialist party split off into opposition as the revolution pursued its course. Otto Strasser, whose ideas had helped to formulate party tactics in the 1920s, was denouncing the leaders from abroad in the first year of the war as 'gangsters' and Hermann Rauschning, former leader of the Danzig senate who had played a big part in the reincorporation of Danzig into Germany, went one better by denouncing Hitler as 'The Beast from the Abyss'.[6] In such circumstances it was not feasible to formulate a strategy requiring many sacrifices from the population nor too great an effort of cooperation with the government. There was no possibility of unifying the nation in a long hard economic effort, as the British government tried to do after the retreat from Dunkirk or the American government after the disaster of Pearl Harbor. Strategy must not weaken the limited political support for the government and if possible, it must strengthen it by bringing early successes.

Finally, strategy had to take account of the fact that within its post-Versailles frontiers Germany was no longer economically a great power in the sense in which the United States was and had

6. O. Strasser, *The Gangsters around Hitler*, W. H. Allen, London, 1940; H. Rauschning, *The Beast from the Abyss*, Heinemann, London, 1941.

control over less raw materials and labour than in 1914. Coal was the only raw material essential for war with which Germany was well-endowed. She had no natural rubber and no oil supply. Her armaments industry depended on an extremely high annual quantity of imports of iron ore from Sweden. She had practically no domestic supply of non-ferrous metal ores such as chrome, nickel, tungsten, molybdenum and manganese, essential for the manufacture of armour plate. Copper and tin supplies depended on imports. Many of these vital imports come from outside Europe, and could not be provided within the German trading bloc. A strategy which implied a continued high level of imports of such materials had to be avoided. The *Blitzkrieg* strategy however could be based on stockpiles of raw materials adequate for a short campaign. This was the policy followed, and the control of foreign trade after 1936 went hand-in-hand with the careful accumulation of adequate stockpiles of strategic materials. Where stockpiling could not serve the purpose, as in the case of oil, investment was directed towards producing high-cost synthetic products. This type of production was the main target for investment in the Second Four-Year Plan which began in 1936.

Thus German strategy concentrated on having a sufficient stock of armaments to ensure immediate superiority over any likely opponent. It was necessary that the armaments should be of a type which permitted a quick mobile campaign so that the opponent could not fight on the defensive for a sufficiently long time to build up a comparable level of armaments. The heavy concentration on the production of tanks, other vehicles and planes indicated the way in which tactics in the field also had to be accommodated to the general strategy. The purpose of the programme to manufacture synthetic materials was to ensure that no vital strategic materials would be in such short supply as to prevent the successful execution of even a *Blitzkrieg* of this limited kind. This was the policy characterized by General Thomas, head of the Economic and Armaments Office of the High Command of the Armed Forces [*Wirtschafts- und Rüstungsamt*] as 'armament in width'.[7] Most military strategists believed that the element of risk was too great and advocated

7. G. Thomas, *Geschichte der deutschen Wehr- und Rüstungswirtschaft (1918–1943/45)* (Schriften des Bundesarchivs, no. 14), Boppard am Rhein, 1966.

instead the policy of 'armament in depth'; a longer term investment in armaments production for a prolonged war. But, as events
proved, Hitler correctly assessed the dangers of a long war of
mass-productive resources against the Soviet Union as greater
than those of a *Blitzkrieg*. Whatever the dangers the *Blitzkrieg*
represented Germany's only chance of success. With such a
strategy Germany conquered most of Europe; from the moment
it was abandoned she was fighting a defensive and losing battle.

Japanese strategy and the economy

There were many superficial similarities between the Japanese
situation and that of Germany and they are reflected in the
strategy adopted. But these resemblances cannot hide the great
difference in economic potential which existed between the two
countries. As in the German case the difference between 'civilian'
and 'war' economy has no meaning for Japan in the thirties.
Certainly from the start of 1937 Japan can be considered to have
been at war, although there was no formal declaration of war to
mark the point at which the so-called 'intervention' in China
passed to the stage of universally recognized 'invasion'. But even
before that stage the Japanese economy, like that of Germany,
had attained high levels of employment. As in Germany, this was
only partly to be attributed to the help provided by military
investment. The 1937 budget, however, marks a clear watershed;
it was 26 per cent higher than in the previous year and 49 per cent
of the total was for military expenditure. Investment for war
purposes, as in Germany, was an integral part of economic policy.
In July 1937 a special secret military budget became a regular
aspect of the government's finances and from the start of 1938
the Annual Resource Mobilization Plan, although far from any
thoroughgoing economic planning, indicated that the demands of
war on the economy had become more than just financial ones.
As a proportion of Gross National Product military expenditure
rose from a constant level of about 6·8 per cent between 1932 to
1936, to 13·2 per cent in 1937 and to 17·4 per cent in 1938.[8]
   Like Germany, Japan was surrounded by a ring of less industrialized and less productive economies, and she could expand at

8. A. Hara, 'L'Économie japonaise pendant la deuxième guerre mondiale',
in *R.d.g.m.*, no. 89, 1973.

their expense with a relatively limited commitment of the economy to war purposes, provided a strategic conjuncture occurred in which the United States could be expected to remain neutral. A relatively high level of armaments, a readiness to strike, and a tactical plan allowing for short mobile campaigns were combined with the minimum degree of economic control necessary to achieve these ends. Unlike Germany, Japan had no far-reaching aims of social and economic policy which in themselves justified the imposition of economic controls, and their development in Japan was far less extensive than in Germany. When purely military expenditure first assumed a dominating role in the German economy there already existed a battery of economic controls devised for other purposes; in Japan such controls sprang mostly from the necessity of war.

The area where such controls were first and most rigorously applied, in foreign trade, reflects also a similarity between the Japanese and German positions, the great dependence of the economy on imports. But in this case the difference in scale of this import-dependence shows clearly how much lower was Japan's economic potential for war and how much more limited her strategic choice. Japan was more dependent on importing strategic raw materials, and the limitations of the Japanese economy in this respect, even when supplemented by the resources of 'greater Japan', were very noticeable. They were a main target of Allied strategy and, in the end, a fundamental factor in the Japanese defeat.

The closed trading arrangements within the Japanese trading bloc had to be combined with heavy investment in the production of goods which could still not be otherwise obtained in sufficient quantities without recourse to the international economy and hard-currency areas. As late as 1936 Japan was still importing 66 per cent of her total oil consumption from the U.S.A.[9] In fact, the domestic Japanese economy on the eve of the war produced only 16·7 per cent of her total iron ore consumption, 62·2 per cent of her steel consumption, 40·6 per cent of her aluminium consumption, 20·2 per cent of her crude oil consumption, and 31·3 per cent of her salt consumption. Although over 90 per cent of coal consumption was domestically mined Japan had no coking coal for steel works. Certain strategic minerals, nickel for example,

9. J. R. Cohen, *Japan's Economy*, p. 49.

were not produced at all in Japan. All the bauxite for aluminium production was imported. Nor could these deficiencies be made up from the underdeveloped regions to the south.

Table 2 gives some indication of how well the Co-Prosperity Sphere could be expected to function as an autarkic bloc. The figures were derived by Japanese military planners and relate to strategic commodities. They should be treated with great reserve as in all such calculations. There are very few raw materials for which there is no substitute when price considerations are set aside. If cost of final output is a factor of relatively low importance and competition in markets is highly restricted the price and quality of inputs are likewise reduced in importance. Also the need to produce a product to 100 per cent specifications is no longer present. Hence inferior raw materials may be substituted for superior ones. In a process like steel manufacturing there is a large possibility of such substitutions, and the same is true of most manufactured goods. Immense ingenuity was shown in this way during the war years in Germany. When cost is reduced in importance aluminium, for example, need no longer be produced from bauxite, and synthetic rubber and synthetic oil may be widely produced. Furthermore the availability of potential resources in an area like the Co-Prosperity Sphere cannot effectively be measured except against the actual demand from Japan once that sphere had been created because the nature of demand within the closed system would have produced significant shifts of production, whereas the estimates of production in Table 2 are based on demand from outside the autarkic area. Apart from one commodity, nickel ore, the planners foresaw no absolute difficulty in obtaining supply. Nevertheless, in order to obtain such high levels of output the Co-Prosperity Sphere would also have required a very high level of capital investment over a very short period when capital was needed at home for the war effort. The process of substitution would in reality have required a greater freedom of economic choice than was likely to be available. The ten million tons of coking coal from North China and Manchuria were only adequate, once all contact with the international economy had been cut off, to enable the Japanese steel industry to work at one third of its full capacity.

To set these ambitious economic plans in perspective it is necessary to compare them with Japanese economic potential

TABLE 2
JAPANESE ESTIMATES OF ANNUAL DEMAND AND SUPPLY OF CERTAIN ESSENTIAL COMMODITIES IN THE CO-PROSPERITY SPHERE FROM 1940 (in thousands of tons)

Commodity	Estimated annual demand	Domestic Japanese output	Prospective supply from						
			Manchuria	China	French Indo-China	Thailand	Dutch East Indies	Philippines	British possessions
Iron ore	10,000	3,950	300	2,700	70	0	0	2,000	1,400
Manganese ore	300	200	0	0	0	0	27	30	32
Nickel ore	1,250	—	0	0	0	0	200	0	0
Copper	200	80	0	0	0	0	0	300*	0
Bauxite	480	50	0	0	40	0	350	0	100
Crude rubber	65	—	—	—	40	25	(400)†	(1)†	(400)†
Industrial salt	1,500	150	400	800	80	70	150	0	0
Rice	100‡	94‡	0	0	4‡	2‡	0	0	0

* Copper ore.
† Production figures.
‡ 1,000 koku (1 koku = 4·96 bushels).

SOURCE: U.S.S.B.S., *Japan's Struggle to End the War*, G.P.O., Washington, D.C., 1946, p. 15.

for war on an international scale. Japan's share of total world output in 1938 was under 4 per cent; Germany's was 13·2 per cent. In terms of those materials consumed in largest quantities in war Japan's share was even lower. Greater Japan in the same year still only produced 4·2 per cent of world coal output and 6 per cent of world steel output. The comparative figures for Germany were 15·5 per cent and 20·7 per cent.[10] Furthermore the stage of industrialization which the Japanese economy had reached was far short of that necessary to sustain anything but the briefest offensive campaign against a state such as Britain, much less the United States, unless that country was already heavily committed elsewhere. Japanese output of capital goods, which are obviously more related to the ability to fight a war than consumer goods, amounted to about 3·5 per cent of world output in 1937 and this may be compared with the United States share of 41·7 per cent. With the possible exception of the Soviet Union Japan, of all the major combatants, had the highest share of her population employed in agriculture, 50 per cent.

Dependence on the Asian trading bloc which she had created and the kind of campaigns necessary to extend this area if the opportunity presented itself implied a large navy and merchant navy. The navy itself, at 906,000 tons (displacement) at the start of the war, was over four times the size of the German navy and twice that of the Italian navy. The total carrying capacity of the merchant marine in 1938 was about five million gross tons, rather bigger than that of Germany but less than one third the size of the British merchant marine. Measured in *per capita* terms the level of Japanese imports was not especially high, about 27 tons per person, about a third of the German level. But in terms of strategic importance Japanese imports were more vital than those of other combatants with the possible exception of the United Kingdom. Britain's higher level of *per capita* imports reflected the very high level of food imports, Japan's that of machinery and other capital goods. Indeed the Japanese armament industries could scarcely function for a long time without supply from the United States.

Although defence industries received the highest level of priority in allocations of foreign exchange for imports and although the levels of priority accorded to consumer goods

10. Hillmann, p. 443.

industries were so low that, for example, after June 1938 imports of raw cotton were provided only to firms exporting a comparable amount in manufactured goods, the dependence on imports for machinery and machine-tools still slowed down rearmament plans. There were effectively only two sources of machine-tool imports; almost 80 per cent of the value of the machine tools entering into international trade was represented by United States and German exports. Given the limited nature of German rearmament Germany still had an export capacity but the Allies found it relatively easy to cut off the supply route between Germany and Japan, depending as it did on a long sea-haul. When the trade treaty with the United States was allowed to expire at the end of 1939 the situation became even more serious, and had to be allowed for in all strategic plans.

As for the non-economic aspects of war potential they too did not seem especially favourable in 1939. Japan was not undergoing the revolutionary turmoil of German society but it was a society in a period of extremely rapid economic and social change. Beneath the authoritarian cover of the alliance of soldiers and business corporations which dominated the government seethed the waters of social discontent, and radical parties of the left and right exerted constant pressures for political and social change. Only those of the right influenced strategic thinking and that mainly because of the example of Germany and Italy.[11] Tensions between some circles in the army and controlling groups in the government prevented the development of complete unity on strategic aims, and the government's doubts about its own standing increased these hesitations.

The strategy which emerged, therefore, was that of a short war to gain a precisely defined amount of territory. The opportunity was provided by the German victories in Europe and the collapse of French and Dutch power in the Pacific, which brought extreme pressures on Britain and the United States. It seemed that a historical moment had arrived which, if it were not seized, would never recur. The assumptions were that Germany would be the victor in the European war and permanently weaken European power in the Pacific and that the United States would be forced by early Japanese successes to make peace because its Atlantic

11. M. Masao, *Thought and Behaviour in Modern Japanese Politics*, Oxford University Press, London, 1963, p. 52 ff.

interests were also threatened. The certainty of early success was guaranteed by the unpreparedness of the United States and the fact that American mobilization would be relatively slow. In this interval Japanese forces would occupy territories within a perimeter whose bounds were Thailand, Indonesia and the Philippines in the south and the nearer islands in the Pacific. These positions would be fortified and it was assumed that the United States would abandon the task of dislodging Japan from them. In the event success stimulated ambitions beyond these boundaries and Japan greatly weakened her strategic position by subsequently committing forces to battle well outside the periphery, in New Guinea, the Solomon Islands, the Aleutian Islands, the Indian Ocean and the Coral Sea.

The strategy and economy of the other combatants

Much less is known about Italian strategic planning and the level of Italian preparations for war. The main weight of Italian rearmament expenditure seems to have gone on the navy and air force. At the start of the campaign in France the Italian army was not sufficiently well-equipped to take up any convincing offensive and its subsequent offensive in Greece suffered also from lack of equipment. There is nothing to indicate that the Italian government had made calculations for a land campaign of any dimensions in Europe. Even for other campaigns Italy's equipment was lacking. Only a third of the 3,000 combat aircraft were in working order.[12] The ultimate decision to declare war seems to have been mainly motivated by the fear of growing German power and the sentiment that if Italy was to pursue her own strategic aims with any chance of success she had to expand her area of territorial control and influence contemporaneously with the extension of German control in Europe. In this respect Italy's strategic position was a curious one. After 1936 it was practically certain that in any future war Germany would be an ally but the realization that this must be so could not alter the fact that there were also serious conflicts of interest in Europe between the two powers.

12. S. Berstein and P. Milza, *L'Italie fasciste*, Armand Colin, Paris, 1970, p. 385; S. B. Clough, *The Economic History of Modern Italy*, Columbia University Press, New York, 1964, p. 263.

The situation was made much more difficult by the great disparity in economic strength between Germany and Italy. The Italian share of total world manufacturing output was lower than that of all other major combatants. She produced practically no coal or crude oil. Steel output, although a large proportion of it was concentrated on specialized high-grade steels particularly suitable for armour plate, was only just over two million tons in 1938, about one third the output of Greater Japan. There were shortages of most strategic materials and stockpiles of oil and non-ferrous metals were so low as to impose limits on any future campaign. Oil stocks at the end of 1941 were sufficient for only one month's consumption.[13] The Italian government had tried to overcome these weaknesses in the same manner as the German government by pursuing autarkic policies aimed at increasing the level of economic self-sufficiency and combining these with the creation of an area of economic domination in Europe and North Africa. That supply would be a problem in any war had been demonstrated even by the limited successes of the trade sanctions imposed by the League of Nations at the time of the war in Ethiopia. The struggle towards autarky in the domestic economy had as its only significant achievement the elimination of wheat imports. The sanctions had also shown how phantasmagorical were Italian hopes of creating their own *Grossraumwirtschaft*. The virtual collapse of Yugoslav trade with Italy in 1936 as a result of these sanctions had been accompanied by a great growth of Yugoslav–German trade. The only European country whose trade with Italy was greater than with Germany, and which could be said to be unequivocally under Italian trading and economic domination, was Albania, whose level of trade and production was too low to affect the situation in any way. In Hungary, Yugoslavia and Greece Italian economic ambitions were thwarted by the German trade drive in south-eastern Europe.

Official propaganda always struggled to maintain the idea that on both sides of the Axis pact there was a fundamental unity of economic interest in the reconstruction of Europe and even went so far as to insist on the basic complementarity of the Italian and

13. The author would like to thank Miss A. Raspin for permission to read the draft of her University of London Ph.D. thesis, 'Some Aspects of German–Italian Economic Relations 1940–43 with Particular Reference to Italy'.

German economies.[14] In 1940 the German Minister of Economics, Funk, actually proposed a close economic collaboration between the two powers, but such a possibility was foreclosed by Italy's desire to pursue her own strategic aims. The verdict of General Favagrossa, president of the Committee for Civil Mobilization, is worth recording. 'Foreign policy', he wrote, 'was in complete contrast to the possibility of carrying it out. With a lightheartedness which beggars description it rushed towards catastrophe.'[15] But with a more wholehearted commitment to rearmament, with a greater level of defence expenditure and with better equipped armed forces Italy's strategic situation would not necessarily have been a better one. What was really lacking in the Italian case was an unambiguous answer to the questions of what war to prepare for, and when? In the event Italy entered the war in order not to be completely displaced from the European scene by Germany. She was instantly identified as the weak link, both economically and politically, in the Axis chain. There was little effective direction of the economy for war and inflationary policies in 1940 were already nullifying the wage and price controls of that year. Armaments production was not stepped up in 1940 sufficiently to keep pace with growing world armaments production and Italy's relative position became an even weaker one.[16]

The strategies of the other combatants had necessarily to be defensive ones. But the question of which of the possible aggressors to defend against had drastic economic implications. After 1934 Germany, Japan and Italy were identified by the British government as strategic threats. Until 1932, however, the Chiefs of Staff had still been acting on the principle of the 'ten-year rule', which stipulated that no 'major war' need be anticipated for a period of ten years in the future. The effect of such a rule had been to put economic and military planning at so low a level that the new prospect of having to fight a war against a combination of three

14. A. de Marsanich, 'Unità economica dell'Europa', in *Economia fascista*, no. 17, 1940.

15. Quoted in F. Catalano, *L'economia italiana di guerra. La politica economico-finanziaria del fascismo della guerra d'Etiopia alla caduta del regime 1935–1943*, Istituto nazionale per la storia del movimento di liberazione, Milan, 1969, p. 62.

16. F. Catalano, 'Les ambitions mussoliniennes et la réalité économique de l'Italie', in *R.d.g.m.*, no. 76, 1969.

aggressors was so daunting as to be thought virtually impossible.[17] Only in 1937 did the Cabinet take the reluctant decision that Italy should definitely be considered a possible aggressor. As late as the summer of 1940 the Chiefs of Staff were still urging all possible steps to keep Italy out of the war, because the large Italian navy blocked the shortest sea communications to the British defence bases in the Pacific.

For no matter whether Germany or Japan were identified as the principal enemy strategic analysis suggested that the main burden of rearmament would be a naval and aerial one. That any war with Japan would be a naval one went without saying. But that plans for a war against Germany should be seen in the same light shows how far the strategic initiative had been conceded. The estimates of the extent of German economic preparation for war were deeply pessimistic and exaggerated. It was assumed by the government that Germany had been preparing for a long time for a massive attack and was so well-equipped that no resistance was possible other than a naval defence against invasion until such time as the level of British war production could be sustained at a high enough level for a long enough period to match that of Germany. It was further assumed that in the circumstances German strategy would be to make a sudden heavy attack in order to utilize her superiority to the full before it was reduced by rearmament in Britain. After the provisions of the Washington naval disarmament treaties lapsed in 1936 the British government therefore embarked on a large naval building programme. Its ultimate, but quite unrealizable, purpose was to produce a navy sufficiently large to cope with that of all three possible antagonists. Side by side with naval production, however, existed the question of air defence. It would not be too great an exaggeration to say that on this question it was thought there was in fact no effective possibility of adequate defence against the bomber. This strategic opinion, which prevailed generally among all the great powers, proved in the event to be somewhere between an over-simplification of the problem and a plain mistake. But it necessarily followed from such an opinion that the only effective aerial strategy would be a deterrent one. Britain would have to be able to match Germany 'bomb for bomb'. So began not only a massive

17. W. K. Hancock and M. M. Gowing, *The British War Economy*, H.M.S.O., London, 1949, p. 63.

programme of investment in the air force but also, as part of this programme, the construction of a large fleet of expensive long-range bombers.

The economic consequences of these initial strategic decisions are worth dwelling on for they were ultimately as important in shaping the economic history of the war as the *Blitzkrieg* strategy in Germany. From the outset Britain gave priority to the production of the most technologically sophisticated and the most costly of available modern armaments, the larger planes and warships. The implications of this decision were far from understood but it was a decision taken with an awareness that the economic resources of Britain could not match those of the possible aggressors and that an adequate defensive strategy could only be sustained by capitalizing on the major advantages of a highly developed economy, research, innovation and modern productive methods. In contrast, these were the very things that the *Blitzkrieg* strategy discouraged in Germany. Long-term research could not be of use for a short war and development was not at a premium when the level of armaments was already considered adequate for victory. At the end of the war Allied interrogators were amazed to discover how slight, inadequate and inefficient had been the administrative apparatus in Germany for fostering research and development, compared with the massive and highly efficient administrative apparatus concerned purely with production.[18] The fruits of these early decisions in Britain were borne in a rich crop as the war did in fact turn into the prolonged struggle which had been anticipated.

In the second place these decisions set the British economy on the path towards 'total war' in the same economic sense in which it had existed in 1917–18. Ironically enough, military strategists were casting about desperately for some way of avoiding this very strategy. The future war was defined in summer 1937 as one of 'limited liability', which seems to be the first use of this now familiar cliché.[19] It had been hoped that by concentrating on naval and aerial defence the tremendous expansion of military supply, and the economic and social problems which this had brought during the First World War, might be avoided. In reality

18. Interrogation of Dipl. Ing. F. Geist at 'Dustbin', Intelligence Report no. 53.
19. Hancock and Gowing, p. 67.

such an attitude was crassly optimistic. The cost of the rearmament programmes already devised would in any case have forced a departure from the attempt to preserve 'business as usual', if they were to be completed on time. And more realistic thinking would have made it clearer that no strategy involving Britain alone had much chance of success. The Munich agreements and the subsequent German occupation of Prague made the war of 'limited liability' ridiculous. There could be no joint strategic planning for defence with France unless Britain was prepared to make a contribution to the defence of western Europe on land. When the occupation of Prague and the threat to Poland forced close strategic cooperation of this kind on Britain and France in March 1939 it became at once more far-reaching than anything achieved between Germany and Italy; almost the first stage in it was that the United Kingdom agreed to equip an army of thirty-two divisions before the end of the first year of war. The rearmament programme had channelled investment away from the army and without a rapid extension of economic controls and a firm direction from the centre there would be no hope of meeting the new requirements. Thus, as the British government was forced to face up to the reality of the situation, it had to add to its expensive rearmament programme the one aspect of rearmament expenditure on which it had hoped to economize. The only way in which the addition could be made was by a return to the economic strategy of 'total war', although this was still not clearly understood.

In the third place the strategic choice had been made for a long war in which the intention would be to maximize all available productive resources in order to out-produce the enemy. The implications of this decision for both the domestic and the international economies were only dimly perceived but the die had, nevertheless, been irrevocably cast for fundamental changes in both. Most economic preparations for the war to come continued to be mainly concerned with avoiding inflation and a disruption of trade, business and social life. Their general drift was negative, concerned more with avoiding problems than with solving them. Strategic decisions had run in advance of economic ones; with each step towards a prolonged war of mass-production economic thinking had reluctantly to bring itself to focus on the problems which such a war implied. It meant in the end an extension of the administration into almost every aspect of social existence and a total priority for 'war' production over every aspect of 'civilian' production.

It had never been assumed that such an effort would draw on the resources of the United Kingdom alone. From the start the Commonwealth and the Empire were seen as supplementary sources from which to draw labour and materials on favourable terms. Naval superiority in the Atlantic was presumed to make it fairly certain that within financial and legal limits the economic resources of the United States could also be drawn on. The extent of these demands on the resources of the rest of the world was not foreseen, but the intention to use the specialized and developed productive capacity of the British economy in this way had important international ramifications. Whereas the strategy of the aggressors aimed at confining and limiting the supply of war material as far as possible to their own autarkic trading areas, British strategy opened the gates of supply to the whole world and ensured from the very start that the economic effects of the Second World War would be world-wide. The maximization of production in Britain would mobilize the resources of a world economy which was wallowing in unemployment and stagnating trade, and sinking rapidly into another severe depression. The Lend-Lease Acts were already implicit in the strategic decisions taken in spring 1939.

It was, therefore, not the available reserves of factors of production in Britain which were at stake in this strategy so much as the available capacity to produce in the widest sense. This would in fact involve, given the new military demands, the most rigidly precise allocation of labour, because imports of labour would be less feasible than imports of raw materials. It would also involve a determined and thorough administrative ingenuity to make sure that plant was utilized to the full. These were problems whose solution lay in the United Kingdom. But there were inherent weaknesses in such a strategy which were to prove much more difficult to solve. Britain was highly dependent on imports and especially on food imports. But it was not only the high *per capita* level of imports which distinguished the British economy from others but the length of haul of these imports. Even when compared to another imperial power like France, a substantial proportion of whose imports was also seaborne, the contrast was very striking, for the average haul per ton of British imports was twice as long as those of France. In spite of the existence of a merchant marine with a carrying capacity of over seventeen million gross tons, there was still the possibility of a shortage of shipping space, which would be greatly aggravated if submarine warfare were to prove as successful as in the First World War. The long hauls were due to the high level of food and raw material imports from distant dominions. About 42 per cent of British imports in 1938 came from the sterling bloc, including the Commonwealth and Empire, an even higher proportion of total imports than Japan drew from her trading bloc. Even if this proportion could be maintained there would certainly be acute payments problems, because of the diversion of manufacturing away from exports to rearmament. There was, in any case, the likelihood of a shipping shortage caused by enemy action.

The British government was justified in its dread of a 'three-power enemy'. The two potential European allies were France and Russia, and the British government could perhaps be forgiven the pessimism which informed its strategic planning in this respect, especially when it is remembered that Germany had relatively few hesitations about launching an attack on either of those countries. The weaknesses of France and Russia were not obvious economic ones; it was rather a question of how far the great apparent economic strength of these two powers could in fact be mobilized for war. The depression had hit France very late and when levels of output and employment were rising in other European industrial economies, and particularly in Germany, France remained in stagnation until 1937. This economic stagnation was accompanied by a profound political unease and a weak and vacillating policy in the face of the apparent German threat. In Russia the Five-Year Plans were accompanied by Stalin's purges of the fighting forces and of the civil service, and industrialization seemed to have been achieved only at the price of an autocratic system which, in the judgement of outsiders, had little chance of holding together in a world war.

Whether this opinion was fair is a matter on which it is quite impossible as yet to pass a reasonable judgement. Historical research is still silent on French and Russian rearmament and strategic planning. It is possible to make some general economic statements about the level of rearmament expenditure, but it has to be said that, whereas only the details of German planning remain to be analysed, in the case of Russia and France most of the economic history of this period is still virtually unknown. Certainly the divisions in the political world in France were no greater than those in Germany, and after the initial defeats Soviet society and the Soviet economy proved cohesive enough to withstand the most savage ordeal. The economic factors in the fall of France and in the successful resistance of Russia can only be indicated in the most superficial way throughout this book, but they are clearly topics of the greatest importance both for the war and for the post-war period.

French military expenditure in the period 1933–8 was little short of that of Britain, although far less than in Germany. As a proportion of national income therefore it was higher than in Britain. What restrained the French government from higher levels of expenditure is not yet known. In the economic circumstances more spending on defence could only have been beneficial and the economic recovery in France after 1937 was in fact associated with the sharp increase in defence expenditure from £215 million in 1938 to £750 million in 1939. Budgetary problems played their part; the Popular Front government was in no position to increase taxation and it was succeeded by governments pursuing stern deflationary policies. The percentage increase in the real value of armaments expenditure in France in the period 1934–8, the very years when the threat from Germany materialized, was only 41 per cent, less than the increase in Canada. It was the consciousness that the economic and military leadership of the continent had passed in this period to Germany that led to the defensive strategic mentality which the Maginot Line symbolized. In the case of the Soviet Union, however, the concept of 'defence expenditure' becomes particularly meaningless. The Russian budget did not have the same functions as the French or British budget. It operated in part as a device for making large-scale general investment decisions and investment in armaments industries in the 1930s cannot be meaningfully separated from the drive to industrialize the economy. Indeed one of the prime motives of the first Five-Year Plan was military strength and the development of economic potential for war.

The strategic thinking which should have governed Soviet policy in the face of German rearmament seems to have been jumbled and vacillating. Chiefly this was because of the inordinate power and authority wielded by Stalin who, after the Russo-German agreements over Poland and the Baltic provinces, remained convinced, in the face of the clearest evidence to the contrary, that the German attack had been diverted to another direction. Russian trade deliveries to Germany, including those of strategic materials, were sustained until the invasion began, and it appears that even after it had begun Stalin at first refused to believe it was the start of a war. Furthermore, the purges of leading officers in the armed forces seriously weakened the quality of strategic planning and the Soviet forces were built up with no clear perception of what sort of war was to be fought. The idea that massive forces would instantly hurl back any invader remained current in Russia in the 1930s although several generals found methods of making public their own perfectly correct views that the changing technology of warfare meant that this was no longer true.[20] The proof of this unpopular opinion was to be demonstrated of course in the most irrefutable fashion. But meanwhile the implications were that, in spite of the high level of armament expenditure, Russian armaments were insufficiently specialized for a war against Germany and that tactical thinking on their deployment and on the structure of the armed forces was equally confused.

The third Five-Year Plan, prepared during 1937-8, was altered to meet some specific armament production tasks which arose from the perception that the Soviet armed forces needed to be equipped to a greater degree for a mechanized campaign against a highly mobile enemy who might penetrate well into Russian territory. But the main weight of the Plan in rearmament was still for general economic potential for war, that is to say for no specific war. The biggest production increases were to be achieved in machine building and in engineering, and as shortages of labour began to make themselves felt the much lower targets for consumer goods production were revised downwards. But there were serious shortfalls also in goods which were to be of vital strategic significance, especially steel and oil.[21] The industrial basis for a

20. J. Erickson, *The Road to Stalingrad. Stalin's War with Germany*, vol. 1, Weidenfeld & Nicolson, London, 1975, especially chapter 2.

21. A. Nove, *An Economic History of the U.S.S.R.*, Penguin Books, Harmondsworth, 1969, p. 255.

powerful modern armaments industry had only begun to be laid in 1928 and it may be that the acceleration in rearmament overstrained the capacity that already existed. Even measured in western terms defence expenditure, that is to say expenditure on the armed forces alone, was high and sustained. In 1934 it was about 6 per cent of national income, by 1937 about 13 per cent and on the eve of the invasion between 25 and 30 per cent. Brown estimates total budgetary defence expenditure over the period 1934–41 at £283 million; other estimates are higher.[22] Defence expenditure therefore was far higher than in any country except Germany and for most of the 1930s Russia was engaged in an armaments race with Germany in which Germany held the important advantage of an early lead which Russia could not wipe out.

Russia's weakness lay not in economic potential for war but in war potential in the wider sense. The total value of capital goods production in the Soviet Union was roughly comparable to that in Germany although their range and sophistication were still less. Her production of basic strategic materials, although still short of that of Greater Germany, was adequate to sustain a massive war effort and was still growing rapidly. Furthermore her vast territory embraced almost every kind of physical resource and the acute problems of foreign trade which dogged German, British and Japanese strategy at every step had little significance for the Soviet Union. But in matters of administrative and psychological organization of the economy and society for war it is clear, reading between the lines of the official histories, that the Soviet Union was unprepared. The conversion of the economy to wartime purposes could not begin until 3 July 1941 and the first 'mobilizational economic plan' was not adopted until one week after the start of the German invasion.[23] Until that time rearmament was still being incorporated into the main priority of Five-Year Plan fulfilment.

The effect of these combined rearmament expenditures on the world economy in general was a favourable one and for some of the smaller primary producing economies it offered the only

22. A. J. Brown, *Applied Economics. Aspects of the World Economy in War and Peace*, Allen and Unwin, London, 1947, p. 30.

23. N. A. Voznesenskii, *The Economy of the USSR during World War II*, Public Affairs Press, Washington, D.C., 1948.

hope of recovery from the depression. States whose governments' inclinations were towards retrenchment and deflation were forced into policies of increased public expenditure by the threat of German and Japanese aggression. Few countries in 1934 devoted more than 5 per cent of their national income to armaments expenditure. Brown's calculations from the League of Nations data which are presented in Table 3 show how steep the

TABLE 3

THE PERCENTAGE INCREASE IN THE REAL VALUE OF ARMAMENTS EXPENDITURE IN CERTAIN COUNTRIES, 1934–8

Germany	470	U.S.S.R.	370	Czechoslovakia	130
Japan	455	United Kingdom	250	Austria	112
Italy	56	France	41	Denmark	115
				Sweden	98
				Netherlands	92
				Switzerland	86
				Poland	56
				Hungary	47
Egypt	280				
New Zealand	172				
South Africa	140				
Australia	123				
Argentina	57				
Canada	55				

SOURCE: A. J. Brown, *Applied Economics*, p. 41.

increase in the real value of armaments expenditure in the years 1934–8 was throughout the world, even in primary producing countries. The figures are probably underestimates since most countries in fact spent more than their published 1938 estimates on rearmament in the course of the year.

The complex nature of the demand arising from armaments production was being felt throughout the international economy before 1939. It was accompanied in the Pacific by the demand arising from the Sino-Japanese war and in that area it had already begun to produce the sort of changes in the economies of primary producers which were to be widely observed after 1940. An important cause of the decline in Japanese rice imports from Korea in 1939, for example, was the movement of Korean labour from agriculture to industry to supply Japanese military needs in China. The strategies of the various powers have been considered primarily as problems in domestic economic policy because they were thought of in such terms at the time, but large rearmament programmes which, with one exception, covered all the most developed economies, inevitably began to change the terms on which even the most domestically orientated and autarkic programme could be carried out.

The exception was the missing counter in the strategy of all the powers, because in terms of economic potential for war the United States, even in depression, dominated all other powers. Hitler eliminated this industrial giant from strategic planning on the grounds that American society would be so unable to withstand the strain of war that its war potential was virtually non-existent, a fortunate misapprehension. The United States produced a bigger share of almost every strategic material than any other combatant and was completely devoid only of rubber. Her steel output in 1938, 26·4 million tons, easily surpassed even that of Greater Germany and her hard coal output, 354·5 million metric tons, was almost double the German level. In certain areas of strategic importance, in the output of aluminium and of synthetic rubber for example, Germany had outdistanced the United States, but even though by 1939 there had been very little rearmament expenditure American industry was still very strong in those areas most relevant to armaments production and nowhere else were there engineering industries of the same scope and sophistication.

United States expenditure for military purposes in 1938 was only 1·5 per cent of net available product at factor cost. Public opinion permitted no steps towards rearmament before that year apart from the Merchant Marine Act of 1936, which provided a framework for the Maritime Commission and the Navy Department to build extra merchant ships. However, the Naval Expansion Bill of May 1938 was the first programme which really affected United States industry, because before that time domestic rearmament was too low and the effect of foreign orders was restricted by the legal difficulties which often confined them to what could not be obtained elsewhere. The Neutrality Acts prohibited the export of materials of war to any belligerent and the export of a wider range of goods to belligerents could take place neither in vessels of American registration nor on any form of credit. Such legislation was, however laudable its intention, a severe obstacle to any effective strategy.

Until the Japanese attack on Pearl Harbor the goal of American strategy was still neutrality. There were alternative paths leading to this goal and the choice between them was not very clearly made. Two extremes of strategy existed: one was for the United States to rearm itself urgently, the other was for it to rearm those states which would bear the brunt of German or Japanese aggression. The second policy demanded modification of the Neutrality Acts, but they were not revised until November 1939 when armaments exports were permitted on strict cash terms. The response was overwhelming and the contracts from the British and French purchasing commissions in the second half of 1940 already amounted to $2,400 million. When, therefore, in June 1940 massive American defence appropriations were made, and a rearmament plan aiming at an army of two million by the end of 1941 was accepted, American industry already had order books full in many cases for several years ahead with original British contracts and with those French contracts which, on the collapse of France, had all been immediately taken over by the British government. Aircraft production for American purposes was to go up to 18,000 a year, with 12,000 aircraft to be in service by spring 1942. Sufficient army equipment for an army of four million was to be produced. The size of these increases can be gauged from the fact that at the outbreak of the war in Europe the American army was only 200,000 strong, with a further 200,000 national guardsmen. There were only 1,800 planes, many of them obsolescent. Most of the army equipment was designed to First World War specifications, including the Springfield rifle. The coping stone of these new programmes was the concept of a 'two-ocean fleet', approved by Congress on 19 July 1940. None of these programmes could be implemented without the most severe clashes over the fulfilment of British contracts.

In truth the rearmament programme of June 1940 represented a decisive strategic change which boded ill for Britain. 'Hemisphere defence', as the new policy was termed, seems in part to have been based on the assumption that further arms for the United Kingdom were probably of no value. Roosevelt's response to Churchill's pleas was to bring pressure for the release of certain American arms which might be spared, but these seem to have been exceptions. It was not until September that aid for the United Kingdom really began again to be thought of as having a strategic value for American defence.[24] It was this change of heart that led to the formulation of a rational strategy both for the United States and her allies. That rational formulation only finally came with the so-called Victory Plan, but from September 1940 onwards the United States was moving towards acceptance of a strategy in which, if she were involved in war, the war would be won through industrial production. The strategic assumption was that over a long period of time the United States must ultimately be victorious if war came to a battle of production, however that production was deployed.[25] And there were powerful arguments for deploying American production in the hands of the Allies. There could be no longer any doubt who those Allies would be. Already their demands had become closely involved with the United States' own defence requirements. Some British armaments orders were already in 1940 being produced to United States specifications because they were so large that American firms had had to get permission to build new armaments factories to meet them. The concept of America as 'the arsenal of democracy' was in fact already formed at a time when neutrality was still the clear aim of the American government.

The lynchpin of this strategy was the lend-lease agreements. By these agreements the United States removed all restrictions on Allied armaments contracts in America including those of immediate payment. Henceforward such goods were supplied against payment to be made after the end of the war. The origins of this complete reversal of policy can be traced to the aid provided on relatively easy terms in 1938 to the Chinese nationalist armies; throughout the period when lend-lease was in operation China remained an important beneficiary. The two main beneficiaries, however, were the Soviet Union and Britain, and it was this that made it necessary to suspend payment for a long term. By the summer of 1940 British dollar reserves had fallen to so low a level that further contracts in the United States on the existing 'cash and carry' basis had become virtually impossible. Even by requisitioning and selling off at knock-down prices the remaining private British investments in the United States and Canada and

24. R. M. Leighton, 'Les armes ou les armées?', in *R.d.g.m.*, no. 65, 1967.
25. R. M. Leighton and R. W. Coakley, *Global Logistics and Strategy: 1940–1945* (United States Army in World War II), G.P.O., Washington, D.C. 1955, *passim*.

by the strictest controls on trade and foreign exchange Britain was not able to sustain her orders in America and her potential as a defensive bastion of the United States was gravely weakened. In these circumstances the Roosevelt administration was hesitant about making a clear strategic choice. One hundred old destroyers were supplied to Britain, but even these were supplied in exchange for Atlantic and Caribbean naval bases which would play their part in 'hemisphere defence'. With the inception of the American rearmament programme in June 1940 the prime force in reviving the American industrial economy had become domestic, rather than foreign, demand and backlogs in the delivery of war material on British contracts soon materialized. The rearmament appropriations of June 1940 followed by the increase in the naval building programme were in fact beginning to achieve in the United States what the New Deal had not achieved.

Yet between the extremes of strategic choice there was still scope for manoeuvre because of the great under-utilization of resources in the United States economy in the 1930s. There were still three million unemployed in December 1941 and not until the later stages of the war did labour become a scarce factor, except for certain grades and in certain areas. Similar capacity existed also in the utilization of domestic raw materials. The opinion persisted that a strategic compromise might be possible, given an efficient administrative machine and a clear definition of priorities. Both these things were lacking in autumn 1940 and no effective machinery to supply them was devised for a further year. Economic strategy swayed according to the tactical developments in the war and the force of public opinion. Not until 30 August 1941, when the President ordered the Inter-Arms Bureau to coordinate secret plans for lend-lease production with domestic rearmament orders, was there any deliberate attempt at a rational strategy pitched between the two extremes, although, thanks to the ease with which the economy had been able to increase its levels of production something akin to this had occurred by accident.[26] The secret programme – the 'Victory Program' – remained a reserve plan until the Japanese attack on Pearl Harbor but from the moment of that attack it could be said that both the rudimentary machinery and the quite definite

26. United States, Civilian Production Administration, *Industrial Mobilization for War*, G.P.O., Washington, D.C., 1947, p. 34 ff.

intention existed for a widespread rational economic collaboration between the Allied powers, something completely lacking on the Axis side. In certain respects and with considerable limitations the Allied economies could be considered as a common set of resources coupled to a common strategic plan.

The plan of course was nothing more than what emerged as a set of loose and general agreements from the various meetings between the American, Russian and British political leaders, and from political compromises between the different national interests. Nor was the intention of economic collaboration thought of as extending one day beyond the end of the war. However large the unpaid bills accumulated under lend-lease it was always intended to present them the moment the joint strategic aim had been achieved. This, in itself, was probably the major obstacle to a rational joint economic strategy. Wars cannot be fought without constant attention to peace, and by summer 1944 the economic nature of the peace had become the main preoccupation. The strategic proposals of the United States army in its submission for the Victory Programme had been initially based on the assumption that Russia would collapse in mid 1942. No proper information about Russia's internal economic situation was ever forthcoming. Russian requests under lend-lease were simply presented as lists of equipment and the American government had to make its own decisions on the justification for each request. These decisions were usually made in an atmosphere of the deepest suspicion and distrust. The competition of national economic interests was also very strong between Britain and the United States. Joint strategic economic planning went no further than what was needed to win the war and as soon as victory was in sight it disintegrated.

The United States had also to adapt its strategy of hemisphere defence to the new situation emerging in autumn 1941. The assumption of all the American armed forces was that the early stages of a future war would have to be defensive ones. The army assumed that the strategic turning-point would come in mid 1943. But the prerequisite for this was that the German economy would have to be weakened by massive aerial bombardment. As in Britain, the main hope of taking the offensive seemed to lie with the development of the heavy bomber. In the Pacific the military campaign would be a defensive one. The army's idea was to use the vast resources of Chinese manpower as the main defensive bulwark and it advocated that one hundred Chinese divisions be armed with American equipment. The weight of the American army itself was to be used in Europe, and it was proposed that ultimately an army of five million men be sent there. The logistic problems set by these proposals were far greater than the general staff understood at the time. The Chinese contribution to the war never approached anything like this magnitude and the shipping shortages were much more acute than these ambitious transport plans supposed. Proposals from the air force were largely in agreement with these strategic ideas. Only the navy dissented and the gist of their dissent was that it would be possible by amphibious campaigns to use the soldiers where the German army could not get at them and thus give the navy a more central role in strategy.

These ideas were vague ones but they contained a great many elements in common, sufficient for certain fundamental economic decisions to be taken. The essential economic aim was to out-produce the enemy, however long it took, and to utilize that production in a framework of international strategic cooperation. Once this decision was made Germany obviously became the main enemy; surpassing Japanese production was no great problem. From this came the idea of the strategic air offensive against Germany. More than in Britain the intention was to focus this air offensive on weakening the German economy by identifying its weak spots and using the heavy long-range bomber as a method of direct intervention in the enemy's economy, rather than as a tactical armament or a deterrent. Finally a massive invasion of Europe would at some stage be launched; it was never assumed that there could be any defeat of Germany without this. Thus from an inconsiderable military power and an economy so bent on neutrality as even to deny itself the possibility of economic recovery through foreign armaments orders the United States moved in two years to a strategy of massive military and aerial intervention, of total mobilization and of the uttermost use of its economic potential. It needed only the bombs on Pearl Harbor to make this strategy public and avowed.

This discussion of the strategies of the various combatants reveals how wide the number of effective economic strategies is.

There are no economic priorities peculiar to a 'war economy'. The range of economic choice is very wide and is governed by a multiplicity of other factors. These initial strategic choices were not always adhered to and where the changes had an important economic significance they will be considered below. But for the most part they defined the framework in which the national economies operated for long periods and they determined the order of economic priorities. There is little point in comparing the economic performance of different countries during the war; the question which must be asked is how successfully the strategic priorities were in fact achieved. Nevertheless certain common economic problems did emerge and the evidence is that there are certain problems peculiar to war whatever the strategic synthesis in which the economy operates. These problems will be considered, not in relation to all the economies involved, but in relation to those which best exemplify the problem. The question of a correct choice of economic priorities was a desperate one where the intention, as in Britain, was to maximize output; it was of less consequence in Germany where economic flexibility was retained. For Japan and Britain problems of trade and supply were more vital than for the United States. For Russia problems of labour were less important than for Germany. To what extent each power had correctly fitted its economy into a strategic synthesis can only be judged on the subsequent history of the war. But it is wrong to think of strategic considerations as influencing the economy only in wartime. The falsity of the separation conventionally made between 'peace' and 'war' economies emerges from the extraordinary changes which began to take place in the United States economy under the impact of the strategies of other powers, and then of United States strategy, while the country was still set on peace and neutrality. Even more does it emerge from the long-term international economic impact of strategic decisions. The great increases of production in the United States, the changes in the world trading system, the revival of trade and production in the underdeveloped world, the structural changes in the European economies, did not have their origins in 1945 but in 1940. They were the result of the particular economic strategic choices made by the powers in the face of war.

3

The Productive Effort

In modern war the great expense of firearms gives an evident advantage to the nation which can best afford that expense; and consequently to an opulent and civilized over a poor and barbarous nation.

In ancient times the opulent and civilized found it difficult to defend themselves against the poor and barbarous nations. In modern times the poor and barbarous nations find it difficult to defend themselves against the opulent and civilized.

Adam Smith,
The Wealth of Nations, 1776

The attempt by Germany and Japan to win a war against major powers while imposing strict limits on the economic effort involved did not succeed, although it did lead in each case to a remarkable period of conquest. When the German armies were finally brought to a halt deep inside Russian territory in the early winter of 1941–2 and the first successful Russian counter-attacks recaptured the city of Rostov-on-Don the war had reached its strategic turning-point, only made more obvious one year later by the German defeat at Stalingrad.[1]

Until the turning-point in January 1941 the two sides continued

1. A. S. Milward, 'The End of the Blitzkrieg', in *Economic History Review*, no. 16, 1964.

to pursue fundamentally very different economic strategies. But with the failure of the *Blitzkrieg* German strategy began to align itself very closely with that of the Allies and this abrupt change of direction took only a short period of time. It was complete by the end of April 1941. In Japan recognition that the original strategy had failed came more slowly and the turning-point came later and is more difficult to identify. But from the attack on Pearl Harbor on 7 December 1941 to the Führer-Order *Rüstung* 1942 issued on 10 January 1942 the economic history of the war saw a decisive change. In this period first the United States and then Germany committed their economies to a strategy of massive increases of certain specialized commodities: armaments, their component parts, other war supplies, and the manufactured goods and raw materials necessary to sustain their production. Japan eventually followed suit. From the start of 1942 to the end of 1944 a torrent of war supplies poured upon the world and the demand for most commodities rocketed relentlessly upwards.

In retrospect the enormous volume of production attained is one of the most remarkable aspects of the war. Once the strategy of the aggressors had failed the strategies of all the major combatants became aligned, and the most important element in each was production. In the United States it was the declarations of war by two powers which triggered this mechanism off. In Germany the process was a more reluctant one and at every hint of a favourable turn in the war Hitler showed signs of hankering for a return to his original strategy of limited economic commitment. The abandonment of the *Blitzkrieg* strategy marked the start for Germany of a battle against hopeless economic odds, the more so as she was giving several years start in long-term investment for war production to a combination of powers which was in any case, in terms of such a strategy, economically more powerful.

In a war on two fronts, requiring different types of armaments, the sudden switches in production priorities which had sustained war production without seriously impinging on civilian production would be no longer possible. Furthermore the quantity of all armaments required in the future would now be much greater. The Führer-Order *Rüstung* 1942 openly acknowledged the new necessities and gave top priorities both to increases in the output of armoured fighting vehicles for use in Russia and to submarines for the battle of the Atlantic. The more clear-sighted officials of the Ministry of Economics, the Wirtschafts- und Rüstungsamt and the Minister for Armaments Production, Fritz Todt, were already firmly convinced that an increase in investment in armaments production was necessary to sustain the war. Although Todt's sphere of authority was a very restricted one, he already had plans in existence to re-design the administration to meet the new contingency.[2] The pressure therefore came from below and Hitler, yielding to the evidence, gradually sanctioned the fundamental changes in the administration of the economy which had as their purpose the creation of a level of war production akin to that of Britain or the Soviet Union, a situation which German strategic planning had sought for so long to avoid. These fundamental changes were carried out between January and May by the two Ministers of War Production, Fritz Todt and Albert Speer, in a remarkable administrative revolution. By May, as German fortunes in the field seemed once again very high, Hitler was regretting the changes, and his reluctance to cut back on civilian consumption appears repeatedly in his conferences with Speer. It needed, however, only the first cold fingers of another Russian winter to push the German economy even faster and further along the road of centralization of administration and maximization of war output.

It is fair to ask what hopes of ultimate success could have inspired German strategy once the idea of *Blitzkrieg* had been abandoned, for viewed in retrospect it seems to have been Germany's only chance of victory. It may well have been that in the minds of the experts these hopes were not very high ones, given the improbability of Hitler's settling for any political compromise acceptable to his opponents. But in so far as post-*Blitzkrieg* strategy was governed by any principle other than the hopeless one of trying to out-produce the Allied powers it was that of 'qualitative superiority'. This seems to have rested on the idea that because of the simplification and standardization inherent in serial production methods, which had been carried much further in the United States and the Soviet Union than in Germany, Allied armaments, although more plentiful, would always be of an inferior nature to German ones. It rested also on

2. Milward, *The German Economy at War*, p. 68 ff.

the size, strength and variety of the German machine-tool and engineering industries, which did in fact prove capable of sustaining high levels of production while adopting constant improvements and modifications to armaments. But these hopes could have been fully justified only if they had been based on an inherent superiority in design and development of armaments. And although German armaments were on the whole of very high quality the difference was not great enough to make the idea of qualitative superiority much more than wishful thinking. Germany, while having a qualitative advantage at the production stage, was very frequently at a disadvantage in the development stage because the original strategy of *Blitzkrieg* meant that relatively meagre funds had been allocated to it. Furthermore, qualitative superiority was not easy to maintain in an economy which was being forced by raw-material deficiencies to substitute one material for another in the manufacturing stage. In many ways the idea of qualitative superiority was a rationalization from the weaknesses of Germany's economic position after 1941. It did not seriously alter the fact that from the start of 1942 Germany was engaged in the same path as the Allies: concentrating the economy on the production of war equipment and cutting back in all other fields of production.

In Japan this turning-point is less evident, probably because the hopes held out by such an alternative strategy were even slenderer than in Germany. The history of the Japanese economy from 1934 is one of a gradual slide into what in Allied terms would have been acknowledged as a 'war economy', so that by 1944 the composition of total output and the level of civilian consumption reflected a desperate struggle for national survival. Each step in this process was a reaction to the crushing series of Allied successes which left Japan no alternative to fighting on alone. In a military sense the turning-points are as visible as the German army's failure to take Moscow, but the economy, impelled by each successive defeat, lurched only gradually away from the original concept of limited war.

With these reorientations of the economy in Germany and Japan all the world's most productive economies found themselves involved in a similar economic process: all the major combatants channelled their productive capacity as far as was possible into the manufacture of those goods whose main purpose was to sustain the war. Equipment for the armed forces accounted for about 66 per cent of total employment in manufacturing in Britain in 1944 and for about 59 per cent in the United States.[3] There were three stages of production during the war. The first began properly with the increased rearmament in Germany and Japan in 1938 and the start of large-scale rearmament elsewhere in the same year. It lasted until December 1941/January 1942 when the change of strategy in Germany gave a further boost to output. From then on economic effort was concentrated more and more on war production until the summer and early autumn of 1944 when the peak of armaments output was reached. After that date armaments output began to fall in Germany and Japan and in the Allied economies resources began once more to be diverted towards peaceful purposes.

The assumption of the Allied powers that time was on their side and that they would be able to produce and bring into action a far greater quantity of war material than their opponents proved a correct one. But their initial false assessment of German strategy meant that they had no appreciation of the extent to which Germany would also be able to increase her own output after the *Blitzkrieg* strategy was abandoned. The overwhelming Allied superiority in 1944 did not result in victory in that year as they had anticipated because, in certain selected areas of armament production, in the first half of the year German output was increasing even more rapidly than that of the Allies and the gap in the relative armaments strength of the two sides was not widening. However, the Allies still produced roughly three times as much combat equipment and armaments as the Axis in 1944, whereas in mid 1941 the comparative outputs had been roughly equal.

By the end of 1944 the value of combined Allied output of combat munitions throughout the war was estimated at $180,000 million; that of the Axis powers at $100,000 million.[4] Such values would have seemed impossible before the war by comparison with the national incomes of countries like Britain and Germany.

3. C. T. Saunders, 'Manpower Distribution 1939–1945', in *The Manchester School of Economic and Social Studies*, no. 14, 1946.
4. United States, W.P.B., *The World Production of Munitions at the End of the War in Europe*, Document no. 25, 1945.

Warfare and economic growth

The war must therefore principally be considered in the light of the sustained increase in production and in national income of most major combatants until 1944. For it was only out of increased national income that such enormous expenditures on war production could be sustained. The problem of how to pay for the war was solved, in the short run, by the transformation of the major economies into markets where production and consumption were paid for by the state. The increases in government expenditure were provided for from the increased production and income which were the result of what was in fact a massive capital-investment programme by the state. In the technical sense the war was a powerful stimulus to economic growth. For some of the combatants in the Second World War the rate of growth of national income was much faster than in pre- and post-war periods. This does not necessarily imply that a well-conceived war will always promote long-term economic growth, for that will require the same stuctural changes in the economy that are associated with economic growth in periods of peace, and may prove very difficult where private consumption is reduced to such low levels as it was during the Second World War. Nevertheless, in some cases the structural changes which took place in major economies between 1939 and 1945 as a result of increased investment and production did in fact play their part in moving these economies to a higher rate of economic growth after the war. Over a short period, war, if well-conceived, may promote economic growth and it is not impossible that it may do so over a longer period. But, passing beyond narrow considerations of the rate of growth of national income, does it also promote economic development? Does it further the development and utilization of resources in the economy in the wider sense?

Writers approaching the phenomenon of war from other standpoints have not been reluctant to point out numerous beneficial aspects of war. Some of these are of decided economic importance. Does not war promote rapid scientific and technological advances which are subsequently of value in peacetime? Does it not further the transfer of labour from low-productivity employment to higher-productivity employment? Does it not – an aspect which many social historians have commented on – open up a wider range of opportunities for many people and in so doing mobilize a greater flow of talent and human ability? By contrast, it is the 'distorting' effects of war which figure more prominently in most economic discussion. The concept of a 'normal' pattern of economic development seems to be deeply embedded in economic thought. The changes in the composition of industrial output which accompany war are usually classified as distortions, on the reasonable grounds that many of them are of a rather different value from increases of output in peacetime. Does the production of armaments, which in prolonged wars becomes the major industry, provide the same basis for economic development as any other industry, or is it a temporary distortion of the economy? The same may be asked of an increase in the output of raw materials which was not sustained after the end of the war because the comparative cost was too high. Large numbers of mines disused for a century were opened up in Europe in 1941 when the cost and difficulty of obtaining imported raw materials became prohibitive. Similar 'distortions' take place in the restriction of the output of goods which are not of great usefulness in warfare. Consumer goods are obvious examples, but certain raw materials important in peacetime production have a lower priority in war. This happened after 1939 with commodities such as lead and zinc.

To these 'distorting' and restricting tendencies of war is usually joined the question of the financial and physical damage done by war. Although a war may well pay for itself out of the increased national product which it occasions, the volume of government outlay on fighting may change the fiscal and financial systems of the economy in an unfavourable direction. The belief of earlier generations of writers that war led to massive increases in the public debt was not a baseless one. The problem of actually paying for the war in the strict financial sense is one of the least of economic problems in wartime, given a correct fiscal and financial policy. But is that correct policy not itself another 'distortion' which will need to be corrected when 'normal' development once more resumes? Similarly, although the national product might grow while the enemy is raining destruction on the population and the fixed capital, does not the effect of that destruction still survive after the war? Will trading connections, long inactive, be reopened? Will the effects of a reduced population not ultimately be felt? Will not the effort to restore damaged cities and destroyed railway lines after the war be further 'distortions'? Even when the productive effort of war leads, as it did in the United States, to such increases in Gross National Product that personal consumption also increases these questions will still apply. The national product, in a war involving a massive production effort, is quite different in its composition and distribution from that of peacetime. The economic development which results from intensive war can therefore be reasonably regarded as a different phenomenon from that which occurs in most economies in peace.

Nonetheless these distortions are often modified by the beneficial effects of war on the economy. The composition of German and Japanese national income after 1933 was more warlike than that of the United States and that in itself was one reason for the better performance of the German and Japanese economies in those years. And even when the national economies were engaged, as they were after 1941, in a productive effort so massive as to involve every possible kind of 'distortion' and damage the question still remains as to how far such 'distortions' and damage did in fact nullify the economically beneficial aspects of the war. The actual armaments with which damage was inflicted on the enemy were only the spearhead of war production. The capacity to produce them had first to be created, involving an increase in the output of a wide range of industrial materials. This in its turn required an initial basic investment in construction, in capital equipment, and in labour training. For example, the Second World War saw an enormous, and, as it proved, permanent, expansion of the world's capacity to produce aluminium because it was the basic constructional material of most aircraft. Unless war demands no armaments beyond those already existing this process is inescapable, as is the accompanying process of technological research and development. To fight against a major economy even with a strategy of *Blitzkrieg* necessitated a long period of preparation and testing. One important aspect of the Spanish Civil War for Germany was that it provided the sort of testing-ground for the development of new armaments that Japan already had at her disposal in China. The consequences of American strategy, which did not have to be seriously changed throughout the war, serve as a good model with which to compare the less fortunate experiences of the other combatants. Furthermore the example of the United States shows that the general tendency to consider war as economically harmful is very questionable, for the United States emerged in 1945 in an incomparably stronger position economically than in 1941. By 1943 the volume of American production far exceeded that of all other powers and by 1945 the foundations of the United States' economic domination over the next quarter of a century had been secured. For the rest of the world the productive effort in the United States was of greater significance than that in other countries; it may have been the most influential consequence of the Second World War for the post-war world.

The war effort in the United States

The wartime productive effort can be observed on three levels: the amount of national product taken by war production and services, the increase in production of certain basic goods and, finally, the increase in armaments available to the armed forces. The Gross National Product of the U.S.A. measured in constant 1939 dollars rose from $88,600 million in 1939 to $135,000 million in 1944. War production in 1939 was 2 per cent of total output, in 1941 10 per cent and in 1943 40 per cent. But the expansion of war and non-war output together was so great that consumers' purchases of goods and services also increased by 12 per cent between 1939 and 1944. This is not to say that the war did not affect American consumers. There were severe shortages of particular items and the general quality of goods deteriorated. But the only items of civilian production and consumption to show a decrease were expenditures on consumer durables and inventories of consumer goods.[5] The great increase in output for war purposes was mainly achieved out of the increase in G.N.P., although capital formation and government expenditure for non-war purposes fell steeply through 1941 and did not begin to recover until 1945.

The expenditure for war purposes is analysed in Table 4, where the timing of the different stages of war production can be seen.

5. United States, W.P.B., *The War Production Program 1943–1944*, Part IV, *Civilian Programs and the National Product*, Document no. 11, Washington, D.C., 1943.

Government-financed construction reached its peak in 1942 and in 1944 had fallen again to well below the level of 1941. The value of armaments production did not reach its peak until 1944 although that was not very much higher than the 1943 level. In 1945 armaments production began to decline. The amount of

TABLE 4

ESTIMATED VALUE OF THE UNITED STATES WAR PROGRAMME BY MAJOR CATEGORIES, 1 JULY 1940 TO 31 AUGUST 1945 (in thousands of dollars)

Category	Total	Calendar year					
		1940*	1941	1942	1943	1944	1945†
Total war programme	315·8	3·6	17·8	57·4	86·2	93·4	57·4
Armaments: total‡	184·5	2·1	8·6	30·5	52·4	57·7	33·2
aircraft	44·8	0·4	1·8	5·8	12·5	16·0	8·3
ships	41·2	0·4	1·9	7·0	12·5	13·4	6·0
ammunition	18·1	0·1	0·4	2·7	4·9	5·8	4·2
combat and motor vehicles	20·3	0·2	1·3	4·8	5·9	5·0	3·1
War construction financed by government: total	31·4	0·8	4·9	12·7	8·5	2·9	1·6
industrial buildings and machinery	16·1	0·2	2·1	6·4	4·7	1·7	1·0
Pay of military and civilians in federal war agencies	71·1	0·5	2·3	7·8	17·5	24·6	18·4

* Six months.
† Eight months.
‡ Physical quantities of production for each year multiplied by standard unit-cost weights of mid-1945.

SOURCE: R. E. Smith, *The Army and Economic Mobilization*, United States Army in World War II, Office of the Chief of Military History, Washington, D.C., 1959, p. 5.

pay to the armed forces and to those civilians working in federal war agencies, however, was much higher in 1944 than in 1943. The importance of armaments output can also be seen from the fact that completed armaments represented a high proportion of the total value of the war programme. In 1941 it was about half the value of the total programme, by 1943 it had risen to two thirds.

The period 1940 to 1944 saw a greater expansion of industrial production in the United States than any previous period. The physical volume of output increased at a rate of over 15 per cent a year. Peacetime periods of similar length seem to have occasionally produced rates of increase which may have been as high as 12 per cent but they were unusual. Industrial output increased at 7 per cent annually during the First World War and the average rate of increase in the period 1896–1939 was 4 per cent. Between 1940 and 1944 the total output of manufactured goods increased 300 per cent and that of raw materials by about 60 per cent. Investment in new plant and equipment, much of it direct investment by the government, is estimated to have increased the productive capacity of the economy by as much as 50 per cent.

The components of this expansion of output were threefold. Firstly came the increased utilization of the available resources. When the Neutrality Acts were repealed and the gates opened more widely to rearmament contracts from Britain and France, there were still 8·7 million recorded unemployed in the United States. The average utilization of working plant was about 40 hours a week. In 1944 18·7 million more people were at work than in 1939 and in war industries the average utilization of plant was about 90 hours a week. Secondly, resources were diverted from other sectors of the economy into industrial production, including construction. Part of the increased employment in industry was accounted for by a movement of labour out of agriculture and other occupations such as housewifery and domestic service, and strict economic controls also diverted other resources into the expanding sectors. The industrial sector accounted for 38 per cent of the national income in 1944 as compared to 29 per cent in 1939. Thirdly, the resources used in the industrial sector were used more productively. The average productivity of labour in industry was estimated by the War Production Board to have increased by about 25 per cent. Some part of this was due to an increase in the working week but the rest was due to a wide range of factors including economies of scale in plant and practice, new capital equipment, pooling of industrial information in a common cause, and better incentives for the labour force including, of course, the incentive to win the war.

Because this expansion did not involve a reduction in consumer expenditure it covered virtually all industries. The only significant exceptions were printing and publishing and clothing. But some industries showed a much greater expansion than others. Towards the close of 1944 about one third of total manufacturing output consisted of armaments and the biggest increases in output occurred in industries directly related to this: aircraft, ship-building, explosives, metal manufacture and engineering, which together came to employ about 20 per cent of all industrial labour by that date. A shift of this kind was only partly in accordance with previous long-term industrial development. In the case of the aircraft industry it did prove a long-term trend, in the case of shipbuilding much less so. The expansion of the engineering industry, although directly related to armaments manufacture, did in fact prove to have an application to post-war economic developments. As for metal manufacturing the United States was equipped by government aid with a large new industry, the manufacture of aluminium. But the pre-war trend, resumed after 1945, was for employment in manufacturing industry to decrease relative to that in services and on that basis the wartime develop-ments were an aberration. On the other hand the level of employ-ment in the armed forces was so high as to make such comparisons rather dubious, especially as industrial workers were more readily exempted from military service.

The rate of increase of industrial production began to slacken in the winter of 1943–4 and on the basis of some measurements may even have been at its fastest in 1941. This would suggest that taking up the slack which existed in the economy was the main factor responsible for establishing a rate of growth of industrial output which was subsequently sustained by transfers of resources and increased productivity. The gains in productivity would perhaps not have been so fully realizable in a less urgent situation. It is possible to work the labour force for longer hours in worse conditions for short periods in war than it is for longer periods in war or peace. There were few extensions of the working week after mid 1942. To the extent that productivity gains resulted from economies of scale this was furthered by a war situation in which output was concentrated on a smaller range of goods.[6] The rest of the increase is therefore ascribable to the

6. United States, W.P.B., Program and Statistics Bureau, General Econ-omic and Planning Staff, *American Industry in War and Transition, 1940–1950*, Part II, *The Effect of the War on the Industrial Economy*, Document no. 27, Washington, D.C., 1945.

greater input of productive factors and in the long run this was probably the more significant since it was not so dependent on the continuation of war.

Nevertheless the gains in productivity are of enormous import-ance in considering the war period alone. The vast superiority of the United States in armaments production – in 1944 it produced about 40 per cent of the world's armaments – was due not only to greater resources but also to higher output per man hour, roughly twice that of Germany and about five times that of Japan. Not only did this have its effect on the battlefield but on the domestic front also. Measured by the official indices, which, as everywhere in wartime, have grave defects, prices of manufactured goods rose by only 20 per cent whereas average hourly wages and raw material prices rose respectively by 50 and 60 per cent. Industrial profits, however, rose by 350 per cent before taxation and by 120 per cent after taxation. A reduction of resources used in real costs per unit of output must therefore have contributed a strong incen-tive to private entrepreneurs to pursue the necessary expansion and also played its part in sustaining the relatively high standards of American consumers during the war. These standards were in fact extraordinarily high for an economy devoting 40 per cent of its G.N.P. to the war effort. The proportion of G.N.P. devoted to war outlay was about 50 per cent in Britain, and at the end of the war even higher in Germany. But between 1938 and 1944 the value of consumer goods and services purchased in Britain fell by 22 per cent.[7] The rapid growth and higher level of productivity in the United States contributed to making that country's experience of the war a less grim one than Britain's.

The changes in the composition of total industrial output were far more rapid than in previous periods. Not only was there a reversal of the pre-war trend for manufacturing to decline in relative importance but there were great changes in what was manufactured. The most obvious of these changes was of course the switch to armaments production. In 1944 55 per cent of the labour force in manufacturing, mining and construction worked on contracts for the armed forces. But much of the output pro-duced specifically for the armed forces also has a wider relevance.

7. M. A. Copeland and others, *The Impact of the War on Civilian Consump-tion in the United Kingdom, the United States and Canada*, G.P.O., Washing-ton, D.C., 1945.

Table 4 shows what a large proportion of it consisted of aircraft and motor vehicles which, although they were produced to strict military specifications, provided a basis for a continuous process of technological learning whose results, particularly in the post-war production of aircraft, were very far-reaching. Furthermore transport and logistical problems are so great in tactical planning that armed forces tend to equip themselves, when they are permitted, with all necessary stores in every place they may conceivably be needed. Hence the 519·1 million pairs of socks ordered for the United States army during the war programme and the 229·4 million pairs of trousers.[8] The German armed forces, not to be outdone, were ordering in 1943 at the rate of half a million pairs of riding boots a year, 4·4 million pairs of scissors and 6·2 million stamping surfaces for ink pads.[9]

In the engineering industry, where the expansion of output was especially large, about half of the contract work for the armed forces consisted of armaments and armaments components.[10] Some part of this would be accounted for by products such as internal combustion engines which were scarcely different from peacetime products. The total quantity of goods supplied by industry in general to the civilian market was in any case no lower than that prevailing in 1939. In addition the exports of all goods other than foods also rose to new heights and in 1944 accounted for 13 per cent of aggregate industrial output. Indices of production of various industries are given in Table 5 and changes in the output of raw materials in Table 6. The prime factor determining the changes was clearly the extent to which production could be applied to war but the range and scope of the increases is still very wide and it covers many of the larger pre-war industries: steel, chemicals, engineering, coal-mining and food-processing. Few industries showed increases of less than 50 per cent and declines were exceptional. Even so the disparities in rates of growth were wide. Aircraft, shipbuilding, explosives, metal manufacture, other engineering trades, chemicals, petroleum and rubber increased their combined share of the labour force from 30 per

8. R. E. Smith, *The Army and Economic Mobilization*, United States Army in World War II, Office of the Chief of Military History, G.P.O., Washington, D.C., 1959, p. 14.

9. Milward, *The German Economy at War*, p. 107.

10. United States, W.P.B., Document no. 27, p. 14.

TABLE 5

FEDERAL RESERVE INDEXES OF OUTPUT OF CERTAIN MANUFAC-
TURING INDUSTRIES IN THE UNITED STATES, 1939–44 (1939 = 100)

	1940	1941	1942	1943	1944
Aircraft	245	630	1706	2842	2805
Explosives and ammunition	140	423	2167	3803	2033
Shipbuilding	159	375	1091	1815	1710
Locomotives	155	359	641	770	828
Aluminium	126	189	318	561	474
Industrial chemicals	127	175	238	306	337
Rubber products	109	144	152	202	206
Steel	131	171	190	202	197
Manufactured food products	105	118	124	134	141
Woollen textiles	98	148	144	143	138
Furniture	110	136	133	139	135
Clothing	97	112	104	100	95
Printing and publishing	106	120	108	105	95

SOURCE: Compiled from United States, W.P.B., Program and Statistics
Bureau, General Economic and Planning Staff, *The Effect of the War on the
Industrial Economy*, Document no. 27, Washington, D.C., 1945.

TABLE 6

OUTPUT OF CERTAIN RAW MATERIALS IN THE UNITED STATES,
1939–45

	Unit of measurement	1939	1940	1941	1942	1943	1944	1945
Bituminous coal	million short tons	394·8	460·8	514·1	582·7	590·2	619·6	577·6
Crude petroleum	million 42-gallon barrels	1,265·0	1,353·2	1,402·2	1,386·6	1,505·6	1,677·9	1,713·7
Iron ore	million long tons	51·7	73·7	92·4	105·5	101·2	94·1	88·4
Manganese ore	gross weight 000 short tons	32·8	44·0	87·8	190·7	205·2	247·6	182·3
Chrome ore	gross weight 000 short tons	4	3	14·3	112·9	160·1	45·6	14·0
Bauxite	000 long tons	375	439	937	2,602	6,233	2,824	981

SOURCE: *Historical Statistics of the United States*, U.S. Department of
Commerce, Bureau of the Census, Washington, D.C., 1960.

cent to 60 per cent. Certain industries which could not possibly
hope to meet the demands imposed by the rearmament programme received government aid and encouragement on an
enormous scale. This happened with the synthetic rubber industry,
because America had no domestic supply of natural rubber, and
with the aluminium industry. When the President's programme

for 50,000 aircraft a year was promulgated in May 1940 there was only one producer of aluminium in the United States (Alcoa) and one more in Canada. Aluminium production had shown a declining trend before 1937, while the German industry had developed into the world's biggest producer. The government expansion programme which began in January 1941 rested on the creation of another firm of the same size (Reynolds) out of a relatively small metal company.[11] Output of aluminium had increased fourfold by 1943.

From this prosperous economy in full expansion, with rising profits and rising hourly earnings (before tax), rising employment and rising productivity, poured a cornucopia of armaments on to all the allied powers but particularly on to the United Kingdom and the Soviet Union. About 60 per cent of all the combat munitions of the Allies in 1944 were produced in the United States. It was the American contribution that ensured a 3:1 superiority in munitions for the Allied powers generally in that year. Germany's inferiority was of course less than that ratio and that of Japan much greater. On the European fronts American munitions were only about 40 per cent of Allied provision and on the eastern European front, where the decisive land battles were fought, they were far less. On that front in fact Germany had a relative equality of armaments provision. The value of Japanese armaments production in 1944 was less than one fifth that of the United States and its scope and variety much less.

Britain was the main recipient of United States aid and many aspects of strategy were based on the assumption, which proved a justified one, that for the period of the war there existed in the two powers a common pool of armaments-manufacturing capacity. The war equipment made in Britain for United States use, together with the construction and services provided for American forces in Britain, represented a considerable return for this aid, but the debts incurred under the lend-lease provisions were still so large by 1945 that, given the very low investment to pay for this imported war material, they could only be repaid after 1945 by virtue of large loans raised in the United States and Canada. Thus, although normal international financial

11. United States, W.P.B., Civilian Production Administration, Bureau of Demobilization, *Aluminium Policies of the War Production Board and Predecessor Agencies*, Special Study no. 22, Washington, D.C., 1946.

settlements were no longer allowed to impede the outflow of war equipment from the United States to Britain after the lend-lease Acts, they were not abolished. The war was a temporary hiatus in their functioning, and the change in Britain's financial position which this hiatus permitted and even encouraged continued throughout these years to be made very clear against the moment when payment would begin. In 1939 about twice as many people were employed in manufacturing for export in Britain as in the United States; in 1944 only a third as many. While British exports were reduced to virtual insignificance, United States exports in 1944, including lend-lease, were two thirds above their 1939 level. The long-deferred credit by which they were maintained was certainly counterbalanced by the immense acquisition of bargaining power in the international arena which they gave in 1945.

The total value of United States lend-lease exports from 1941 to September 1945 was $32,515 million. Of this total $13,842 million went to Britain and $9,478 million to the Soviet Union. The total value of all exports to Britain, including lend-lease, was $15,956 million over the same period.[12] There were practically no exports to the Soviet Union outside the terms of the agreements. No other economy drew on the provisions of the agreements to anything like the same extent, although about $2,000 million of supplies went both to Egypt and to India. Of all munitions of war supplied to British forces in 1941 11·5 per cent by value came from the United States, in 1942 6·9 per cent, in 1943 26·9 per cent, in 1944 28·7 per cent, and in the second half of 1945, 21·2 per cent. In 1944 the proportion represented by purchases outside the framework of lend-lease had fallen to only 1½ per cent. The composition of this lend-lease aid to Britain alone is difficult to isolate but to the British Commonwealth as a whole the biggest item between March and December 1941 was foodstuffs (29·1 per cent) with ships, equipment and repairs second (14·1 per cent). After 1941 aircraft and aircraft equipment was always the biggest item rising to 27·7 per cent in 1945.[13] The other major items were foodstuffs, vehicles and their equipment and, especially in 1943, ships and ship repairs. As a proportion

12. United States, Foreign Aid Statistics Unit, Foreign Economic Section, Office of Foreign Liquidation, *Lend-Lease Export Summaries*.

13. R. G. D. Allen, 'Mutual Aid between the U.S. and the British Empire, 1941–5', in *J.R.S.S.*, no. 109, 1946.

of United States production these exports to the British Commonwealth were very high when it is considered that the United States was itself desperately in need of munitions of war of all sorts. The proportions can be seen from Table 7. The total values of British reciprocal aid to the United States amounted to $5,667 million, made up largely of military stores, services and petroleum. In proportion to the size of the economy this was in fact

TABLE 7
UNITED STATES LEND-LEASE SUPPLIES TO THE BRITISH COMMON-WEALTH AS A PERCENTAGE OF TOTAL UNITED STATES PRODUCTION, 1942–5

	1942	1943	1944	1945 (first six months)
Aircraft and equipment	12·4	11·9	13·5	11·8
Ships, equipment and repairs	5·5	11·8	6·7	5·4
Ordnance and ammunition	10·4	10·0	8·8	4·6
Vehicles and equipment	9·8	26·7	29·4	12·1
All munitions	7·6	11·2	11·7	7·6
Foodstuffs	4·3	4·4	5·4	3·9
Other agricultural produce	4·3	5·6	4·4	5·0
Machinery	2·6	5·7	7·1	4·2
Metals	3·9	4·2	3·4	3·5
Other manufactured goods	0·7	0·6	1·1	0·7

SOURCE: Allen, p. 258.

similar to the value of United States aid to Britain, representing in both cases about 4·75 per cent of national income.

United States aid to the Soviet Union was a more agonizing affair for the American public and government. There was no joint planning of what was needed except what occasionally emerged from the meetings of the heads of state. The Soviet government normally presented lists of its requirements and left the lend-lease authorities to work out how acute the priorities actually were. On the other hand it was in Russia and largely with Russian resources that the decisive combats against Germany were taking place, and, whatever the political predilections involved, the economic sense of supplying aid in large quantities to the Soviet Union was obvious. The exact composition of these deliveries has still not been established, much less their importance in total Russian supply. British and American supply is said to have represented about 10·5 per cent of all tanks, and over 11 per cent of all aircraft.[14]

Foodstuffs, however, were an equally vital commodity for the Soviet Union and received equal priority with aircraft in lend-lease shipments at some periods. Even in 1944 about 2 per cent of United States food supply was shipped to the Soviet Union.[15] Over the period of the agreements as a whole over 700,000 tons each of flour and sugar were sent to Russia and almost that volume of canned meat, which provided a significant part of the Red Army diet. The total value of machine-tools exported was $306 million. The volume of copper provided was equivalent to three quarters of Soviet production over the period, that of steel one seventeenth. The Ford Motor Company installed a large tyre plant, which produced nothing during the war, however, and a large oil refinery began to be built there in 1945. Sufficient railway equipment was provided for 7,669 miles of track, together with 1,966 locomotives.

In its productive effort the United States of course had advantages in terms of size of labour force and raw material supply that were shared only by the Soviet Union, or would have been had not so much of Russia been in German hands. Nor was there any active interference by the Axis powers in the workings of the United States economy apart from sinking its ships and killing its citizens, whereas a considerable amount of industrial plant in the Soviet Union and the United Kingdom was reduced to rubble by the German armed forces. Yet there can be no doubting the importance of productivity in the American production achievement. The high level of productivity in American manufacturing industry in general was exemplified by the comparatively higher level of productivity in armaments industries, where it might seem that other economies had equal need of high productivity and equal opportunity to achieve it. It is by no means obvious why such a wide difference existed; it cannot be explained on the sole grounds that the United States economy was safe from interference. Most armaments, in all countries, were made by extremely modern mass-production methods.

14. Institut Marksizma-Leninizma Pri Tsk. KPSS, *Istoriya velikoy otechestvennoy voyny Sovetskogo Soyuza 1941–1945*, vol. 6, Moscow, 1965, p. 48.

15. R. H. Jones, *The Roads to Russia*, University of Oklahoma Press, Norman, 1969, p. 268.

Part of the explanation, however, lies in the technological differences in production which will be considered later, in Chapter 5.

It can be seen from Table 4 that aircraft and ships together accounted for about half of the value of United States armaments production. In five years almost 300,000 military and special purpose aircraft were produced. Of these 97,800 were bombers, the most technically advanced of all the armaments with which the war was fought, apart from the two awful bombs which ended it, and 100,000 were fighters. Over the same period naval vessels with a displacement weight of 8·5 million tons and merchant ships weighing 51·4 million tons deadweight were built. To this tally should be added 86,700 tanks. For purposes of comparison, Germany produced 44,857 tanks and assault guns over the same period and in the years 1934–44 111,767 aircraft, of which only about 32,600 were bombers, mostly of much lighter types and shorter range.[16] Britain produced 123,819 military aircraft between September 1934 and June 1945.[17] In Japan, where shipbuilding was absolutely necessary for survival, 7,366 naval ships were built in the period 1942–4. From January 1941 to August 1945, 69,910 aircraft were produced there.[18] The Soviet Union produced 136,800 aircraft during the war, very few of them bombers, and 102,500 tanks and self-propelled guns, thereby out-producing Germany in both of these vital areas.[19] But the number of motor vehicles produced for the armed forces was relatively insignificant and in this area the Soviet Union depended heavily on lend-lease supply.

The war effort elsewhere

Other economies could not approach the level of production of the United States. This was not by any means due to their smaller available resources, although such physical barriers in further production might well have been encountered at some point. But

16. U.S.S.B.S., Overall Economic Effects Div., *The Effects of Strategic Bombing on the German War Economy*, Washington, D.C., 1945, appendix tables.

17. H. D. Hall, *North American Supply*, H.M.S.O., London, 1955, p. 424.

18. U.S.S.B.S., Overall Economic Effects Division, *The Effects of Strategic Bombing on Japan's War Economy*, Washington, D.C., 1946, Table 13, Table C-162.

19. Institut Marksizma-Leninizma, *Istoriya*, vol. 6.

the constraints on production in the Second World War were more of the nature of those discussed in Chapter 2 than absolute economic barriers. Granted that the United States had peculiar advantages in quantity of resources, in freedom from intervention by the enemy, and in the great amount of slack which existed in the economy before 1940, it remains a logical and revealing approach to ask precisely why the productive effort in other economies fell short of that in America. The incidence of warfare on the economy is so complex that such a question would be too difficult to answer satisfactorily even if all the necessary information were available. But it is the question which opens up the most avenues of exploration into the economies of the different combatants. And, strategically, it is the vital question because in the event the *Blitzkrieg* strategy failed and the war was decided by the weight of armaments production.

For Germany after 1943 figures for Gross National Product are unreliable. In any case it was not only national product that was at stake; German strategy was supra-national and was based on the mobilization of the resources of the occupied territories. Nevertheless it still emerges clearly how in Germany itself – leaving aside the occupied areas – expenditure on war, at first a much lower part of the G.N.P. than in America, developed to the same proportion and by the end of the war was even larger. All available evidence points to the fact that Germany, which had begun the war with a strategy designed to restrict the effect of the war on the economy, ended it with her economy as committed to war as any other combatant. Consumer expenditures in 1940 were still higher than war expenditures and only in 1942 did they become markedly inferior. It was also in 1942 that the share of G.N.P. taken up by government expenditure increased more sharply. The figures for government expenditure in Table 8 include *all* government expenditure. In 1939 government expenditure on war was about two thirds of all government expenditure, by 1940 it was five sixths of it and thenceforward almost the whole of it.

Because the war at first involved little extra productive effort in Germany Gross National Product grew only slightly. Once the economy had been forced to adopt a strategy of mass-production, however, G.N.P. began to increase at a rate comparable to that in the United States. The consequence of the slow growth of G.N.P. in the first period of German strategy was that inroads were in fact made into consumer expenditures beyond what the government would have wished. Over the period from 1938 to 1942 the fall in real consumption was comparable to that in Britain although of course German consumption started from a higher level thanks to the higher level of employment in the 1930s. The standard of living of the individual consumer was still higher than in Britain. Only in 1944 did this cease to be the case and to that extent the economic strategy was justified. But Germany was unable, unlike the United States, to increase her war outlay

TABLE 8
WAR EXPENDITURE AND CONSUMER EXPENDITURE IN THE GROSS NATIONAL PRODUCT OF GERMANY, 1939–43 (in thousands of millions of 1939 Reichsmarks)

	1939	1940	1941	1942	1943
Gross National Product	129	129	131	136	150
Government expenditure	45	62	77	93	109
Consumer expenditures	71	66	62	57	57

SOURCE: Klein, p. 257.

out of her national resources without eventually making inroads into consumption. How far this was nullified in the earlier period of the war by the conquest and exploitation of other states is a complicated question which has to be reserved for discussion in Chapter 4. But after the summer of 1943 the amount of occupied territory available for exploitation began to decrease and its decrease coincided with an increase in the proportion of G.N.P. devoted to the war effort. Thus as the inroads into consumption became much greater the mitigating effects of the occupation and exploitation of other territories became much less.

The strategy of *Blitzkrieg* therefore imposed important constraints on the functioning of the whole economy. Until 1942 the benefits of rapidly expanding output were forgone. After February 1942 output began to rise steeply for a relatively short period until summer 1944, and then it began to fall again. Between 1938 and 1942 there was a reduction in numbers employed – excluding the armed forces – of about 5 per cent, obviously attributable to the draft into the armed forces. This was offset by the increase in the average working week from 46·5 hours to 49 hours. The expansion in total output before 1942 must have been mainly due to a shift in the structure of production in favour of manufacturing industries. In fact industrial output increased between 1939 and 1942 by about 20 per cent whereas total national output increased by only 6 per cent. In manufacturing industry productivity increased about 15 per cent over the same period. From 1941 onwards the situation was completely changed by the massive influx of labour into Germany, some voluntary and some drafted, from all over occupied Europe. The ideal of the *Grossraumwirtschaft* was brought nearer to fruition in an unexpected way as the drive to increase production in Germany filled the industrial core of Europe with a pullulating army of foreign workers. By September 1944 there were seven and a half million foreign workers in Germany of different legal status and of almost every available nationality.[20] They formed one fifth of the total German labour force, a situation surely without historical parallel. How productively they were used is another question. In 1944 less than half their number were employed in industry and before that only about one third were so employed. But even when employed in agriculture they were releasing German workers for employment elsewhere.

Because increases in production in Germany were not achieved without decreases in consumption the shifts in production were more marked than in the United States. The number of people employed in all industries other than basic materials, metal working and engineering and construction fell from 3·5 million in May 1939 to 2·39 million in May 1944.[21] There are few figures for physical output of consumer goods before 1943 but it can safely be inferred that increases in productivity in consumer-goods industries were not such as to nullify the effect of this decline in employment. The industries where employment developed were the same as those in the United States. The decline in consumer-goods output was a more general one than in the United States but one major difference was the decline in foodstuff industries, an index of whose total output falls from 100 in 1940 to 82 in 1944. A similar index for leather, textiles and clothing falls over the same period to 79.[22]

20. E. L. Homze, *Foreign Labor in Nazi Germany*, Princeton University Press, Princeton, N.J., 1967, p. 232.

21. U.S.S.B.S., *The Effects of Strategic Bombing on the German War Economy*, Washington, D.C., 1945, pp. 210–11.

22. ibid., p. 130.

The division of industrial production by categories in Table 9 shows that non-armaments production did not sustain its total share of net industrial output. The significant decline was in investment goods and construction more than in consumer goods. There was a considerable expansion of capacity which began in 1942 but it had to take place in the most urgent circumstances and by 1943 pressure was already building up to reduce investment in armaments-producing capacity in favour of immediate output. As far as investment in basic industrial production was

TABLE 9

PERCENTAGE SHARE OF DIFFERENT INDUSTRIAL GROUPS IN NET
INDUSTRIAL PRODUCTION IN GERMANY, 1939-44
(contemporary territorial area)

	1939	1940	1941	1942	1943	1944
Basic industries	21	22	25	25	24	21
Armaments	9	16	16	22	31	40
Construction	23	15	13	9	6	6
Other investment goods	18	18	18	19	16	11
Consumer goods	29	29	28	25	23	22

SOURCE: Petzina, *Autarkiepolitik*, p. 187.

concerned the main weight in the period from 1938 to 1942 fell on the effort to fulfil the Four-Year Plan programmes. That basic investment was already bearing fruit in the increased output of petroleum, aluminium, synthetic rubber, chemicals and explosives. After 1942 the expansion of capacity was mainly an expansion in the capacity to produce armaments. Yet, in spite of the more biased expansion of industrial capacity and output in Germany as compared with the United States, at the end of the war, after the tremendous destruction wrought by the Allied powers, German productive capacity in basic industries and investment goods industries was about the same size as at the start of the war.[23] The significance of that fact for the post-war world needs no more emphasis; the currency reform two years later activated that capacity for West Germany.

The industries whose output expanded were similar to those in

23. R. Krengel, *Anlagevermögen, Produktion und Beschäftigung der Industrie im Gebiet der Bundesrepublik von 1924 bis 1956*, Duncker und Humblot, Berlin, 1958, p. 94.

the United States (Table 10). The curve of expansion does not reveal the change of strategy in 1942 because the expansion of capacity in certain areas had been a necessary part of the *Blitz-krieg* strategy and of the policy of autarky. The largest new plants in Germany, such as the Leuna synthetic fuel works or the Hermann Göring steel works, were part of the pre-war Four-Year Plan, while comparable works in the United States such as the basic magnesium plant in Las Vegas which cost the American government $132·6 million had to be undertaken as part of the

TABLE 10
OUTPUT OF CERTAIN GOODS IN GREATER GERMANY, 1939–44
(in thousands of metric tons)

Goods	1939	1940	1941	1942	1943	1944
Steel	23,733	21,540	28,233	28,744	30,603	25,853
Petroleum spirit	n.a.	3,963	4,849	5,620	6,563	4,684
Synthetic rubber	22	39	71	101	119	93
Iron ore*	4,920	5,698	10,822	10,189	10,884	7,848
Coal†	240,300	267,700	315,500	317,900	340,400	347,600

* Fe content.
† Coal years. March 1938–9, 1939–40, etc.
SOURCE: Deutsches Institut für Wirtschaftsforschung, *Die deutsche Industrie im Kriege 1939–1945*, Duncker und Humblot, Berlin, 1954.

war programme. But when the output of finished armaments is considered the change is obvious.

Indices of armaments production for the period 1939–41 show violent short-term movements between armaments types but very little overall increase of output. This was perfectly in accordance with the strategy of *Blitzkrieg*. Because the economy was not geared to long-term production in huge quantities of particular armaments types it was possible to switch the emphasis in the production of armaments very quickly from one type to another. Table 11 shows the doubling of the output of army ammunition which accompanied the land campaign against France and the speedy reduction after the victory in the level of output – which was not reached again for another two years. Equally striking is the fall in output of army equipment in the last quarter of 1941. Consistent with strategy reductions in output were ordered after the great successes in Russia. When Moscow had been taken the armaments production would be already concentrated on naval and aerial armaments for the further stages of the war. As the first Russian counter-attacks were prepared the German army was receiving its lowest share of total ammunition output since the start of the war. The decline in bomb production after the Battle of Britain was a similarly logical development.

TABLE 11

INDICES OF PRODUCTION OF CERTAIN ARMAMENTS IN GERMANY, 1939–41 (average of monthly indices, Jan./Feb. 1942 = 100)

Period	Ammunition	Explosives	Bombs	Army weapons
1939 4th quarter	74	38	41	n.a.
1940 1st quarter	82	41	40	86
2nd quarter	125	88	146	101
3rd quarter	139	101	179	97
4th quarter	102	82	124	101
1941 1st quarter	105	93	122	127
2nd quarter	106	107	117	144
3rd quarter	100	103	106	132
4th quarter	95	111	100	90

SOURCE: U.S.S.B.S., *The Effects of Strategic Bombing on the German War Economy*, Washington, D.C., 1945, pp. 283–6.

What happened after this policy of switching was abandoned can be seen from Figure 1. The general index of German armaments production rose remarkably until July 1944, but not evenly. There are three distinct periods of expansion, each of which increased production by about half of the previous level. The first was in February to July 1942, the second in October 1942 to May 1943, the third in December 1943 to July 1944. Thereafter total armaments production fell although the output of weapons and tanks continued to increase until the end of the year. Within the two and a half years of the rising trend German armaments output increased threefold, that of tanks almost sixfold. The success of this effort is testimony to the extraordinary productive capacities which a highly developed economy seems to retain in the face of every difficulty. Interference of a massive and growing kind by the enemy, the administrative problems of converting the economy to a much higher level of war output while actually fighting the war, the difficulties presented by a narrow raw materials base which tended to diminish in the period when increases in output were most needed and finally the loss of German territory to the invader had all to be contended with and were all, in the short run at least, overcome.

Figure 1. Indices of German Armaments Production, 1941–45

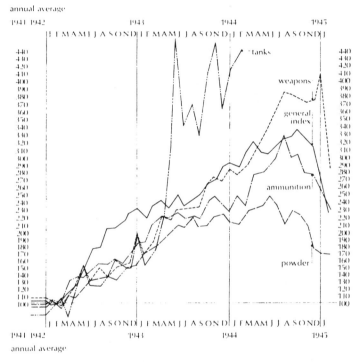

SOURCE: Milward, *The End of the Blitzkrieg.*

To decide which of these factors or what combination of them was finally responsible for halting the growth of national income and production is a hopeless task. But there is no evidence that shortages of raw materials or other resources were in themselves responsible until the territorial area controlled by the German government was reduced to well below its 1937 extent. The Ministry of War Production did have a definite idea of the extent of territory which would permit, economically, a continued possibility of defence. The Nibelungen Line, behind the shelter of which General Guderian wished in 1945 to organize a last desperate defence of the Reich, was ruled out of order by the Minister himself. The retreat, Speer thought, would be synonymous with the extinction of the fighting capacity of the troops only a few weeks later. Without the Ruhr and Upper Silesia Germany could no longer fight. 'After the loss of Upper Silesia German armament will no longer be even remotely in a position to meet the requirements of the front for munitions, arms, and tanks and the demands for new lists of equipment to replace losses. The material superiority of the enemy can therefore no longer be balanced by the bravery of our soldiers.'[24]

But loss of territory only affected armaments output when it had already begun to fall steeply. The inadequacy of the resource base cannot account for the delay in increasing output, nor for the fact that productivity was so much lower than in the U.S.A. Germany had no desire to increase armaments output until it became a matter of survival. The subsequent obstacles which twice caused the graph of armaments production to flatten out before resuming its upward trend were related to technological, administrative and political problems, and on these problems were superimposed the difficulties caused by the vigorous intervention of the Allies in the working of the German economy. Theoretically, if not in the real world of warfare, the German productive effort had not reached its outermost limit when it began to falter.

The same factors which restricted the growth of German output also had the most force in restricting the productive effort of the other major combatants. It is sometimes implied that Britain did in fact come up against the physical limits to further production because no further labour could be mobilized. In 1944 labour was drafted back from the armed forces into the civil economy. But the physical limits to output are, given the possibilities of substitution of factors, not set by one factor alone and even at the extremely high level of employment prevailing in the United Kingdom it might still have been possible to combine the factors of production differently. In the Soviet Union the loss of so many resources through enemy invasion may have brought perilously close a situation where there was no longer a sufficient base of manufacturing capacity to sustain a campaign on such a scale.

24. Speer to Hitler, 'Wirtschaftslage März/April 1945 und Folgerungen', 15 March 1945.

By the end of November 1941 63 per cent of pre-war Russian coal production, 58 per cent of steel production, 60 per cent of aluminium production and 41 per cent of the railway track had been in territory now controlled by the German army and in addition the great manufacturing centre of Leningrad was isolated from the rest of the economy. How near the Soviet economy was to the ultimate production limits cannot be assessed because we lack sufficiently detailed knowledge. As for Japan the deficiencies of the raw material base were so great that it is sometimes virtually impossible to decide whether shortages of raw materials at certain stages were inherent or due to Allied policy or caused by transport difficulties. The constraints which brought the increase in Japanese output to a standstill were as tangled and inextricable as those in Germany, but a physical shortage of resources was one of them only in a few sectors of production. The degree to which national product could be increased was governed more by the success of economic policy and administration, by the level of productivity, flexibility, and responsiveness throughout the economy, and by the ability to withstand the enemy's attacks on the economy than by inherent, absolute and unavoidable economic barriers.

In Japan the response to the growth of Allied armaments output was as decisive as in Germany once it had become clear that the United States was not readily going to make peace and that Germany was not necessarily going to win the war; Japanese production began to decline only in autumn 1944. Invading armies did not set foot on the home islands before the decline began but the retreat from the Co-Prosperity Sphere meant acute import difficulties. A poorer country with a smaller and less-developed industrial sector, short of the level of human and mechanical technological resources in which Germany abounded, Japan was much more vulnerable to economic warfare than was Germany, but the Allies never pressed home their strategy of economic warfare with the same determination they used against the more difficult target, Germany. When all attention was concentrated on Japan a number of alternative offensive strategies was available. But on all the economic evidence Japan's capacity to continue to fight had become very questionable before the bomb exploded over Hiroshima.

The proportionate growth of G.N.P. in Japan over the war

years seems in fact to have been slightly greater than in Germany, which had also started from a high level of industrial production and employment. But between 1940 and 1942 it remained relatively stable, its rapid growth after that time reflecting the urgency of the war for survival. For the first sixteen months of the war with the United States G.N.P. barely grew. Plant and equipment expenditures in the munitions industries declined between 1941 and 1942. The increased amount of war output in these years was obtained by restrictions on consumer expenditures and non-war investment. The percentage of total production accounted for by government war expenditures and private capital investment in armaments rose from seventeen in 1940 to more than thirty in 1942. United States war outlays rose from a lower point to a slightly higher proportion of G.N.P. in the same period and at the same time total output was greatly increased. After 1942 when Japan's only hope of a negotiated peace lay in maintaining a long war of attrition in the Pacific the rate of growth of G.N.P. was still outdistanced by that in the United States. The increase in capital investment in armaments industries in 1943 and 1944 (Table 12) was a large one. But in the circumstances it was inevitable that capital investment in Japan should be biased more towards producing armaments than extending the productive capacity of the basic industries. By 1944 the ratio of war expenditure to G.N.P. had climbed to 50 per cent and Japan's war effort had become more intense than that of the United States. The severe drop in consumer expenditures shown for that year does not fully reveal the hardship which prevailed in Japanese civilian life.

Total employment in manufacturing and construction increased by about five million during the war but the increase may not have been at the expense of the agricultural sector. The three million males who left agricultural employment between October 1940 and February 1944 for the most part left their farms to be worked by their female kin. There was, however, a shift of labour out of other low productivity occupations such as domestic service. On balance the improvement in productivity was lower than elsewhere. The increases in output shown in Table 13 were probably more than in other countries the result of concentrating resources on those priorities at the expense of other sectors and the 'distorting' effects of war on production are particularly in

TABLE 12

GROSS NATIONAL PRODUCT OF JAPAN, FISCAL YEARS 1939–44
(in thousands of millions of 1940 yen)

	1940	1941	1942	1943	1944
Gross National Product	39·8	40·3	40·6	45·1	49·3
Government war expenditure	4·7	6·6	9·9	14·5	20·2
Private capital formation in armaments industries	4·5	4·3	3·4	5·1	5·3
Consumer expenditures	26·7	26·0	23·8	22·4	18·8
War expenditure abroad	1·0	2·2	2·5	3·4	7·1

SOURCE: U.S.S.B.S., *The Effects of Strategic Bombing on Japan's War Economy*, Table 3.

evidence in Japan. But all alterations in the composition of industrial output were not necessarily distortions of development. The shift from cotton manufacture to metal manufacture and engineering was in line with the path of Japan's economic development, and the war speeded up and positively helped this change. In discriminating against textile manufacturers and making bank loans on guaranteed terms available to aluminium producers the Japanese government was furthering the process of economic development which was already under way before the war and was completed after it.

The rate of growth of Japanese armaments production is shown in Table 14. Until 1944 production expanded at an increasing rate for most categories. Motor-vehicle production declined after 1941, tank and combat vehicle production after 1942. War production reached its peak in September 1944 and between then and

TABLE 13

OUTPUT OF CERTAIN GOODS IN JAPAN PROPER, 1940–44
(FISCAL YEARS)

Goods	Unit of measurement	1939	1940	1941	1942	1943	1944
Steel	metric tons	5,549	5,384	5,120	5,166	5,609	4,320
Coal	000 metric tons	52,409	57,309	55,602	54,178	55,538	49,335
Aluminium	metric tons	29,559	40,863	71,740	103,075	141,084	110,398
Iron ore	000 metric tons	850	993	1,334	2,059	2,708	3,587

SOURCE: U.S.S.B.S., *The Effects of Strategic Bombing on the Japanese War Economy*, appendix tables.

July 1945 it fell by 53 per cent. The growing importance of production for air warfare is an obvious aspect of the whole; in 1945 52 per cent of all war production was for this sector. The Japanese economy did not merely move away from textile production to capital-goods production, it moved to capital-goods production on the most demanding technological level. The destruction caused in Japan by the defeat did not take away the technological expertise acquired during the war years. Although far too small to turn the tide of battle the level of armaments output was a remarkable achievement for such an economy.

TABLE 14

INDICES OF VALUE OF ANNUAL JAPANESE ARMAMENTS PRODUCTION IN 1945 PRICES, FISCAL YEARS 1941–5 (1941 = 100)

	1941	*1942*	*1943*	*1944*	*1945*
Aircraft	100	171	341	465	338
Army ordnance	100	133	167	221	143
Naval ordnance	100	151	286	512	242
Merchant ships	100	135	351	414	111
Naval ships	100	110	145	207	120
Motor Vehicles	100	62	45	39	16

SOURCE: U.S.S.B.S., Military Supplies Division, *Japanese War Production Industries*, Washington, D.C., 1946, p. 5.

The joint economic planning which enabled the United States and British economies to supplement each other was quite lacking between Germany and Japan. There was indeed very little contact at all between these two economies. Germany's economic contacts with her allies were confined to those weaker European powers whose economies she was increasingly obliged to support as the war continued. The great acquisition of diplomatic strength which Germany's conquests had brought her after the destruction of Czechoslovakia gave her the opportunity, which she seized, to redefine her economic relationship with central and south-eastern Europe very much more in her own interests. To the extent that this area of Europe, without Soviet territory, could comprise the larger economic space which the German government sought, the trade agreements negotiated in 1939 and 1940 foreshadowed a much closer subjection and integration of the whole area to the German economy. The German–Romanian trade agreement of March 1939 allowed free transit zones in Romania for German goods with further destinations and led to a great increase in Romanian oil exports to Germany and strong German pressure for the sale of French, Belgian and British capital holdings in the Romanian oil companies to Germany. The agreement with Hungary on 9 October 1940 contained practical measures to ensure closer agricultural cooperation between the two economies. In 1940 44 per cent of Romanian exports went to Germany, compared to 19 per cent in 1937. In the same year 59 per cent of Bulgarian, 49 per cent of Hungarian, 38 per cent of Greek and 36 per cent of Yugoslav exports also went to Germany.[25]

The need for armaments drove these states further into Germany's orbit. In 1941 the Hungarian government imposed legal measures to compel a cropping scheme which would be more in accordance with the food-export guarantees which had been given to Germany. Nevertheless Hungary was quite exceptional among the German Allies in 1942 in running a substantial export surplus with the Reich. By this date the hope of sustaining the German war economy by contributions of raw materials from allied powers had disappeared in face of the need to sustain the military effort of these powers by exports of armaments and other manufactured goods from Germany. In 1942 Germany had an export surplus in each case of more than 200 million current Reichsmarks with Romania, Italy and Finland, the price of keeping them in the war.[26]

Italian trade in 1941 and 1942 was virtually monopolized by Germany which provided an average of 61 per cent of Italian imports over those two years and took about half of Italian exports.[27] The biggest item of Italian exports to Germany was foodstuffs, accounting in 1942 for 515 million RM, over four times their value in 1936.[28] The volume of armaments provided

25. Ministerul Finantelor, Directinnea Statisticei Generale, *Comertul, Exterior*; Direction Générale de la Statistique, *Annuaire Statistique du Royaume de Bulgarie*; Office Central Royal hongrois de Statistique, *Annuaire Statistique Hongrois*; Ministère de l'Économie Nationale, *Statistique du commerce de la Grèce avec les pays étrangers pendant l'année 1940*; Statistique Générale d'État, *Annuaire Statistique du Royaume de Yougoslavie*.

26. Milward, *The New Order*, p. 283.

27. Istituto Centrale di Statistica, *Statistico del comercio speciale, 1941–42*.

28. K. Hunscha, Eidesstattliches Gutachten, 'Die wirtschaftlichen und finanziellen Beziehungen Deutschlands zu den von ihm besetzten Ländern Kontinentaleuropas 1940–1944' (unpublished document).

by Germany in return in these years is not known; neither is the accurate composition of German exports to Italy. But in 1939 and 1940 coal and coke were the most important items followed by iron manufactures and by machinery. After 1939 the Italian war effort was completely dependent on Germany maintaining supplies of coal. The unforeseen demand for coal in Italy was a prime cause of the constant problems of supply in Germany of the one raw material with which Germany seemed to be adequately provided before the war.

TABLE 15
ITALIAN IMPORTS OF COAL FROM GERMANY, 1937–43
(in thousands of metric tons)

	Total coal imports	From Germany
1937	12,572·8	7,628·0
1938	11,915·0	7,003·8
1939	11,154·7	6,513·4
1940	12,428·2	10,685·9
1941	11,428·0	11,386·2
1942	10,462·7	9,722·4
1943*	6,096·0	5,217·0

* First six months.

SOURCE: Statistisches Reichsamt, Der Aussenhandel Italiens 1939–43, cited by A. Raspin in her unpublished Ph.D. thesis, 'Some Aspects of German–Italian Economic Relations 1940–43 with Particular Reference to Italy' (University of London).

Even in the Hungarian case, where Germany was on balance a net importer, German capital was often financing the industrial development which permitted this level of Hungarian exports. The Manfred Weiss munition works built a new plant four fifths of the capital for which came from Germany. Joint German–Hungarian investment in aircraft factories provided Hungary with an important new industry. The Danube Aircraft Construction Company and the Hungarian Wagon and Machine Factory were merged to turn out modern warplanes, whereas before 1940 only old-fashioned trainers had been built in Hungary. Between the end of 1943 and summer 1944 700 modern German aircraft and about 1,000 engines were produced. The constructional materials were provided from the Danube Alumina Factory built with German capital in 1942 and from two new aluminium factories.[29] Before the war German policy had been to prevent Hungary processing its own bauxite. Although after 1941 the output of consumer goods ceased to grow it would not be unfair to characterize the years 1938 to 1944 in Hungary as an industrialization boom produced by Hungarian and German military demand. The growth of output of manufacturing industry in the period 1938 to 1940 was greater than the total growth achieved between 1918 and 1938. At the peak of production in 1943 industrial output was 38 per cent higher than before the war. The share of capital goods industries in this total output also grew rapidly. It was during the war that for the first time Hungarian manufacturing industry made a greater contribution to the national income than agriculture.

After 1943 about half of the artillery and ammunition output of the Hungarian armaments factories was for German use. But otherwise the industrial contribution made by Germany's allies was small. This of course does not include Bohemia and Moravia which were virtually absorbed into the German war economy. It is estimated that between 1939 and 1943 Czech coal production increased by more than one third, electric current production by 44 per cent and the output of steel by 11 per cent. At fixed prices the total output of the industry of the Protectorate was 18 per cent above pre-war levels.

In the United Kingdom as in the United States, the increased output was financed by a growth in national income, which rose 64 per cent between 1939 and 1945. British economic strategy for the war did not crystallize until 1940; before then discussion in the Treasury ranged over the older question of who should pay for the burden of the war, present taxpayers or taxpayers still to come. Considerations of public finance still loomed large and fiscal policy was regarded as being a prime determinant of economic strategy rather than being a tool by which it could be implemented. Thus the policy of 'business as usual' had a particular appeal if it meant that export levels could be maintained at so high a level as to permit part of the costs of the war to be paid out of the earnings of an export surplus. Hence the extraordinary

29 I. Berend and G. Ránki, 'Die deutsche wirtschaftliche Expansion und das ungarische Wirtschaftsleben zur Zeit des zweiten Weltkrieges', in *Acta Historica*, no. 5, 1958.

fact that an 'export drive' received top priority in the winter of 1939–40. It had not yet been understood that the financial cost of the war would be so huge as to be beyond all possibility of payment out of such means plus taxation. It was Keynes in his trenchant newspaper articles who forced thinking towards the concept of national income and its wartime growth and placed the problem of 'how to pay for the war' in its true economic setting, where it appeared much more solvable.[30] Once the problem of paying for the war had come to be seen not as merely a budgetary one but as a matter of the deployment of the total national income strategy remained with only one significant interruption firmly attached to a period of basic capital investment in extending productive capacity.

Of the total national product government consumption for both civil and war needs was taking about one half when the war effort reached its peak. Since that consumption was overwhelmingly for war purposes a rather greater share of the available product was going to those purposes than in the United States. However this was accompanied not only by the consumption of capital but also by a drop in consumer expenditures. In 1943 civil consumption had fallen about 21 per cent below its 1939 level. A higher proportion of the *increase* in national product was therefore devoted to war outlays in the United Kingdom than in the U.S.A. This trend did not continue in 1944 although even in 1945 the war was still being fought out of capital consumption.

It would be repetitious to analyse at length the pattern of increases of production in Britain. The output of consumer-goods industries declined sharply and that of certain other manufacturing industries increased in accordance with the pattern already observed in the United States. Indeed the direction of this trend by the central government was much easier in Britain because the large proportion of industrial raw materials which was imported could be controlled at the ports and issued to manufacturers under licence. But the output of two basic industries, steel and coal, did not increase and in the case of coal fell consistently throughout the war. The steel industry was dependent on imports of iron ore whose unit cost of carriage and, more importantly in wartime conditions, whose consumption of shipping space per ton was

30. J. M. Keynes, *How to Pay for the War*, Macmillan, London, 1940.

very high. British and Russian steel production combined in 1942 was less than that of Germany and in the British case this did impose certain constraints on armaments production. As for coal it was a sorry story, on every count more was needed and in every year less was mined.

The Ministry of Supply indices of munitions production all show consistent increases. Capital investment seems to have been heavily biased towards extending the capacity of plant to produce finished armaments. At the time when the initial decisions on expansion were taken no one realized how drastic the restrictions on imports would eventually be and it is hard to resist the impression that the expansion plans assumed a higher level of imports of basic metals and semi-manufactures. Certain major armaments have been included in Table 16 to indicate how successful manufacturing industry was in these respects. The number of

TABLE 16
OUTPUT OF CERTAIN GOODS IN BRITAIN, 1939–45

Goods	Unit of measurement	1939	1940	1941	1942	1943	1944	1945
Steel	000 tons	13,221	12,975	12,312	12,764	13,031	12,142	11,824
Electricity	m. kW hours	27,733	29,976	33,577	36,903	38,217	39,649	38,611
Coal	000 tons	231,338	224,299	206,344	204,944	198,920	192,746	182,773
Aluminium	000 tons	24·96	18·95	22·67	46·78	55·66	35·47	31·90
Iron ore	000 tons	14,486	17,702	18,974	19,906	18,494	15,472	14,175
Cotton yarn	m. lbs	1,092	1,191	821	733	712	665	597
Total aircraft	number	7,940	15,049	20,094	23,672	26,263	26,461	n.a.
Specialized bomber aircraft	number	758	1,967	3,275	5,439	7,352	7,903	n.a.
Tanks and self-propelled artillery	number	969	1,399	4,841	8,611	7,476	n.a.	n.a.
Bombs	short tons	n.a.	51,093	147,848	211,048	233,807	309,366	n.a.

SOURCE: United Kingdom, Central Statistical Office, *Statistical Digest of the War*, H.M.S.O., 1951, *passim*.

medium and heavy bombers produced, compared to Germany, and Japan, for example, was extremely high. In Germany and Japan these were armaments whose manufacture was virtually abandoned in 1944 and the Russian output was always low. But although the air production programme occupied the front of the stage the supporting roles were forcefully played. Production of small arms and of shells and bombs increased tenfold between the end of 1939 and the first quarter of 1943, of guns seven and a half times, of high explosives five times, and of wheeled vehicles three and a half times. Well over one thousand merchant ships were completed in every year in the period from 1941 to 1944, four fifths of them in every year having a weight of over 1,600 gross tons. By 1945 the British economy was turning out armaments at an annual value of about $15,000 million in spite of the reductions which had been taking place since summer 1944. This was about $5,000 million less than the value of Russian output and less than one third that of the output of the United States.

Alone of all the major combatants the Soviet Union had to fight the war out of a diminishing rather than a rapidly increasing national product and from an industrial base much smaller than the pre-war one. As a result of the invasion gross industrial output did not again reach its 1941 level until 1944 and national income in that year was still below the 1941 figure. It is obvious that for the Soviet Union the problems to be faced were unique in their severity and that they could only be solved by the utmost sacrifice by consumers. The great capital investment programmes of the previous decade which had equipped Russia with the basic industrial capacity to resist the German onslaught had already caused downward movements in consumption and Russian consumers had far less capacity for further sacrifices than those of the other Allies. That these sacrifices passed beyond the bearable may be understood from Table 17; gross agricultural output in 1943 was

TABLE 17
INDICES OF ECONOMIC PERFORMANCE IN THE SOVIET UNION, 1940–44

	1940	1941	1942	1943	1944
National income	100	92	66	74	88
Gross industrial output	100	98	77	90	104
Output of armaments industry	100	140	186	224	251
Gross agricultural output	100	62	38	37	54

SOURCE: A. Nove, *An Economic History of the U.S.S.R.*, Penguin Books, Harmondsworth, 1969, p. 272.

just over one third its 1940 level. Such a shortfall could not be made up from lend-lease food imports and the old, infirm and unfortunate on occasions starved to death. Furthermore the huge emphasis on capital-goods production under the Five-Year Plans meant that consumer-goods industries were often so small that the drastic cuts freed comparatively few resources for other forms of industrial production. The share of engineering and metal working in total industrial output was 57 per cent in 1942. Consumer-goods production in some areas virtually stopped altogether. An index of consumer-goods production with 1940 equal to 100 gives a value of 54 for 1943, 59 for 1945 and does not again reach 100 until 1949.[31] The output of footwear fell from 211 million pairs in 1940 to 63·1 million pairs in 1945, of cameras from 355, 200 to practically nil in the same period and the output of sewing machines ceased altogether.

The Soviet budget is a better guide to investment and to total expenditure within the economy than the budget of the capitalist states because the level of private investment, which played, for example, so big a role in the Japanese armaments industry, does not have to be considered. It is fortunate that this is so because the budget is one of the few accurate and available sources of information about the Soviet Union during the war. Table 18 indicates

TABLE 18
CHANGES IN THE SOVIET UNION BUDGET, 1939–45
(in thousands of millions of roubles)

	1939	1940	1941	1942	1943	1944	1945
Government revenue	156·0	180·2	191·4	165·0	202·7	268·7	302·0
Turnover tax	96·9	105·9	93·2	66·4	71·1	94·9	123·1
Direct taxation	7·0	9·4	10·3	31·5	28·6	37·0	39·6
Loans	7·6	9·4	10·9	13·2	20·8	29·0	26·7
Government expenditure	153·3	174·4	203·2	182·8	210·0	263·9	298·6
Military expenditure	39·2	56·8	90·5	108·4	124·7	137·7	128·2
Financing of national economy	60·4	58·3	51·6	31·6	33·1	53·7	74·4

SOURCE: S. Prokopovitch, *Histoire économique de l'U.R.S.S.*, Flammarion, Paris, 1952, p. 613.

the huge increases in taxation which were necessary to sustain production on Russian territory. The decline in the turnover tax, the principal Soviet tax, is to be attributed to the fall in production. In its place came swingeing increases in direct taxation. The loans referred to were effectively forced savings out of workers' earnings. In 1945 real wages were only 40 per cent of their 1940 level.[32] The fall in consumption in Britain, Germany or Japan was far less by comparison.

31. Institut Marksizma-Leninizma, *Istoriya*, vol. 6, p. 45.
32. Nove, p. 282.

The indices in Table 17 reveal that in such desperate straits it was still possible to increase armaments output. It increased by 40 per cent between 1940 and 1941. In 1942 aircraft output increased threefold and that of tanks doubled. This could only have been achieved by giving such output the most absolute and overriding priority. Clearly the Soviet Union faced a unique strategic problem in that it had to create the capacity to sustain a continued increase in armaments output to match German production at a time when industrial output was declining, while at the same time finding the resources for investment to halt that decline. This necessarily implied ruthless cuts elsewhere; indeed the armaments industries were the only ones to avoid catastrophic falls in output. The official Soviet histories give Russian aircraft production during the war as slightly higher than that of Germany and tank production as almost twice as high. The difficulties of comparing armaments production are such as to make comparisons almost meaningless but in the case of tank production there are grounds for valid comparison for Russian and German tanks were very similar. The comparison with aircraft is probably in Germany's favour if weight and complexity of type are taken into account. American estimates of Russian arms production also put it at roughly equal to that of Germany.[33]

The consequences of such an effort on industrial production in circumstances where in many industries over half the plant was captured by the enemy were inescapable. Steel production in 1943 was less than one half its 1940 level and coal just over half that level. Production of metal-cutting lathes fell from 58,400 in 1940 to 38,400 in 1945, of forging and pressing machines from 4,668 to 2,871.[34] There was no major industry whose level of output in 1945 was as high as before the German invasion (Table 19). In that sense the Soviet Union's experience was the opposite of that of the United States. The U.S.A. emerged in 1945 into a world of exhausted nations with its enormously expanded industries working at full capacity and at higher levels of efficiency than ever before, and with its population enjoying a higher standard of

33. United States, W.P.B., Program and Statistics Bureau, General Economic and Planning Staff, *World Munitions Production 1938–44*, Document no. 21, Washington, D.C., 1944.

34. R. A. Clarke, *Soviet Economic Facts 1917–1970*, Macmillan, London, 1972, pp. 69, 71.

living; Russia entered the post-war world after the most appalling population losses with an enormous armaments industry operating only amidst the wreckage of the Five-Year Plans.

TABLE 19
PRODUCTION OF CERTAIN GOODS IN THE SOVIET UNION, 1940–45
(in millions of metric tons)

	1940	1941	1942	1943	1944	1945
Coal	166	154	75·2	92	118	149·3
Oil	31	28·5	15·2	15·8	17	19·4
Steel	18·3	17·8	8	8·4	10·8	12·2
Electricity*	48·3	46·5	23	28	35	43·3

* 000m.kilowatt/hours.

SOURCE: P. Sorlin, *La Société soviétique, 1917–1964*, Armand Colin, Paris, 1964, p. 261.

That the Soviet Union could sustain even these levels of production was due to the most remarkable geographical shift in production of the whole war. It is quite common for war to alter the regional distribution of industrial production. Shifts of this kind in the United States were more significant than in peacetime. Had California's labour force merely kept pace with its pre-war rate of expansion it would have been 400,000 smaller in 1944 than it actually was. The origins of the post-war industrial development of the south-western states and of California and Utah lies in the expansion of defence industries there during the war. But most new defence plant in the United States was created in existing industrial centres because there the labour, the skills and the basic materials were most easily collected together. In the Soviet Union there was a forced removal of plant to the Urals and Siberia, carried out with the utmost ingenuity.

Nor did this constitute the continuation of an existing trend because in the 1930s most investment had continued to go to the western regions. Between July and November 1941, 1,360 large-scale industrial enterprises were evacuated eastwards. One such factory evacuated in this period had already produced 30 MiG aircraft on its new site by the end of the year. About ten million persons also took part in the evacuation and the scale of the whole operation shows, perhaps more than any other incident of the war, the extraordinary capacity which industrialized economies have for adaptation to the most seemingly impossible situations.

The Stalin gun factories were moved from Moscow and re-erected in Miass in the Urals in the middle of winter in temperatures far below freezing point. The Putilov armament works evacuated from Leningrad produced 18,000 heavy tanks in the southern Urals.[35] The transfer eastwards of the steel works from Zaporozhe required 8,000 railway trucks. It is not surprising that the railway system could not properly cope with removals on such a scale; the total volume of transfers has been estimated at one and a half million wagon loads.[36]

It quickly became the practice to transfer only the most essential machines. Had the eastern regions been completely unindustrialized before 1939 or had they had no resources this extraordinary redistribution of the productive capacity could never have succeeded. But the developments were not on virgin land: Siberia already produced one third of Russian coal, iron and steel. And the biggest movement was to the Urals which was already becoming an industrial area. During the war it was transformed into the country's major industrial area. Investment there over four years was at a level 55 per cent above that of pre-war levels and the industrial output of the region increased threefold.[37] About 40 per cent of the output of all war industry was supplied from that region alone. Even so the increases in output in Western Siberia, in Kazakhstan and in Central Asia were remarkable. In Western Siberia the value of engineering output increased elevenfold in the period from 1940 to 1943.

Many of the products – aircraft, machine-tools, tanks, ball-bearings and electrical equipment – were quite new. This redistribution was made possible by the large amount of railway construction and improvement which accompanied it. In the whole period of the war about 10,000 kilometres of new railway were built, and in 1943 19,000 kilometres of recaptured track were reconverted to the Russian gauge. Forty-five new power stations were built there and ten new blast furnaces, including the big extensions to the Magnitogorsk steel works. Two new metal-producing centres appeared, Petrovsk-Zaibalski east of Baikal

35. J. Chardonnet, *Les Conséquences économiques de la guerre, 1939–1946*, Hachette, Paris, 1947, p. 49.

36. A. M. Belikov, 'Transfert de l'industrie soviétique vers l'est', in *R.d.g.m.*, no. 41, 1961.

37. Voznesenskii, p. 28.

and Komsomolsk on the Amur river. New oil-wells were opened in Daghestan and the output of the Emba field in Kazakhstan increased from insignificance to two million tons by 1945. Even bigger was the so-called 'Second Baku' between the Volga and the Urals. There are obvious advantages to space in warfare; the German government occasionally attempted similar evacuation policies during the retreat on the eastern front but one of the major obstacles was finding a place to re-erect the plant.

The decline in national product in the Soviet Union at the start of the war was the consequence of the loss of territory and the economic disruption caused by the invasion. In Italy Gross Domestic Product at market prices was not increasing even in the period of victories. After 1942 it began a catastrophic fall. In 1945 it had sunk to the level of the first decade of the century. The immense investment and productive effort which characterized the war effort of the other combatants did not take place in Italy and it fell rapidly behind the other powers. Government and economy alike were utterly unsuited to resisting the Allied onslaught. Stagnating production and raging inflation soon made Italy's situation hopeless. The fascist experiment, whose economic foundations had been shaky at the best of times, collapsed into occupation and penury. None of the economic benefits of war were reaped in Italy; its disasters were reaped in full.

The poor response of the Italian economy to the challenge of

TABLE 20
GROSS DOMESTIC PRODUCT OF ITALY AT MARKET PRICES AND NET NATIONAL INCOME AT FACTOR COST (in millions of lire)

	G.D.P. at market prices	N.N.I. at factor cost
1938	165,053	133,173
1939	176,790	142,291
1940	175,040	143,774
1941	173,617	142,471
1942	169,757	140,926
1943	150,766	129,770
1944	120,579	109,353
1945	96,297	85,866

SOURCE: G. Fuà, *Notes on Italian Economic Growth 1861–1964* (E.N.I. Publicazione n. 26, Scuola Enrico Mattei di Studi Superior sugli Idrocarburi), Milan, Giuffrè, 1965.

war even before the invasion shows how varied the economic experience of war was. Italy was at the opposite end of the spectrum from the United States. The other economies, although they were able to fight the war out of the increase in national product, were unable to emulate the American experience and were forced substantially to reduce consumption to below its pre-war standards, although in Germany that was a feature only of the closing period of the war. Although therefore all the major combatants, except for the Soviet Union, experienced a period of economic growth during the war, their collective experience from the wider viewpoint of economic development was a varied one. Even in the United States the path of economic development revealed the familiar 'distortions' of wartime. Everywhere the degree of success with which the productive effort was undertaken determined the extent to which inroads had to be made into consumption. Where the degree of success was highest, in the United States, it is surely impossible to consider the war except as a stimulus to growth and development. Where the success was lower and the obstacles greater there is more room for debate. It was not resource deficiencies which prevented other economies from emulating the American success but other obstacles. The effect of these obstacles to increasing national production must be looked at before any more definite answers can be given to the questions posed at the outset about the relationship between war and the economy, although the positive influence of war on economic development is certainly very much in evidence when examined from the macroeconomic viewpoint.

4

The Direction
of the Economy

Another great war will plunge the world into a sort of military
communism, in comparison with which the control exercised
during the recent war will seem an Arcadian revel. Personal
freedom and private property are condemned by the exigencies
of a modern war.

E. M. H. Lloyd,
Experiments in State Control, 1924

The movement away from market mechanisms

The differences between the political societies involved in the
Second World War were very wide. Once commitment to a war
involving a high level of economic effort was accepted, however,
the economic problems to be solved were often very similar. A
comparative study of the machinery by which these economic
decisions were taken and enforced indicates that common decisions impose to some extent common administrative solutions.
This is not to say that such common administrative solutions
work equally well in every form of political society; the evidence
of the war is that they do not. The acceptance of war on such
a scale wrought profound changes in the administration and
direction of the major economies, with the possible exception of
the Soviet Union. Everywhere the price mechanism came to be

regarded as a method of allocating resources which was too slow and too risky. A variety of mechanisms of economic control and direction were devised to supplement and speed up the normal workings of the market. The circumstances were regarded as wholly exceptional but the successes achieved left those concerned with the direction of western economies with markedly different attitudes to the economy from those with which they had entered the war. No longer did they feel themselves to be the helpless victims of economic forces beyond their control. Economies were positively and successfully directed into different paths in the war period. By 1945 a great wealth of administrative experience and of economic confidence had been gained. After 1945 this was to be firmly applied in an effort to avoid the cyclical disasters which had followed the First World War. The war widened the scope of economic understanding and it had this effect particularly in government circles. But more than this, it brought the pressure of society to bear to change political will in the direction of constructing a more humane economic society, a society which was prepared to influence and master economic events rather than suffer from them.

In spite of the existence of two economies – the Soviet Union and Germany – which had relied heavily on physical controls rather than prices during the 1930s, the other economies moved away from allowing markets and prices to determine the allocation of resources reluctantly and only under the pressure of great danger. This is not surprising because the basic conception of war which had prevailed since the eighteenth century was a financial one. War was seen as a financial loss. The almost universal assumption was that expenditure of resources of any kind on war was a waste, necessary, perhaps, but a waste, in the sense that there was no return to the economy from these expenditures. Therefore every war had its cost, which could be expressed in a financial calculation. It followed from this that the main task of economic strategy was to decide at the outset how much could justifiably be expended on any war. This question decided, the next question was how that sum would be obtained. Was it better to raise it in taxation during the war itself or by loans to be repaid after the war? The assumption was that wars financed out of current income bore on the generation fighting them, those financed by loans bore on generations still to come.

The huge and unforeseen costs of the First World War had made it quite impossible for it to be fought out of current income. After 1918 considerable ingenuity was spent on calculating exactly what the loss to the combatant economies had been and how the burden of this loss had been distributed. The items considered as loss were various. In the first place there was the value of the actual physical destruction inflicted by the enemy. This had also to embrace the human capital lost, each item of human capital representing a certain sum invested by the economy in education and training, and also a loss of hypothetical future income and production after the war. Added to this were the sums of money set aside as war 'expenses' which could be taken as an approximation for the real resources 'wasted' on war, that is to say diverted from what was considered the normal path of production. A typical procedure for establishing these 'expenses' was to calculate the difference between the sums raised and spent by the government during a period of war and those raised and spent during a preceding period of peace of equal length.

The conception that government expenditure in peacetime has little to do with government expenditure in war seems now to belong to a happy and very distant past. The two types of expenditure could not meaningfully be distinguished in National Socialist Germany. Even for nineteenth-century Britain the distinction seems in retrospect closer to the methodological conveniences of a counting-house than to economic and political reality. Furthermore there are theoretical issues raised by the assumption that capital destroyed in war is a loss. They may be summed up in the following way. Suppose a practically uneducated and unskilled labourer to have been killed at an early age while serving with the fighting forces in 1918, what was the loss to the economy? It must surely depend on the post-war conditions of employment and on the production function, in the widest sense of the term, remaining unchanged after the war. In this case it is all too likely that he would have been unemployed for long periods after 1918 and his future hypothetical consumption greater than his production. His death would not be a loss to the economy but a gain. It might be argued with almost equal cogency that had he been unemployed before the war, a quite likely event, his death could also have been a gain. The suggestion is now frequently made that Germany and Japan gained during the war because so much fixed capital was destroyed and replaced with more productive plant where necessary. Beyond these considerations lies a more important one still. Is it true that the expenditure entailed by war is wholly a loss? Is not some part of it actually beneficial in stimulating future production and employment?

Clearly it is. But so long as war was conceived only in terms of cost the central economic administrative machinery of war had to be a financial administration which finally governed all decisions on the allocation of resources. This administrative practice survived intact, although by no means undented by the events of the First World War in the United States and in Britain. When war demanded that central economic decisions be made about the allocation of real resources these decisions were initially made, when they were made, by the central financial administration.

The assumptions on which financial control was seen as the central mechanism for the economic mobilization of factors of production could not long survive the economic realities of the Second World War. They had in any case been eroded by the development of Keynesian economic theory and of national income accounting as a tool of economic management, as well as by the growth of more 'planned' economies elsewhere. After 1939 they were dealt mortal blows. It was impossible to suppose in the aftermath of the defeat of France that Britain had any possibility of sustaining the war against Germany short of the most absolute and immediate utilization of every resource, whatever the cost. The aim of any rational financial policy could only be to make this utilization easier. But even the most pessimistic calculations of the volume of resources necessary were soon seen to have fallen far short of what would actually be required. The cost of the war was virtually limitless and virtually irrelevant. The primary economic decisions were seen to be decisions about the immediate utilization of real resources and the priorities to be established in their utilization. Once it was perceived to be a question of the order of priorities it was equally clear that the order could be more quickly determined by methods of control other than financial. Control of the economy by the Treasury in Britain came to an end in May 1940.[1] Until the fall of France the illusion prevailed that the

1. D. N. Chester, 'The Central Machinery for Economic Policy', in D. N. Chester (ed.), *Lessons of the British War Economy*, N.I.E.S.R., Cambridge University Press, 1951.

resources for the war might be provided from a balance of payments surplus. When orders for war equipment swamped industries producing for export and when it was comprehended how much war equipment was needed realities could no longer be evaded. There were two periods during the war when the Chancellor of the Exchequer was not even a member of the War Cabinet.

In the United States public bodies with control over allocation of raw materials and empowered to take certain planning decisions over priorities in their use were developed before Pearl Harbor. The Advisory Commission, which depended on the inactive Council on National Defense, became the focus for defence-spending decisions in May 1940 because of general uneasiness that such decisions needed to be taken outside the normal political arena. In June the President was permitted to order higher levels of priority for contracts for the armed forces, but with firms producing for a normal peacetime market now in full expansion it was difficult to get such contracts accepted. The mechanism chosen to solve this problem was still a financial one. Congress empowered the Reconstruction Finance Corporation to make loans to industrialists for defence and to allow the borrower to deduct the costs of construction from taxable profits over a five-year period. Both the War Resources Board and Bernard Baruch, who had been the main figure in industrial mobilization in the First World War, recommended in 1939 that there should be a central control of economic resources in the economy. But, as in Britain, changes had to wait on political opinion, and it was only after Roosevelt's re-election in November 1940 that controls came slowly into being to cope with the growing backlog in defence contracts and armaments production.

The machinery that was devised was not very effective. The Office of Production Management, headed by William S. Knudsen, the President of General Motors, and the trade unionist Sidney Hillmann, never came to terms with the situation. Theoretically it exercised the rights of the Advisory Commission over industrial production, raw materials and priorities in the allocation of resources, and subsequently it took over the work of the Adviser on Employment. But like the Advisory Commission it tried to act on the assumption that the primary task was policy-making and that the administrative enforcement of the policies would look after itself. But policy-making was not centralized in one body. The main influence was the armaments programmes which the military declared to be necessary. Neither the military nor the Office of Production Management had enough facts to determine the feasibility of these programmes and their effect on the economy as a whole. The industrial effort in 1941 was already having an effect on remote and obscure businesses throughout the economy. The military organizations were competing economically on the market with each other, with civilian organizations, and with foreign military purchases, to get their orders completed. In reality, the extent to which policy was fulfilled was being determined by thousands of separate local decisions by businessmen.

The first real break with financial control only came in August 1941 with the establishment of the Supply Priorities and Allocation Board which could mediate between existing levels of priority laid down by the Office of Production Management and the ordnance departments. It marked the administrative acknowledgement that the overriding issue was now, as it had become in the United Kingdom in May 1940, the order of priorities in which resources were made available. The Board's duties were to estimate, outside the conception of cost, exactly what resources were needed for defence and to make them available even at the expense of restricting other activities. Donald M. Nelson, Chairman of Sears Roebuck, was made Executive Director and it was he who was later to become head of the War Production Board. But the size of the military programmes was constantly increasing and there was still no agreement to restrict production for civilian purposes. The Supply Priorities Board tended towards financial assistance towards its priority choices rather than to imposing unpopular restrictive controls on the types of production that clashed with them. Only with Priorities Regulations 10 and 11, issued in June 1942, was the decisive step to interfere with markets finally taken. The first regulation established a method of identifying the final use of all raw materials allocated; the second established the principle that raw materials would be controlled and allocated according to whether their final use corresponded with the priorities of government policy.

The role of financial policy

With these regulations financial policy had ceased to be the determining issue in the economies of all the major combatants. But that did not mean that it became an unimportant one. Except in the Soviet Union, where juggling with incentive wage rates did little to disturb the basic system of planning by physical controls, economic administration everywhere became a mixture of physical controls and financial incentives and deterrents. The role of financial policy, although no longer central, remained a positive one. The transfer of resources between sectors continued to depend to some extent on price and wage mechanisms and could therefore be speeded up by the pursuit of a correct financial policy. The productivity of the resources transferred also depended to some extent on financial decisions. So did the volume of resources which could be obtained from abroad. Nor could the state of the economy after the end of the war be entirely left out of consideration and as far as possible financial policy had also to offer positive guidance for the peace to come.

The most universal example of the need for a positive financial policy as an aid to physical controls was in the control of inflation. Warfare and inflation have been virtually inseparable in modern history. The sudden increase in demand for raw materials and foodstuffs raises the price of imports for the combatant powers and this is exaggerated by the higher costs of carriage and insurance. This early inflationary tendency is then boosted by the efforts of the powers to mobilize every available resource, efforts which are expressed in the great increases in government expenditure. Not all these resources are used productively, and to that extent the earlier conception of war as a waste of capital was not wholly wrong. To keep resources channelled in the directions required by government for wartime purposes there has to be a constant pull in these directions from government expenditure.[2] At the same time as this necessarily inflationary situation is developing, the quantity of goods available for general civilian consumption tends to drop while money earnings tend to rise because of higher employment. The general dislocation of established markets and trading practices adds a further element of inflation by permitting speculators to operate in new ways.

2. R. S. Sayers, *Financial Policy*, H.M.S.O., London, 1956, p. 5 ff.

Wage-earners are in a strong position to demand higher earnings to meet these situations because their labour is in high demand. For physical controls to cope with this situation unaided by financial policy requires a government of massive power and efficiency and a population largely in agreement with its policies.

As the war pursued its course financial policy became increasingly concerned with moderating the effects of the incurable tendency to inflation. It was not only considerations of the post-war world that caused governments to struggle against inflation. An unmitigated rise in prices could have had serious consequences for the effective mobilization of resources. It would have caused changes in the distribution of income and rewards which might have led to serious social disruption. This had happened in Germany and Britain during the First World War, where in each case economic strategy had failed to achieve the level of social acceptance necessary for success. In neither the First nor the Second World War did the bargaining power which groups could exert in this inflationary situation exactly coincide with the optimum allocation of resources in war, and financial policy was called to the aid of physical controls after 1940 in rectifying this situation. Finally, there was the threat that money might have lost its value to the point where the population would have ceased to save from their higher earnings and ceased to lend to the government. That was also a not-too-distant memory in many European economies. The disasters which were often envisaged as the result of wartime inflation were more remote than many other threats to the working of the economy. In Vichy France the price of gold and other black market goods soon soared above the meaningless official price indicators.[3] The volume of physical production in the economy dropped and total liquidity increased. The political standing of the government and the state was not such as to impress many people with confidence in their survival. Yet throughout the Vichy period the government was easily able to mop up the surplus liquidity by borrowing at low interest rates. The threat of inflation was more one of inefficiency; it could be fought, and it was in this battle that financial policy had to struggle everywhere.

3. France, Institut National de Statistique et des Études Économiques, *Le Mouvement économique en France de 1938 à 1948*, Presses Universitaires de France, Paris, 1950, p. 72.

Taxation was the main instrument. In the United Kingdom the burden of taxation grew rapidly heavier until 1944 when it appeared to be so heavy as to be acting in some cases as a disincentive. Both in Britain and in the United States taxation also became more progressive, partly out of necessity and partly out of a desire to mitigate social inequalities. But the realities of the political situation in the United States prevented the government from raising out of current income a proportion of government expenditure comparable to that in Britain and Canada. The programme recommended by the Wallace anti-inflation committee in March 1942 was for 42 per cent of war costs to be paid out of taxation; the programme submitted by the Treasury to Congress was for about 30 per cent to be so raised; the Revenue Act of 1942, which became law in October, permitted 26 per cent of 1943 war expenditure to come from taxes. The comparable figure in the United Kingdom was 53 per cent and in Canada 55 per cent.[4] The fiscal year 1943 was the peak year for government borrowing in the United States. After that the balance shifted towards taxation, which provided two thirds of federal funds in 1944 and four fifths in 1945.

For Germany the problem was quite different in scope because of the receipts from occupied territory. Occupation payments replaced borrowing rather than revenue from taxation, which accounted for about 48 per cent of government revenue throughout the war.[5] But rates of personal taxation, particularly on higher incomes, remained noticeably lower than in Britain. Large financial institutions were obliged to take treasury bonds against their funds, a form of borrowing which depended less on public opinion than the publicly subscribed war loans of Britain or the United States. Employees were forced to open savings accounts and accumulate credits which were wiped out after the war with the collapse of the government and the release of the suppressed inflation. These stern financial measures were needed to cope with the immense volume of government expenditure required to keep Germany in the war. In the first year of war total expenditure was

4. United States, Bureau of the Budget, *The United States at War. Development and Administration of the War Program by the Federal Government*, G.P.O., Washington, D.C., 1946, pp. 238–9.

5. D. Petzina, 'La politique financière et fiscale de l'Allemagne', in *R.d.g.m.*, no. 76, 1969.

twice the revenue. By the fifth year of the war it had increased more than two and a half times and was 150 per cent of revenue.[6] The public debt rose from 37,400 million RM to 380,000 million RM during the war, and after 1940 its annual rate of increase was far above that of the income from taxation. The long-term debt increased five times, the short-term debt was 57 per cent of total debt, compared to only 27 per cent in the United States.[7]

The German example shows what support financial policy can give to other controls. The success was perhaps only a short-term one, but as long as the war lasted the problems of finding the finance for the war were solved while inflation progressed less rapidly than in any other economy.

In Italy, where the war expenditure was much lower, the official cost-of-living index increased by 169 per cent in the period 1938–43. Black-market prices for basic foodstuffs in June 1943 were ten times the official prices and the amount of money in circulation quadrupled as the volume of goods available shrank. There was no real modification of the tax system and tax frauds continued to be officially connived at.[8] Although Germany was at the point of financial exhaustion in 1945 skilful financial administration avoided the mistakes made in Italy and stopped financial problems from interfering with the workings of the war economy. But with the onset of unmistakable defeat the house of cards collapsed bringing loss of confidence, administrative breakdown and penury, ushering in a period of monetary collapse.

In the financial disaster that overtook Germany and Italy, however, a primary cause was the lack of government after defeat. Occupied territories were subjected to even more inflationary circumstances but they did not all succumb. The Greek currency collapsed under the strain, but elsewhere the German administration was careful to enforce financially prudent policies so that the stream of occupation payments could be kept up. Grave problems were being stored up, as in Germany, for the end

6. R. Andexel, *Imperialismus, Staatsfinanzen, Rüstung, Krieg. Probleme der Rüstungsfinanzierung des deutschen Imperialismus* (Schriften des Instituts für Wirtschaftswissenschaften, no. 25), Akademie Verlag, Berlin, 1968, p. 113.

7. P. Jacobson, 'Le financement de la guerre en Allemagne', in *Kyklos*, no. 1, 1947.

8. F. Catalano, 'Les ambitions mussoliniennes et la réalité économique de l'Italie', in *R.d.g.m.*, no. 76, 1969.

of the war, but they could be solved by bold action. The Belgian government recalled the whole currency after liberation; the French government chose to struggle on through a series of financial crises resulting from the German depredations. In the Allied economies the apparent rate of inflation was higher than in Germany, but the recourse to short-term borrowing, particularly in the United Kingdom, was far less. And with very little resort to compulsory savings schemes the British government was able to borrow remarkably cheaply. Because of the shortage of non-government investment possibilities the government was able by skilful operations on the money market to keep the interest rate around the 3-per-cent mark at which it had stood in the previous decade. In spite of inflation it was a 'cheap' war.

Raising the revenue to fight the war as cheaply and certainly as possible might be described as the first aim of financial policy and the one where it acted most independently. In its secondary aims it acted together with physical controls and these aims might be described as ensuring that the movement of money and prices at no time took a path conflicting with that of physical controls. In these secondary aims financial policy was in a subordinate position. But the evolution of a machinery of economic direction which properly replaced financial control was a hesitant and fumbling business which brought into question many of the deeper issues which lay at the heart of the war. These administrative questions were more significant than the details of financial administration.

Planning and economic controls

In the early stages of the war it seemed simple enough to sketch out certain basic degrees of priority for armaments and other manufactures in accordance with overall strategic aims. But the first machinery for establishing priorities everywhere created more problems than it solved. The very large quantity of components, for example, that went into any finished armament, especially into aircraft, which had high priority everywhere, meant that once initial high-level priorities had been defined their order had to extend into more detailed questions of production. From there they reached into the availability of raw materials, for without the basic materials priorities in the allocation of labour or plant were meaningless. Furthermore it was soon found that there were priorities within priorities and further priorities within those. The manufacture of one top-priority armament could conflict with that of another if both competed for scarce components or other resources. It was a common experience everywhere that after a short period of war such a multiplicity of priorities developed that the lower ones were positive discouragements and the upper ones clashed with each other in such a way that practical business decisions were still made at a lower level and were often quite different from the intentions of the policymakers.

The decisions to be made on priorities were decisions of extreme importance and significance, only to be made by the possessors of great political power. In their hands had to be concentrated an extreme centralization of priority decisions and a full knowledge of the facts on which to make these decisions. Secondly, to implement these priority decisions there had to be administrative organizations under their control which could properly and efficiently supervise the use of physical resources throughout the economy. Thirdly, this demanded a much greater and more precise knowledge of the economy. The war gave an immense impetus to the collection of economic statistics and to their use in practical management. Fourthly, these developments required the use of experts, whether administrators, businessmen or economists, to a far greater extent in government service. Lastly it required a change of will and outlook on the part of government itself, the will to act consistently to pursue a particular line of policy and the courage to create, rather than merely hope for, the desired economic future. In large part this change of outlook was provided by the experts drafted in from outside the civil service for they came from areas where to attempt to manipulate the future was already a matter of importance.

In the Soviet Union economic decisions were already made on the basis of the allocation of physical resources, although they do not seem to have been based on a very realistic, nor perhaps very knowledgeable, assessment of the possibilities. In Germany machinery for controlling raw materials had existed throughout the 1930s but it did not prove comprehensive enough nor adequate in an administrative sense to satisfy these new demands. The machinery for controlling physical resources in Italy and Japan was rudimentary in 1939 and in the United States and Britain non-existent. From their various standpoints, however, these economies all were faced with the need for these same developments and obliged to fit them as best they could into their own political framework.

The centralization in a few hands of the control over priorities was politically a very difficult problem for all societies. In Britain and the United States it meant the creation of a body which would take the most fundamental decisions outside the purview of the elected representatives. In Germany it meant investing some authority or person with such a degree of economic power as to make a significant rival to the Führer himself. One reason for opting for the *Blitzkrieg* strategy had been to dodge this very problem and so long as the *Blitzkrieg* strategy was maintained the problem was avoided. In the democratic countries it was present from the start although it was certainly not squarely faced up to until events compelled a solution. Until May 1940, the decisions on priorities in Britain were still financial ones and the Treasury remained the controlling body. From May until December, although control had passed out of the hands of the Treasury, the decisions on priorities were handled by a series of committees. Only when the Lord President's Committee in January 1941 was given an overriding power over the other committees was an effective central machinery for making long-term priority decisions devised. The Lord President's Committee became a parallel Cabinet in which most domestic matters were finally decided. Its membership fluctuated according to the area in which policy and priority decisions were to be made, but it remained very small. Underneath it were placed the other economic committees, the Food Policy Committee, the Economic Policy Committee, the Home Policy Committee, and the Production Council. The ultimate decisions on priorities were therefore made by high-ranking politicians who could presume on the political support of both parties in the House of Commons. Nevertheless the actual degree of control which the elected representatives could exercise over the Lord President's Committee and their knowledge of what happened there were both very small. The House of Commons virtually abandoned its watchdog role, and what emerged was almost as far from democracy as the government of Germany or Italy.

The greater fragmentation of authority in the United States government, once it had been delegated by the President, made the process a more painful one there. It was not fully attempted until the formation of the War Production Board at the end of 1942. Even then labour was exempted from the area of the Board's power to make priority decisions. The Board's control over physical resources was further limited by the existence of powerful independent ordnance departments of the armed forces. Nevertheless it did bring clear decisions to the question of priorities in production plans and programmes. There were weekly meetings of all the organizations concerned in running the economy and binding decisions outside the sphere of production itself could sometimes be reached.

But it was soon apparent that the second stage, the creation of a detailed control machinery, was not possible if it had to be under the direction of an organization which basically consisted of businessmen temporarily in the government's service. A higher central policy machinery body emerged in May 1943 with the creation of the Office of War Mobilization which could take priority decisions binding on all the other economic agencies. Its power resided in the important political figure chosen as its head: James F. Byrnes was a New Deal politician having close ties with the President himself. The strength of his political position more than compensated for the administrative clumsiness and weaknesses of the new arrangements. The War Production Board had never had control of manpower, and decisions on the allocation of labour were still taken by a plethora of organizations. As unemployment was absorbed the question of the allocation of labour moved to the centre of the stage and the trade unions would probably never have accepted the right of the War Production Board to handle it. Furthermore there remained very strong military pressures against the War Production Board. Military procurement agencies were still independent of its operations and, indeed, of each other. Admirals went on occasions directly to the President to overturn or influence decisions of the War Production Board.[9] It was from the demands of the service procurement agencies that the grand outlines of the production programmes were formulated and these demands were made by

9. H. M. Somers, *Presidential Agency: The Office of War Mobilization and Reconversion*, Harvard University Press, Cambridge, Mass., 1950, p. 137.

the services in a hurried and improvised way with practically no effective planning nor any respect for economic feasibility. The Office of War Mobilization acted in this situation as a supreme umpire over the powerful. The executive machinery which enforced its decisions, however, was not its own but had to be painfully built up on the basis of experience already gained by the War Production Board. And the most vital piece of this machinery, the Controlled Materials Plan, was only put into effective operation in 1943.

Once it became necessary with the abandonment of the *Blitzkrieg* strategy to take similar firm decisions over priorities in Germany the same dislike of military control over such decisions manifested itself as in the western democracies. However, the army in Germany had an organization, the Wirtschafts- und Rüstungsamt which was an economic agency as well as merely a service procurement agency, and was concerned with the estimation and provision of raw materials capacity to fulfil the military strategy. In spite of this, however, there were occasions when its demands for raw materials were no more realistic than those made by the United States armed forces. What is more its head, General Georg Thomas, was an implacable opponent of the *Blitzkrieg* strategy, which he considered risky and inadequate.[10] Drawing a contrast between what he called 'armament in width', as he termed the conception of *Blitzkrieg*, and 'armament in depth', capital investment in armaments production for a longer war, he argued that only the second was adequate to deal with a war against a major economy.

Two other economic agencies also determined priorities in the *Blitzkrieg* stage, the Four-Year Plan Office and the Ministry of Economics. The Four-Year Plan Office had been created in 1936 under the leadership of Hermann Göring to take charge of the so-called 'second' Four-Year Plan. Essentially it remained concerned during the war with increasing the domestic output of strategic materials, particularly oil and rubber. Investment in high-cost domestic production of these materials remained a high priority and the purpose of the Four-Year Plan Office was to see that these priorities were maintained and the targets achieved. The personal importance of Göring in the economic administration was greater than that of other ministers, including Funk, the

10. G. Thomas, *Geschichte*.

Minister of Economics, by virtue of his role as Commander-in-Chief of the Air Force. But his personal competence and the trust in which he was held by Hitler both had greatly declined by 1941. The sphere of competence of the Ministry of Economics tended to be confined to the field of external economic relations and raw material controls. It was the head of the network of corporate organizations in the German economy through which raw material control was exercised, and its minister was still nominally the chief adviser to the Führer on all economic questions. The Ministry of Economics and the Four-Year Plan Office between them had control over the priorities in foreign trade, including strategic materials.

Whatever difference the coming of war made was made by Hitler's own Führer-Orders. These were directives on general strategy.[11] Once issued, it was the job of the economic agencies to translate their implications into economic policy within the framework of economic controls inherited from peacetime. Such a system could only work providing the demands expressed in the Führer-Orders in terms of numbers of divisions, numbers of aircraft and ships and so on, did not put such a strain on the economy as to necessitate a different administrative system. There were two areas of particular difficulty. One was the difficulty of joint control over strategic raw materials which were needed urgently in response to Führer-Orders, the other was the difficulty of achieving sudden increases in munitions production through the untidy and competing controls exercised by the armed forces.

This fragmentation of control was even harder to overcome in the National Socialist state than in a democratic country because there was a more basic incompatibility between National Socialist political ideas in action and the centralization of economic control. Committee government was not acceptable in a National Socialist state and the only alternative was to raise an individual to so high a degree of power that he might become politically dangerous to the Führer himself. As particular problems arose therefore the solution adopted was to create additional lower-level personally controlled administrative machines to solve limited problems. In February 1940 Hitler named Fritz Todt, who had successfully

11. W. Hubatsch, ed., *Hitlers Weisungen für die Kriegführung 1939–45, Dokumente des Oberkommandos der Wehrmacht*, Bernard und Graefe Verlag, Frankfurt am Main, 1962.

built up an organization to carry out the Autobahn projects of the 1930s, as Inspector-General for Special Tasks in the Four-Year Plan. Essentially he was to act as a trouble-shooter and to reduce the consumption of copper by munitions industries while eliminating the other bottlenecks which had appeared in munitions production. In March he became established as Minister of Munitions and thereby added another warring party to the economic administration.

The organization of an economy demanding a rational allocation of resources and a rigid disposal of them according to predetermined principles posed a direct threat to the National Socialist revolution in Germany. The collapse of the *Blitzkrieg* therefore raised the possibility of the collapse of the revolutionary state by internal changes as well as through external force. A temporary administrative solution had to be found, until by accommodating itself to the same strategy as its opponents, the National Socialist state could finally achieve its victory. The solution was much like the one adopted in the Allied economies.

Göring was in decline, the extension of military control over the economy was unacceptable and the Ministry of Economics still carried within it too much of the despised bureaucracy of the bourgeois state. The remaining possibility was the Ministry of Munitions. In December 1941 a series of decrees extended into a wider range of industries the methods of control which Todt had already begun to introduce into armaments production. By the end of December Todt had transformed certain of the raw-material control organizations into production 'rings' and committees with a clear line of authority from the Ministry of Munitions and the capacity to survey the manufacture of certain products, like tanks, from raw material to finished article.[12] Once the *Blitzkrieg*, by the Führer-Order of 10 January 1942, *Rüstung* 1942, had been tacitly abandoned, a fierce power struggle began for an important place in the administrative changes that were bound to ensue. By the end of January the matter had been decided. Wirtschafts- und Rüstungsamt, which had so long advocated this very change of strategy, did not benefit from it. The necessary central controls were to be exercised by Todt's ministry. On 6 February 1942 he called the first meeting of all the

12. A. S. Milward, 'Fritz Todt als Minister für Bewaffung und Munition', in *Vj.f.Z.*, no. 14, 1966.

chairmen of the new production rings and committees to establish an effective central control mechanism. Two days later he was killed in an air crash.

His death brought to prominence one of the most remarkable and able figures in the history of the war, Albert Speer. Speer was still a young man, a personal friend of Hitler's, and the chosen architect for the reconstruction of Europe's cities. By copying Todt's original methods and by skilfully widening the scope of the power which Todt had been given by the Führer he turned the Ministry of Armaments and Munitions into the central administrative machine of the German war economy. This was publicly recognized in 1943 when the Ministry's title was changed to that of Ministry of War Production. In a state such as National Socialist Germany efficiency was an achievement, extreme efficiency such as that of the Ministry of War Production utterly exceptional; it needed the combination of a brilliant minister, an able ministry and fortunate political circumstances.

From his appointment to the end of the war Speer or his deputy held frequent personal conferences with Hitler which ranged over a wide set of extremely detailed questions of armaments, a subject on which Hitler was both knowledgeable and inexhaustibly interested. The decisions recorded in these conferences replaced the former Führer-Orders as priority decisions and were implemented in the same way as the Führer-Orders by a subsequent elaboration of their consequences for the rest of the economy.[13] The economic system continued to accommodate itself to the *Führerprinzip* by allowing initial decisions on these detailed questions to lead only at a second stage of administration to more fundamental questions of the allocation of resources. Only rarely was the Führer himself consulted on these fundamental issues and, indeed, there is no evidence that he was consistently interested in them.

But it was still necessary to construct a formal machinery to turn into concrete form the verbal decisions extracted from the Führer. This was created on 4 April 1942 when Hitler agreed to the formation of the committee called Zentrale Planung. It consisted of only three members, Speer himself, Paul Körner from

13. Milward, *The German Economy*, p. 75 ff.; W. A. Boelke, ed., *Deutschlands Rüstung im zweiten Weltkrieg: Hitlers Konferenzen mit Albert Speer 1942–1945*, Akademische Verlag, Frankfurt am Main, 1969.

the Ministry of Economics, and Field Marshal Milch of the Air Force. This small group exerted a tight control over raw-material allocation throughout the economy and by so doing enforced a system of economic priorities throughout the civilian as well as the military sectors of the economy. All claimants for raw materials had to appear before the committee to present their case and the committee then made comprehensive and binding allocations on a quarterly basis. Thus Zentrale Planung, in spite of its name, was not a planning committee, but a committee which forced the production committees, the armed forces and the civilian economic ministries themselves to plan.

Once the control over raw-material priorities was firmly established the powers of Speer's ministry rapidly increased as those of the other economic agencies withered away. In May 1942 Wirtschafts- und Rüstungsamt was transferred to the control of the Ministry of Munitions. In June 1943 many of the remaining powers of the Ministry of Economics were also transferred. In the previous month the navy had transferred their shipbuilding programmes. In March 1944 came a further transfer of powers from the armed forces with the creation of the Fighter Staff (Jägerstab). This was a joint team from the Air Ministry and the Ministry of War Production whose function was to increase the output of fighter planes. These accretions of power were not valuable only on the lower level of enforcing control priorities outside the original sphere of authority of the Speer Ministry; the *Führerprinzip* made personal power and authority vital and the success of the Ministry depended on the extent of the powers which the minister extracted from the Führer.

In Japan this process was begun later and it was never finally resolved in a politically acceptable way. The Japanese government did not have the massive capacity to repress dissent which existed in Germany. Neither did it have that large measure of general support for its war aims which permitted the British and American governments to suspend the normal constitutional practices in favour of arbitrary and speedy decisions. Until November 1942 all the Japanese ministries with responsibility for the economy functioned independently of each other and the Cabinet no more provided a suitable vehicle for resolving their conflicts than it had in 1939 in Britain. An experiment in November 1942 with a ministerial coordinating committee did not improve the position and as the scale of the economic effort to be made in 1943 became apparent the political difficulties mounted. It was in these circumstances that the Prime Minister, Marshal Tojo, introduced proposals in January 1943 to give himself quasi-dictatorial powers over the Cabinet and the war economy. He would be endowed with special powers to make all priority decisions concerning five industries, shipping, aircraft, coal, iron and steel, and non-ferrous metals. After a bitter struggle imperial approval was accorded in March, but only as the result of a further political compromise. The Prime Minister was obliged to exercise his special powers in association with an Advisory Council of seven leading members of the Industrial Control Associations, that is with the representatives of the large industrial trusts (*Zaibatsu*) which effectively controlled planning policy in the industries in question.[14]

The Zaibatsu continued to implement most basic industrial decisions after these changes and frequently to thwart prime ministerial policy. No central machinery adequate to make the whole range of priority decisions was devised until November 1943. The existing Ministry of Commerce and Industry was then divided and control over the industrial sector handed to a new ministry, the Ministry of Munitions. This was the same acknowledgement as in other economies that the goal of industrial production had become the manufacture of armaments. But it was also a drastic political restructuring designed to make the Prime Minister's special powers more effective. The new Ministry exercised all the basic planning functions which had lain with the Cabinet at the start of the war, together with the implementation of priority decisions and the allocation of raw materials, previously in the hands of the Industrial Control Associations. Firms engaged in any sector of the industrial economy related to armaments were designated as 'munitions companies' and transferred to the control of the new Ministry. The Prime Minister himself became Minister of Munitions and all orders emanating from the ordnance departments of the armed forces had first to be screened by the new Ministry. These changes came too late for perfect success and Tojo himself fell from power nine months after their introduction; the necessary controls to make them

14. T. A. Bisson, *Japan's War Economy*, International Secretariat, Institute of Pacific Relations, New York, 1945.

completely workable were then still being introduced. To the end the armed forces retained a strong influence over armaments production and the Zaibatsu still occasionally thwarted overall economic planning.

The institution of an effective political body for deciding economic priorities by no means meant that these decisions would be carried out. It meant that certain areas of production which did not receive high priority could no longer compete for resources. But it did nothing in itself to answer the question of what resources were available. Military programmes everywhere were based on greatly exaggerated ideas of the availability of raw materials and labour. The priority machinery cut them down to a more realistic size, but before the stage of the production of finished goods there was still no systematic attempt to find out the precise quantity of inputs available.

> The questions of paramount importance which should have been answered at the highest echelon in the Pentagon Building were being answered every day, through accident or ignorance, by the managers or even by the stock-room clerks in thousands of industrial plants all over the United States.[15]

This was a problem much more easily solved in theory in Britain and Japan than elsewhere. A very high proportion of raw materials used in the war effort there was imported and controls over imports and shipping space came close to being controls over raw-material allocation. After the passage of the Lend-Lease Acts there was very little private importing into Britain from the United States, so that the major source of imports fell automatically under government control. Furthermore, the quantities to be imported from all sources were determined at the highest government level because they affected a most vital strategic issue, that of the availability of shipping space. It was in some ways fortunate that this was so. For there was very little rational thinking in Britain about how an effective raw-materials control could be imposed; if the controls were reasonably effective that was often because the pressures from outside Britain, especially from the United States, were so great. In February 1942, for example, the British government was forced to make a thoroughgoing appraisal of its raw material needs by the formation of the Combined

15. D. Novick, M. Anshen and W. C. Truppner, *Wartime Production Controls*, Columbia University Press, New York, 1949, p. 136.

Raw Materials Board in Washington, consisting of the deputies of the Minister of Production and of the Chairman of the War Production Board. Indeed it was the function of this international raw-materials control agency which was decisive in the creation of the Ministry of Production in Britain to act as the capstone of the raw-material control organizations. In June 1942 came the Combined Production and Resources Board and the many sub-committees which proliferated from it. In November was formed the Raw Materials Committee of the Commonwealth Supply Council. In so complex an international framework it was not possible for the United Kingdom to persist in the haphazard and improvised methods of raw-material control which had existed until then.

But by that time the machinery of control in Britain had become set and the weaknesses which it incorporated survived to the end of the war. It rested on the industrial *status quo* as it had existed before the war. The organization controlling each raw material was the trade association or, in the case of a material not imported, the business organization of the industry mainly responsible for its wartime consumption. In the case of a material whose imports were severely restricted, like timber, the trade association would sometimes handle the allocation of the domestic resources.[16] Such controls were only devised as each raw material became scarce; rubber, for example, was not controlled until April 1941 and the first allocation by its controlling committee only made in January 1942.[17] The advantages of having allocation made by businessmen turned temporary civil servants were obvious. They were each experts in that particular business. The dangers were equally obvious. Even if they could distance themselves from their own firm's interests, which was not always the case, and even if they could win the complete confidence and trust of their pre-war competitors in the same trade, which was also not always the case, they found it particularly difficult to accept that a wider national interest should sometimes lead to decisions clearly against the short-term interests of their own trade or industry. Men whose lives had been devoted to increasing the consumption of a particular commodity were now asked to work full-time at reducing its consumption.

16. F. H. House, *Timber at War*, Ernest Benn, London, 1965.
17. J. Hurstfield, *The Control of Raw Materials*, H.M.S.O., London, 1953, p. 414.

Had the priority decisions at a higher level been more firmly made in the early years of the war this might have mattered less. The Raw Materials Department, although an integral part of the Ministry of Supply, functioned virtually as a separate organization except at the very highest level of the Ministry. Since most decisions were decisions of detail they were made below that level by civil servants with little expertise in the field. They found themselves at a disadvantage against an army of professional experts whose interests were perhaps not so neutral and who acquired relative independence because they knew more about what they were doing. Perhaps no better solution could have been found. The higher-grade personnel in the civil service were simply not equipped by their education to deal expertly with a range of problems of this kind. After the establishment of the Ministry of Production and the international Combined Boards better statistical knowledge often meant that the decisions to be taken were much clearer. But the main force in making the business community function as civil servants in a way not too divorced from the national interest was scarcity, arising from world shortages of materials and from the much firmer machinery for enforcing priority decisions elsewhere in the economy. It was futile to continue to allocate raw materials to industries which could get hold of virtually no other resource from the government. In this light the acute labour shortage and the drastic labour controls in Britain appear as even more important. They were the check on the rather haphazard method of raw-material control.

The control which the trade associations exercised in Britain cannot, however, be properly compared to the position of the Zaibatsu in Japan, whose power and interest pervaded every area of the industrial economy. It would have been an impossible task to devise any method of controlling physical resources there that did not operate through this structure, and to impose curbs on the Zaibatsu in the wider national interest proved extremely difficult. Two years before the Ministry of Munitions came into existence some of the control associations already controlled allocation for more than 500 companies and a much higher number of factories. The directive compelling the armed forces to submit all orders first to a central council created in the Ministry of Munitions to vet such orders was difficult to enforce because of the intimate ties that had grown up between the industrial associations and the armed forces. Fujihara, who became Minister of Munitions in July 1944, conveyed the reality of his position to his interrogators after the war. 'What I am saying in effect is this – I was Munitions Minister but my function actually was that of conciliator between Army, Navy and Air people.'[18] What had emancipated Speer from this position was the effectiveness with which his ministry could enforce its orders through Zentrale Planung. Although the agencies through which Zentrale Planung operated, businessmen's associations, were similar to those at the disposal of the Japanese Ministry, the relative power relationships were different. The National Socialist party occupied a clear position of power above that of the business and industrial associations and in spite of its often close alliance with them it could and did bend them to its will in cases of conflict. In Japan the industrial control associations retained the capacity to thwart and impede government policy in their own interests to the very end. The allocation of physical resources at company and plant level fell well below the level of efficiency and rationality which a study of the central machinery for determining priorities would suggest. It could still happen in Japan even in 1945 that a factory would accept a large and unvetted order from the armed forces in return for documents guaranteeing access to the necessary, but no longer existing, stocks of raw materials. The inefficiencies of this system were mitigated, as in Britain, by the fact that so many materials had to be imported that controls began before shipping space was allocated.

The fundamental difference in the United States was the apparently lavish availability of domestic resources. As far as raw materials were concerned that proved in the event to be deceptive because the United States was involved by 1943 in a global economic strategy which made the demand for her own raw materials much higher than foreseen. In the heyday of economic expansion after the declaration of war lorry factories were converted by companies into aircraft factories when the future demand for lorries was as great as for planes. Locomotive works were turned into lorry factories in spite of the fact that within a year American locomotives would be required in many parts of the globe. Completely new factories were built with government

18. Cohen, p. 79.

help when there was no possibility that they would ever get the necessary raw materials to sustain their planned production. This situation was exaggerated by the absence of economic planning in the armed forces. The best efforts of the War Production Board, and afterwards of the Office of War Mobilization, could not enforce priority decisions when so high a proportion of the programmes emanating from industry and the armed forces were unrealistic in their conception.

In these circumstances allocation of raw materials sometimes consisted of making a fixed percentage reduction in all demands and thereby encouraging an even greater level of unreality in the original request. The navy insisted on aluminium being made available for furniture on its ships instead of being allocated to aircraft manufacture and also fought strenuously against all raw material allocations to the Soviet Union. The root of the problem was the lack of a sufficiently expert staff in any of the armed services to undertake the detailed economic planning which was indispensable in mobilizing over eleven million people to fight. The Office of Production Management reported:

> In so far as the Navy is concerned most of the estimates we have received represent guess work. There is neither the basic material for doing the job satisfactorily nor the inclination to develop the staff needed for estimating raw materials needed in the Navy Department. Time after time a check of the estimates has indicated the need for almost unbelievable revision upward or downward in the originally submitted figures.[19]

The central priority decisions were only made effective by the introduction of the Controlled Materials Plan. In devising the methods of materials control and in making them work the clumsy but massive bureaucracy of the United States intervened successfully at a stage where the British civil service had abandoned the task to others. In fact the Controlled Materials Plan owed its success, like Zentrale Planung, to the fact that it was not a plan but a method of forcing all consumers of raw materials themselves to plan. The movements of stocks of materials about the country had henceforward to be fully recorded and no order could be accepted until the manufacturer had provided the Requirements Committee of the War Production Board with an

19. United States, Bureau of the Budget, *The United States at War*, p. 81.

exact statement of his raw material requirements. The subsequent allocations were made quarterly by the Committee. For the first time the armed forces procurement agencies were forced to consider their future demands within the context of long-term strategy. Had this not been so the necessary quantities of steel to meet the emergency landing-craft programme for the invasion of France could not have been met at short notice.

In all these cases the economy in question had been unplanned in every sense of the word before 1939. In the German case, however, some elements of planning had existed and among the controls on which the planning was based there was an extensive if ineffective mechanism for the control of materials. After the formation of Zentrale Planung this mechanism was subordinated to the Ministry of Armaments and to Zentrale Planung. Raw-material control in Germany had its origins in the foreign trade and exchange controls which had developed in the economic crisis of 1929. Its original purpose was only that of economizing on foreign exchange. As National Socialist economic policy developed into deficit financing and rearmament on a bigger scale raw-material controls extended from imports to the allocation of foreign exchange and strategic materials within the domestic economy. This was done through the National Socialist corporate businessmen's organizations (Reichsverband der deutschen Industrie). As instruments of planning they left much to be desired, for they were basically the former trade associations of businessmen in each industry given some ideological stiffening. The new Fachgruppe Werkzeuge, for example, was simply the old machine-tool manufacturers' association with new notepaper and a new master. The importation and allocation of raw materials, as well as the nominal supervision of the businessmen's associations, lay with the Ministry of Economics. But in effect business associations exercised relatively independent control over allocation once foreign-exchange certificates for imports had been granted. They met to settle all disputed questions as equals in a small collegial committee.[20] If that committee succeeded in arriving at a political compromise in any question of raw-material allocation

20. J. S. Geer, *Der Markt der geschlossenen Nachfrage, eine morphologische Studie über die Eisenkontingentierung in Deutschland 1937–1945* (Nürnberger Abhandlungen zu den Wirtschafts- und Sozialwissenschaften, no. 14), Duncker und Humblot, Berlin, 1961, p. 120.

it still had no proper executive body to implement the compromise fully. Its quarterly meetings were the only coordinating instrument that existed below the Führer's own erratic interventions.

One of Todt's principal achievements as Minister of Munitions was to breathe a new spirit into this method of quarterly allocations of raw materials. The system of production rings and committees which he gradually introduced into certain armaments industries combined the method of raw-material control with introducing technological cooperation between the firms involved. The committees were also associated directly with the allocation and sharing of other resources and capital equipment. Speer pursued this policy with even greater energy and extended the rings and committees throughout manufacturing industry.[21] In theory their membership was made up from experts from firms which had the most efficient production process although in reality they seem often to have preserved the existing power structure in each industry rather than to have rationalized it in the interests of the war economy.[22] It was 'through the rings and committees that Zentrale Planung enforced its decisions. Raw material allocations were made quarterly to the Head Committee in each industry and from there the resources were in turn allocated to the committees dealing with each product in the industry concerned. Each industry was therefore forced first of all to justify its raw-material demands before the three judges of Zentrale Planung and then to cooperate on the most detailed level in the utilization of the quarterly allocations of raw materials it received. Ultimately it was responsible for achieving the targets set by the Ministry of Munitions. The longer the committee system survived the greater was the quantity of accurate information fed back to the central deciding body and the more accurate the allocation decisions made there. For all its faults and the deep suspicion with which it was viewed by the more radical wing of the National Socialist party it proved its flexibility in the rapid growth of output of war material in Germany after 1941 which so confused Allied strategy.

The remaining stages in the development of economic administration in the major combatants can be dealt with much more

21. G. Janssen, *Das Ministerium Speer. Deutschlands Rüstung im Krieg*, Ullstein, Berlin, 1968.
22. Eichholtz, *Geschichte*, p. 121 ff.

succinctly for they followed automatically from the establishment of a full machinery of economic control. In Britain 'in the early days of the war many government statistics were extremely confusing, conflicting and incomplete. It was extraordinarily difficult to get a simple, overall picture of what was happening.'[23] This was true almost everywhere and it became a life and death matter to change it. Churchill built up his own statistical advisory section at the start of the war and this became the Prime Minister's Statistical Section in May 1940. It advised him mainly on the economics of new scientific and technological possibilities. But these activities naturally took its inquiries into most branches of the wartime economy. Although economic statistics were widely available, in Britain and elsewhere they were not the particular statistics required by the war effort. The Statistisches Amt was created within the Speer Ministry, for example, in order to enable Zentrale Planung to make more accurate priority decisions by providing for it the missing statistical information. It was built up by the statistician and economist Rolf Wagenführ to whose work all historians of the war years are deeply indebted.

Judging from the *Statistical Digest of the War* published after the event under British government auspices there were still decided limitations on the range and meaningfulness of the statistics collected and used during the war in the United Kingdom, limitations which in the United States and Germany the War Production Board and Statistisches Amt seem to have overcome.[24] There was nothing in Britain comparable to the overall indices of armaments and industrial production which guided these other organizations from 1942 onwards. On the other hand much greater progress was made in Britain in national-income accounting than in Germany, where it was still in its infancy in 1945. The immense gaps which exist in our statistical knowledge of the war in Italy are probably not due to the loss or unavailability of the evidence but to the fact that it was never collected at the time. Even so, the war brought great advances in this regard to most combatants, as may be seen from a comparison with what happened in France. The beginnings of an improved government

23. G. D. A. Macdougall, 'The Prime Minister's Statistical Section', in D. N. Chester, ed., *Lessons*, p. 62.
24. United Kingdom, Central Statistical Office, *Statistical Digest of the War*, H.M.S.O., London, 1951.

statistical service there were cut short with the occupation and after 1944 France was still virtually without the necessary information to plan her recovery.[25]

The legacy of wartime administration

The need of government for new kinds of professional expertise was very high. Economists were recruited to many wartime government agencies in the United States and also in Britain. Scientists and engineers were even more in demand. It was not merely that the scope of governmental activity was much wider but also that the tasks it undertook were much more complicated. By April 1940 the newly created Ministry of Food in Britain already employed 3,500 people; by 1943 it employed 39,000. In 1941 the Berlin office of Wirtschafts- und Rüstungsamt had a staff of more than 1,000, a larger number than the economic staff of the army in 1918 when it had had a far more extensive control over industry. Both military and civilian activity in wartime consists ideally of a meticulously coordinated and planned set of activities; many people in all countries felt that during the war for the first time their particular expertise, however small, was used and valued.

But the expert most commonly recruited everywhere outside the Soviet Union was the businessman. It had already been noticed in the First World War how the recruitment of businessmen in large numbers into government administration imbued that administration with a different outlook. For good or ill the tendency of businessmen was to look to the future; that of career civil servants was to look to the present. The extent and vigour of planning for peacetime reconstruction during the war was remarkable. Equally noticeable was the extent to which government everywhere was forced to apply itself to the post-war problems of industry. The relationship between government and industry in western Europe underwent a decisive change as a result of these wartime developments and the two worlds of business and government administration were never again seen as the separate worlds they had still been in the thirties. The hope that the economy could be managed, and the political will that it should

25. A. Sauvy, 'Heurs et malheurs de la statistique', in *R.d.g.m.*, no. 57, 1965.

be managed, were greatly reinforced by the knowledge of the more detailed workings of business and industry which central governments were forced to acquire between 1939 and 1945. That is perhaps the most immediately obvious historical consequence of the changes in the direction of the economy during the Second World War. Capitalist economies had been made to function in a very different way and it is easy to see in the plans for reconstruction that their economic shibboleths had been much altered by the war experience. Governments were persuaded that their economic powers were much more extensive and their economic duties more compelling. Their knowledge of the economy was incomparably larger in 1945 than in 1939. The range of feasible economic options open to them appeared wider.

The picture painted by Soviet and east European scholars is that during the Second World War capitalist economies fell completely into the clutches of businessmen and produced the apotheosis of 'business-fascism'. As far as the Axis powers were concerned the western democracies were not wholly out of sympathy with this interpretation at the end of the war. In Japan the American occupiers were convinced that the Zaibatsu were incompatible with a future democratic Japan and carried out a thoroughgoing programme of 'Zaibatsu-dissolution'. In Germany there were long legal processes against big firms such as the Krupp and Flick industrial empires. However, the last year of the war in Germany had already witnessed a vital shift in power away from the business interests in the National Socialist state.

The business organizations which the Ministry of War Production had harnessed to its own purposes functioned very much like their equivalents in Allied economies. Indeed both Todt and Speer justified the system as a method of breaking through the bureaucratic hierarchy of the new state by giving executive power to neutral technical experts. Neither minister seems to have understood this initially as a challenge to the political nature of the régime, to whose political principles they were both loyal. Todt actually presented his reforms as a product of the new society, the technocrat freed from the prejudices and hierarchies of history at grips with modern problems, while thinking and writing about them in terms of the new world-outlook. Scholars have accepted that this was an increase in the efficiency of the state and Speer has himself portrayed it in the same way in his memoirs.[26] But how far was such an increase in efficiency permanently possible in a state imbued with the National Socialist world-outlook?

The opposition to the growing centralization of economic controls and to their administration by businessmen was very strong and was by no means simply one of obscurantism or vested interest. To the inner core of the National Socialist party and to the SS. the so-called 'Self-Responsibility of German Industry' was a threat to the continuation of the National Socialist revolution in Germany. Each political system within the strategic synthesis has its own optimum level of economic efficiency, and if friction is to be kept to a minimum the economy must operate near to that optimum level. The changes in economic administration associated with the development of the Ministry of Munitions in Germany were mainly a response to desperate necessity and by pulling against the mainstream of National Socialist thought they were condemned to a short life. The administrative friction which resulted in the closing stages of the war made that in other wartime economies look insignificant by comparison.

Sauckel continued with Hitler's support to pursue a labour policy that had lost all economic meaning. The SS. continued to build its own massively inefficient economic empire. Local party bosses brought every influence to bear on the Führer, through Bormann and the party organizations, to thwart the new economic controls. It was only possible for Speer to resist these attacks as long as his policies were justified by their strategic results. As the enemy forces rolled towards Germany in summer 1944 the National Socialist revolution began to flow again in more revolutionary channels. Speer fell from favour and the ultimate stage of inefficiency was reached when the Ministry of War Production secretly conspired against the scorched-earth policy which Hitler and the SS. wanted, and tried to preserve as much as possible of Germany's industry for the post-war world by issuing weapons to factory managers to defend their works against party militants. The new Germany and the SS., embryo of the new Europe, were relatively untouched by the drive to economic rationality of which the Ministry of War Production was the spearhead. Such concepts

26. A. Speer, *Erinnerungen*, Ullstein, Berlin, 1969.

existed only to win the war; that done, they, like the Speer Ministry, would no longer be wanted. The political irreconcilabilities of the National Socialist state were already destroying its administrative power in 1944. As they did so the political position of business in the German state declined, and the less pragmatic supporters of the National Socialist state drove boldly forward to embrace the economic chaos which their beliefs invited.

Elsewhere the triumphant feeling that the economy had been successfully bent to the purpose of victory led to the idea of bending it to another purpose, 'reconstruction', in which the interests of all might play a part. In spite of the limitations on the expression of public opinion during the war it succeeded in exerting considerable influence on the often reluctant minds of government as to what reconstruction should consist of. The sense of common purpose had politicized opinion in the western world in favour of certain economic and social changes, thought of as improvements on the pre-war world. The main ones could be summed up as the certainty of employment and a reasonable income, both of which had been provided by the war. Before the war governments had been equipped to deal with such complexities in only a fumbling way. There was practically no economic planning during the war in the sense in which that phrase is now used.[27] What existed was elementary forecasting and the rigid control of resources combined with a definition of priorities which excluded most of the priority choices available in a peacetime economy. There was little in the wartime machinery of economic direction to enable it to cope with a situation in which a wider range of choice would have to be considered and a greater number of interests balanced.

The legacy of the war was a consciousness that the economy could be directed into the desired channels, some knowledge of how to direct it, and the acquisition of a great store of facts about the economy. To this was added some degree of political and economic agreement about the aims of the economy in peacetime. In the closing years of the war and in its immediate aftermath there was a conscious attempt to use the machinery of economic

27. E. Welter, *Falsch und richtig planen. Eine kritische Studie über die deutsche Wirtschaftslenkung im zweiten Weltkrieg*, Veröffentlichungen des Forschungsinstituts für Wirtschaftspolitik an der Universität Mainz, no. 1, Heidelberg, 1954.

direction to further the strong, but vague and ill-formed, aspirations and yearnings which the experience of war had brought to the forefront. With a new consciousness of their power over the domestic economy governments turned eagerly to the task of building an international economic system which would replace the international economic anarchy of the 1930s.

5

The Economics
of Occupation

Conquests made by New Zealanders have some sense in them;
while the conquered fry, the conquerors fatten. Conquests
made by the polished nations of antiquity, conquests made by
Greeks and Romans, had some sense in them. Lands, movables,
inhabitants, everything went into the pocket.

Conquests made by a modern despot of the continent have
still some sense in them. The new property, being contiguous,
is laid on to his old property; the inhabitants, as many as he
thinks fit to set his mark upon, go to increase his armies; their
substance, as much as he thinks fit to squeeze from them, goes
into his purse.

Jeremy Bentham,
Principles of International Law, 1839

Occupation in history

German and Japanese strategy were each based firmly on the
assumption that it is possible to exploit an occupied economy to
the advantage of the occupying power. The boldness of such an
assumption is less apparent today, but before 1939 the assumption
that occupied territory could not in the long run be successfully
exploited still prevailed in economic thought. In the First World
War Belgian law had forbidden any economic cooperation with
the occupying German forces. For the most part Germany had
accepted this situation and the Belgian economy had functioned

at a very low level while the population was kept alive by food supplies organized from the United States with German permission. Such an attitude was quite incompatible with German strategy in 1939 and also with the National Socialist *Weltanschauung*. If German territorial aims could only be achieved by war, and if the war was not to involve a further level of commitment of the economy to war production, the occupied territories would have to be regarded as a supplement, whether temporary or permanent, to Germany's own economic resources. The strategy of *Blitzkrieg* meant that occupied territories were seen at the very least as sources of economic booty and, where business interests were more pressing or Germany's deficiencies more noticeable, as a more regular and consistent source of supply to the German economy. Beyond the immediate considerations of the war lay those of the reconstruction of the European economy and society which Germany wished to bring about. Some changes in the economic relationship of the other European states to Germany would be inevitable after a peace settlement based on a German victory and the nature of those changes had already been clearly indicated in Germany's trade agreements with weaker states in 1939. The dominance of the German economy and the assertion of a specific National Socialist economic policy would mean that many European economies would be reduced to a situation scarcely distinguishable from that of permanent exploitation on a more organized basis. The ultimate fate reserved for many South-East Asian economies and areas of China hardly seems on present evidence to have been different.

It was only with the weakening in the eighteenth century of the assumption that warfare was a psychological necessity for mankind that the economic value of occupying territory came to be challenged. Increasingly economists contrasted foreign conquest with domestic development as alternative investments. Domestic development policies, however, in the eighteenth century, were conceived very much in terms of agricultural development and in that light the settlement of population in uncultivated lands abroad offered better returns than the extension of the cultivated area at home because the most fertile lands in western and central Europe were already in cultivation. This of course was one component of Hitler's own theories. 'Yet I think,' Vanderlint wrote, 'that there is one case in which making war on other Nations may be justifiable, viz. Fighting for Territory when we are over-peopled, and want Land for them, which our Neighbours have, but will not part with on amicable and reasonable Terms.'[1] And this exceptional case could well be compared with Hitler's questioning in 1920 whether it was right 'that there is eighteen times more land per head for every Russian than there is for a German',[2] a theme he was later to develop into a basic idea of *Mein Kampf* and which lay at the heart of the idea of *Grossraumwirtschaft*.

Undoubtedly, in an age when the possibilities of increasing labour productivity depended on the agricultural sector, whether conquest and occupation were a correct economic choice was to some extent a function of the ratio of population to land area. But in an age of increasing industrialization conquest also came to be seen as a way of acquiring the necessary raw materials to sustain industrial development. That it was the best way to do so was refuted by the main stream of classical economic theory.

Say's law of markets, by establishing the proposition that the demand for commodities was very closely in proportion to their supply removed one theoretical reason for conquest by making capital accumulation appear a self-regulating process. In explaining the persistence of wars of conquest in the nineteenth century most writers took the view that such wars were anachronistic and should be attributed to the imperfections of political society. The benefits of conquest, it was argued, went to a ruling élite, whereas its costs were borne throughout the economy. The ideas which inspired *Mein Kampf*, however, were brought once more into prominence by Darwinian conceptions of struggle and, well before Hitler wrote, they had begun to be incorporated into classical economics. De Molinari argued that there had been a stage when conquest was the foundation of human economy and of the economy of an organized state, but that in the nineteenth-century economy conquest would price itself out of the market as no longer being a satisfactory investment decision by the state.[3]

It is not certain that the relative cost of conquest increased in

1. J. Vanderlint, *Money Answers All Things*, ed. J. H. Hollander, Baltimore, 1910 (first published London, 1734).

2. R. H. Phelps, 'Hitler als Parteiredner im Jahre 1920', in *Vj.f.Z.*, no. 11, 1963, p. 289.

3. G. de Molinari, *Esquisse de l'organisation politique et économique de la société future*, Guillaumin, Paris, 1899; *Grandeur et décadence de la guerre*, Guillaumin, Paris, 1898.

the nineteenth century. The French government had mitigated the tax burden of sustaining the Napoleonic Wars by successfully exploiting the occupied territories. The peace terms of the Franco-Prussian War included a war indemnity to repay the cost of Germany's temporary occupation of France which was relatively easily paid. Many of the imperial conquests of Britain, France and the United States were achieved with a capital outlay which must have been quite insignificant as a part of national product. However, the cost which must be considered is not the relative cost of conquest over time but the relative opportunity cost, and there is no doubt that the scope of other investment possibilities greatly widened in the nineteenth century. The political stance of the German and Japanese governments in 1939, that conquest was profitable, therefore challenged liberal thought at a point where it was not on particularly strong ground. How successful in fact were these policies of conquest? Did they justify the capital expenditure involved? How well did the *Grossraumwirtschaft* and the Co-Prosperity Sphere function as economic units? Did the historical experience of occupation in the Second World War justify the conclusions of economic theorists on the economics of conquest? Or should it lead us to modify these conclusions?

The profitability of occupation

The exploitation of conquered territory by the German economy was governed by German strategy. So long as that strategy was based on the idea of a short war exploitation in the interests of fighting the war was of a short-term kind. It consisted mainly of the seizure of stocks of strategic goods and of securing the use of particular goods or plant which could bring some immediate support to the German war effort. When strategy changed at the start of 1942, and the certainty of a long war was accepted, the attitude to the exploitation of occupied territories also changed. The German occupiers now became interested in organizing a substantial and continuing contribution from the occupied territories to Germany's war economy, or as they preferred to call it, 'the European war economy'. It was some time before these changes took effect in the occupied countries because there was still a great deal of slack to take up in the German domestic economy in 1942 and the main immediate task was one of domestic reorganization. But as resources became scarcer in Germany pressure on the occupied economies mounted. In spring and early summer it came to a head with a determined effort on the part of the German Ministry of War Production to stop all short-term plunder and exploitation of the occupied countries and to integrate their economies into a common long-term productive effort.

Both the short-term policy of exploitation and the attempt to create 'a European war-economy' which followed it were policies designed to make the best use of the conquered territories in the interest of Germany's war effort. But both strategies took place against the background of a deeper policy question which raised even more serious issues. Considering the war only as a temporary state of affairs what was ultimately to be done economically with the occupied territories? This question aroused most interest when the war could reasonably be seen as a relatively brief phenomenon, but when the *Blitzkrieg* was abandoned interest rapidly faded away because the war and survival became the overriding issues. Interest then focused on how far and how long the conquered territories could help Germany to survive. The more revealing aspects of Germany's plans for other economies were therefore in the forefront of economic policy when, ironically enough, interest in the occupied economies as an addition to Germany's war resources was at its lowest. And when a small degree of coordination between Germany and the occupied economies, rather than mere exploitation, was forced on Germany, the longer-term politico-economic considerations of European economic planning came to appear in the circumstances merely fanciful. But the two strands of economic policy in occupied territory nevertheless existed side by side throughout the war. These two strands were by no means always compatible with each other and, given the conflicting policies within the National Socialist government as well as the tendency to appoint occupation governments with a great degree of independence in decision making, it is not surprising that economic policy in the occupied territories was often confused and contradictory. The most glaring example is the relentless pursuit of a 'racial' solution to Europe's problems by the wholesale murder of Russians and Jews in the Soviet Union while at the same time attempting to win the allegiance of the inhabitants away from the Soviet government.

But before examining these contradictions further the issue of the economic value of the conquered territories can first be considered. The evidence in this case is quite unambiguous. Although not every conquered territory was profitable, the conquered areas as a whole were. They represented a great addition to Germany's own productive effort. The most profitable was France where the returns to the capital invested in conquest and occupation were very high. France provided the largest single component of the financial income coming from abroad into the German treasury. The most regular component of the financial income from France was the so-called 'occupation costs' levied by the German government. These were originally fixed at twenty million RM a day and although there were subsequently brief periods when the total was slightly reduced or, towards the end of the occupation, increased, this enormous sum obtained throughout. For purposes of payment the franc was valued against the Reichsmark at 20:1 as it was for all other commercial agreements between the two countries during the occupation. This represented a very substantial over-valuation of the Reichsmark. No genuine equilibrium exchange rates had existed before 1939 between Germany and other countries so that the precise extent of the over-valuation of the Reichsmark is difficult to measure. The rates specified in the pre-war bilateral agreements negotiated by Germany were usually about 25 per cent below the official exchange quotations. If we assume the nearest true rate to have been the previous dollar exchange rate of both currencies in June 1940 the new valuation probably represented an over-valuation of the Reichsmark by about 50 per cent. If the previous exchange rates against the pound sterling are used the over-valuation appears as high as 63 per cent. The over-valuation seems to have been higher in France than in most other occupied countries and there was even a drain of the occupation currency, the Reichskreditkassenschein, from south-eastern Europe to France where its purchasing power was higher.[4]

The occupation costs were far greater than the sums of money required to maintain the German army in France. What the actual cost of maintaining the army of occupation was is not

4. A. Munz, *Die Auswirkung der deutschen Besetzung auf Währung und Finanzen Frankreichs*, Veröffentlichungen des Instituts für Besatzungsfragen, no. 9, Tübingen, 1957.

known; there was very little need to work it out when the occupation costs could be fixed high enough to make the Bank of France print the bank-notes necessary to meet all Germany's demands. The Economic Delegation to the Franco-German Armistice Commission was simply presented with a total sum established by the German armed forces, with no breakdown of what it covered, and instructed to force the French to pay. The average cost of maintaining a French soldier in the field in the Second World War was twenty-two francs a day. On the same basis the occupation costs would have paid for an army of occupation of eighteen million men. The payments covered black-market operations by the German commissariat in France, the cost of the German troops in North Africa, the building of the West Wall against an Allied invasion, and secret service and intelligence costs.

This method of levying 'occupation costs' became standard practice for the other occupied territories. For the whole period of the war the German income from occupation costs in all countries was about 40 per cent of the income from taxation. In the financial year 1943–4 income from taxation began to decline and income from occupation costs increased so that in that financial year it actually accounted for 38·4 per cent of total treasury income.[5] Of this foreign income 42 per cent came from France over the duration of the war as a whole. In each of the first four years of the war the increase in the foreign contribution to Germany's total available product was in fact greater than the increase in the domestic contribution. If the yield from occupation is considered as one mechanism by which cuts in consumers' expenditure could be avoided, a role which it was certainly intended to play in German strategy, its effectiveness until the end of 1942 is demonstrable. The greatest single contribution to the increase in government expenditure in that period came from occupation levies.

But this traditional method of levying occupation costs was allied to a more sophisticated method of exploitation. The costs were paid through the clearing mechanism set up to handle the trade between Germany and the occupied territories. Each country was obliged to negotiate from a hopelessly weak position

5. F. Federau, *Der zweite Weltkrieg. Seine Finanzierung in Deutschland*, Rainer Wunderlich Verlag, Tübingen, 1962.

a bilateral trading agreement with Germany of the kind that had increasingly governed German trade after 1933. The balance of the trade was kept in clearing accounts while each country paid its own exporters in return for credits entered to its account. In the situation of 1940 the German government could not only overvalue its own currency but it could also ascribe arbitrarily low prices to the exports from other countries covered in the agreements. No direct clearing was allowed between occupied countries except between Denmark and Norway. All transactions were centralized in the Deutsche Verrechnungskasse in Berlin, which thus controlled the funds for European trade and governed the commodities exchanged. Trade with France was controlled by the clearing agreement of 14 November 1940 which established the new exchange rate and the wartime commercial pattern. All occupation costs were entered in the clearing accounts as German credits. In all occupied territories therefore, and particularly in France, Germany had an enormous open-ended purchasing power, the more so as there was no longer any means of compelling her to diminish the debt in which she could maintain the account. The occupation levies represented a crushing weight of purchasing power, created by the French government itself, and suspended over the French economy. The size of the clearing deficit was as much financial gain from occupation as the levies themselves. The contribution of the two items together to Germany's wartime product is shown in Table 21. Such measurements cannot be strictly accurate because of the deficiencies of wartime data but they do show the substantial nature of the financial return alone from the conquest of France.

Table 21 shows the high level of France's contribution. It also shows how the rate of contribution increased after 1942 and continued to increase, since the 1944 contribution only covers six months. What proportion of the available resources of France did these contributions to the German economy represent? Over the period as a whole France effectively transferred to Germany a cash sum equivalent to 169 per cent of her income from taxation. The payments to Germany were 49 per cent of total French public expenditure over the years 1940–44, which is a longer period than the occupation, and in 1943 they were as high as 60 per cent. About one third of these transfers were covered by taxation, the rest by currency creation and borrowing. The opportunities for

TABLE 21
OCCUPATION COSTS AND OTHER PAYMENTS FROM FRANCE IN
RELATION TO GERMANY'S GROSS NATIONAL PRODUCT

Year	French occupation costs (m. current francs)	Total payments from France including clearing deficit (m. current francs)	Occupation costs as a percentage of German G.N.P. at wartime exchange rate	Total payments as a percentage of German G.N.P.	
				at wartime exchange rate	at 1938 exchange rate*
1940	80,000	81,600	2·8	2·8	3·0
1941	121,500	144,300	3·9	4·6	5·3
1942	109,000	156,700	3·4	4·8	5·5
1943	194,000	273,600	5·7	8·0	9·1
1944†	126,900	206,300	3·6	5·9	6·7

* Estimated at 176 francs and 10 RM to the pound sterling.
† First six months.
SOURCE: Milward, *The New Order and the French Economy*, Oxford University Press, London, 1970, p. 27.

capital investment in wartime France were relatively limited and the rate of saving much higher than in peace. Germany had interest-free access to French capital. Unfortunately estimates of French national income for these years lack precision. If we use the more accurate estimates of total available product in 1938 we can estimate that the total payments from France to Germany in 1940 were equivalent to 9·3 per cent of that product. In 1943 they had risen to almost one third. Table 22 shows these measurements.

TABLE 22
PAYMENTS TO GERMANY FROM FRANCE AS A PROPORTION OF
FRENCH RESOURCES, 1940–44

Year	As a percentage of French national income in 1938 at 1938 prices	As a percentage of total available product in 1938 at 1938 prices
1940	10·9	9·3
1941	19·3	16·5
1942	20·9	17·7
1943	36·6	31·3
1944	27·6	23·6

SOURCE: Milward, *The New Order*, p. 273.

Some check may be made on these calculations by assuming that the proportion of occupation costs paid by France out of total occupation costs received by Germany, 42 per cent, is the same as the French proportion in the 'total foreign contributions' to the German economy estimated by the United States Strategic Bombing Survey.[6] The Survey's estimates include the occupation levies paid by France, the Netherlands, Norway, Bohemia and Poland, the net deficit in Germany's foreign trade balance, purchases made from foreign countries by invasion currency (which was fairly quickly withdrawn in many areas) and the net product of the annexed areas after consumption and capital formation had been deducted. The Survey may not have taken sufficiently into account the growing difference between foreign prices and prices in Germany, where price control was more effective, and may thus have arrived at slightly too high an estimate. On the basis of these calculations the French share, if it was 42 per cent, would appear as 2·6 per cent of German G.N.P. in 1940, 5·4 per cent in 1941, 8·3 per cent in 1942, 8·2 per cent in 1943 and 7·4 per cent in 1944.

The order of magnitude of the French contribution as it appears in Table 21 may therefore be assumed to be reasonably correct provided the financial contribution in addition to the occupation levies and the clearing levies is not too great. The fact that this second calculation makes the French contribution in 1942 appear more important is probably a reflection of events in other territories. Certainly the assumption that the French share of the total foreign contribution to the German economy, measured in this wider sense, was also at least 42 per cent is not an unreasonable one, as will be seen. But it is at this point that there are conceptual difficulties in deciding what constituted France's contribution beyond the financial element.

The estimates of 'foreign contributions' made by the Bombing Survey do not include the value of the goods and services consumed without payment outside Germany by German troops. Nor do they include the value of booty. What is more they omit the contribution of foreign workers in Germany, and French workers made the biggest contribution of all foreign groups. The contribution of French workers in Germany in fact is considered

6. U.S.S.B.S., Overall Economic Effects Division, *The Gross National Product of Germany 1936 to 1944*, Washington, 1945.

within the convention as a part of German G.N.P. From the claims made by the French Reparations Commissioners after the war the value of German booty from France together with the value of transport and entertainment services provided free can be estimated at 154,523 million 1938 francs.[7] This is about the same sum as the financial contribution including the unpaid German clearing deficit in 1942. It is still, however, an under-estimate. Except for the value of the captured Belgian gold reserves, it does not include the use of goods and capital in France belonging to other countries in a state of war with Germany. It does not include the value of goods seized from expelled or murdered people of Jewish descent, nor of the output of certain large farms operated purely for German purposes. Neither does it include the value of persons seized and transferred to Germany.

A correct estimation of the contribution of French workers to the German economy would depend on knowing the precise level of their productivity. But it is in any case too large an item to be ignored. A survey by the Reichswirtschaftskammer in 1944 esti-mated the productivity of French male workers at between 90 and 100 per cent that of German workers.[8] If this figure is correct French workers in Germany were certainly more productive than in France. In France labour productivity fell to very low levels in 1944 partly through the depreciation of the capital equipment, the growing food shortages and the long working hours, but mainly through the unwillingness of the labour force to work for a cause in which they did not believe. It is understandable that in these circumstances there would be a gain in productivity by transferring the labour to Germany where depreciation of the capital equipment was less, food supply better and possibilities of compulsion far greater. The Strategic Bombing Survey esti-mated that the productivity of labour in Germany rose by 10 per cent during the war.[9] It has already been noted that because of the greater capital-intensiveness of the economy in a long war and also perhaps because of the greater care taken of the labour force

7. Milward, *The New Order*, p. 81.
8. Homze, p. 259.
9. U.S.S.B.S., Overall Economic Effects Division, Special Paper no. 8, *Industrial Sales, Output and Productivity, Prewar Area of Germany 1939–1944*, G.P.O., Washington, 1946.

this phenomenon is a general one. It is not, however, general to an occupied economy. There the opposite economic circumstances apply.

The Reparations Commissioners calculated that the loss to the French economy of that part of the French work-force working in Germany, together with those workers forced to work in France for German agencies, was 13,000 million hours of work.[10] The calculation is based on the average income per hour of work devoted to domestic production in France in 1938 and it is equivalent to one third of the working hours of the production of 1938. But to allow for differences in productivity of French workers in France and Germany the Commissioners reduced the cash value of the hours of work by estimating seventy-two hours work in wartime Germany as the equivalent of forty-eight hours work in France in 1938, surely a miscalculation. The financial value which the Commissioners ascribed to these hours of work, 71,000 million 1938 francs ought, if the foregoing productivity estimates are nearer to the truth, and a wider range of factors than patriotism influenced productivity, be revised upwards to about 100,000 million 1938 francs. This estimate may, in spite of its upward revision, be an underestimate. It does not include the loss of those prisoners of war, one million of them, either immobilized in Germany or at work in the German economy. Piatier does include the prisoners of war in his calculations estimating the loss at 9·7 million worker years.[11] If we assume the thirty-six-hour week of 1938 as a basis of the calculation this would imply 16,000 million hours of work lost. But whether in most armies the amount of work done even in wartime is the equivalent of a thirty-six-hour week is no doubt a matter on which readers will have their own opinion.

So far we are expressing only the purely financial benefit to the German economy of the occupation of France. To what extent could these sums of money be exchanged for goods and services? One of the primary purposes of the occupation levies and the

10. Commission Consultative des Dommages et des Réparations, *Dommages subis par la France et l'Union française du fait de la guerre et de l'occupation ennemie (1939–1945), Part imputable à l'Allemagne*, vol. i, chapter 7, Imprimerie Nationale, Paris, 1947.

11. A. Piatier, 'La vie économique de la France sous l'occupation', in *La France sous l'occupation*, Esprit de la résistance, P.U.F., Paris, 1959.

clearing agreements was to obtain a greater flow of goods and services from the French to the German economy. The total value of such goods and services in the period 1940–44 can be estimated at 1,151,056 million current francs or 538,589 million 1938 francs.[12] The value of the manufactured goods obtained from France throughout the war, omitting the military equipment seized under the terms of the armistice, was 5·5 per cent of German G.N.P. in 1943 on the basis of the wartime exchange rate, which clearly underestimates the true contribution. The value of the agricultural produce so obtained was 3·9 per cent of 1943 G.N.P., of raw materials 3·1 per cent. If services are also included the total gain was greater and could be represented as roughly equal to one quarter of German G.N.P. in 1938.

Looked at from the viewpoint of the precise needs of the German economy in this period the true value of the French economy is perhaps no better expressed by the total value of goods and services which it contributed than by the stream of cash which was obtained from it. In the framework of Germany's economic plans it was not so much the average level of French industrial or agricultural output obtained which mattered most but the control over certain specific categories of production. For example, Germany took for her own purposes three quarters of France's iron-ore supply. In 1943 over half of French bauxite production went to Germany and, although there was an acute coal shortage in France, 15 per cent of coal production also went to Germany. In December 1941 two thirds of the total train movements in France were for German purposes, in January 1944 85 per cent.

There can be no doubt that, whatever the inherent difficulties of exploiting an occupied economy, the yield to Germany from the French economy was extremely high. Nor are there any indications that returns began to diminish. On the contrary, the proportion of French output diverted to German purposes and the contribution of that proportion to total German output increased in 1943 and 1944.

What was the cost of this conquest to Germany? Here the conceptual problems are more difficult than in estimating the gain, and accurate information harder to come by. If the whole

12. Milward, *The New Order*, p. 276.

of German military expenditure from 1934 until the end of the conquest of France is considered as the cost of all Germany's conquests until that time and it is assumed that this expenditure fell equally between the conquests of Czechoslovakia, Poland, Belgium, Luxembourg, the Netherlands, Denmark and Norway (omitting the conquest of Austria as comparatively inexpensive) the average expenditure for each territory was 13,300 million R M. This average expenditure is less than the financial payments alone from France in 1943. But there is also the cost of maintaining the conquest. If we assume that the occupation costs met exactly this purpose, when in reality they covered other purposes also, the net profit to Germany could be estimated at the gross profit less the total of the occupation levies, represented in Table 21, plus 13,300 million R M. But that is to estimate the profitability of the conquest at its lowest level. Finally, if conquest is considered as an investment choice, in a period of massive unemployment and low investment, the opportunity cost of a rearmament programme was scarcely a cost in the sense in which we are now using the word. It was part of the programme of economic reinvigoration and employment creation.

But we are dealing in the case of France with a rich and well-endowed economy which was effectively under German control for four years. (The demarcation line and the existence for the first two years of a nominally independent government in Vichy did not greatly impede German economic plans in France. The economic pressures which the Germans were able to bring to bear were extremely strong, especially when backed up by the constant threat of military force. The regular meetings of the Franco-German Armistice Commission at Wiesbaden were dominated by economic issues and in German eyes the most important function of the Commission was to ensure that Germany's economic writ ran with almost the same force in Vichy territory as in occupied France.) Even in the early period of the occupation of France, before French manufacturing industry was extensively used for German purposes, Germany could still benefit extensively from diverting French raw material resources such as bauxite and iron ore in large quantities to German war industry. But what about a smaller highly developed economy whose functioning depended on a constant availability of international supply and a close integration into the international economy? An economy like Norway's, for example, had very few raw material resources which could be exploited. Its manufacturing industry, although highly developed, was, for the most part, insignificant in terms of total output by the side of that of Germany. The level of economic activity could only be maintained by organizing a regular supply of raw materials most of which had, before 1940, come from areas outside German control. There was practically no surplus labour which could be shipped off to Germany. And the population was dependent on food imports for survival. Did an economy of this kind bring any worthwhile reinforcement to Germany's productive effort?

Occupation levies were imposed there as in France and the *per capita* burden of these payments was set at a higher level. The average burden of these payments on the individual Norwegian in the first two years of the occupation was 1,842 Norwegian kroner per inhabitant. In France it was 779 Norwegian kroner and in Denmark only 579.[13] The difference is mainly to be attributed to the great size of the army of occupation relative to the Norwegian population. The total sums paid out in occupation costs averaged about one third of national income for each year of the occupation. The total share of Norwegian national income lost to the country rose from about 25 per cent in 1940 to about 40 per cent in 1943 and may have been higher still in 1944.[14] It was therefore rather less than in France but still so great as to leave no doubt whatsoever about the effectiveness of German policies of exploitation.

Even so a total loss to Norway of 12,440 million 1938 kroner, plus 5,000 million pre-war kroner, the estimate of Germany's gain from depreciating Norway's capital stock, almost certainly an exaggeration, made only a slight difference to the German war effort. It was about 6 per cent of German G.N.P. in 1944 at the wartime exchange rate. On the same exchange-rate basis French payments to Germany in 1944 alone amounted to 5·9 per cent of German G.N.P. in that year. When it is considered that a large army of occupation had to be kept in Norway the profitability of the occupation of Norway seems much less clear cut than that of France. This comes out more clearly if the trading connections

13. Milward, *The Fascist Economy*, p. 280.
14. O. Aukrust and P. Bjerve, *Hva krigen kostet Norge*, Dreyers Forlag, Oslo, 1945, p. 48.

are considered. Only in 1944 did Norway have an export surplus on the clearing account with Germany. In the three years 1941 to 1943 she had a substantial import surplus, occasioned by the cutting-off of the pre-war food imports from elsewhere and also by the presence of so many members of the German armed forces. As a brief comparison France had an export surplus to Germany of 858 million current Reichsmarks in 1942, Norway an import surplus of 130 million current Reichsmarks. Of course this is to accept the official German valuations of goods traded and the Norwegian import surplus may represent the arbitrary values which Germany ascribed to commodities in the trade treaties. However, there were certain strategic raw materials, such as titanium ore, and certain manufactured products, such as aluminium and magnesium, whose real value to the German war economy was higher than the price ascribed to them. But Norway's contribution to the German war economy does not suggest that in strictly economic terms the occupation was profitable.

Belgium provides an intermediate example of an economy with greater raw material resources, in particular coal, and a larger manufacturing capacity, especially in steel, non-ferrous metals and engineering, which could be coupled to the German war effort. From the start of the occupation to the end of 1943 about half of Belgian production was for German purposes. In 1943, after the change of policy by Germany, some more important Belgian industries were completely dominated by German orders. Three quarters of the value of the output of the metal-working industry in 1943 was represented by German contracts. But at the same time the level of production in Belgium remained very low. Industrial production during the war was about two thirds its pre-war level, which had already been a very depressed one. Raw materials and capital were difficult to obtain. In many ways the industries which could have made the most significant contribution to the German war economy were those processing non-ferrous metals. But they were dependent on raw material imports and the only branch whose wartime output was significant in terms of German output was copper refining. Iron and steel output was only 50 per cent of its pre-war level. Total steel output varied between 5 and 7 per cent of production in the Reich. And although Belgian coal was exported to Lorraine and Luxembourg, both incorporated into the Reich, total output, which remained very low during the war, was less than one tenth that of Germany.[15]

Nevertheless Belgium in 1942 had an export surplus with Germany of 412 million current Reichsmarks, and the Netherlands came not far behind. If this is taken in consideration with France's enormous export surplus to Germany the paradoxical reversal of pre-war National Socialist economic ambitions becomes clear. In 1942, while economic policy in western-occupied territories was still governed by the ideas of short-term exploitation and improvisation, it was nevertheless those developed western economies whose contribution to the German economy was dominant. As for the east, from which so much had been hoped, its contribution was relatively unimportant by the side of that of France, Belgium and the Netherlands. When the policy of exploitation changed this situation became even more marked. Once it was a question, in 1943, of systematically exploiting the productive capacities of the national economies without looting them it was to the western economies, with their greater flexibility and variety of manufacturing industry and greater range of skills, that the German Ministry of War Production turned. The value of German imports of manufactures and semi-manufactures from France in 1943, even at the undervalued exchange rate then prevailing, was twenty times its 1938 level. Over the whole period of the war France even made as large a contribution to German food supply as the eastern occupied territories. The eastern goose that would lay the golden egg proved to be only a myth; the richest pickings were in the west.

One reason for this was the constant warfare in the east. The battlefronts swept to and fro across Russian territory. The Soviet government put into practice a systematic scorched-earth policy. Military requirements predominated over questions of economic reorganization and the stable administrative machinery which controlled the western occupied economies could never be

15. The author would like to acknowledge here the kindness of two scholars who allowed him to consult Ph.D. theses which they had just submitted and which were otherwise not available, J. Gillingham, author of 'The Economic New Order in Belgium', submitted to the University of California in Berkeley, and P. F. Klemm, author of 'German Economic Policies in Belgium 1940–44', submitted to the University of Michigan. It is from their works that this passage and certain subsequent remarks about Belgium are taken.

installed in the east. Economic policy was always concerned, as in the first two years of occupation in the west, with the ruthless short-term exploitation of the economy to satisfy German needs. The prime need was foodstuffs, for it was the rich lands of the Ukraine that were to make the Greater-German economy effectively autarkic. But there were also reserves of strategic materials of great importance, the oil of the Caucasus and the iron ore and manganese deposits of Krivoi Rog and Nikopol, so important that they even affected decisions on the direction of the German campaigns.

The extent to which Germany was able to divert the foodstuff resources of this eastern area to her own purposes is considered in Chapter 8. The raw material resources proved more difficult to obtain. The oil-fields as well as the Krivoi Rog iron ore mines had been comprehensively put out of commission by the retreating forces. After the first capture of the coalfields east of the Dnieper it was estimated that only between 10 and 20 per cent of pre-war production could be obtained. Railway equipment and electric power were in acutely short supply. Coal production in fact proved inadequate even to supply the needs of the troops on the spot. By the end of 1942 only 347,000 metric tons of iron ore had been delivered from Krivoi Rog compared to the 17·4 million tons obtained from France in that year. But with manganese ore it was a different story; during the occupation of Russia 90 per cent of German consumption came from that source, 475,000 metric tons of concentrate and 660,000 metric tons of ore.[16]

National Socialist occupation policy

However, it was not only the fighting in the east which impeded German exploitation. It was also the fundamental confusions of National Socialist policy and political attitude. Where policy remained unchanged, as it did in the case of the ally Hungary, control over raw materials proved very effective until 1944. Hungarian bauxite production doubled between 1938 and 1943, reaching one million tons, and crude oil output increased from a mere 42,000 tons to 842,000 tons. About 90 per cent of the bauxite and half the oil went to Germany. But in general the

16. M. Riedel, 'Bergbau und Eisenhüttenindustrie in der Ukraine unter deutscher Besatzung (1941–1944)', in *Vj.f.Z.*, no. 21, 1973.

eastern states were at first regarded as permanently agricultural areas peopled by inhabitants of a lower capacity. Accordingly the most atrocious and seemingly pointless cruelties were regularly practised. If the population was to produce for Germany it was to do so in the most abysmal conditions and under the most extreme terror. Policy wavered between sustaining sufficient organized productive capacity there to help the German war economy and destroying the fabric of all organized economic life.[17]

There were elements of this destructiveness in the early stages of occupation in the west. They coincided with the stage of exploitation when loot and booty were the main German objectives there also. But they were quickly replaced by a proper administrative machinery. This machinery depended either on civilian governments as in Norway or on the military administration as in France. Its immediate function was to ensure that there were properly maintained economic controls in these countries, to facilitate the placing of German contracts there, and to ensure that no financial or social policy was pursued which would endanger the advantageous trading and payments mechanisms which Germany had set up. Allowing that such policies were wholly in the German interest, they were on the whole pursued with restraint and in the case of Norway the Reichskommissariat provided a sensible economic check on the wilder schemes of the Quisling puppet government. The main object was not to kill the milch cow. Within this framework the various German economic agencies, including the armed forces, dealt directly with the ministries or businessmen involved. There was no centralization or nationalization of contracts or policy, the occupation government looked after its own affairs and the rest was up to the conflicting interest of the German ministries.

Once it became a question of integrating the western economies into the German war effort on a more planned and comprehensive basis this would not do. From late 1942 onwards the Speer Ministry tried to integrate the captured economies into the machinery of German production planning, and to reinvigorate them by making more materials available, by placing more German contracts there, and by stopping the direct looting of labour and resources. By a gradual process of administrative

17. A. Dallin, *German Rule in Russia, 1941–1945*, Oxford University Press, New York, 1957.

change the Ministry of War Production tried to reverse the previous policy of exploitation while keeping the relationship as much in the German interest as ever.

At the end of October 1942 all restrictions were removed on the quantities of steel which could be allocated for German contracts in Belgium. The decree of the Four-Year Plan Office of 10 January 1943 gave a unified control of the armaments economies of all the occupied territories to the Ministry of War Production and enjoined on the minister 'the exploitation of every possibility of an increase in German armaments-potential in the occupied territories'.[18] The consequence of this was seen in February when a sharp upward movement began in the number of contracts placed in Belgium. After March the French and Belgian economies were treated for all purposes of production planning as part of Germany. As far as the Speer Ministry was concerned policy was that increases in consumer-goods production in the western occupied territories would release capacity in Germany for more vital manufactures.

It had become clear that the restrictions on supply in the occupied territories and, even more, the compulsory drafting of labour to Germany were working against the interests of the German war economy. Furthermore the growing effectiveness of the strategic air offensive meant that there were certain advantages in organizing production outside Germany. But the main consideration was the failure of the older policy of exploitation. This was made clear by Hans Kehrl, the head of the Planning Office (Planungsamt), when he sketched out Speer's reasoning.

> If even by the use of violence I cannot bring people from France to Germany in the necessary number, something which is obvious from what is happening, and at the same time I run the risk that through fear of being seized by force people leave the firms where they are working, then only the lesser evil is left for me, to try to employ these people in France or Belgium, and in that way I no longer need a German force to bring them over the border. . . . In this way a change in production policy began.[19]

The culmination of this change was the visit of the French Minister of Industrial Production, Jean Bichelonne, to Berlin in

18. Reichskommissar für das Vierjahresplan, 'Anordnung über die Steigerung des Rüstungspotentials in der besetzten Gebieten', 10 January 1943.

19. Minutes of Zentrale Planung, 1 March 1944.

September 1943 and the agreement there between him and Speer. By the agreement the production committees and rings which controlled German war production were extended into France by the creation of similar machinery there, so that raw material and other resource allocations could be made, at least in principle, jointly for the two economies on the basis of a common war production programme. This common programme posited a great increase in coal and iron-ore output in France for the use of French industry and it also posited on the German side certain financial, administrative and technical aids to bring this about. In November Belgium was also integrated into the committee system which enforced economic controls in Germany. But the new production targets set for both countries were never reached. The proportion of industrial output for German purposes was higher in both economies in 1943 than 1942; in Belgium it rose from 32 per cent to 48 per cent. But by the time of the Speer–Bichelonne agreements shortages of resources, combined with the refusal of the German labour agencies to stop drafting labour even from 'protected' factories, were starting to bring down production in occupied western territories from the peak it had reached in autumn 1943.

These changes in policy were bound to have an even more limited effect in eastern Europe where they ran more violently against the general principles of National Socialist thought. Göring's original directives for the treatment of the Polish economy even envisaged reducing all the railways to single track in order to provide more rail for Germany, taking away the power stations and dismantling the telephone system. But these absurdities were soon replaced by a general policy of increasing the output of raw materials and food for German purposes while maintaining a low level of industrial production to keep the economy functioning. When a greater volume of war production was required both from occupied Poland and the small, nominally independent, General-Government of Poland it was much less easy to switch policy than in the western occupied territories. It is almost impossible, because of the territorial divisions, to sort out Polish statistics for the period but the only industries which showed any increases in output for German purposes were those producing raw materials. Coal production increased from thirty-eight million tons in 1939 to fifty-seven million tons in 1943, but the general level of output of mining and industry together may have fallen by as much as 60 per cent. Ruthless looting and seizure of food and raw materials continued there side by side with the attempts at a more organized policy.

German plans for Europe

Beyond the clear intention to exploit the occupied territories another aspect of German policy emerges, the interest in reconstructing the subject continent in accordance with the political and economic ideas prevailing in Germany. This was what the National Socialist party implied by the 'New Order', a phrase popularized by the Reichs Minister of Economics in July 1940. What the New Order would have meant is not easy to see. As the war became more pressing there was less time and energy for such grandiose schemes, although they were, even so, never entirely lost sight of. At the height of German success in Russia Hitler's talk circled about these great schemes but after that less and less is heard of them. But it is not only that the war took precedence over social reconstruction. Any discussion of, let alone attempts to implement, a New Order revealed the inherent contradictions in the National Socialist economy itself. These contradictions appeared even more sharply against the background of economies and societies not sharing the same pattern of development as Germany. But in spite of the many contradictions there were some persistent tendencies in German occupation policy which show that wider issues concerning the future of the European economy were at stake.

The most important of these tendencies was the attempt to integrate European trade and production more completely into a pattern where it was dominated by the demand of the central Greater German area. It was inevitable that this would happen during the period of the war itself and this was, indeed, all that was meant by the phrase 'the European war economy'. But this new pattern of production and commercial exchange in Europe was no temporary wartime phenomenon; the break between Germany and international economic influences was to be made permanent and more complete by initiating structural changes in the other European economies which would cut them off from international economic movements and tie them more closely to

Germany. This would in turn increase Germany's own level of self-sufficiency. Secondly, this policy was to be furthered by creating a zone in the underdeveloped area of south-eastern and eastern Europe where only German capital and German commercial interests would hold sway. The geographical boundaries of this zone roughly coincided with those sketched out by the theorists of *Grossraumwirtschaft*, except that it was obviously intended also to include large areas of the Soviet Union. Thirdly, the extension of the influence of German private companies in Europe was to be helped provided the nature of their business or the geographical area of their interests coincided with the interests of the German government. Finally, the ultimate goal of a social and racial reconstruction of the continent was not lost sight of, and the more radical theories of the National Socialists in these respects were put into practice everywhere on the continent. All these tendencies of policy clashed at times with the strategic aim of economic exploitation of occupied territory and the fact that they were allowed to continue in spite of these clashes also suggests that there were long-term plans for a reformulation of the European economy, however vaguely conceived.

The first of these tendencies may be seen in the economic policies pursued in Norway. Soon after the occupation it was decided to create a large aluminium industry there to serve the needs of German aircraft production. Norway was to be as great a supplier of aluminium to the German air force as Germany itself. The economics of aluminium production in Norway were very favourable in spite of the need to import all the raw material. The main factor in the cost of production was the huge quantity of electric current consumed in the manufacturing process and hydro-electric current was cheaper in Norway than anywhere in Europe. Norway was already a producer on a medium scale before the occupation, with an output of 28,900 metric tons of finished aluminium in 1938. The 'aluminium plan' agreed between the German Air Ministry, Vereinigte Aluminiumwerke and, subsequently, the Junkers Aircraft Company was designed to increase Norwegian production to 119,000 metric tons of aluminium within one year of the plan's commencement and to 243,900 metric tons annually when the further stages of the plan were completed by June 1944.[20] This was little short of Germany's

20. Milward, *The Fascist Economy*, p. 177.

own level of production in 1942. The plan also envisaged an immediate increase in the output of alumina, the intermediate stage between the raw material (bauxite) and aluminium.

The aluminium plan was remarkable, not only because of its magnitude, but also because of its assumptions about the future. The first stage involved building four new aluminium factories and extending the four existing ones; the second stage involved six new factories. The new factories would demand eight new hydro-electric power stations to supply them. Since Norwegian bauxite imports came almost entirely from outside Europe the assumption was that in future Germany would herself have perpetual control over extensive bauxite deposits, which could only have been in France or Hungary, and that she would be able to ship this bauxite in large quantities to Norway. From the establishment of the Franco-German Armistice Commission one of the main interests of the German team had been to secure a regular bauxite supply from unoccupied France.[21] The capital invested in bauxite mining and aluminium production in Hungary has to be seen in this continental perspective. The sum to be invested in Norway itself was 1,200 million RM and it was never anticipated that more than a small proportion would be raised in Norway.

This was only one of the items in the German capital investment programme in Norway which evolved during 1941. There was also to be investment both of capital and agricultural expertise in extending the area of land used for food production and thus increasing the total food output of the country in order to make it less dependent on food exports from German-controlled Europe. An investment programme to turn unused moorland into pasture and thereby economize on fodder imports was started. It was due to run for twenty years. Concurrently with this programme there were to be long-term readjustments in Norway's livestock economy in order to reduce further the level of imports of animal feed. Poultry stocks, for example, were to be reduced by half and sheep stocks to be increased and fed on the natural heathland which covered so much of the country. A five-year plan was initiated to increase the number of sheep from 1·7 million to almost four million.

21. *La Délégation française auprès de la Commission Allemande d'Armistice*, Imprimerie Nationale, Paris, 1947, vol. 3, p. 104.

The one foodstuff Norway could contribute to Europe in return was fish. There were plans to process a greater proportion of the fish catch into fodder to help German agricultural planning and to increase the total catch, so that more fish could be exported to Europe. 'It is clear', wrote the German administration in its annual report even in 1942, 'that developments involving so great a reorientation of Norwegian fishing can only proceed under German influence and German capital participation. The Norwegian economy can never produce enough capital strength to perform the great tasks which grow before it in the future.'[22] The major obstacle to increasing fish exports was the low proportion of the catch which was frozen and the high proportion which was dried or salted and exported to shrinking low-income markets. By another capital investment programme the German administration intended to increase the number of fish-freezing plants and to improve the basic capital equipment of the fishermen, whom, like the peasants, it regarded as a pure reservoir of Aryans for the Europe of the future.

In these plans Hitler included the magnificent addition of an Autobahn to link Trondheim with Berlin, the completion of the southern railway to Stavanger from Oslo, and the building of a railway into northern Norway and the Arctic. The last idea had been long mooted in Norway but always postponed because of shortage of capital. The railway, had it reached its ultimate objective of Narvik, would have been the costliest of all these investment projects. It was an iron monument to the European dimensions of the Greater German Empire, in which, it seems, Trondheim would have been no mean city. But the need to fight the war soon made serious financial inroads into these schemes. The northern railway made some progress, the road none at all. One of the major new aluminium factories was completed and two of the power stations. The programmes to revive agriculture and fishing were overtaken in 1942 by financial restrictions and shortages. In the changing circumstances of the war the Reichskommissariat in Norway saw this programme of capital investment as inflationary and unsound and likely to weaken the capacity of the Norwegian economy to pay the occupation costs.

Plans of this kind naturally attracted the interest and support

22. Reichskommissariat für die besetzten norwegischen Gebiete, 'Ein Jahr Reichskommissar', 'Fischwirtschaft'.

of those companies which might benefit. The attempt by German business to turn the new political situation to its own advantage strengthened interpretations of National Socialism as a stage of state capitalism, and behind the advance guard of soldiers, SS. men, and party rhetoricians were seen advancing the real holders of power in Germany, a phalanx of highly organized businessmen out to subject the business of other European nations to their own control. The decree of 2 August 1940 of the Four-Year Plan Office indicated that 'one goal of German foreign economic policy is the increase of German influence in foreign enterprise'.[23] Two weeks later Göring indicated to the Minister of Economics that Germany should aim to control the capital in 'key' firms in the occupied areas.[24]

These were the lines which some larger German firms – such as I.G. Farben – had followed in their contingency plans.[25] Other firms were more interested in raw-material deposits elsewhere in Europe; Mansfeld demanded special rights over foreign copper deposits, especially those in Norway.[26] Vereinigte Aluminium-werke brought pressure to bear to gain control of the bauxite deposits in Yugoslavia on which the Yugoslav government had developed a small alumina works in the inter-war period. They also signed a secret agreement with the Croatian Ustaše party in exile in Italy that after any coup Croatian bauxite deposits would in future be exploited only in conjunction with Vereinigte Alu-miniumwerke.[27]

Not all these objectives were furthered by government help and not all of them were attained. Although individual businessmen were of course eager to seize their opportunities, the pattern of German intervention in foreign capital holdings and business had a certain consistency. Attempts to acquire firms and capital in the western territories received full support only where a vital

23. *Documents on German Foreign Policy*, H.M.S.O., London, vol. 10, no. 278.

24. O. Ulshöfer, *Einflussnahme auf Wirtschaftsunternehmungen in den besetzten nord-, west-, und südosteuropäischen Ländern während des zweiten Weltkrieges insbesondere der Erwerb von Beteiligungen (Verflechtung)*, Veröffentlichungen des Instituts für Besatzungsfragen, no. 15, Tübingen, 1958, p. 41.

25. See Chapter 1, p. 12.

26. Radandt, *Kriegsverbrecherkonzern*, p. 226.

27. Milward, *The Fascist Economy*, p. 193.

strategic interest was at stake. Otherwise German companies, although offered certain facilities, were left to fend for themselves against the administration and the business circles of occupied western territories. In eastern Europe, however, there was a conscious policy of eliminating the influence of foreign capital and transferring these assets to German ownership. In spite of the domination of German trade in eastern Europe in the inter-war period German capital holdings had been much less important there than those of Britain, France and Belgium. In the Europe of the future the eastern countries would have been reserved for German control and development.

The biggest single acquisition was that of the French capital holdings in the Yugoslav copper mining company, Les Mines de Bor – 1,800 million 1941 francs. Strategic interests were also involved here. The French government had used its control early in 1940 to pre-empt the whole Yugoslav copper supply. French, Belgian and British capital holdings in the Romanian oil industry were a prime target. French shares in one of the companies, Concordia, were transferred to the Deutsche Bank in return for city of Paris loan certificates. The same bank bought out in under-valued francs the holdings of the Union Parisienne and of the Belgian Société Générale in the Bancă Commercială Română. The Franco-British Danube transport companies which handled the oil traffic were bought out in March 1941, together with French capital holdings in the General Hungarian Credit Bank. In this case the payment was made in 1939 French rearmament loan certificates captured in the Netherlands. French holdings in the Czech Hutni Bank suffered the same fate. Between June and October 1941, when the French government temporarily relaxed its opposition to these proceedings, shares in a variety of Polish banks, mining companies, steelworks, and the Silesian Zinc Company were transferred to German ownership. In this period the payment was simply made by increasing the German clearing debt.

Where areas passed directly into German control, as in Bohemia and Moravia or Poland, the direct acquisition of firms was readily pursued without scruples. It was here that the devices of 'trusteeships' exercised by German firms were most used. The Hermann Göring Works in this way took over the Vitkovice steelworks, the Škoda armament and vehicle factories, and six other major companies. The Dresdner Bank took control of the Tatra car factories and the Mannesmann interests took over the Prague Railway Company and a steelworks in Ostrava. About half of the industrial share capital in the Protectorate of Bohemia and Moravia passed by various methods into German control and almost all the share capital in coal-mining, oil, cement and paper.[28]

In western Europe German business did occasionally also force concessions of this kind. The most obvious was the joint creation of a new dyestuffs combine in France, Francolor, but in the circumstances the resulting agreements were hardly in the worst interests of the French industry. The French negotiators accepted a 51 per cent German capital holding in the new combine but the German negotiators abandoned all claims to use the agreement as a precedent and abandoned also their insistence that the new company should have monopoly rights of all innovations on the French market. The new company had the French and the French colonial market reserved to itself in return for relinquishing the right to export elsewhere. German exports, however, were to have a completely free run in south-eastern Europe. The situation was summed up by Hemmen, the chief German negotiator, 'For you will have your place, but not such that you may permit yourselves the uncontrolled competition of before the war. Besides, that is the line of our general economic policy towards France.' And later he widened the issue. 'Note that, set in the framework of our programme of European reorganization, these proposals are economically very advantageous for you. They are in your interest. . . . They are above all in the interest of Europe, since, essentially, it is a question of reorganizing the continent of Europe.'[29]

Even a very low level of economic coordination demanded some control over strategic industries. The usual legal device in this case was either the appointment of a trustee (*Treuhänder*) to manage the firm in the German interest or technical supervision and control by a similar firm in Germany. The Saarland steel manufacturer Hermann Roechling became the effective controller

28. V. Král, *Otázky hospodářského a socialniho vyvoje v Českých zemich 1938–1945*, Nakl. Československé academie věd., 3 vols., Prague, 1957–9.

29. *La Délégation française auprès de la Commission Allemande d'Armistice*, A. Costes, Paris, 1947, vol. 2, p. 527.

of the large French steel industry in Lorraine. Krupp was given the run of the productive capacities of several steel and armaments works in eastern Europe. In cases where the captured firm was controlled by British or American capital trusteeship was more usual. In western Europe these arrangements contained enough legal force to preserve the nominal independence of such firms as far as was possible when the orders and the raw materials to supply them were largely controlled by Germany. In eastern Europe they were tantamount to the seizure of the firm and its equipment.

What Hemmen called 'the line of our general economic policy towards France' appears to have applied also to the other western countries. They, too, would have had their place. German and Belgian business were able to work together in some harmony as soon as it became clear that the exploitation of Belgium involved maintaining production there. The agreements over the foundation of Francolor and for the participation of German firms in the French artificial textile industry, although they reflected a situation where German firms were in a strong bargaining position, were on balance commercial agreements between major firms from which the French partners also drew important benefits. The arguments about relative shares in capital participation were of the same nature as similar peacetime negotiations. This was even more strikingly the case in the disputes between German firms as to their relative degree of involvement in the Norwegian aluminium programme. The Reichskommissariat in Norway in the circumstances applied very little pressure to curtail these business squabbles, safeguarded on occasions the interest of Norwegian firms, and always pursued its own government policy without any subservience to the financial interests involved. In retrospect it is extraordinary that the investment plans should have been so long delayed by business disputes more proper to peacetime.

As far as the plans for expansion of German business were concerned they were vigorously and even brutally supported by the National Socialist government where they applied to eastern and south-eastern Europe. The increase in the proportion of the foreign trade with Germany between 1934 and 1939 had already brought difficulties because of the relatively low level of German foreign investment in the area compared to that of the other western economies. After 1939 Germany completely dominated the exchanges of these countries and in the normal course of events there was no reason to tolerate the potential opposition there of foreign capital interests, especially where they controlled a resource of vital strategic importance like Romanian oil. But the policy of the German government was more consistent than a mere series of reactions to this situation or occasional surrenders to heavy pressure from the business world. In some cases – as in France – western Europe was undergoing a temporary military occupation which provided the opportunity to reduce certain business interests to a scale more suitable to a future European economy dominated by Germany. At the same time the situation afforded a good opportunity to pay off some old business scores. In other cases – such as the Netherlands and Norway – the possibility of a complete political integration with the Reich was always present, and here economic policy was concerned with a general reorientation of the economy which had to become less 'international' and more 'European'. This reorientation had to start from the same basic principles that can be discerned in the German economy itself – a high level of control, especially of foreign exchanges and labour, and an insistence on autarkic development where it was strategically important. But everywhere in western Europe occupation was used to remove the barriers which western capital could erect to the creation of a German economic empire in the east.

Because such far-reaching considerations about the future nature of the European economy could be discerned behind the day-to-day pressure of economic exploitation the political opposition to the Axis alliance in Europe was obliged also to state its opposition in pan-European terms. If a repetition of the dismal events of the inter-war period, which had seen Germany's peaceful connections with the other European economies diminish and had given birth to her attempt to solve her own and Europe's political and economic problems by brute force, was to be avoided economic relationships between the European states would have to be set in a more coherent and durable frame. Both inside Germany and among her opponents Nazi policy therefore posed after 1939 the question of what sort of European economy and society was to emerge once the fighting had stopped.

For the German government itself this was a very difficult

question to answer. The priority given to domestic economic policy in Germany after 1933 and the controls which had sustained that priority had created a growing gap between the level of prices and wages in the German economy and those elsewhere in Europe. After 1939 this was a major obstacle to any closer integration with the other European economies. The idea that, providing the connections between the smaller western European economies and the extra-European world were broken, Germany could dominate European exchanges implied a harmony of domestic economic policies which was far from present and a relaxation of German tariffs and exchange controls which, after 1936, had become impossible without a drastic interference in the management of the occupied economies. To Reichsmarschall Göring it was

> particularly important . . . that even before the end of the war as intensive as possible a penetration of, in the first place, the Dutch and Belgian, but also the Norwegian and Danish economies, should be attempted by German capital on a very wide basis, and in return it should be open to Dutch and Danish interests to participate economically and to place their capital in Germany with the aim of creating in the shortest time common economic links and connections of interest between Germany and these countries.[30]

The group of publicists, bankers and businessmen around Walther Funk in the Ministry of Economics who were responsible for publicizing the concept of a 'New Order' in 1940 thought in terms of a tariff-free zone in western Europe accompanied by the economic integration of the west European economies to a central core of European manufacturing industry in Germany.[31] Immediately after the occupation of the Low Countries and northern France, before any definitive occupation policy. was settled, Funk advocated the removal of the national tariffs over the whole area and it is clear that this policy was briefly considered.[23] But the *Blitzkrieg* strategy meant it was incompatible

30. Göring to Funk, 17 August 1940. Riksarkivet, Norway. Reichskommissariat für die besetzten norwegischen Gebiete. Diverse, Pakke 10. Hauptabteilung Verwaltung (VP 13875/5).
31. W. Funk, 'Wirtschaftliche Neuordnung Europas', in *Südost-Echo*, 26 July 1940.
32. Reichskommissariat für die besetzten norwegischen Gebiete, Abteilung Finanzen 2500, 'Bericht über öffentliche Finanzwirtschaft', 8 August 1940.

with the immediate economic exploitation of these lands and it was vigorously opposed on these grounds by Göring, who thus revealed himself a true National Socialist in the fundamental contradictions of his economic ideas.

Once the *Blitzkrieg* had failed, however, and been replaced by the idea of a 'European war economy' the idea was bound once more to reappear. When the Ministry of Armaments and Munitions began to turn in 1943 towards the policy of increasing production in the occupied territories it was obvious that such increases would only be achieved if raw materials and labour were diverted from Germany to the other industrial areas of Europe. Speer and his officials began to consider European 'planning' as an essential part of German war production; the apogee of this policy was attained in the agreements reached between Speer and Jean Bichelonne, the French Minister of Industrial Production, in 1943. 'It would have been the supposition', Speer told his interrogators after the war,

> that the tariff was lifted from this large economic area and through this a mutual production was really achieved. For any deeply thinking individual it is clear that the tariffs which we have in western Europe are unbearable. So the possibility for producing on a large scale only exists through this scheme.[33]

Even in western Europe there were tendencies in German economic policy which were clearly opposed to such a solution. The support given by the Reichskommissariat in Norway to the under-capitalized fishing and farming sector of the economy implied, for example, a high level of economic protection through tariffs and closed trading agreements with Germany for a substantial period of time. Even thirty years after these events, in far more propitious circumstances, Norwegian farmers and fishermen were clearly unconvinced of the advantages of the type of Europe envisaged by Speer and Bichelonne. The support for these sectors in Norway came from those members of the German administration whose view of National Socialism was more ideological than that of Speer. They admired the Norwegian peasantry, seeing them as a pool of uncorrupted Aryan blood and a bastion against the more insidious pressures of international 'plutocracy'.

33. Interrogation of Albert Speer, 21 July 1945, Intelligence Report EF/AM/6.

But it is the nature of the intended economic empire in the east which most reveals the fundamental contradictions of German policy. It was not difficult for the business groups around Funk to incorporate this into their idea of a New Order. They proposed a close economic symbiosis between Germany and underdeveloped Europe governed by an exclusive set of economic agreements in which the underdeveloped lands provided raw materials and food-stuffs against German capital, expertise and manufactured goods. Seen from the standpoint of south-eastern Europe this simply meant that those commodities such as oil and chrome which they had been able to sell on free international markets even in the 1930s would now become tied to the German market and that they would lose the economic independence for which they had fought so hard. They did not accept that the *Grossraumwirtschaft* was an arrangement which would accelerate their own economic development; rather they saw it as a proposed colonial exploita-tion. In this respect they were quite right, for German policy, whatever the future arrangements for developed western Europe, always maintained a sharp demarcation between west and east. And behind the Ministry of Economics and the concept of *Gross-raumwirtschaft* lurked all the more sinister implications of National Socialist racial ideology.

In the east this ideology was firmly translated into policy and this constituted the most flagrant of all the contradictions in German economic policy. The start of the invasion of the Soviet Union was also the start of the 'final solution' to the Jewish problem. The savagery of the German administration in Russia and Poland produced an economic chaos which both prevented any rational economic exploitation of those territories for war purposes and any rational planning for the economic future there. These contradictions appear more sharply in the context of labour policy which is examined in Chapter 6. However, as far as the economic future of Europe was concerned the apocalyp-tic vision of a racially purified society went hand in hand with the idea of the Slav races as inherently inferior and fit only for the lowest forms of economic activity. It was on these racial ideas that economic policy in Poland was initially founded.[34] It was

34. See the interesting analysis in M. Broszat's *Nationalsozialistische Polenpolitik 1939–1945* (Schriftenreihe der *Vj. f.Z.*, no. 2, Deutsche Verlags-Anstalt, Stuttgart, 1961).

these ideas which permitted Gauleiter Koch his bestial excesses in the Ukraine. And it is in the context of these ideas that proposals for the future of western Europe have to be seen also. The attempts to bring about the German millenium in the east were not mere incidents of policy but were integral to German economic policy throughout Europe. They did not offer a very welcoming horizon to German businessmen and they were convincing evidence that the National Socialist movement had its own directions independent of those of the business interests which went along with it. The ultimate destination of the National Socialist movement was far from being merely identical with the expansion of German state capital. The New Order ended with Fritz Sauckel's agents deporting to Germany at great cost and by main force any small group of potential workers they could get hold of and with SS. groups trying to destroy Germany's own capital equipment; the last demonstrations, apart from the Führer's own Valhalla, of the efficacity of violent action in resolving political and economic doubts.

Japanese occupation policy

Japan never controlled a developed economy and the economies of the countries that were occupied by Japanese forces were not so completely subjected nor controlled for so long as the western European economies were by Germany. The successful seizure of the southern areas in the first year of warfare did, as intended, correct certain raw material deficiencies in the Japanese economy. Imports of crude oil from the Netherlands East Indies in 1942 were the equivalent of about four months of the forecast consumption for that year and an amount equal to half the forecast annual consumption was consumed in the area itself.[35] Bauxite imports similarly rose to a level well above that of 1939 as a result of the occupations. But the purpose of the invasions was not simply to acquire materials in this way; it was the extension of a policy of commercial expansion pursued in these areas with particular energy in the 1930s. In 1940 Japan already owned 82 per cent of the paid-up industrial share capital in Korea, with virtually total control of the chemical, cement, metal and cereal-

35. U.S.S.B.S., *The Effects of Strategic Bombing on the Japanese War Economy*, p. 18.

milling industries.[36] The industries which the Japanese government particularly wished to encourage were directly subsidized. These, however, were all industries of special strategic significance, such as synthetic oil and alumina manufacture. Otherwise development was regarded as a joint operation involving private companies and the government.

The biggest company involved was the long-established Oriental Development Company, whose close cooperation with and financial help from the Japanese government created the Korean synthetic oil industry. Its interests were numerous and widespread, ranging from cotton production in China to rubber plantations in the Netherlands East Indies. Its importance in the Korean economy can be judged from the fact that a subsidiary company involved in making nitrogenous fertilizer for Japan had been responsible for almost the whole of the electrical-power generating industry there. This was the pattern of Japanese business activity in all the dominated areas except Manchuria. There the influence of more fascist political ideas on the Kwantung army deterred businessmen from participation on these terms and the first steps in the creation of industries for Japanese purposes were undertaken by a corporation depending more directly on government finance and support, the Manchurian Industrial Development Corporation. The puppet Manchurian government guaranteed a 6 per cent return on all investment in the Corporation's subsidiary companies. The difference, however, was more one of degree than of kind; in China proper both the North China and the Central China Development Companies received half their capital from the Japanese government.

But these development operations over so wide an area were also taking place in countries which were as yet scarcely industrialized. Korea was the only area in the Co-Prosperity Sphere whose industrial production was more than 5 per cent of the Japanese total. The future development of these areas by Japanese capital required a period of peace and stability. In the constant warfare it was inevitable that Japanese efforts should be concentrated entirely on economic objectives that were of immediate strategic value. Furthermore the area of exploitation was also determined by ease of transport. The sea routes to Korea were

36. Cohen, p. 36.

shorter and safer than to most other occupied areas and the result was that the most developed of the occupied territories became the one in which Japan was most interested during the war. After the battle of Guadalcanal the worsening shipping situation persuaded the Japanese to develop the Mozan iron-ore mines in Korea; the imports from this source in 1944 were over 200 per cent higher than in 1943 while imports from China declined.

Seen simply as a source of strategic supply the territories of the Co-Prosperity Sphere played a vital role, and when supply from them could no longer arrive the Japanese economy was in severe difficulties. Table 23 shows this decline in imports. In the case of

TABLE 23
IMPORTS OF STRATEGIC MATERIALS INTO JAPAN, 1941–4
(in thousands of metric tons)

Commodity	1941	1942	1943	1944	1945
Coal	6,459	6,388	5,181	2,635	548
Iron ore	6,309	4,700	4,298	2,153	341
Bauxite	150	305	909	376	15
Iron and steel	921	993	997	1,097	170
Raw rubber	68	31	42	31	18

SOURCE: U.S.S.B.S., *The Effects of Strategic Bombing on the Japanese Economy*, Appendix, table C-106.

iron ore, coking coal, non-ferrous-metal ores and bauxite these reductions were virtually reductions in the total supply. Nor was the reduction in supply solely due to the shipping shortage. Wartime restrictions also affected production outside Japan; aluminium production in Manchuria did not increase after 1941 and in 1944 was still far below the target set by the Five-Year Plan. But the effect could also go the other way. Coal production in Karafuto in 1944 was only 41 per cent of its 1941 level because Japanese shipping resources were concentrated on bringing coking coal from North China. The propaganda of the Co-Prosperity Sphere sounded with a hollow ring during the war. Even as a source of strategic materials to be exploited the area diminished in usefulness as the war continued.

For China and South-East Asia the merging of the war into a world struggle retarded rather than advanced the realization of Japanese plans for the area, slowed down the export of Japanese capital and expertise and diverted it into narrower channels more related to Japan's immediate military needs. Nevertheless the incursion of Japanese armies, administrators and businessmen produced changes of attitude in Asian countries whose true significance was to be seen only after 1945.

6

War, Technology and Economic Change

Les vaisseaux de guerre qui sont des moyens d'aggression bien plus que de défense, sont d'une dépense énorme et d'autant plus regrettable que cette machine gigantesque et coûteuse où se sont épuisés tous les efforts du génie industriel de l'homme, est bornée dans sa durée à quinze ou vingt ans, même lorsqu'elle n'a essuyé aucun accident.

[Warships, which are offensive rather than defensive weapons, involve an enormous expenditure which is the more regrettable as this gigantic and costly machine wherein all the efforts of man's industrial genius have been exhausted is limited in its duration to fifteen or twenty years, even when it has met with no accident.]

J.-B. Say, *Cours complet d'économie politique pratique*, 1829

Technology in modern war

Even the most ardent economic critics of warfare frequently concede that in one respect war brings economic benefit, in its tendency to promote technological and scientific innovation. The argument seems to be based on the well-known consequences of technological innovations in peacetime and the assumption that such innovations occur with greater frequency in war. However, in the light of the history of the Second World War this assumption appears as a glib simplification of the economic situation.

There are benefits in war, but it is by no means certain that they are in the area where they seem so readily acknowledged.

Technological innovation can have far-reaching consequences in peace and it can be readily agreed that there is no inherent difference between innovation for peaceful purposes and war purposes. During the Second World War, for example, the development of the long-range bomber and of the jet engine provided the essentials of the modern long-distance passenger aircraft. If war does in fact speed up technological change, as is often argued, it may well be that in so doing it also promotes economic development. Technological innovation has had profound effects on modern economies in changing the size and distribution of industry, in changing the relative importance of different raw materials, in changing the pattern of social and working activities and in increasing incomes. Indeed it has sometimes been argued that in increasing incomes technological innovation in the widest sense of the phrase has played a bigger role than the increased use of capital and labour. Is there a greater incentive to such innovation in war?

The most obvious incentive lies in the field of combat. The tendency of modern fighting is to become increasingly capital-intensive. One measurement of this is the amount of capital expended on killing one enemy; this has been estimated as roughly ten times as much in the Korean war as in the Second World War.[1] It does not by any means follow, however, that victory will go to the side best able to accommodate itself to this trend and the United States experience in Vietnam has made a commonplace of the observation that capital-intensive economies are obliged to use capital-intensive strategies even when they may be inappropriate to bring victory. But the success of the much more labour-intensive strategy of the 'Communist' side should not disguise the fact that, for so poor an economy as North Vietnam's, the amount of capital per unit of labour used in the armed forces is extraordinarily high. There is everywhere the incentive to produce superior armaments because they bring great rewards and the penalties of inferior armaments are also very great. There exists also the perpetually tempting possibility of the armament against which there is temporarily no defence.

1. A. Morsomme, *Anatomie de la guerre totale*, Pierre de Meyère, Brussels, 1971, p. 14.

The tendency of armaments research is therefore always towards the capital-intensive. The mushroom cloud over Hiroshima was not an isolated event, it was the logical process of the trend of modern warfare. In the First World War the recruitment of vast quantities of fighting men had emphasized the futility of labour-intensive campaigns ending either in defeat, as in the case of the huge Russian armies, or in stalemate, as on the western front. Furthermore, by tightening the pressure on the labour market it provided a greater incentive to find a strategy less expensive, less wasteful of humankind, and able to bring victory sooner.

The trend towards capital-intensiveness in warfare means that in the armaments industry there is often less scope than in other industrial sectors for suiting the nature of the technology to the nature of the economy; once they are engaged in pitched battle even North Vietnamese soldiers must fight with complex modern machines. There is certainly room for manoeuvre and for marginal adjustments, and it is not necessary to have *all* the best available armaments technology, but there are many strategic situations where no amount of labour will compensate for certain kinds of technological deficiencies. Japan was poorly provided in the Second World War with designers, engineers, draughtsmen, mechanics and pilots but it was still necessary for her aircraft to equal the best in American design and to be deployed in a basically similar way. The Russian armies were very much more prodigal of manpower in battle than the German armies, as befitted a country with larger reserves of unskilled labour, but the basic technological equipment of the army campaigns and the way it was used were both directly derived from the German model. It was, for example, only in the Soviet Union that heavy tanks comparable to those manufactured in Germany were successfully produced and used in battle.

The production of modern armaments beyond a certain level of complexity is only possible in states which possess the best-equipped, largest and most innovative engineering industries. Since it is also in such countries that most of the technological innovations in armaments design take place, the process is a self-reinforcing one in which most powers can only struggle to maintain a level of armaments technology which does not fall too far behind the best. The first Canadian division in the war had to be equipped almost entirely in the United Kingdom. Subsequently Canada developed the capacity to produce some categories of armaments on a very large scale, but these categories always fell short of the most complicated and advanced armaments types. Total aircraft production there between 1935 and 1939 numbered about forty planes. In the one year, 1944, it reached over 4,000 including a small proportion of the more complicated types; but the largest planes were faithful copies of British specifications. The main effort in Canada, and also in Australia, had to be in the production of ships, ammunition and small arms designed to British or American specifications. The increasing pace of armaments development and increasing technological complexity widened the gap between those countries whose engineering industries could respond fully to the situation and all the others. This was only a little modified by the international pooling of information and the great trade in armaments. Japanese aircraft matched up to United States aircraft until 1942 only because the designers had been trained before 1939 in the United States, because the designs had for the most part been purchased from the United States, and because the planes were made on United States machines. As the war pursued its course the Japanese were unable to keep pace with aircraft development elsewhere and found themselves at an increasingly serious disadvantage.

By 1944 significant differences had appeared in the capacity of combatants whose engineering industries were much more highly developed than Japan's. As United States war production continued to rise American technological capacity came clearly to exceed that of the United Kingdom in spite of the longer period of effort in Britain. The gap could be seen both in design capacity and in productive capacity. American armaments output passed that of Britain in summer 1942 and by 1944 was six times greater. Few British innovations were in fact incorporated into American weapons. Some kinds of tank turrets, several aircraft engines and one or two guns were adapted from British experience or copied directly. Otherwise American equipment either proved better, or was easier to produce in large quantities while not being inferior in quality. This was particularly true in the design of transport vehicles, copied almost wholesale by the British army, and in naval design, where high-temperature, high-pressure turbines proved more satisfactory than anything that could be made in Britain. Nor was there any British equivalent of the jeeps and amphibious vehicles used by the American forces.

By no means all technological innovation in wartime however was in the armaments industry. Much of it resulted from the desire to widen the bottlenecks in production which appeared in other industries which were called on to expand very rapidly. New methods of mass-production were devised to cope with the sudden rush of demand and with the acute labour shortage that often accompanied it. Shortages of raw materials, or a great escalation in their comparative cost, also stimulated research into new production techniques. This was especially the case in an industry like steel-making where the greater sophistication of demand resulting from the exacting specifications to which armaments steel had to be manufactured coincided with great changes in the relative costs and absolute availability of many raw materials, causing a long period of intensive metallurgical research in all countries. Its results were nowhere more striking than in Australia, where in the course of the war ferro-alloys and high-speed tool-steel, not previously made, were manufactured to higher standards than in Britain or the United States.[2] The increased use of machinery in many industries often raised the level of learning of the labour force. At the start of a war the demand for skilled labour is higher than for unskilled labour, because it is engineering and related capital-goods industries which expand most rapidly. Labour training programmes in all the major combatant powers were more active in the first year of war than in the preceding peace. It is not only the labour force which learns, however, in such situations. In the economies of all the major combatants it became an important role of the economic administration to bring all production techniques up to the best available by forcing firms to pool their knowledge and in some cases even their equipment. The inefficient entrepreneur and the inadequate firm could find little shelter when efficient production methods might be synonymous with national survival. And no matter how dependent they were on the cooperation of private firms, governments still had to place severe limits on the extent to which firms could guard their secrets during the war in order to maintain their competitive positions after it. The war therefore everywhere resulted in a great diffusion of technical knowledge and managerial expertise.

2. E. R. Walker, *The Australian Economy in War and Reconstruction*, Oxford University Press, New York, 1947, p. 136.

There were however definite limits to the exchange of technological information between allies, and even between firms in the same country. These were most strikingly seen in the development of the atomic bomb. In autumn 1941 the United States government was keen to enter into an agreement to manufacture it jointly with the United Kingdom but the British government held back. By spring 1942 the boot was on the other foot and development was going ahead full blast in the United States with the United Kingdom now advocating, but failing to get, a joint project. In the event British and French scientists who had played a very prominent part in the early stages of development played only a very minor part in the later ones of production. As for the Russians, they were kept in complete ignorance of what was going on. The lavish use of resources to produce the bomb involved an advance on several competing fronts, as, for example, in the four separate processes for slowing down neutrons, all of which were fully financed. But the policy of 'compartmentalization' of knowledge imposed by the American military security services prevented any disclosures except the most essential ones between the various teams of scientists and engineers involved.

Nevertheless, to admit the fundamental tendency towards technological innovation in modern war should not obscure the limitations imposed by the nature of the combat. The search for the armament against which no defence exists can prove an exhausting one, leading easily into technological fantasies. The gigantic and terrifying 'landwalker' envisaged for the American army of the future and illustrated at the New York World Fair in 1964, plunges its mechanical leg into a fast-flowing river while steadying itself against a pine-tree with what is obviously a hand.[3] Its derivation from the Martian war-machines of H. G. Wells' *The War of the Worlds* is all too clear. The fantasy of the insuperable mechanical giant is only one of the many will o' the wisps which military research has been cheerfully tempted to chase. Research and innovation will both be abortive unless the nature of the combat and the nature of the strategy determine the path of advance. And there is a wider question raised by these limitations. Will not a particular war (for all wars have their own strategic requirements), while speeding up technological inno-

3. Illustrated in I. F. Clarke, *Voices Prophesying War 1763–1984*, Oxford University Press, London, 1966

vation, at the same time divert its main thrust away from those objectives which economists usually consider desirable? Is technological innovation in all strategic syntheses the same thing, from the standpoint of economic development, as technological innovation in peacetime?

Before 1940 research into nuclear fission, in so far as it had any practical application, might have been directed towards the production of energy. It was rearmament and war which concentrated this research on the making of a bomb. Werner von Braun's early research into rockets was seen as having a practical application in the speeding-up of international postal services. Research and development formerly spread over a wide front were increasingly concentrated on a small number of absolute strategic priorities after 1939. And in spite of the ecstatic accounts of the achievements which such a concentration of resources brought in all economies,[4] it is in fact not at all established that the so-called 'spin-off' from armaments development into more peaceful lines of scientific and industrial development was superior or even equivalent to what would have occurred without the pressure of war. That war is a forcing-house of technological development is undisputed, but what are the plants which flourish?

Technological research and development

The long period of time which is required for the development of new armaments is basic to the situation. Viewing the major economies together it could be reasonably said that only in 1944 did armaments show fundamental differences of technological principle over those existing before 1939. From this process of development Japan and Italy can be virtually eliminated. Their equipment was for the most part imitative and, as the war continued, inferior in design. New types of army equipment, amphibious vehicles, proximity fuses, homing bombs, armour-piercing incendiary ammunition, recoilless rifles and the bazooka emerged in 1944 only as the result of a major concentration of effort in the more technologically endowed economies. But the most dramatic advances were not in equipment for ground fighting. They were in aerial warfare. Increases in the range, speed and carrying

4. As, for example, A. M. Low, *Benefits of War*, The Scientific Book Club, London, 1945.

capacity of aircraft rendered pre-1940 designs quite obsolete. Before the end of the war the jet engine, the pilotless plane, the rocket and the atomic bomb had announced a new epoch of warfare. These major developments were quite beyond the reach of smaller economies. A complete set of plans and a model of the first German jet fighter, the Messerschmidt 262, were sent to Japan. It seems that only the plans arrived and, in spite of the great advances which the Japanese aircraft industry made during the war it was unable to get such a plane even into the prototype stage. In spite of its extremely important role in the early research into nuclear fission, industrial production of an atomic bomb proved ultimately beyond the United Kingdom's capacity unless the project were to lead to the virtual cancellation of all others. Had the bomb been manufactured in Britain many other lines of development, some of them more vital and pressing, would have been consigned to limbo.

This long period of development has to take in every branch of the armaments industry and much of it, as in the case of the atomic bomb, is also dictated by fears of what the enemy might be developing. A curtain of secrecy over the years between 1939 and 1945 greatly reduced the extent of accurate knowledge about the enemy armaments industries. Allied research on nuclear fission was lent wings of urgency because German progress along the same lines was overestimated. The German scientists for their part, however, could not at first bring themselves to believe that the United States had actually succeeded in manufacturing a nuclear bomb. The Allies, on the other hand, underestimated the extent of German progress on rocket technology.

The main lines of armament development tended in the same direction in all economies. In the first place there was a constant tendency towards greater mobility in warfare in an attempt to avoid the futile trench warfare of the First World War. This tendency went even to the extent of the complete motorization of all United States forces. Research therefore was heavily concentrated on aircraft, tanks, all other forms of armoured fighting vehicles, tank transporters, and more powerful and efficient road transport. Secondly, there was a constant attempt to improve firepower per man. By the end of the war hand-armaments which far exceeded the rifle in destructive capacity were being produced, and artillery, although not greatly changing in principle, developed in rapidity and accuracy of fire. One consequence of this was the concentration of research on better propellants and explosives. These developments led by a natural reaction to a third, the attempt to provide better protection. Before 1940 armour plate had, except in the case of warships, been designed for the most part to resist only small-arms fire. By 1945 it was produced to far more demanding and advanced standards. No amount of research in that direction, however, could provide adequate protection against aerial bombardment; research had to be concentrated here to find better methods of anti-aircraft defence. Fifthly, as the bomber came to be seen as the weapon of victory, unflagging attempts were made to produce bigger and better bombs and better methods of delivering them. The small bombs dropped on British civilians by the Luftwaffe had been transformed into 12,000 lb. blockbusters for use by the British air force against German civilians by 1945. Not content with this the British were actively preparing a 22,000 lb. 'Grand Slam' bomb in 1945 while the United States, by copying the designs, was ambitiously at work on a 44,000 lb. bomb. Finally, the economic pressures forced research in all countries in the direction of conserving raw materials, substituting one raw material for another and generally manufacturing to high standards with great economy in raw-material consumption. The substitution of special plywood in aircraft manufacture for aluminium, for example, is estimated to have saved 30,000 tons of aluminium over two and a half years in the Soviet Union.[5]

Substitution of raw materials was the development most obviously applicable in peacetime conditions. There were numerous examples of technological ingenuity of this kind. It was successfully practised on a large scale in the manufacture of oil and rubber, where new manufacturing processes created synthetic versions of the natural product. In both cases the free market price of the natural product was much lower than the cost of simulating it by manufacture but the strategic importance of both commodities was such as to overcome any hesitations on economic grounds. Indeed, as far as natural rubber was concerned Malaya had come close to being the only large-scale world supplier and the danger for both Germany and the Allies was that they would be shut off from that supply. For the continental

5. Voznesenskii, p. 41.

European powers and Japan the possibility of being cut off from adequate supplies of crude oil was also very real. After 1933 the production of oil from coal and other raw materials on a large scale was pioneered in Germany. By September 1939 production of oil products from coal was running at an annual level of 2·3 million metric tons. Several processes were involved, the older ones of the distillation and carbonization of coal tar to make fuel and oil and the newer methods of hydrogenation and the Fischer–Tropsch process. Of these methods hydrogenation was the most fertile, producing 1·3 million metric tons of oil products in 1939. Seven hydrogenation plants existed of which one, the Leuna works, had an annual capacity of 400,000 metric tons.[6] Five more works were in the process of construction, with a combined capacity when completed of 1·3 million metric tons. The whole programme represented an extremely costly investment in terms of high tariffs, protective taxes on oil consumption, government subsidies and tax concessions – so costly that it had not been copied in less autarkic and less controlled economies. The war slowed down this investment programme in Germany apart from four smaller special installations to process aviation fuel. But the basis of an industry now existed, which, given economy in consumption, could continue to supply the economy with oil even if all foreign supply was cut off. In 1943 5·7 million metric tons of oil were produced from all synthetic processes combined, about half the total supply. Even in the period of maximum extent of substitution for other products this represented the consumption of about ten million metric tons of bituminous coal and fifty million tons of lignite. It required about four tons of hard coal and between eight and ten tons of lignite to make a ton of oil products. Had the full programme of the Four-Year Plan been completed it would have needed about 7·6 million man days of labour to construct the synthetic works, although once they were functioning, their labour utilization was small.[7] Even with this level of synthetic production very little petrol was available for civilian transport. But here also it was possible to substitute. In Germany, in occupied Europe, and on a small scale in Britain

6. W. Birkenfeld, *Der synthetische Treibstoff 1933–1945*, Musterschmidt-Verlag, Göttingen, 1964, p. 138.
7. U.S.S.B.S., *The Effects of Strategic Bombing on the German War Economy*, p. 76.

also, vehicles were equipped with generators towed behind them which burned gas and solid fuels.

The manufacture of synthetic rubber had also been begun in Germany by the same costly methods of protection and subsidization, and at the outbreak of war the two plants working, Schkopau and Leverkusen, produced 27,500 metric tons annually, slightly more than a quarter of the total supply. The war in this case speeded up the investment process and by early 1943 two more large plants were in operation. In 1942 synthetic rubber production was higher than total domestic production plus imports had been in 1938. The artificial product, buna, did not have the same endurance at high pressure but by the end of the war its quality was almost the equivalent of natural rubber. The hydrogen and gas needed in its manufacture were supplied from the synthetic oil plants so that the process also depended partly on coal as a basic raw material.

The buna process had come to the United States through agreements on patent-sharing in the 1930s between I.G. Farben and Standard Oil but it had made little headway without the government subsidization that existed in Germany. Neoprene, a commercially more useful but even more expensive product patented by the Du Pont company, had made more headway. Faced with the possibility of being cut off from natural rubber supply the United States government began to finance the synthetic processes in June 1941. This involved forcing the competing interests into some compromise. After Pearl Harbor the government directed all efforts into buna processes and agreed to finance a programme to produce 400,000 tons a year in 1944. The anti-trust laws had to be suspended to permit the necessary technical cooperation to take place.[8] In September 1942 cooperation was further enforced by the appointment of a Rubber Director, William M. Jeffers. But it could not extend to the political world: Congress repeatedly retarded development by legislating for a greater use of alcohol produced from grain in the manufacturing process, in a successful attempt to get something for the farmers out of the new programme. The Canadian government also initiated a programme to make 30,000 tons of buna a year.

Although the other main lines of development concerned

8. F. A. Howard, *Buna Rubber. The Birth of an Industry*, Van Nostrand, New York, 1947, p. 181.

armaments only their effects spread throughout the whole industrial sector; the process of armaments development by 1944 had resulted not merely in new weapons but in large-scale new industrial processes. But the impression which pervades much literature on the subject, of lightning technological breakthroughs effected under the tremendous pressure of war, is a misleading one. There is no convincing evidence that the overall speed of technological advance was greater in wartime. The concentration of research on particular tasks greatly accelerated their achievement, but this was always at the expense of other lines of development. And in the armaments industry itself, which acted as the spearhead of this technological thrust, the process of turning out a satisfactory final product is in fact a very long-drawn-out one compared to most other manufacturing industries.

It involves three prolonged stages, none of which can be circumvented without the gravest risks. Although these three stages have a great influence on each other they must still be distinguished, and each one remains necessary. The first is that of basic research and development, the second is the actual production of armaments on a large scale, the third is their deployment in combat. All three stages are essential to a satisfactory armament, the third no less than the other two because the lessons learnt in use must constantly be applied in modifications to the basic design and production method in order to produce a satisfactory weapon. It was the length of time necessary for the completion of these three stages, before which the initial stage of development was not concluded, that meant that in armaments technology, and in all the so-called 'spin-off' effects which came from it, the most striking advances were visible only after 1943 and often even later. The concentration of the development stage on certain priorities therefore had drastic effects on overall development.

The re-equipment of the United States forces with a new rifle required 20,000 hours of preliminary engineering study to plan its mass production and 200,000 hours of engineering and design time to prepare the necessary tools.[9] The design and development of a weapon like a heavy bomber took an enormously greater effort in terms of man hours. Although the faith in bombing as a weapon of victory in the British Air Ministry lent great urgency to the attempt to get heavy bombers into effective production as

9. Smith, *The Army and Economic Mobilization*, p. 17.

early as 1940, those that were safe to use in action only appeared in service in 1941. By spring 1943 the total available, 3,500, was only what it had been expected to be in April 1942. For two of them, subsequently the most used by the Royal Air Force – the Halifax and the Lancaster – the longer development period was well worth it for the improvement. For the third, the Stirling, it was not.[10] Yet the British government had in fact given top priority to the manufacture of a fleet of heavy bombers as early as 1936. The failure of the German aircraft industry, only switching to this priority early in the war, cannot be wondered at, although it was sharply criticized by Göring who, even from the position of Commander-in-Chief of the Air Force, was unable to comprehend the length of development time required. The aircraft designers reminded him not 'of men to be taken seriously, but of jugglers and magicians, they seemed to him like a circus'.[11] The plans were abandoned in 1943 after only one and a half years. With the exception of the period immediately following the appointment of Lord Beaverbrook as Minister of Aircraft Production in February 1942, the United Kingdom refused to sacrifice development time and funds in aircraft production to obtain the satisfaction of higher production figures. When Beaverbrook insisted on production rather than development during the Battle of Britain it caused serious delays in producing better equipment later. One other such attempt to shorten the period of development, the rush development and production of the Churchill tank, was also a failure. The tank was developed in nine months in 1940 and 1941 and subsequently proved much too unreliable in use.

The inter-related nature of the three phases of manufacture, however, must not be forgotten. Had there been a sufficient previous experience of tank production the use of short cuts in the development stage might have been more feasible. The later German Tiger tanks were deliberately rushed through the development stage into production because previous basic designs had proved so successful and because there had been a long learning process using heavy tanks in the field. Even so, although the modified Tigers were certainly an excellent design, the speed with

10. M. M. Postan, D. Hay, and J. D. Scott, *Design and Development of Weapons*, H.M.S.O., London, 1964.
11. Messerschmidt Papers, 'Industriebesprechung beim Reichsmarschall in Karinhall'.

which they were pushed through development still led to a far higher proportion of breakdowns in the field than in other designs. Here of course it is necessary to ask for how long an armament is actually likely to survive in combat in good working order. The technological ingenuity which produced American tanks whose mechanical components were specified to last for forty hours under battle conditions and which were comfortable enough to spare the driver from undue fatigue during that time was misplaced. The fourteen hours for which Russian tanks were designed under such conditions proved about right. The specifications for armaments can often be lower, as far as duration is concerned, than those for another product.

That the lessons learned in the third stage – use in the field – were crucial to the development stage could be clearly seen in the success of Allied aircraft production and the relative failure of tank production. The greater wealth of pre-war experience in aircraft design and development in the United States, arising from the much greater development of civil aviation there, meant that even the early war planes such as the Tomahawk and the Kittyhawk were highly successful designs. This superiority was maintained throughout the war. By contrast early American and British tanks were produced with ordinary commercial engines because it was mistakenly thought these would be adequate in combat use. The General Staffs in both countries acted on the assumption that an enemy tank, no matter how heavily armoured, could always be stopped, and thus light armouring and greater mobility of action were the desiderata. In the field such vehicles were heavily outgunned by German tanks, which with their heavy armour sought the tank-to-tank duels which the Allies had hoped to avoid. The consequence was that the thickness of armour plate on the British and American models had to be increased, and this brought the tanks to a weight where the engines were no longer powerful enough for the tank to fulfil its original purpose. It was not until 1944 when the Meteor engine, a version of a Rolls-Royce aircraft engine, was fitted to the new Cromwell tank, that the British and Americans had an armament equivalent to the German Panzer II and Tiger or the Russian T34 and KVI.

Most basically new concepts were evolved in the development stage, and their purpose was always a military one. The extent to which technological research was concentrated on this stage was very much a function of assessments of the value of the existing equipment. In the Soviet Union the dilemma was more acute than elsewhere and it is clear that prolonged research of this innovatory kind in the development stage had frequently to be sacrificed; the emphasis in development had to be on the modification of existing basic types of armament. Development was in any case everywhere subject to many delays of a non-economic nature. The major questions were the nature of the strategy and, within that strategy, the tactical deployment of armaments. There was very little room for last-minute improvisation or crash programmes for equipment the need for which had not been seen a long time in advance. One exception to this was the 'Mulberry' harbours, constructed out of prefabricated materials and used in the D-Day landings to get equipment on shore where there were no ports. Even on such a large emergency project as this the largest labour force directly employed was never more than 45,000, about 2 per cent of the total labour force engaged in munitions production at the time by the two departments concerned.[12] The extra demand for steel was roughly commensurate. Apart from such exceptions development, and therefore innovation, was dependent on decisions taken a long time in advance. The delay in developing a satisfactory heavy tank in Britain can basically be attributed to the tactical conception of tank warfare, which was different from that prevailing in Germany or the Soviet Union. This was not the only reason, however: the British General Staff originally insisted that tanks should be built within such dimensions that they could be transported by rail. This requirement was only finally relinquished when tank-transporters were imported from the United States.

It followed also from the tight limitations which strategy placed on development that resources were very seldom available to foster research on projects which would not reach the production stage until after the forecast end of the war, no matter how valuable those projects might be for peacetime. The last stage of German strategy was marked by the decisions in April 1944 to concentrate all effort on those weapons already in series production and to remove resources from the development of new

12. M. M. Postan, *British War Production*, H.M.S.O., London, 1952, p. 282.

armaments. This decision was made comprehensive by the Concentration Order of 19 June 1944 which brought to an end most development projects which could not be ready for series production within another six months.[13] Throughout the war all combatants were faced with the agonizing problem of exactly what proportion of resources could be devoted, in a highly dangerous situation, to research and development for the future, and all had to make arbitrary decisions about the distance of that future.

Production technology

Although innovation at the stage of series production was less frequent, a different range of innovations, usually of more obvious application in peace time, made their appearance there. These stretched from differences in plant lay-out through differences in managerial technique to more mechanized and standardized methods of production. Sometimes the whole production process had to be virtually redesigned from scratch to cope with the much greater volume of demand. Ultimately production was, of course, the overriding task. At the beginning of the British aircraft construction programme in 1935, for example, virtually any plane, even if it was known to be inferior in design, had to be built. And in all countries in 1939 a considerable production effort was being made to turn out armaments which were admittedly obsolescent. In an industry like the British aircraft industry, whose output of finished planes before the war had been relatively small, there was also a temptation to concentrate the innovative effort on production techniques in order to get somewhere near the production targets. Throughout the war United States aircraft manufacturers, for example, employed a higher proportion of the workforce on development. In the end the typical British aircraft firm which had entered the period of expansion very largely as an experimental, or very nearly experimental, organization turned in the later years of the war into a vast manufacturing concern with a relatively modest establishment for design and development.[14] Vast, but not so vast as an American aircraft factory. Whereas between 3,000 and 15,000 were employed in a

13. Milward, *The German Economy*, p. 128.
14. Postan, Hay and Scott, p. 39.

British aircraft factory the typical figure for an American factory rose to between 20,000 and 40,000. An American works would turn out an average of sixty aircraft a week, a British works ten, although the maximum weekly output was much higher in both countries.[15] The whole American aircraft industry had turned out less than fifty transport planes a week in 1937. In 1938 the French aircraft industry in full expansion was producing only fifty aircraft a month.[16] It is particularly in an armament like the modern aircraft that the absolute necessity for innovation in the production stage can be seen. The original Ford V-8 engine had 1,700 separate parts; the early bomber engines of the Second World War had 11,000, the planes themselves about 70,000.[17] The annual demand for aircraft by each of the major combatants was roughly equivalent to the world's total stock of aircraft in 1937.

The organizational and innovatory effort needed to achieve levels of output which would have been deemed quite unobtainable in peacetime often came into direct conflict with the more basic scientific and technological innovations of the development stage. Frequently it was the more practical and less innovatory design which was most successful in the stages of production and deployment. An aircraft like the Mosquito, for example, which embodied very little that was conceptually new, was not only produced with relative ease through a large number of modifications but was also very versatile in use.

Similarly, innovation and reorganization on the factory floor, because it was altogether less dramatic than the emergence of a new concept like the jet engine or the rocket, and also because it is much harder to detect, has received much less attention from historians than invention. But the improvements in managerial technique, in the fixed capital, and in the productivity of both labour and capital were probably of more significance during the war in all countries than the development of new concepts, and their value was no less after the war. In the economies of all major

15. Postan, p. 39.
16. J. Truelle, 'La production aéronautique militaire française jusqu'en juin 1940', in *R.d.g.m.*, no. 73, 1969.
17. R. Wagenführ, *Die Flugzeugindustrie der Anderen* (Schriften des Instituts für Konjunkturforschung, Sonderheft 46), Hanseatische Verlagsanstalt, Hamburg and Berlin, 1939, p. 12.

combatants they brought about a decisive shift to a higher level of productivity. In the U.S.A., a merchant vessel took only fifty days' work in 1943 whereas one of the same basic type took thirty-five weeks before the war. The time taken to make an Oerlikon gun fell from 132 hours to thirty-five hours. The cost of constructing a long-range bomber in the U.S.A. fell from $15.18 per hour in 1940 to $4.82 in 1944.[18] In the Soviet Union the manufacture of an Ilyushin 4 aircraft required 20,000 man hours in 1941, 12,500 in 1943. In the same period the time needed for a 152 mm howitzer dropped from 4,500 man hours to 2,400, for a large calibre machine-gun from 642 to 329.[19] In the closing stages of the war effort in Britain contracts often went to firms with a proven good management team rather than to firms with manufacturing experience in the particular field. It was often entrepreneurial and organizational talent which counted most in the production stage, as in the case of the large chocolate manufacturing firm which made rockets or the football-pools firm which made gun carriages.

One central question that arose in production and affected the rate of innovation was that of how good a job was to be done. It was a universal experience that the gain in output was far greater than 10 per cent if an armament was produced to only 90 per cent, rather than to 100 per cent, of the specifications. Whether this should be done or not was basically a strategic question. It was open to the United States to sacrifice some quality in production for quantity, but Germany could not compete in quantity production and opted to produce armaments nearer to perfect specifications in the hope that this might give some tactical advantage. If any strategic concept predominated in German thinking after the defeat at Stalingrad it was that of 'qualitative superiority'. By maintaining a very high standard of armaments it was hoped to compensate for the inevitable and growing disproportion in the size of final output. Equipment was produced as nearly as possible to full specifications and until the Concentration Orders a continuous effort was also made to stay in advance of the enemy in basic armaments concepts. Out of this strategy were born the two 'secret weapons', the V-1 and the V-2. Such a strategy

18. P. Grand-Jean, *Guerres, fluctuations et croissance*, Société d'Édition d'Enseignement Supérieur, Paris, 1967, p. 100.
19. Voznesenskii, p. 68.

put a higher premium on fundamental innovation. But, ironic- ally, it was on the development side that the German organiz- ation was weakest, certainly weaker than in the United States where it mattered less. Where equipment was manufactured up to 100 per cent specifications technological innovations were concentrated in machine-tools and metallurgy; where size of output was more important they were concentrated more in production organization and layout. It is impossible to say which was more valuable for the peacetime economy; but the point is a choice had to be made and one field or other of inno- vation sacrificed. This was partly due to the nature of the machine- tool industry; since in many ways this industry lay at the heart of the changes in productivity and production it is as well to consider it more closely.

The production of armaments and of all other equipment which the armed forces needed implied a change in the compo- sition of the final output of the engineering industry, which, in its turn, implied in most countries a large-scale re-tooling of factories and workshops. The world machine-tool industry was dominated by the United States and Germany, the only large economies with a significant export capacity. Even countries with highly developed engineering industries like Britain and France witnessed a rise in machine-tool imports from the United States in 1939 and 1940 sufficient to cause foreign-exchange worries. In Japan the Machine Tool Industry Act of 1938 enacted complicated tariff legislation to protect machine-tool producers and encourage them to under- take more ambitious projects. One result of the war was a great increase in the number and variety of machine-tools produced by all the major combatants but this was especially marked in Britain and Japan where a new range of skills had to be mastered. The annual output of machine tools in Britain in 1939 was 37,000, in 1942 it was 95,788. The proportion of the annual supply of machine tools provided by imports from the United States, less than a quarter before the war, rose to over half in 1940 and then declined to less than a seventh in 1944.[20] Once they had an adequate market, and the protection which the rapid increase in the domestic demand for machine tools in the United States in 1941 automatically provided, machine-tool manufacturers in

20. Postan, p. 207.

Britain were able to manufacture a wide range of products which they had not made before the war. In Japan the annual output of machine tools increased from about 15,000 in 1936 to 67,260 in 1938. There was no increase in numbers during the war but the types of tool made came to include tools which had only been imported in 1938. Before 1938 Japanese machine tools had been mostly general purpose tools and of a rather low standard compared to American machine tools. Even in 1943 special-purpose tools were still only 1 per cent of total production; by 1944 they accounted for 15 per cent.[21]

This increase in special-purpose tools represented a great change in the productive process. A special-purpose machine tool is usually used only for the manufacture of a single piece or for the performing of a single function and cannot easily be converted to the manufacture of some other product. Its lack of versatility is compensated for by its high rate of output. The time needed for its design and construction is longer, however, and is justified only where there is stability in production programmes. The rapid advance of special-purpose tools in Japanese war industries in 1943 and 1944 indicates therefore a rapid shift towards more standardized mass-production and towards higher productivity. Above all, it was by the use of such methods that the United States armaments industries achieved levels of productivity so much higher than all others. The composition of the stock of machine tools in the United States shows that the proportion of special-purpose tools was far higher than elsewhere. It was established practice in the United States before the war for machine-tool designers to collaborate closely with the designers of the final product to be manufactured. This practice was carried on even more extensively in wartime, whereas it was quite common in Britain and Germany for machine-tool producers to be excluded from armaments factories because of the security risk. Of course, to produce armaments in this way also means that the demand for new tools and the delay in providing them are both greater at the beginning of rearmament; the United States was in reality obliged to produce by the methods within which its industry already operated and this meant an intense period of innovation and a sudden and enormous increase in the output of machine tools.

21. U.S.S.B.S., *Machine-Tools in Japan*, Office of Strategic Services, Washington, 1946.

In many ways production by special-purpose tools might seem more suitable to an economy like Japan with a less skilled labour force because the task for the machine operative is simpler. But the obstacles to innovation which exist in peace are by no means always removed in war, and the ability to produce completely new ranges of special-purpose tools in large quantities was confined to an economy like the United States where the necessary manufacturing skills were present in sufficient quantity.

Above all it is the example of the German machine-tool industry which shows that only in certain precise circumstances does the experience of war stimulate technological innovation. For it is a curious fact that of the world's two great machine-tool industries that in the United States was literally forced into innovation whereas for the German industry innovation was needless. The number of employees per machine tool in the metalworking industries in Germany did not significantly change between 1939 and 1944. The ratio was in fact remarkably low, about 2·35, whereas in the United Kingdom in 1943 it was 5·7.[22] The explanation of this is that the German machine-tool inventory was about two thirds greater than that of Britain in 1943. It is clear that the only increase in the utilization of machine tools in Germany during the war came from a longer working week, otherwise machines were seldom worked for more than one shift, whereas in Britain and the United States three shifts were quite common. Increases in munitions output in Germany came more from rationalization on the factory floor than from greater use of machines. But beyond this it is also clear that very few new machines were produced in Germany in these years and there was no significant shift to special-purpose machine tools on the American pattern The startling contrast between Germany and the United States is shown in Table 24; it suggests that the explanation for what happened in Germany cannot lie only in the fact that German machine-tool output was already very large.

Germany's position in 1939 was almost the opposite of that of the United States. Instead of having a large inventory of machine tools of which a high percentage could not be converted to armaments production, Germany had a large inventory of universal machines which could be switched over to armaments production

22. U.S.S.B.S., *Machine-Tools and Machinery*, Office of Strategic Services, Washington, 1946.

with very little difficulty. Until 1942 there was little increase in armaments output and little continuity in the production programmes. Even after 1942 the investment of time and funds in the production of special-purpose machine tools was hardly justified in view of the low rate of utilization of the existing machine-tool capacity, and by the end of the war special-purpose tools were barely 8 per cent of the total output, a much lower proportion even than in Japan. Manufacturers preferred the more adaptable universal machine-tools which, although they were a handicap

TABLE 24
INDEXES OF MACHINE-TOOL OUTPUT IN THE UNITED STATES AND GERMANY, 1939–44 (1939 = 100)

	U.S.A.	Germany
1939	100·0	100·0
1940	221·0	116·3
1941	387·5	129·5
1942	662·2	125·7
1943	599·0	116·0
1944	244·1	102·5

SOURCE: U.S.S.B.S., *Machine Tools and Machinery*, p. 14.

to increasing productivity, were easier to adapt to the changing armaments programmes and also, of course, would be more useful once the war was over and armaments no longer in such demand.

This is not to say that there was no innovation at all in the German machine-tool industry. Some bottlenecks in armaments production could only be solved by the use of special-purpose tools. Ball-bearing fabrication machines were produced under government orders by firms whose normal machine tools were of less applicability in wartime and several kinds of specialized bearings which had previously had to be imported from Sweden were now made in Germany. Similarly, special crankshaft machines on the American model were also made because the saving in time on the final product was about 500 per cent. But on the whole the war did not accelerate the rate of innovation in the German machine-tool industry and as a consequence it did not significantly change, except in fairly simple organizational ways, the methods of production in Germany.

Some techniques of production, however, made great strides in all countries because they were not dependent on major capital re-equipment but only on the adoption of a new process. This was often facilitated by the disruption and dislocation of the established labour force. One such development which gained ground everywhere was the use of welding, particularly in shipbuilding. In all countries there was a great demand for welders throughout the war, a demand seldom satisfied. It is very doubtful whether in peacetime it would have been so easy for entrepreneurs to get the training and employment of women as welders accepted by the established labour force, especially where, as in shipbuilding, they displaced riveters. The use of welding in shipyards was particularly associated with the American steel magnate, Henry Kaiser, and the Liberty ships produced in his yards. The first was produced in December 1940 and showed the way to a far more rapid method of construction. But it was not until 1943 that the British Admiralty was prepared to abandon the older techniques of riveting and then only under the pressure of the acute shipping shortage. The Shipyard Development Committee set up by the Admiralty in November 1942 undertook a wholesale modernization of the equipment and methods in British shipyards with the particular aim of introducing the techniques of construction by prefabrication and welding. Without the extraordinarily rapid modernization which ensued the two successful emergency production programmes, that in 1942–3 to produce escort vessels and that in 1943–4 to produce landing craft, could never have been achieved.

Technology in combat

The production stage was affected in its turn by the third stage of armaments manufacture, the experience of deployment in combat. The specifications laid down for armaments production by the users were extremely exacting, though they frequently had to be modified to take into consideration what could practically be achieved in the manufacturing process. The two-and-a-half-ton truck made for the United States army was far superior in its performance to any commercial vehicle. It had to be able to climb a 65° hill fully loaded from a standing start, it had to be stable enough to cross the face of the hill without falling, and it had to be able to drive through a grove of two-and-a-half-inch trees.[23] To achieve these results it had to have drive on all wheels and this necessitated a completely new components industry before it could be produced. This was a common enough story. Before 1939 the stock-in-trade of British radio manufacturers was the ordinary household receiver; they had very little experience with more complicated items. Radar, and the radio equipment with which bombers were equipped, posed a whole new range of problems for them.

But in spite of meeting these initial specifications the experience of battle required constant modifications to even the best-designed armament. An armament once used in battle does not stay secret long. The foil strip 'window', used in the raids on Hamburg in July 1943, when the radar defences were thrown into complete confusion, worked only once and was immediately copied by the Germans. German development and research in fact were based on the concept of keeping one step and only one step in front of the enemy, because of the ease of copying. The constant competition provoked in armaments and the changes in their specifications deriving from combat experience meant therefore that it was impossible to maintain long uninterrupted flows of production. There were at least 19 different 'marks' of the Spitfire and nearly 1,100 technical modifications to the design from 1938 to the start of 1945.[24] The top speed rose from 356 to 460 miles per hour in the same period. In order to avoid interrupting production to make such modifications it was the practice in American aircraft factories to freeze long batches of production without incorporating any modifications and where necessary to send the plane from the factory to a 'modification centre' before final delivery. This practice certainly resulted in higher output figures, but the backlog of planes requiring modification became so enormous that the actual delivery figures to the user were much lower and the 'modification centres' functioned like large factories. It should be added that it was usually very much in the interests of firms to resist both new designs and modifications to existing ones and that the pressure for change was only from the armed forces.

The experience of combat, like the experience of production, often discouraged the more advanced technological innovations.

23. Smith, *The Army and Economic Mobilization*, p. 16.
24. Postan, Hay and Scott, p. 125.

On the whole the fighting forces were recruited from the unskilled mass of the labour force; workers with technical skills were retained in the economy. There were therefore inherent limitations to increasing the complexity of the equipment which the labour force could use. Tank crews in the United States army approached the technical élite of the world's fighting men but nevertheless, rather than master the expensively designed and even more expensively produced gyrostabilizers fitted to the later American tanks, they disconnected them. When the gyrostabilizers were used by crews trained for a longer period of time a special team of maintenance engineers had to be kept just behind the lines to repair them. Such obstacles were frequently encountered in the United States forces; they must have been even more common elsewhere. A weapon like the proximity fuse, which could be set by a trained American soldier to explode in the proximity of a target which the projectile did not actually hit, might well have been virtually useless in some other armies because of the incapacity of the labour force to handle it. Only where an innovation met both the demands of production and of combat, therefore, was it produced effectively in wartime. This had the consequence of restricting the area of basic research even more and putting an even greater emphasis on innovations in production methods rather than development.

The technological legacy of the war

There were therefore at least as many forces inherent in the armaments and munitions industries in wartime retarding technological innovation as stimulating it. It was the complicated interconnections between the three stages of development, production, and use which imposed restrictions on innovation. These restrictions were exaggerated by strategy and wartime shortages as well as by the usual forces of conservatism. For an innovation to be appropriate it had to satisfy a wide range of conditions. When it did so the tendency was for all efforts and resources to be concentrated on it. And at that point, of course, other developments, possibly of greater significance for economic development in general, had to be neglected. Whether innovation of the kind which occurred was in the long run beneficial is a question which, however academic in the context of war, cannot be avoided. The expansion of output in wartime was not always in industries whose long-term tendency was towards development. The huge destruction of shipping between 1939 and 1945 produced a rapid growth in an industry whose long-term tendency in many countries was towards a contraction of output. In Japan the contraction of the textile industry and the expansion of an industry like machine-tool engineering or aircraft manufacture can clearly be seen as an acceleration in the development of the economy. But the pattern of consumption of armaments in war was not always completely in accordance with the trends of industrial production; the enemy could always impose a choice of armaments which was, from an economic point of view, some way from the optimum choice. The extent to which innovations in armaments had a beneficial applicability in peacetime varied according to the innovation.

The best-known innovation to satisfy the necessary conditions and also the most significant for the post-war world was the atomic bomb. The full period of development in this case embraced a history of scientific research in many countries over at least thirty years. But that this research could produce an explosive bomb only became a firm idea after an extraordinary series of theoretical discoveries in 1939, just in time to be internationally communicable, and it was not taken seriously in Britain until the Peierls–Frisch memorandum on this subject in spring 1940. Only in autumn 1940 did the British government lend its official but very slight financial support to the development stage. Although the main focus of development was in Britain some developmental work was also being done in the United States and there was discussion in 1940 of shifting the emphasis to that country. This faded in 1941 with the advance of research into the properties of uranium and the slow conviction that a nuclear bomb was a production possibility. It was the decision of the Scientific Advisory Committee's panel on the question in July 1941 to push ahead with building a uranium-235 bomb in Britain that first made United States scientists take seriously the pressure from the armed forces to explore such a weapon.[25] The estimated time needed to produce such a bomb in

25. R. G. Hewlett and O. E. Anderson, *The New World 1939–1946*, vol. 1 of *A History of the U.S.A.E.C.*, Pennsylvania State University Press, Philadelphia, 1962, p. 42.

Britain was two years provided that if a separation plant were to be built to obtain heavy water it could be constructed in Canada or the United States where it would be safe from attack.[26] Already the need for technological and scientific cooperation on so vast a project was realized. But the full cost of putting an atomic bomb into production was far from being recognized.

The enormous advantages of the United States, able to pursue every possible path of development in the project rather than have to select one only, very soon shifted the development lead to the United States, the more so as after Pearl Harbor the work already done in Britain was readily made available and the scientists involved went to help in the American project. Subsequent American production of the bomb could not be said, however, to have depended on British development work. It represented a determined decision to allocate maximum priority to an inordinately expensive production project. In September 1941 a Presidential committee was set up to see if the bomb was in fact a practical possibility at the stage of production. In the year in which the committee sought to establish the fact that it was, it discovered that the construction tasks imposed were so great that the only possibility in wartime was to have them undertaken by the army. On 28 December 1942 Presidential approval was given to a priority production effort. It was assumed that there was a good chance, if all went well, of having a bomb in the first half of 1945. It was also assumed that by that time Germany might already have had a similar weapon for six months.[27] Four separate processes for isolating uranium-235 were each backed at great expense to find the most feasible one. Of the two bombs ultimately delivered against Japan only one was a uranium bomb and the other, used at Nagasaki, the more lately conceived plutonium bomb.

The possibilities of producing independently in Britain or of constructing a plutonium plant in Canada were still actively canvassed in 1942, but by April 1943 the United States had a lien on all Canada's supplies of heavy water and uranium. Furthermore it was thought the war in Europe would be over before an independent British project could produce a bomb. It has been

26. M. M. Gowing, *Britain and Atomic Energy 1939–1945*, Macmillan, London, 1964, p. 102.
27. Hewlett and Anderson, p. 115.

estimated that total United States expenditure on the project was about $2,000 million, and this fact alone indicates the economic difficulty that would have faced Britain or Germany in actually going into production with such an armament. As far as Britain was concerned its strategic value was in any case not likely to have been greater, by the time it was ready for use, than other weapons. Indeed, its strategic value in ending the war against Japan has been endlessly discussed in the United States, where many historians would not be prepared to justify the decision to use the bomb even on the evidence available at the time, by no means all of which was correct. The exact circumstances in which the decision was taken were confused, but one factor which weighed very heavily was that the bomb *had* been produced and was available. It must also be remembered that it was considered only as an explosive weapon about the equivalent of the huge blockbuster bombs being developed in Britain in terms of high explosive capacity, although, it was also realized, far more devastating in its effects. The biological consequences of exposing so many people to radiation and the genetic dangers of fall-out received hardly any mention at the time.

The knowledge acquired in manufacturing the bomb pervaded many areas of post-war existence and it was mostly acquired in the short space of four years from the start of serious development in the United States. The raw material survey of 1943, aimed at getting maximum information on all possible ore deposits, synthesized the contents of 30,000 volumes.[28] The British scientists who went to work on the project obviously learned technological and scientific information which was later important in British nuclear development. Nor did they all keep their knowledge to themselves in spite of the draconian security, and by 1945 the Soviet Union seems also to have benefited, by altogether more devious routes, from this stock of knowledge. After August 1943 some information, but not much, was made available to Britain by official agreement; the slow neutron pile constructed in Canada received United States financial help. The engineering problems overcome in the production stage certainly had benefits beyond the mere making of the bomb itself and by 1945 the strong possibilities for the less belligerent use of nuclear fission had

28. Gowing, p. 303.

emerged very clearly, possibilities which had seemed too costly to be considered in 1939. Even so, in the words of H. L. Stimson, 'The entire purpose was the production of a military weapon; on no other ground could the wartime expenditure of so much time and money have been justified.'[29]

Of the other major technological breakthroughs which had an immediate impact on the post-war world several were also connected with air warfare; the jet engine, the pilotless plane, and the rocket. It is not surprising that research should have been concentrated in this field. Already in the First World War aerial bombing had come to seem the best way to launch a decisive offensive strategy, since mutual slaughter by rifle and artillery appeared capable of infinite prolongation. In the restless search for the winning weapon it was always assumed that it would be despatched through the air and, as a result, in this sector of warfare technology advanced more rapidly. In fact, the major developments cannot properly be isolated from the great improvements in navigational systems and in safety and accuracy of flight, which were also fundamental in the rapid development of air transport after 1945. Most of these systems, such as H2S, Gee, and Oboe were based on the prior invention of radar. Radar itself, however, was initially conceived as purely a defensive system. Its success was established by the construction of the Home Chain of radar detection stations in Britain which played a vital part in the Battle of Britain. Its subsequent evolution into more complex methods was partly the result of joint development in Britain and the United States after 1940 which produced innovations such as centimetric radar on which the new navigational systems were based, and of the rapid development of radar defences in Germany which stimulated the search for a more positive use of radar among the Allies. To these innovations should be added the great increases in the range and lifting capacity of aircraft as well as the great improvements in their more orthodox radio equipment.

The jet engine achieved its post-war impact only when conjoined with all these other improvements. Once again the length of the development period is very striking. Sir Frank Whittle took out his first patent to use a gas turbine for jet propulsion in 1930.

29. H. L. Stimson, 'The Decision to Use the Atomic Bomb', in *Harper's Magazine*, February 1947, p. 98.

Throughout the 1930s parallel research was carried on in Germany and also in Switzerland by the engineering firm of Brown Boveri. Again it was the year 1939 and the coming of the war that concentrated effort and cash on these projects. In the same year the Northrop Aircraft Company made the first serious effort in the United States with government support to apply gas turbines to flight. But in the fluctuating strategic situation of the war, constant support was not given to these developments in Britain and the United States, where the main effort even in 1943 had to be in the direction of producing long-range fighter aircraft. The jet planes which could have been brought to the production stage would not have been able to fly safely beyond Britain. Although information on the Whittle engine was released to the United States in July 1941 neither Britain nor the United States had an operative jet plane until July 1944, when the Gloster Meteor was first launched into combat. Neither that nor its earlier German equivalent, the Messerschmidt 262, played an important role in the war. But the joint development of the jet in Britain and the United States laid the basis for an important American post-war industry making jet engines, many of them under licence from Britain.

The first jet planes were preceded by the so-called V-1, the 'flying bomb', which was a pure jet propulsion unit, although pilotless. It was also noteworthy for its gyromagnetic automatic pilot. It was an easily mass-produced weapon involving less precision work than a piloted plane. It took only 800 man hours to build, apart from its warhead.[30] The first designs for the V-1 were produced by the German Air Ministry in 1936 but production did not begin until September 1943. Despite its effectiveness and cheapness, it was already intended that the flying bomb should be replaced by rockets when it first went into production. The type of rocket subsequently produced and launched against Britain, called V-2 by the Allies and A4 by the Germans, has also had its special significance since 1945: it is the basis of all modern space exploration. In fact its designer, von Braun, was whisked away to the United States at the end of the war to a highly important post, a twist of fate reserved only for distinguished scientists and secret police officials. The rocket was propelled by a reaction jet motor using alcohol pumped to the jet by a steam turbine. The

30. U.S.S.B.S., Aircraft Division, *Industry Report*, Washington, 1947.

steam was produced by a mixture of chemicals, for only enough fuel for one minute's powered flight was necessary; after that the rocket followed the normal course of a ballistic missile. In many ways the electronic system which controlled the rocket during its ascent was more startling and complex than the rocket itself. As an achievement it was beyond question a great technological advance, although like the jet aircraft its immediate value as an armament was more questionable. At peak production each rocket cost about 56,000 RM, and over the project as a whole 250,000 RM.[31] The cost of concentrating effort on such high-level technology can be gauged from the fact that 3,000 units had to be used experimentally before the rocket became operational. After it did so it gave endless trouble in manufacture and use. It often burst in the air. The maximum number produced in one month was 700, and at the cost per unit over the project as a whole six standard fighters could have been produced for each rocket.[32]

It is the considerations raised by projects as complex as the V-2 or the atomic bomb that indicate the extent to which the most advanced economies with the most sophisticated engineering industries were able to outdistance other economies in these years. Technological advance which takes place in wartime through the medium of the armaments industry is limited not only in its area of application; it is also limited to a small number of economies. This is not to say that the Second World War did not produce significant technological innovation outside the economies of the major combatants; it did. But the technological gap existing between those economies and the major combatants was widened rather than closed by the emphasis on armaments research. This may be seen from the history of armaments production in three countries where the full demand of the Allied war effort was felt and from which large quantities of armaments were obtained: Australia, Canada and India.

Of these three Canada was the best equipped for the development of sophisticated armaments manufacture because it alone had a car industry. On the other hand, the car industry there depended very heavily on the import of component parts from the United States, which compensated for the lack of a properly developed general engineering industry. In the course of the war

31. Milward, *The German Economy*, p. 106.
32. U.S.S.B.S., *Industry Report*.

this lack was continually to impede the production of new armaments in Canada.[33] Australia had no comparable mass-production engineering industry. But it had certain advantages lacking in Canada. In the First World War it had developed a shipbuilding industry capable of producing ocean-going vessels. That industry had collapsed in the inter-war period but the Australian government had contrived to maintain the rudiments of an aircraft industry and as a result of these earlier developments there existed a machine-making industry of a more sophisticated kind than in Canada. In India the presence of large fighting forces meant that the government arsenals manufactured large quantities of small arms before 1939, although many of the optical parts had to be imported. All three countries for good economic reasons were keen to produce armaments, all were safe from air raids, two of them were near to theatres of war.

After some initial hesitations on the part of the British government the demands of the war prevailed and large armaments industries were developed in all three. But the technological limitations of what could be done became increasingly obvious. These limitations proved less restricting in Australia because of the prior development of machine-tool manufacture there. In 1939 there were only three machine-tool manufacturers, one making lathes and the other two power presses. In 1943 there were about one hundred firms making a variety of milling machines, drilling machines, grinders and planers.[34] The manufacture of optical instruments and sophisticated radio equipment including centimetric radar developed. The Australian shipbuilding and ship-repairing industry which had so briefly flourished in the First World War was revived by the Australian Shipbuilding Board. In Canada and Australia aircraft manufacture began on a considerable scale. Canada, by the end of the war, was making Lancaster heavy bombers. Planes of this size were not manufactured in Australia but because of the greater capacity for machine-tool manufacture, the Australian aircraft industry made one significant advance which proved impossible in Canada, the manufacture of aircraft engines.

Active plans had been canvassed for an Australian aircraft

33. H. D. Hall and C. C. Wrigley, *Studies of Overseas Supply*, H.M.S.O., London, 1956, p. 49.
34. Walker, p. 137.

industry since 1936. The war provided the opportunity for their realization. The Commonwealth Aircraft Corporation produced its first training plane, a copy of an American design, in 1939. On the strength of this success the United Kingdom government agreed to have the Beaufort bomber, a British design, built in Australia. But in June 1940 the supplies of component parts from Britain on which its production depended were cut off. The Commonwealth government decided to continue with its pro-duction – in the circumstances of the Australian economy a vast production task. The subcontracts affected about 600 firms and much of the equipment involved manufacturing processes quite new to Australia. Most significantly it involved building the American engines. The war thus produced the extraordinary situation of a country which manufactured aircraft engines but did not manufacture car engines.[35] It was almost three years from taking the decision to build until the first 'all-Australian' Beaufort was built. Later in the war the de Havilland assembly works also began to construct Mosquitoes. In June 1944 the Australian air-craft industry employed 44,000 people.

No armament, however, was produced in any of these countries that was not an American or British design or a modification of one. The production of the Beaufort involved the transport of 250,000 specifications and drawings from Britain. Furthermore, the Australian aircraft industry was dependent on imports of alu-minium from Canada. Neither aircraft engines nor tank engines were made in Canada during the war. The Canadian car industry was not converted to other purposes like its American counterpart and its armaments output was mainly trucks, of which the more specialized versions were made in the United States. The bulk of the armaments made in Canada and Australia consisted of basic army supplies. In India it proved impossible even to sustain the planned level of basic army supply. Shortages of skilled labour, shortages of supervisory and managerial ability, rampant inflation in a country where a large part of the population could only just sustain human life and the intolerable strain placed on an economy where the substructure of manufacturing industry and services was inadequate to sustain an expansion of the armaments industry meant that Indian armaments output had to be scaled down in

35. D. F. Mellor, *The Role of Science and Industry*, Australian War Memorial, Canberra, 1958, p. 381 ff.

1944 to protect the economy from worse problems. No aircraft were made in India although they were assembled there in small numbers. The Indian government's plans to build warships were turned down because the engines would have had to come from Britain.

Government control of technological innovation

One final aspect of technological innovation in these years remains to be considered, the extent to which it was monopolized and controlled by government. Projects such as the flying-bomb, the rocket and the atomic bomb involved government in applying the utmost sanctions to control the scientists and engineers who worked on them, and in all areas of armaments research it was civil servants or officers of the armed forces who everywhere made the essential decisions about which research should continue. The intimate connections between economic development and technological change therefore forced government into an area of activity from which it was never able to withdraw after 1945, however reluctant it was to remain involved and to acquire the necessary expertise to make rational decisions in a new field. This process was the more inescapable because of the increasing cost of the more complicated technologies and the vital security aspects which they occasionally involved. In 1943 the British chemical cartel, I.C.I., was prepared to consider the construction of a heavy-water plant as a commercial venture with the technical help of refugee experts from the Norwegian company Norsk Hydro, but in Britain, as in the United States, it was felt necessary to keep all atomic energy developments under the control of a specially created government authority. There is still little research on the effects which the intervention of government has had on the direction of technological research, but it is hard not to feel that they have been restrictive in so far as the total range of government objectives at any time is far smaller than the range of all the research objectives existing in a complex highly developed society. Disputes about the aims of technological research have become a commonplace since 1945 and there are certainly many instances of wasteful decisions and even serious misjudgements by government in this area. The government's answer to this must, perfectly correctly, be that the cost of technological development does not become easier to bear with the growth of G.N.P. But government control of research was much more restrictive during the Second World War when economic controls gave government greater power and when the decisions were greatly simplified by the tendency of war to eliminate instantly a very large number of possible economic choices. There were extraordinary examples of actively discouraged private development and even private production proving better than that sponsored by government.

For example, the early work on the jet engine in Britain was carried on only through the unshakeable conviction of Sir Frank Whittle over many years that his patent was of extreme military value and through the support which it achieved from private backers. At the start of the war it would surely have foundered without government support; but once government became fully convinced of its value and allocated it a priority in funding, further development was compulsorily taken out of Whittle's hand and transferred to the Rover car company. The company refused to acknowledge Whittle's patents and refused even to permit his cooperation in the development stage. The result was that the development done by government and company so seriously delayed the production stage of the gas turbine that it had to be transferred elsewhere so that Whittle's familiarity with the problems involved would be used. Aircraft were seldom developed in government arsenals but by private firms with government help. Even when the French aircraft industry was partially nationalized in 1936 private engine and frame manufacturers were deliberately left in order to stimulate competition. In Britain these private firms sometimes persisted with successful ideas which were discouraged for long periods by government. The refinement of the not very successful Manchester heavy bomber into the excellent Lancaster was only achieved through the persistence of A. V. Roe at a time when government support was flowing to two competitors, the Halifax and the Stirling, both destined to relative failure. The inspiration for the Mosquito long-range fighter escort, which rescued the Allied air forces from the consequences of their false assumption that heavy bombers would be able to conduct safely precision-bombing raids over Germany without escorts, was also largely private. Wood and fabric were the basic constructional materials and the British Air Ministry was for a long time sceptical of the value of a wooden plane.

The strength of private research and manufacturing capacity in armaments before 1939 varied greatly between countries. In the United States armaments design was wholly the province of the ordnance departments of the armed forces and there were no private armaments manufacturers other than those who made small-arms. In Britain and France, by contrast, there were powerful private armaments firms like Vickers or Schneider with widespread international connections and the capacity to manufacture the heaviest armaments. Such firms had always cooperated closely in the way of business with the ordnance departments of the armed forces of their own countries but they were by no means prepared to abandon private developments which found no domestic market. In the course of the war, however, most private firms in all the major combatant powers were reduced to armaments manufacturers existing only on government orders even though the capacity of the government-owned ordnance factories and naval workshops nowhere served as any more than the basis for armaments production. New armaments manufacturers were frequently manufacturing products wholly designed by government. Apart from the established pre-war armament makers very few firms offered anything beyond the capacity to produce to orders. The aircraft industry was again an exception even though in France and Britain it was scarcely larger in 1939 than in 1918. Many small firms offered many different designs. In Germany, Japan and Italy, however, the existence of a large domestic military market had already revolutionized the structure of the industry during the thirties. In Germany the firms with the stronger design teams, Junkers and Messerschmidt, came rapidly to dominate the industry by securing government orders after 1933. Weaker firms came to exist mainly to produce aircraft designed by the leading firms. This process was hastened by government insistence on the pooling of technical information and the industry, although nominally private, was quickly transformed into a dependency of the government.

There were certain mitigating factors in this process. The armed forces were always obliged to maintain the vital interests of the firms which had become their virtual dependents. In Germany, an attempt in January 1942 to limit the new development of all required types of planes to only one or two firms had to be abandoned because it would have inflicted irreparable damage on the companies which had been passed over. Contracts had to be spread around in order to keep everyone who was needed in business. In the United States this led to special legislation to compel the award of armaments contracts to small firms which had tended to lose by the preference of government for larger firms with a more varied capacity. The smaller aircraft firms survived in Germany through the need for incessant modifications and repairs to existing models and the industry continued to contribute a range of private initiative and experience. In Japan under the same pressures four firms, Nakajima, Mitsubishi, Kawasaki and Tachikawa, had come to provide two thirds of the industry's total output in the thirties.[36] But as in Germany the plethora of different designs and specifications required by the Air Ministry meant that ninety separate basic types were manufactured; many in small numbers only. Even in the United States, where the standardization of types was taken furthest, the refusal of ordnance boards to compromise on the obvious truth that an aircraft designed to do a specific job did it better than any other aircraft maintained a similar structure of output to that elsewhere. A restricted number of very successful designs, like the Spitfire, the Messerschmidt 110, or the Flying Fortress, were produced in large numbers, but in all countries many specialized and less successful types were produced in numbers hardly varying from pre-war levels of output.

It has been fairly remarked by both British and American official historians that in such a situation private and government development were not alternatives but complementary to each other. So they were; but the weight of advantage was all on the government side in economies where the capital was provided by the government and every unit of labour and materials required an official certificate. In Britain in 1943, the Ministry of Aircraft Production undertook a complete revision of the structure and managerial capacity of the aircraft industry and firms with poor production records were forced to change all their controlling personnel. In Germany in March 1944, when top priority was given to fighter production a special organization, the Fighter Staff, was given overriding control over all firms in the production stage with the objective of maximizing the number of fighters produced. Although they had no specific control over development

36. U.S.S.B.S., Aircraft Division, *The Japanese Aircraft Industry*, Washington, 1947.

the natural consequence was a sharp reduction in the number of aircraft types called for in the new production programme issued in July, for this was the easiest way to increase the monthly output figures. This programme was the death of several private projects which had ceased to be of strategic value but would have enabled German aircraft design to keep abreast of the type of development which proved so important elsewhere after 1945. It was, for instance, finally decided not to go into production with the Heinkel 177 long-range bomber. In spite of the complementarity of private and government initiative, the trend everywhere was towards an increasing dominance of all development by government. And the evidence is that, although often for the best reasons, this also resulted in a narrowing of the range and scope of innovation.

The discussion has been closely confined to armaments and the industries directly related to them. The technological impact of war was a wider one than this. It is only necessary to consider the innovations in the art of patching up the damaged human capital, civil and military, so that further use could be made of it to see how wide the war's ramifications were. Most wars bring advances in surgical techniques but the Second World War was more distinguished in medical history for its advances in chemotherapy. The development of sulphonamides, penicillin and other anti-infective agents, such as the anti-malarial drug mepacrine and the scrub-typhus vaccine, played their part in keeping the deaths in the armed services below the gruesome heights of the First World War. After 1945 these benefits were extended to civilians. In the short run the development of D.D.T. also improved the state of the harvests, if not always of the people who ate them.

But even these advances had a direct military purpose. The much-discussed benefits of technological 'spin-off', whereby the methods used to solve a particular problem prove ultimately to have a more universal applicability, are apparent in relation to a limited number only of the technological innovations of the Second World War. The evidence is rather that the concentration of innovation on an extremely narrow range of priorities limits the benefits of 'spin-off' as much as it limits the immediate forms of technological innovation. Between 1939 and 1945, although disrupted by enemy intervention, industry could still achieve increases in productivity. It may well be that, where there is immunity from enemy interference, war does lead to more rapid improvements in productivity than peace. But these improvements were made up from a wide range of managerial and organizational changes as well as from technological innovation in the narrower sense. If technological innovation is a benefit the evidence of these years suggests that it may be numbered as much among the benefits of peace as of war.

7

War, Population and Labour

The number of those who can go to war, in proportion to the whole number of the people, is necessarily much smaller in a civilized than in a rude state of society. In a civilized society, as the soldiers are maintained altogether by the labour of those who are not soldiers, the number of the former can never exceed what the latter can maintain, over and above maintaining, in a manner suitable to their respective stations, both themselves and the other officers of government and law whom they are obliged to maintain. In the little agrarian states of ancient Greece, a fourth or a fifth part of the whole body of the people considered themselves as soldiers, and would sometimes, it is said, take the field. Among the civilized nations of modern Europe, it is commonly computed, that not more than one hundredth part of the inhabitants of any country can be employed as soldiers, without ruin to the country which pays the expense of their service.

Adam Smith,
The Wealth of Nations, 1776

Demographic response to war

Malthus was not the first economic theorist to establish connections between population behaviour and warfare, but he has become the most influential. He considered warfare as an endemic 'check' on population growth, of the same order as famine and disease. Unfortunately, in doing so, he left the door wide open to numerous authors who have subsequently sought to connect theories of the incidence of war with theories of the cyclical behaviour of the human population. Such studies properly belong to the field of mysticism rather than to history. Such is the case for example with Kulischer's attempts to explain the periodicity of war by 'frustrated migration movements'.[1] It has not been established that there are any observable cyclical patterns in the incidence of warfare nor that there is any correlation between the incidence of international warfare and demographic behaviour. The only recurrent demographic phenomenon relating to all or most wars over a long period is the fact that war kills many people.

This is not to say that the state of any war may not be accurately and sensitively reflected by the behaviour of the population. But in this case behaviour of the population reflects particular and unique situations. Among the unique aspects of the Second World War was the fact that it was launched by a power intent upon a political and racial restructuring of the European continent. Mainly because of this huge numbers of Europe's population were moved by force from one area to another. This resulted in permanent changes in the distribution of the population and a wave of intra-European migration surpassing even the movements in the nineteenth century in scope. Furthermore, in re-ordering the racial structure of Europe the National Socialist party made considerable headway in one aspect of these plans, the extermination of the Jewish race. This alone argues for the uniqueness of the demographic history of the years 1939 to 1945.

As regards the impact of the war on population behaviour the apparent connections observed on a national scale look less convincing when international comparisons are made. The upward movement of the birth-rate in Britain and in France in the early years of the war, a movement which reversed the trend of the 1930s, has been interpreted in both countries as a deep sign of optimism for the future. But this phenomenon was common to most west European countries in the same period, although obscured by the fluctuating and abnormal death-rates which occurred in the first year of the war. Both the birth-rate and the

1. E. M. Kulischer, *Europe on the Move: War and Population Changes 1917-1947*, Columbia University Press, New York, 1948.

net reproduction rate moved upwards steeply in Norway and Denmark in 1941. In the Netherlands the same upward movement occurred, obscured by the sharp rise in the death-rate in 1943 and in 1944, but resumed in 1945. Nor was this phenomenon limited to combatant and occupied countries. It was also to be observed in neutral countries such as Sweden, Switzerland, Spain (where the distorted age structure of the population due to the Civil War caused it to slow again in 1944) and even in Ireland.[2]

In Germany, on the other hand, a fall in the rate of natural increase began in 1939, principally due to a decline in the birth-rate. It would be foolish to deny that these population trends in Germany were influenced by people's views of the human condition there after 1939. But elsewhere the broad similarity of experience suggests that a more determining factor in the population behaviour was the previous pattern of population behaviour. In eastern Europe, where the inter-war pattern had been different, with falling but relatively much higher rates of natural increase, the wartime experience was also different. The pre-war trend of a rising population but a falling rate of population increase was generally maintained in eastern Europe, whereas in western Europe the pre-war tendency of population to show a falling trend was reversed. The continent as a whole, except Germany and Italy, showed after 1941 a surge of population growth which was to make the gloomy predictions of demographers of the 1930s seem fantastic to the planners of the 1940s.

The loss of life attributable to the war cannot be estimated with even reasonable accuracy. People died and were killed in huge numbers in anonymous and terrifying circumstances. Even setting aside those whose deaths are not statistically attributable to war, as those who died from undernourishment or emotional shock, it is still impossible to establish the number of civilians and military whose death was directly caused by the war. It could have been as high as forty million, more than three times the loss in the First World War. Of this total 4·6 million were deported and murdered mainly because they were of the wrong race and about another 4·5 million mainly because they were of the wrong politics. The most grisly harvest was reaped in the Soviet Union. Stalin publicly

2. G. Frumkin, *Population Changes in Europe since 1939*, Allen & Unwin, London, 1951, pp. 14–15.

declared in March 1946 the loss of life in the U.S.S.R. at 7 million people. But Soviet statisticians have remained silent on the subject and the figure of 7 million is usually regarded as too low. About 3 million Russians met their death on the battlefield and a further 5 million were taken prisoner, of whom as many as 3 million may have subsequently died through bad treatment. In occupied Russia the estimates of deaths due to the war go as high as 8 million, in unoccupied Russia 3 million. Such figures, if exaggerations, may be so only to a small degree; 650,000 civilians, for example, died in the siege of Leningrad. The total loss of population in the Soviet Union may therefore have been as high as 17 million. German military casualties amounted to 3·25 million; total casualties to more than 6 million. In addition one million German prisoners of war remained in the Soviet Union after 1945. In Poland between 2·3 million and 2·9 million Jews alone were killed and the death-toll among non-Jewish Poles must also have been appallingly high. Japanese military casualties were reported after the war to be 2·1 million; 289,000 civilians lost their life in Japan through 'military action'.[3] Chinese casualties must have been even higher. In France a total of 497,000 civilians and military lost their lives due to the war. If the increase in wartime mortality rates over the previous trend is taken into account a further 300,000 deaths in France may be attributed to the war.[4] Total casualties in the British Commonwealth were 611,596, in the United States 323,688, and in the Netherlands 209,648.[5]

The extent to which these casualties resulted in a long-term overall population loss is a complex issue and perhaps too hypothetical. In western European countries the increase in the birth-rates during the war, prolonged after 1945, meant that population recouped itself numerically much more rapidly than after the blood-letting of 1914–18. The immense migratory movements begun during the war were in some countries sustained on such a level as to dominate the general population

3. I. B. Taeuber, *The Population of Japan*, Princeton University Press, Princeton, N.J., 1958, pp. 334, 335.

4. J. Vincent, 'Conséquences de six années de guerre sur la population française', in *Population*, no. 3, 1946.

5. H. Bernard, *Guerre totale et guerre révolutionnaire*, Brepols, Brussels, 1965, vol. 3, table 298.

behaviour in spite of the casualties of the war years. In West Germany for example immigration from East Germany and from eastern and southern Europe was on such a scale as to cancel out many of the post-war effects of the terrible death toll. After 1945 the Allies set themselves the task of repatriating the Japanese population from the former empire back to the Home Islands. None the less, on balance the population still fell short by one million men after the losses, both direct and presumed, due to the war. This may have been no bad thing in the circumstances of the economy after 1945. However, it also resulted in a net surplus of women over men of more than 400,000, which obviously tended to restore population losses more quickly.[6] In most countries the return of the fighting forces to civilian existence and the return of settled conditions produced a short sharp upward movement in the birth-rate which also tended to cancel earlier population losses. The real and durable effects of the deaths in the war were seen and felt not in the absolute numbers of the population but in its age distribution. Again this was most obvious in the Soviet Union: the seven million military casualties there, equivalent to almost 10 per cent of the employed labour force, were not replaced, despite the great territorial extension of the Soviet Union after 1945. In 1959 there were still seven women between the ages of thirty-five and fifty for every four men.

Physical transfers of population

For the post-war world the effect of these demographic changes was often more significant than for the war years themselves; this was perhaps also true for the enormous physical transfers of population which took place in the war years. As early as October 1938 Germany began to deport Jews over the Silesian and East Prussian borders into Poland. After April 1940 the Jewish ghettoes in Poland were re-created and early in 1941 the policy of starving their inhabitants to death began. This was followed by the policy of working Jews to death in labour camps such as Auschwitz (Oswięcim). This in turn was succeeded by the systematic deportation of Jews to extermination centres. From early 1943 the only limits imposed on this extermination seem to have been administrative and technological ones, breakdowns of the

6. Taeuber, p. 361.

gas plant, disruptions of the railway system, the difficulty of disposing of so many corpses and so on. The number of Jews killed in the war was less than that of Russians or Germans. But they were massacred systematically, without regard for sex or age, only with a certain haphazard regard for ability and standing in the community, both good qualifications for death. The total number killed and their distribution by nationality remains unknown. The best estimate is between 4·2 million and 4·6 million.[7] Of these over 2·3 million were inhabitants of Poland in 1939, over 700,000 of Russia, Estonia, Latvia and Lithuania, and about 250,000 of Czechoslovakia. The Jewish 'problem' was distinguished from that of other races because there were possible areas of settlement for all other races. One clear difference between post-1945 Europe and pre-1939 Europe was the great reduction in the size of racial minorities. After 1945 national frontiers corresponded much more closely to linguistic and ethnographic frontiers than they had before. The planned population transfers which took place are difficult to distinguish from the general phenomenon of 'displacement'. The second involved greater numbers and was often temporary. About twelve million Russians, for example, fled eastwards in front of the advancing German armies and of this horde some subsequently settled permanently in Siberia. Millions of French and Belgians fled into central and southern France in June 1940 to escape the German forces and of these, too, many settled permanently.[8] In addition there were those from all occupied countries who escaped to fight against Germany and who after the war no longer wished, or were no longer permitted, to return to their own country. There were still 1·4 million 'displaced persons' at the end of 1945, mostly in Germany.

The deliberate transfer of population was a permanent act usually involving smaller numbers, and there was some mechanism for aiding the reception and settlement of the transferred population in their new country. In certain instances, however, the numbers were very large. About 400,000 people of German descent in the Volga region of the Soviet Union were transferred

7. G. Reitlinger, *The Final Solution*, Valentine, Mitchell, London, 1953, appendix I.

8. J. Vidalenc, *L'exode de mai–juin 1940*, Presses Universitaires de France, Paris, 1957.

in autumn 1941 to Siberia and central Asia. The same number of people of Finnish race were moved from Russian Karelia into Finland in 1940 after the transfer of sovereignty there. About 160,000 Hungarian-speaking inhabitants of Transylvania were settled in Hungary proper in the period from 1940 to 1943, and 100,000 German-speaking inhabitants of the South Tyrol were resettled, under the terms of a treaty signed in October 1939, in the Austrian north Tyrol, Lorraine, Luxembourg and Styria. It was the resettlement of the German population of Europe in a contiguous German-speaking area that formed the most significant part of these transfers. In the winter of 1939–40 128,000 *Volksdeutsche* from those parts of Poland annexed by the Soviet Union were settled in the areas annexed by Germany. In the autumn of 1940 93,500 from Bessarabia and Russia were settled in Poland and in Germany proper. Poland was a 'problem' of almost as great a magnitude as the Jews. Various solutions were canvassed, including liquidation on the same scale as the Jews. In July 1941 the Jewish 'problem' began to be solved separately and no solution so brutally comprehensive was attempted with non-Jewish Poles. However, people who could be considered German were needed to colonize the annexed areas. Many of those settled there were German in only the most theoretical sense, many were in fact classified as 're-Germanizables' (*Wiedereindeutschungsfähige*).[9] The settlement continued until summer 1944, when 135,000 so-called 'Transnistrian' Germans were settled in the parts of Poland still occupied.[10] As the area controlled by Germany shrank the settlers and what remained of the German-speaking population of eastern Europe poured back into it. Probably 1·2 million people came back from eastern Europe, often after a century and a half of settlement there, to swell the population of the two German states which eventually emerged. Of these two states and also of Poland it may be said that their population history effectively started all over again in 1945. This is particularly true of the Bundesrepublik, which received massive inflows of people from the German Democratic Republic. In 1950 almost one third of the population of the Bundesrepublik

9. R. L. Koehl, *RKFDV: German Resettlement and Population Policy 1939–1945*, Harvard U.P., Cambridge, Mass., 1957.

10. J. B. Schechtman, *European Population Transfers 1939–1945*, Oxford University Press, New York, 1946.

had not been born in the territorial area of the existing state. Ironically, the population of Germany, as much as Israel, was a creation of the Second World War.

Excluding the Soviet Union from the calculation, together with the territories which it subsequently annexed, the population of Europe fell between the end of 1938 and the end of 1945 from 380·4 million to 372·5 million. This drop includes five million prisoners of war who had not yet been repatriated, of whom a certain proportion subsequently returned home. The evidence points to the fact that this net loss of between three million and eight million was, at least numerically, recouped in 1946 and in 1947, by which time the population was greater than in 1938. The absolute loss between 1939 and 1945 was borne mainly by Germany, eastern Europe and Russia; most other areas gained in population. Territorial changes were also more significant than the abnormal death-rate of the war years in changing the national pattern of population after 1945. This was the biggest factor in reducing the population of Poland from 32·3 million at the end of 1938 to 23·7 million at the end of 1947. The density of the population of Finland increased by 19 per cent over the same period, and that of pre-war Germany by 15 per cent. By contrast the density of population in Poland fell by 27 per cent, in spite of the decrease in territorial area.[11] In Japan also the main economic significance of the war for the future as far as population was concerned was not the abnormally high death-rates, but, as in Europe, the physical redistribution which it brought about. About three million citizens of Japan and the Ryukyu Islands in 1950 had been 'repatriated' by the allies from the far-flung territories of the Co-Prosperity Sphere.[12]

Labour demand and supply

So much for the demographic legacy of the war. The population which some combatants had at their disposal changed considerably during the period. The proportion of the available population which should be assigned to do the actual fighting is a question which economists have long debated. The range of strategic choice available suggests that the optimum proportion

11. Frumkin, p. 165 ff.
12. Taeuber, p. 361, n. 72.

might vary widely. But the evidence of the Second World War leaves little room for these niceties, for the proportion of the employed labour force in the armed forces was strikingly similar amongst the major combatants. As a proportion of the total population the armed forces showed more variation, but these variations were mostly due to the differing age structures of the populations. There was very little difference before 1945 in the definition of the section of the population liable to conscription into the fighting forces. In Japan at first the minimum age for conscription for males was twenty whereas elsewhere eighteen was the norm. The upper limit varied from forty-five to fifty. The number of women in the fighting forces was relatively low in all countries. The proportion of the total active labour force engaged in the armed forces in the United States and Japan in 1944 was in each case about one in six. However after February 1944 the same number of men were drafted in Japan as in the whole period from 1937 to 1943, so that the proportion by autumn 1945 was probably nearer one in five. In Britain in 1943 it was about one in five. In Germany in 1942 it was about one in four and a half, but as foreign labour was more and more used in the domestic economy the proportion became in 1945 nearer to one in five, although the proportion of native Germans serving was of course much higher.

These proportions represented an immense increase in overall employment. The numbers engaged were so enormous as to make any possibility of providing them by transferring labour from other sectors of the economy out of the question. There were over 12 million in the United States armed forces in 1945 and in June of the same year over 5 million in the British armed forces. In February 1944 the Japanese armed forces were 4 million strong. In September 1944 the German armed forces numbered 9·1 million and by that date a total of 13 million Germans had been mobilized into the fighting forces over the whole period of the war. It is sometimes argued that German labour mobilization during the war was less comprehensive than in Britain or the United States, and in one sense this is true, but it did not affect the ability of the Wehrmacht to call up a higher proportion of males in the prime age group than in any other combatant economy with the possible exception of the Soviet Union. Effectively in all these economies the armed forces were responsible for the biggest increase in employment since 1918.

No wonder that everywhere the military sought general control over labour policy, and also that politicians, justly fearing that such military control would inflate the armed forces at the expense of the economy, resisted it. The industrial mobilization plans of the United States army during the 1930s certainly envisaged some such element of control and these ambitions were never entirely given up throughout the war.[13] For the last year and a half of the war the army had more men than had been authorized without anyone being able to work out where they had come from.[14] In Japan it may be said that military and politicians came to a draw on this issue and thereby prevented the creation of any central administrative body with overall powers to decide labour allocation. Allocation depended on the application of numerous piecemeal decrees and in areas where local military commanders were particularly powerful or ruthless key workers could be called up. In some areas for instance coal miners were actually called to the colours and replaced by inexperienced men.[15] When the German economy emerged from the *Blitzkrieg* phase in 1942 the aspirations of the military, the Ministry of Munitions, and the German Labour Front to control labour supply were all disappointed and a new organization under the former Gauleiter Fritz Sauckel was created with responsibility only to the Führer. As the Allied forces drove into Germany from both sides and planned economic organization became almost impossible a new labour policy was forced on the German economy. In September 1944 a small circle of party figures around the Führer decided to arm and train all available manpower and create a national militia, the Volkssturm.[16] Production in factories was interrupted for compulsory periods of military training. At this point Germany had passed into a stage of labour utilization where manpower for hand-to-hand fighting was now allocated a priority above manpower for production. This decision marked the last

13. B. Fairchild and J. Grossman, *The Army and Industrial Manpower*, United States Army in World War II, Office of the Chief of Military History, Washington, D.C., 1959.

14. A. A. Blum and J. Grossman, 'La lutte pour une armée nombreuse et les problèmes de main-d'œuvre industrielle', in *R.d.g.m.*, no. 66, 1967.

15. Cohen, p. 300 ff.

16. H. Kissel, *Der deutsche Volkssturm 1944/45* (Beiheft 16/17 der Wehrwissenschaftlichen Rundschau), E. S. Mittler & Sohn, Berlin, 1962.

stage of German strategy. Such a position was never reached in other economies, where the pressure on labour supply gave rise to increasingly complicated planning and regulations to preserve the labour force in more productive sectors of the economy in order to sustain output. This was the more necessary as the expansion in employment after 1939 was not solely due to the growth of massive armed forces, although this was everywhere the biggest factor. The amount of production needed to keep the forces fighting also grew and provided an additional demand for labour and this, too, was too great to be met by transfers from other sectors of the economy. How much extra employment was generated by the war? And from what sources was the labour found?

The United States could have expected on the basis of pre-war trends an extra 3·25 million people over fourteen to come on the labour market in the period 1939 to 1944, although on the basis of the same trends there was little likelihood that all of them would in fact have found employment. The sudden expansion in employment meant that this average number of 900,000 people per year was easily absorbed and there was an 'extra' expansion in employment of 7·3 million over the same period. This extra expansion represented as much as 14 per cent of the employed population in 1940. In the United Kingdom the total employed population increased by 2·9 million, about 14·5 per cent, in the period 1939 to 1943. Only half a million of this could be ascribed to the natural population increase. In Canada the total increase in the employed population in the period 1939 to 1945 was 880,000; of this 300,000 represented the natural increase in the population, which was at once absorbed into employment. What might be called the 'war-induced' increase was thus about 14 per cent of the pre-war employed population, as in the United States. A similar proportion, about 13 per cent, or 300,000 people, was brought into full-time employment in Australia.[17] The Japanese labour force expanded by 3·2 million between October 1940 and February 1944, considerably more than the natural increase in the population, and in the next year and a half it may have expanded by a further four million. The sources of this expansion were the absorption of pre-war unemployment, the employment of women, the young, such as schoolchildren and students, the old and foreigners.

17. Saunders.

In all the western countries the pre-war unemployed were now employed. In 1943 unemployment in the United States was 7·4 million less than in 1940, almost sufficient to account for the increase in civilian employment since the same year. In Britain the decrease in unemployment by 1943 over 1940 was 1·2 million, 400,000 more than the increase in civilian employment over the same period.[18] By 1941 in Britain and by 1943 in the United States the unemployment which had seemed to have become endemic in these two economies had disappeared. This was not short-term as in the First World War, but an economic change which would last for a quarter of a century.

In no country did women provide so large a part of this increase in employment as in the United Kingdom. Eighty per cent of the total addition to the labour force in 1939 to 1943 consisted of women who had previously not been employed or had been housewives – two quite different categories which economists and government statisticians have conspired to treat as the same. About two and a half million workers came from 'non-industrial classes', mainly housewives and domestic servants, into industrial employment.[19] The war affected the economic position of women in Britain very forcefully and if it did not bring about a permanent change in their role in the economy it did so in their aspirations. The United Kingdom was the only country where the government also took full powers to conscript and direct women, and un-married women in certain age groups were in fact conscripted to work in war industries. This decision was not copied elsewhere, although in Japan from 1943 onwards women at work in vital industries were prevented by law from leaving. The proportion of women over the age of fourteen employed in Britain rose from 27 per cent in 1939 to 37 per cent in 1943. The permanent increase was much smaller; by December 1945 the proportion had already fallen to 31 per cent, but with the long period of full employment which followed it gradually rose again. About half the addition to the labour force in the United States during the war consisted of women. As a proportion of women in work before the war the change was more striking there, but the expansion of female

18. C. D. Long, *The Labor Force in War and Transition – Four Countries*, National Bureau of Economic Research, Occasional Papers no. 36, New York, 1952.

19. H. M. D. Parker, *Manpower*, H.M.S.O., London, 1957, p. 482.

employment attributable to the war was only about three million jobs and the proportion of employed women over fourteen rose from 26 per cent in 1939 to only 32 per cent in 1944. Compared to the United Kingdom the United States had greater available numbers of unemployed people and a far larger population at school and college which could be drawn on. Similar figures have not been calculated for the Soviet Union where female full-time employment was already a much more usual phenomenon in the inter-war years, but such evidence as exists suggests that the employment of women continued to develop there in the war years. Women were 38 per cent of the civilian labour force in 1940, 53 per cent in 1942. Everywhere women were successfully trained to meet the sudden increase in demand for welders but in the Soviet Union almost a third of the welders were female in 1942, as well as a third of the lathe operators and 40 per cent of the stevedores.[20] Women tractor-drivers, rare in 1940, accounted for almost half the drivers in the communal tractor stations in 1942.

Germany was the one exception to the rule that the war brought about a great increase in the employment of women. In Japan the apparent increase was not very great but the drafting of peasant smallholders into the armed forces meant that many farms were operated entirely by the peasant's wife and children. In spite of the insatiable demand for labour in Germany the social ideas of the National Socialist party prevented any fuller mobilization of women. Since race and blood were paramount in the creation of the new society breeding was vital. General arguments in favour of the sanctity and stability of the family were raised in all countries against an increase in employment of women, but in Germany they had a particular force. The stock of Aryan women had to be preserved from risk of death and injury for even to the optimists it must have seemed rather small to do the job required of it. Imprisoned in its own illogicality the party left relatively untapped a large part of the country's labour resources. The maximum number of women in the labour force, attained in 1943–4, was scarcely higher than in 1939 and only 600,000 above the low point of 1941. Social allowances for wives and dependents of servicemen were relatively higher in Germany than in the other major combatants. Indeed it was possible to survive on them,

20. Voznesenskii, p. 65.

whereas in Britain and the United States they were at a level low enough to push women on the labour market.[21] In September 1944 there were still 1·3 million female domestic servants, most of whom were of German nationality, at work in Germany. The contrast with Britain where the war virtually ended domestic service as a source of employment could not be more absolute.

Accurate information on the employment of younger and older people is harder to come by. In Germany in 1945 males of fifteen were drafted into the Volkssturm and certain para-military organizations. It is certain that what in peacetime would have been the school and college population of the United States made a greater contribution to the war-induced increase in employment than did the employment of previously 'idle' women. In the last two years of the war in Japan schoolchildren were used extensively for agricultural work. By 1945 three million students had been assigned to war work. Those under eighteen were 6 per cent of the active labour force in the Soviet Union in 1939, in 1942 they were 15 per cent. In the same period those over fifty rose from 9 per cent to 12 per cent of the employed. At the peak of labour utilization the number of men and women still in industrial employment in Britain beyond the normal peacetime retiring ages of sixty-five and sixty could well have been as high as one million.[22]

Germany, where full employment existed in 1939, recruited fewer unemployed and fewer women to the labour force than the other major combatants. As a result the demand for labour could be met in only one way, by the employment of foreigners. The war began the influx of immigrant labour into the central manufacturing core of Europe which was also to be one of the most economically significant aspects of the post-war world. The post-war immigration, however, was not of the same scope as that of 1939 to 1945, which transformed the German labour force into a babel of nationalities and tongues.

Exact figures for the number of foreigners employed in the German economy during the war have never been established. The highest officially recorded number is 7·1 million employed on 31 May 1944. A great deal of double counting was involved in

21. Long, *The Labor Force in War and Transition*, p. 42.
22. Sir G. Ince, 'The Mobilisation of Manpower in Great Britain in the Second World War', in *The Manchester School of Economic and Social Studies* no. 14, 1946.

the confused administrative procedures for registering and allocating labour and this has prevented more accurate estimates being made. But an equal and more appalling barrier is the administrative 'loss' of a number of people approaching one million, both Russians and Jews. The economic foolishness of such methods is not worth commenting on by the side of the monstrous inhumanity which it reveals, except in so far as it again shows the extent to which the political ideas of the National Socialist party prevailed over established economic thought.

Most of the foreign labour employed in Germany was already there in May 1943. The total foreign employment, including prisoners of war, is shown in Table 25. It shows a marked shift in the type of employment for which foreign labour was used after 1942. In May 1942 45 per cent of the foreign civilian workers and 54 per cent of the prisoners of war were employed in agriculture. By May 1944 the bigger share was employed in industry; 45 per cent of the civilian workers and 44 per cent of the prisoners of war.[23] Their significance as a proportion of the active labour force is also shown in Table 25.

The recruitment of foreign labour began with the conquest of Poland and was a part of the plans for the dismemberment of that country and the projected reduction of its people to an agricultural way of life. After the subjugation of Czechoslovakia these questions had not been raised and indeed Czechs and Slovaks played little role in the foreign labour force in the Reich at any time. To what extent the occupation of Poland coincided with definite economic decisions taken in Germany about labour supply, to what extent the debate about the economic status of the Poles raised the question of their being brought to Germany in large numbers as agricultural workers, to what extent the migration was mainly a function of the extremely low level of employment in Poland caused by the dismemberment, are questions to which no satisfactory answer has yet been provided by research. But the 110,000 Polish workers who had already crossed the frontiers into Greater Germany in October 1939 were the first wave of a torrent to come from all parts of the continent.[24]

23. Homze, p. 235.
24. E. Seeber, *Zwangsarbeiter in der faschistischen Kriegswirtschaft* (Schriftenreihe des Instituts für Geschichte der europäischen Volksdemokratien no. 3), Deutscher Verlag der Wissenschaften, Berlin, 1964.

TABLE 25
NUMBER OF FOREIGN WORKERS EMPLOYED IN GERMANY ON 31 MAY, 1939–44,
AS A PERCENTAGE OF THE ACTIVE LABOUR FORCE (000)

Foreigners employed	1939 no.	1939 %	1940 no.	1940 %	1941 no.	1941 %	1942 no.	1942 %	1943 no.	1943 %	1944 no.	1944 %
Total	301	0·8	1,148	3·2	3,020	8·4	4,115	11·7	6,260	17·1	7,126	19·7
Agriculture	120	1·1	681	6·4	1,459	13·6	1,978	17·6	2,293	20·3	2,478	22·1
Industry	110	1·0	256	2·6	965	9·5	1,401	14·3	2,829	25·7	3,163	29·3
Handwork	29	0·5	108	2·6	310	7·7	296	8·5	430	12·7	537	16·4
Transport	16	0·7	35	1·8	97	4·5	171	7·7	289	12·6	407	17·4

SOURCE: U.S.S.B.S., *The Effects of Strategic Bombing on the German War Economy*, p. 206.

Poles constituted by far the majority of the foreign workers in May 1940. But of the total of 1·1 million foreigners a further element had been added in that 344,000 of them were prisoners of war, also mostly Polish. In its use of prisoners of war for labour in this way the German war economy established an important precedent by which it was to abide throughout the war. After the armistice with France about one million French prisoners of war were retained in Germany and until the end of 1943 most were used in the German labour force. Even this number was eclipsed by the numbers of prisoners of war taken on the Russian front, which has been estimated at 5·1 million. What happened to them is obscure. The largest number recorded as employed in Germany at any one time was the 594,000 at work in February 1944.[25] Very large numbers died of ill-treatment before they could make any real contribution. The highest number of prisoners of war of all nationalities recorded at work in Germany was 1·9 million in February 1944. During the course of the war the earlier inhibitions about using prisoners of war in manufacturing industry fell away. When it was finally decided to bring labour from Russia to Germany one motive was to permit the transfer of French prisoners of war to the more skilled employment for which they were often qualified. But prisoners of war were not a full substitute for civilian foreign labour because the legal and security implications of using them in armaments factories were drastic. Of the Polish prisoners of war 70 per cent still worked in agriculture in 1944 while the Russian prisoners of war were used mainly as miners. Even among the French prisoners more than half were used as agricultural labour.

In contrast, civilian foreign labour was increasingly used in armaments manufacture. It comprised 30 per cent of the labour force in the armaments industry in November 1944. Airframe factories, where the work was repetitive assembly-line operations, were suitable for the employment of foreign workers and 31 per cent of the labour force in all aircraft factories was foreign by that date. More than a quarter of the labour force in machine-building and in the chemical industry was also foreign.[26] Of these workers the greatest part arrived after the German victories in the west.

25. J. Billig, 'Le rôle des prisonniers de guerre dans l'économie du IIIe Reich', *R.d.g.m.*, no. 37, 1960.
26. H. Pfahlmann, *Fremdarbeiter und Kriegsgefangene in der deutschen*

The conditions which induced them to migrate were basically the same as in Poland, acute unemployment at home and high employment in Germany. At the end of 1940 there were already 220,000 workers from the western countries in the Reich. As employment improved in occupied lands the movement slowed down and at the start of October 1941 there were still less than 300,000 such workers in Germany. In the intervening period the main contribution had been made by German allies, particularly Italy from where 272,000 workers had come.[27] The demand for labour, as well as the wish to preserve a normal level of peacetime economy for the citizens of the Third Reich, even forced Hitler to relax his prejudices and permit the importation of Russian labour as early as July 1941. But this relaxation did not extend to the politically active (who were murdered), nor to 'Asiatics' and 'Mongols'. Later in the war Hitler conceived an abortive scheme for liberating German housewives for part-time work by importing Ukrainian domestic servants. They were required to be blond.

The use of foreign labour developed in this way because it was politically easier than implementing a comprehensive labour policy at home. The moment of decision did not have to be met until the failure of the *Blitzkrieg* strategy. But, however great the available foreign resources in spring 1942, they had from the first to be considered in relation to domestic labour resources. The result of this consideration was a systematic attempt to recruit foreign labour on a larger scale in conjunction with native labour. The appointment of Fritz Sauckel as Plenipotentiary-General for Labour systematized what had been up to that moment only a mixture of ad hoc decisions and the natural consequences of the slack economic conditions created in occupied territory. In a series of 'actions' Sauckel recruited labour by a mixture of incentives and sheer force from the whole continent. In the first four months of 1942 a further 1·6 million workers arrived and in the next six months one million more. Taking the year as a whole 80 per cent of the additional input of labour into the economy was foreign. It was impossible to sustain such a movement, both because of the opposition of other governments and because of the growing employment in the occupied economies. By the start of

Kriegswirtschaft 1939–1945, Beiträge zur Wehrforschung, vol. XVI/XVII, Wehr- und Wissen Verlagsgesellschaft, Darmstadt, 1968, pp. 232–3.
27. Homze, p. 57.

June 1943 a further 846,000 workers had arrived, but already a slowing down in the rate of departures was noticeable and by September in countries like France it had become almost impossible to obtain labour even by compulsion. Setting aside all considerations of rationality, Sauckel's plans for 1944 took no account of the new social and economic situation. He set about the task of acquiring a further 1·5 million Italians, one million French and 600,000 workers from the east.[28] By July, even with the use of the most brutal methods, only about 500,000 had been obtained. The economics of the military and police effort needed to obtain them did not bear too close an inquiry, to say nothing of the influence of such tactics on public opinion in the occupied countries nor the number of potential recruits to resistance forces whose minds were made up by seeing the alternative of deportation to Germany placed before them.

As the 'actions' continued the element of compulsion grew and what had started as a labour migration was now a deportation. Compulsion had always been present from the outset; outside the framework of legal migration many politically active Poles and Jews had been deported to Germany. The Sauckel-actions in the occupied territories were in fact the logical culmination of a policy of compulsory work for 'undesirables' which had begun in the German economy before the outbreak of war. It was only the need of the unemployed to find employment in Germany and the high numbers of prisoners of war available that prevented compulsion from becoming an important factor in labour migration at an earlier date. The extent to which compulsory work was economically useful, and the numbers of people involved, are very difficult to establish, but its existence profoundly influenced policy towards labour brought from the east.

Camps for political prisoners had always existed after the National Socialist takeover but until the beginning of internment for racial reasons in the late 1930s they played little part in the economy. From the start of large-scale internment, however, the intention was always to use the labour, in some degree, for production. The so-called concentration camps in which the prisoners were detained were under the control of the SS. which

28. A. S. Milward, 'French Labour and the German Economy, 1942–45: An Essay on the Nature of the Fascist New Order', in *Economic History Review*, no. 23, 1970.

regarded the inmates as its own labour supply, separate from the normal reserves in the economy. Because it was the germ of the society of the future, the SS. kept aloof from the politically compromised ministries running the war economy. Himmler's intention was to have the Waffen SS., the armed wing of the movement, equipped and supplied ultimately only from factories controlled by the SS. Those unfortunates imprisoned by the political police became in this way the foundation of a separate economic empire. The maximum number of people in concentration camps at any one time was 750,000 in January 1945. But of the total number who passed through such camps in the Nazi period one million died.[29] There was in fact a fundamental contradiction between the philosophy underlying the existence of the camps and the idea of using the labour detained in them productively. The camps were operated for inmates considered to belong to the 'anti-race' to instil into them a deep conviction of their unworthiness to live. The efforts made to reduce mortality in the camps in 1943 in order to increase the productive labour derived from them were useless in the face of these basic conceptions. The work was often silly and slipshod, badly performed by workers dying of hunger and maltreatment. Furthermore, the spirit which informed these camps spread into the foreign labour programme through the links created during the war by the use of some camps for even more sinister purposes. Two of them, Auschwitz and Majdanek, contained extermination units, for use in the 'final solution' to the Jewish problem. If those executions, together with those of political internees from foreign countries, are counted, about 3·2 million people died in concentration camps, while there were only rarely more than 500,000 actually at work. Once again the predominance of political dreams of the future over the realities of the economic present in Germany emerges with a fearful clarity.

The SS. itself managed several large concerns run on concentration-camp labour, notably the German Earth and Stone Works (D.E.S.T.), which developed also small assembly plants for bombs, rifles and aircraft parts, and the German Equipment Works (D.A.W.), which turned its hand to several armaments.[30]

29. J. Billig, *Les Camps de concentration dans l'économie du Reich Hitlérien*, Presses Universitaires de France, Paris, 1973, p. 99.
30. E. Georg, *Die wirtschaftlichen Unternehmungen der SS.* (Schriftenreihe

Even in 1944, however, while Sauckel was seizing workers from French factories producing for Germany for work on essentially the same production in German factories, the greater part of the labour force of D.E.S.T. was quarrying stones for the cities of the new Germany. Into this situation the Ministry of War Production forced a certain rationality by organizing the recruitment of concentration camp labour into war production factories. Even then the wages went to swell SS. funds. By 1945 slave labour of this kind had spread into many German industrial concerns.

In such an atmosphere it is hardly surprising that the laws governing workers from the east and the conditions in which they were housed and fed were such as to lower their economic usefulness. *Ostarbeiter* were worse paid and worse treated, had to wear distinguishing marks, and, even if skilled industrial workers, usually employed in repetitive drudgery. As the campaigns on the eastern front turned against Germany the status of these workers declined to the point where they were practically prisoners.

The productivity of labour

Such conditions raise the question of the relative productivity of the work force in the different economies. Foreign workers in Germany were less efficient than German workers, but there were great differences according to nationality. Speer's personal impression was that French workers and Russian women workers approached levels of native productivity while Dutch workers were barely half as productive. But later surveys indicated that the French workers were as indifferent to their work as others. The prevailing attitudes among all were 'a widespread psychological regression, i.e. a collapse of adult norms and standards in speech, behaviour and attitude, and a reversion to less mature patterns'.[31] I.G. Farben estimated the efficiency of newly trained foreign workers at about 70 per cent of German workers.[32]

der *Vierteljahrshefte für Zeitgeschichte*, no. 7), Deutsche Verlags-Anstalt, Stuttgart, 1962, p. 42 ff.

31. E. A. Shils, 'Social and Psychological Aspects of Displacement and Repatriation', in *Journal of Social Issues*, no. 2, 1946.

32. H. L. Ansbacher, 'Testing, Management and Reactions of Foreign Workers in Germany during World War II', in *American Psychologist*, no. 5, 1950.

Germany was the only economy where the use of either compulsory or foreign civilian labour was so important. But the direction of labour in the British economy rested on legal powers which were not too different from those governing the draft into the army. In Japan after 1939 about 1·6 million workers were drafted into war production plants. In many economies the labour force in particular occupations was not permitted to change jobs. In Britain Italian prisoners of war were brought from Africa and later from Italy for agricultural work. German prisoners of war were less used because they were considered a more dangerous security risk. At the end of the war 224,000 prisoners of war, including 131,000 Italians were at work in the British economy.[33] Irish workers were more numerous. Their number is not accurately known but after summer 1941 recruitment from the Republic of Ireland was on a semi-official basis. By the end of the war about 1·5 million Koreans were working in Japan. Over seven thousand prisoners of war were at work in Japanese coal-mines.[34]

Although extra inputs of labour into all economies were the main mechanism by which the extra production was obtained longer hours worked by the labour force and higher productivity per employee were also important. The average working week in the United States increased from thirty-eight to forty-five hours during the war. Increases of this order were almost universal and in most countries the work-day was lengthened to a point beyond which declining productivity would have set in. In the Soviet Union, and in 1944 in German aircraft factories, working weeks of over seventy hours were achieved for short periods by making special welfare arrangements in the factories. On the other hand, the use of shift working, which might have brought an increase in the productivity of capital, was much less well-developed. This was partly because, for technological reasons, the productivity gain was sometimes less than it might theoretically seem. Night work remained socially very unpopular everywhere. Three-shift working was usually only a feature of war production industries which were under heavy pressure to fulfil orders against time. Most significant of all, however, was the fact that capital was rarely the scarce factor; it was usually labour that was in short supply.

33. Parker, p. 348.
34. Cohen, p. 301.

Evidence of the increased productivity of labour in most industries during the war is abundant. New plant, economies of scale, pooling of information and the incentive to win the war played their part everywhere. The productivity of labour in the United States rose by about 25 per cent between 1939 and 1944. In the Soviet Union the average number of hours worked per month went up by 22 per cent in the first two years of the war but the contribution made by higher productivity was equally important. The increase in output per labour unit of time is estimated at 19 per cent in 1942 and at 7 per cent in 1943.[35] The United States War Production Board estimated that the improvement in labour productivity was responsible for about one third of the total increase in the output of finished goods in the period 1939–44, the rest of the increase being attributable to the increased input of productive factors.[36] Allowing for the exaggerations of enthusiasm the contribution made by better productivity was still a striking one. In spite of the use of foreign labour the productivity of labour in Germany rose by between 10 and 12 per cent during the war.[37] The evidence from armaments industries in other economies suggests a similar process at work there.

The part played in this higher productivity by the will to win was probably less than the real changes in methods of production which the war forced on all economies. At this point the economics of war bore directly on the daily lives of workers and managers alike. There was no time to allow working routines and social habits to adjust gradually to the implications of technological and organizational change, nor did governments readily allow firms to delay change in the interests of business safety. In Germany the rings and committees which controlled the allocation of raw materials to manufacturers were specifically enjoined to favour those manufacturers with the most efficient production process. Improvements in the productivity of labour and capital were therefore largely confined to industries where substantial technological and organizational changes could be made. Where this was impossible no amount of goodwill could improve the position.

35. Voznesenskii, p. 67.
36. United States, W.P.B., Document no. 27, Washington, D.C., 1945.
37. U.S.S.B.S., Overall Economic Effects Division, Special Paper no. 8, *Industrial Sales, Output and Productivity, Pre-war Area of Germany 1939–44*, Washington, D.C., 1946.

This may be seen from the wartime history of the coal-mining industry in all economies. The importance of coal for war production could scarcely be overestimated. It was still the most important source of energy for industrial production. But in no economy were any significant improvements in productivity obtained and in some there were falls in production. The experience everywhere was of constant labour troubles and of falling output per man employed and even per coal-face worker. In the inter-war period the picture had been quite different. The introduction of coal-cutting machines and mechanical picks had brought about rapid improvements in productivity. By 1939 the possibilities of further mechanization were exhausted and during the war the basic geological fact that as mines get older and deeper they become less productive asserted itself. Between the first quarter of 1939 and the last quarter of 1943 the quarterly output per wage-earner in British coal-mines declined by almost nine tons in spite of all efforts to reverse the trend.[38] Over the same period in France quarterly output per wage-earner fell by 6·6 tons and in Germany the Russian miners drafted into the mines did not succeed in reversing a similar falling trend. The slump in coal-mining after 1929 had left the industry everywhere with an ageing and a discontented labour force. In a period of full employment it was hard to get coal-miners although exemption from the armed forces was guaranteed almost everywhere. Men and boys were drafted down the pits in Britain, foreigners in Germany, Japan and the occupied countries. The bitter labour relations between companies and men of the inter-war period could not so easily be forgotten in a common patriotism, especially in a period when longer working hours and worse working conditions were demanded.[39] Wherever such a response was possible the industry was racked by strikes. Coal-miners' strikes accounted for about half of the total working days lost in Britain through strikes in 1943 and about two thirds of those lost in 1944.[40] The miners' strikes in 1941 in the United States wrecked

38. W. H. B. Court, *Coal*, H.M.S.O., London, 1951, p. 110.
39. E. Dejonghe, 'Problèmes sociaux dans les houillères du Nord et du Pas-de-Calais pendant la seconde guerre mondiale', in *Revue d'histoire moderne et contemporaine*, no. 18, 1971.
40. P. Inman, *Labour in the Munitions Industries*, H.M.S.O., London, 1957, p. 397.

the National Defense Mediation Board and produced a spate of local anti-union legislation. The most effective strikes in occupied Europe were those of miners in the Franco-Belgian coalfield in February, May and June 1941.

Where war stimulated an increase in output in older industries the potentiality for productivity improvement was limited, because the industry, like coal-mining, had passed that point on its growth curve where such improvements were likely. But improvement was not impossible. Sheet-metal beating, a skilled craft long established, was replaced by new automatic production methods because it could no longer respond to the higher demand. The history of the expansion of the shipbuilding industry in the First World War reveals few substantial improvements in productivity, but the use of welding and the manufacture of the standard 'Liberty Ship' in the Second World War indicates that war can sometimes shift productivity upwards even in an older industry. In this case, however, the introduction of welding in shipyards came up against the deeply prejudiced conservatism and entrenched procedures of both management and workers, which in Britain held back possible improvements in productivity. Riveting was neither rated nor paid as skilled labour outside Britain but the opposition of 'skilled' British riveters to welding first delayed the introduction of welding and then led to welders being also rated as skilled workers although the period of training was even shorter. Outside the older industries and crafts this sort of opposition was much less so that in spite of the varied origins of the labour force sustained improvements in labour productivity were an important aspect of the war.

Effects of the war on labour

It will have become clear in the foregoing discussion that in spite of the massive inputs of extra labour into the productive process, of the improved productivity of labour, and of the longer hours worked, the volume of war output would often not have been so large without substantial reductions in the number employed in other industries and other sectors of the economy. The male agricultural labour force in Japan between the ages of fifteen and forty fell by over one million during the war and the consequences of this both for agriculture and for the economy in general are discussed in Chapter 8. In Canada the labour force employed in industry increased by 900,000 between April 1939 and April 1944, the agricultural labour force decreased by 225,000. In June 1944 the number employed in industry in the United States was 8·3 million higher than the monthly average of 1939, the number employed in agriculture 1·3 million lower. Such shifts were by no means the same in all economies. In Britain, where the economic and strategic importance of agriculture was almost as high as armaments manufacture, the agricultural labour force rose slightly during the war. The number employed in textiles fell from one million in 1939 to 634,000 in 1945 and by 1948 had risen to only 835,000. In distributive trades the number employed fell from 2·89 million in 1939 to 1·96 million in 1945.[41] Employment in the textile industry in Japan fell from 1·5 million in October 1940 to 717,000 in February 1944.[42]

In spite of these movements between industries the general tendency everywhere was to an increase in employment in the manufacturing sector. The effect of this depended on the stage of development of the economy concerned. In mature economies like the United States and Britain where the long-run tendency was for the service sector to grow, this was a temporary movement. In rapidly developing economies like Japan and Canada it was a permanently effective acceleration of the development process. The same can be said of the shifts of employment within industry. The movement away from employment in the textile industries proved permanent in Britain and Japan because it was an acceleration of a long-term trend. But in the case of industries where employment expanded in the mature economies this was rarely permanent. The requirements of the armed forces in 1944 accounted for 66 per cent of the total manufacturing employment in the United Kingdom, 60 per cent in Canada and 59 per cent in the United States.[43] The increased demand for labour came principally from those industries directly concerned with military supply. The number employed in the aircraft industry in France rose from 82,300 in 1939 to 250,000 in June 1940. Employment in the machine-tool industry in the United Kingdom increased more

41. United Kingdom, Central Statistical Office, *Annual Abstract of Statistics*, no. 86, 1938–1948, p. 97.
42. Cohen, p. 299.
43. Saunders.

than threefold between 1935 and March 1943.[44] The corollary of such increases was a sharp decline in employment in other industries. This was most marked in Britain, where certain consumer-goods industries such as furniture and pottery were compulsorily rationalized to produce a set of standard products within the framework of the 'utility' scheme, and the quantity of those products was determined by the government as a part of the general rationing policy. New munitions factories were sited on the edge of towns where the labour force had before the war been heavily engaged in consumer-goods industries. In the Soviet Union employment in consumer-goods industries seems in some cases to have practically disappeared.

In spite of this extensive redistribution of labour and in spite of the possibilities of longer hours of work and higher productivity, labour shortages were a constant factor in the war years in all the major combatant economies. The reason why this was so was only rarely that there was an absolute shortage of labour. Given that Germany was able to import labour, it is probably fair to say that only in the United Kingdom was labour so absolutely scarce as to be the determinant factor in economic planning. In 1942 the 'manpower budget' became the main instrument in planning war production in the United Kingdom and after the end of that year future munitions production was based, not on estimated munitions demand, but on estimated future supplies of labour. Between 1935 and May 1940 the main problem was the shortage of skilled engineering workers. But the shortage was not at that stage an absolute one; there were still many engineering workers not in war production and as yet there had been little labour dilution. In the next two years the shortages of skilled labour became more acute and occupied the forefront of government attention. Behind them was developing a much more serious problem, an absolute shortage of unskilled labour. With more comprehensive and rational planning of manpower resources at the start of the war this could have been foreseen. It was revealed fully by the first attempt at comprehensive planning at the end of 1942. Labour at once became the decisive factor and as the overall size of the industrial labour force declined during the war, while the number employed in engineering and metals, explosives, chemicals and shipbuilding increased from 2·74

44. A. N. Hornby, *Factories and Plant*, H.M.S.O., London, 1958, p. 338.

million in June 1939 to 4·85 million in June 1943, the allocation of labour resources became a vital decision for the economy as a whole rather than for the particular sector involved.[45] The contraction of employment in industries which were not essential to the war effort, including export industries, had to be far more drastic than in the United States or Germany.

There was no comparable labour shortage in the United States until 1944. In that year for the first time the allocation of military contracts began to depend on whether labour was available locally. But difficulties in meeting the demand for skilled labour were always present there, as elsewhere. It is these problems which make the general assertion that only the United Kingdom had an absolute labour shortage a rather hollowly theoretical one. For war production it was essential that there should be sufficient labour of the right kind in the right place at the right time. It was inherent in the mechanism of war production that this would not be the case. The industries which expanded the most rapidly were often, like shipbuilding, aircraft, machine tools and electronics, industries in which the proportion of skilled to unskilled labour was exceptionally high. Of the proposed new intake of labour into the United States shipbuilding industry in 1940 it was estimated that over one third would be skilled labour and over one third semi-skilled.[46] Of the quarter of a million workers needed by the aircraft industry in 1941 an even higher proportion would consist of skilled labour.

It was not possible for economies to provide such a sudden increase in skilled labour at such short notice. All economies invested in accelerated training schemes and similar devices. In Britain 300,000 workers were trained in government training centres during the war.[47] But the only effective solution was what had come in the First World War to be called 'dilution' of labour. This consisted essentially of two processes. The first was that of breaking a skilled job down into its separate component parts so that some or each of the parts could be performed by unskilled or semi-skilled labour with the aid of new machines. The second

45. Inman, p. 5.
46. A. F. Hinrichs, 'The Defense Program and Labor Supply in the United States', in *Canadian Journal of Economics and Political Science*, no. 7, 1941.
47. Inman, p. 71.

process was that of upgrading workers to do jobs previously reserved for skilled employees. The labels attached to labour were only administrative and managerial tags and the actual degree of skill in a skilled job could vary enormously. It was not so much the actual skill of labour which was under attack as the status and pay which went with the label. But in a period when completely unskilled labour was able through full employment and long hours to obtain a substantial increase in money earnings considerations of status and pay differentials within any industry became very important. In those economies where labour retained some possibility of independent action without incurring ferocious penalties the shortage of skilled labour in the first two years of the productive effort was accompanied by labour disputes of an acute severity. Underlying these disputes was the improvement in the bargaining position of labour which the constantly rising demand tended to produce. Changes in the tempo and organization of work and in the status of workers had to be carried through at a time when the economic position of workers was passing from a weak one to a strong one.

In all economies except Germany money wages and earnings rose substantially above pre-war levels. Average weekly earnings in all industries in Britain rose by over 80 per cent between October 1938 and July 1944. In industries where the demand for labour was greater the increase in average earnings was also greater. It was over 90 per cent in metal industries, engineering and shipbuilding; in printing, where the opposite conditions prevailed, it was barely 50 per cent.[48] The same applied generally to other economies: workers even in industries where production was restricted received substantially higher earnings but there was also a substantial redistribution of earnings in favour of workers in those industries more directly associated with war output. Between January 1941 and July 1945 average weekly earnings in manufacturing industry in the United States rose by 70 per cent. In the Soviet Union average monthly earnings increased by 53 per cent between 1940 and 1944. In coal-mining and in the iron and steel industry the increase was about 90 per cent.[49] The calculation of earnings in Japan is a complicated matter, even more so than in

48. United Kingdom, Central Statistical Office, *Annual Abstract of Statistics, no. 86, 1938–1948*, H.M.S.O., London, 1949.
49. Voznesenskii, p. 73.

the Soviet Union, because of the issues of status, seniority and length of employment in the same firm of which wartime wage rates continued to take cognizance. However money wages are estimated to have more than doubled there during the war years. This makes the case of Germany unique, for both Japan and Germany had full employment in 1939 and yet Japanese wage rates continued to rise, while in Germany the increase was very slight. Between 1939 and 1944 wage rates in Germany rose only 1·8 per cent. Weekly earnings rose by only 9·6 per cent.[50] The rate of increase of hourly and weekly earnings fell after 1941 compared to the period 1932–41. Indeed after 1943 the evidence points to an actual decline in earnings.

The conversion of these figures into real wages is statistically very difficult and the figures given by so many authorities for wartime real wages ought to be accepted with less confidence than they are given. All governments instituted price and wage controls of fluctuating severity and effectiveness. In Japan there was no effective central control over wage rates and local wage rates varied considerably. The army escaped entirely from these controls and the high wage rates paid on military construction sites attracted labour from manufacturing industry in the immediate locality. A similar situation existed in Norway where the fishing industry, vital both to Norwegian and German food supply, was depleted of key labour by the high wages paid by the occupying forces for construction work on air strips and military camps. Only in Germany were these controls genuinely effective for the duration of the war. The difference created by National Socialist economic policy between price and wage levels there and levels prevailing elsewhere was exaggerated in the war years in spite of the occupation of so many other European territories. The bilateral trading agreements and the central clearing mechanism in Berlin were able to impose international trade prices on the occupied economies and also to insulate the German economy from the rampant inflation which occurred elsewhere in Europe.

But even in Germany it is difficult to arrive at a meaningful figure for real wages because of one price control policy which the German government shared with those of Britain and the United States. In all these countries statisticians had evolved a

50. G. Bry, *Wages in Germany 1871–1945*, National Bureau of Economic Research, Princeton University Press, Princeton, N.J., 1960, p. 239.

cost-of-living index based on pre-war consumption levels which was officially used to deflate money wages into real wages. In Britain the index also became a prime instrument of anti-inflationary policy. Government subsidies after 1941 were used to keep stable the price of the goods used in compiling the index. Thus those goods which comprised a typical pre-war shopping basket were stabilized in price, other goods were not. The cost-of-living index was similarly used in Germany and the United States as an aid in price control policy. Because patterns of consumption may have changed quite drastically during the war as a consequence of the shortages of goods, the reorientation of supply and the increases in earnings, the cost-of-living index tended to become only a vague guide to real wages. In Britain for example tobacco and alcohol were not rationed and part of the increased earnings was channelled into this form of consumption by a deliberate act of policy. The part of these goods in a typical working-class budget therefore grew as the part of basic foodstuffs, which were efficiently and drastically rationed in quantity and completely controlled in price, fell. The effect of full employment and higher earnings is always to change the pattern rather than simply increase the level of consumption and in a period when output of certain consumer goods was much restricted these changes of pattern were probably exaggerated.

Even allowing for these unavoidable statistical inaccuracies the evidence for an increase in real wages in the United States during the war can hardly be gainsaid. Average real weekly earnings in manufacturing industry in 1939 prices rose from $24 in 1939 to $36·72 at their peak in 1944. Real hourly earnings rose less, from 64 cents in 1939 at 1935–9 average prices to 81 cents in 1944, indicating that, as everywhere, overtime was a major item in increased earnings.[51] In Britain the situation was less clear. Real earnings showed a definite increase; real wage rates, however, rose more slowly than the cost-of-living index. In so far as there was an improvement in real earnings, therefore, it was attributable to longer hours of work.[52] In Germany, where there exists, thanks

51. United States, Department of Labor, Bureau of Labor Statistics, *War and Post-war Wages, Prices and Hours, 1914–23 and 1939–44*, Bulletin no. 852, Washington, D.C., 1945.

52. J. L. Nicholson, 'Employment and National Income during the War' in *Bulletin of the Oxford University of Statistics*, no. 7, 1945.

to the labours of Bry, an adjusted version of the inadequate official cost-of-living index, there was an insignificant increase in real weekly earnings between 1939 and 1941 and then a slight fall such that in 1944 the level of real weekly earnings was again at that of 1938.[53] The Soviet government pursued a consumption policy analogous to that of Britain by allowing prices on the free *kolkhoz* market to rise steeply while freezing the prices of basic and rationed foodstuffs. As a consequence prices of vegetables on the free markets rose more than twelvefold in the period 1940–43.[54] The money expenditures of the urban population were much greater than their money incomes in the first two years of the war; the reverse was probably true for the rural population. But the problem in estimating real wages is a greater one, not only because so much is obtained in the Soviet economy by the earner without recourse to his wage packet but because the practice which had developed in the 1930s of using this to provide extra incentives was extended during the war. Thus the rationing system was directly tied to the concept of real wages. It was ruthlessly biased in favour of workers who 'overfulfilled' the production norm set for their job. Production episodes, later to be copied in German aircraft factories in 1944, where workers worked a seventy-six-hour week while being fed and tended at the work-bench, were widespread. In such circumstances the concept of a real wage becomes even more distorted from its usual peacetime significance. Lastly, it has to be asked what could be bought for the increased real wage. In Britain the answer was tobacco and alcohol. Elsewhere, too, shortages diverted the increased earnings into whatever government policy made available, or into savings. In such circumstances the wartime gain in real wages was not comparable to a similar movement in peacetime.

This shift in economic bargaining power was not translated into any fundamental alteration in the balance of political power. In Britain, when the new government was formed in 1940, Ernest Bevin, Secretary of the Transport and General Workers' Union, the largest trade union, entered the government as Minister of Labour. In this capacity he was dealing with what became the most important area of the British war economy. His own mas-sive abilities made the role a more decisive one. It may be that

53. Bry, p. 264.
54. Voznesenskii, p. 76.

such drastic labour policies could only have been put into operation by a lifelong labour leader. His forbidding presence did not prevent a persistent increase in strike activity, but it did symbolize a political change of that gradual kind which British historians occasionally lapse into calling a revolution. By 1944 Bevin had developed an 'obsession' that wartime strikes were caused by Communists.[55] The same political steps in the United States were less successful. Sidney Hillmann, President of the Amalgamated Clothing Workers, was appointed as one of the seven original members of the National Defense Advisory Commission, which had the special task of monitoring labour disputes. In December 1940 he became one of the two Directors-General of the Office of Production Management. This, however, was the high-water mark of labour's personal political influence on the war economy. The eventual creation of the War Production Board, directed and staffed largely by businessmen, had as one of its causes the relative failure of the Office of Production Management. Once the War Production Board was established labour had no real say in the formulation of important economic decisions, except in the framework of the National War Labor Board, which handled only labour questions.

One reason why few trade union officers in either country acquired more political power during the war was that they were often great experts in a very narrow field, collective bargaining, and it was precisely in that field where they would be most compromised by taking government office. Where economic power could actually be taken and shared in the war years was in the day-to-day organization of production, for there were few arguments that could be raised against any set of managerial and organizational readjustments which would have made the production process run more smoothly. But in that area labour leaders were not so expert, nor, perhaps, sensitive enough to the opportunities which existed. Where the work force was involved in a common effort to produce, in order to beat what few British or United States workers could fail to perceive very clearly was their enemy, the involvement was generally of that spurious kind whose main features were ineffective works councils and a suggestion box. The War Production Board in March 1942 urged on

55. Parker, p. 471.

all contractors the formation of joint labour and management production committees, but like similar efforts in Britain they were publicity for an idea rather than the practical application of it.[56] The functions of the Joint Production Councils developed after 1942 in Britain were never properly defined. Whether any executive action was taken as a result of their decisions depended entirely on the management.

The main effort of the trade unions was therefore spent on collective bargaining, in a climate where the political circumstances of collective bargaining were likely to change all the time simply because of the emergency powers exercised by the government. In Britain strikes were illegal during the war; in the United States they were banned by mutual agreement and subject to fierce legal penalties. But the reality of the situation was that the demand for labour was exploited as a counterweight to the danger of government abusing its executive powers. Governments also were sensitive to the political realities and themselves provided many labour benefits out of their own executive power. In Britain the conditions of work were altered in many factories by a government-financed programme to install factory canteens; in general the social care of workers and an improvement in their conditions came to the forefront of labour policy. In the United States where employers were still fighting against the labour legislation of the 1930s the government was directly instrumental in enforcing the strict conditions of this legislation. The National Labor Relations Act (the Wagner Act) was used to force the most recalcitrant employers into accepting collective bargaining by the threat of withholding war contracts. The Committee on Fair Employment Practice heard evidence against employers practising racial discrimination and promoted full employment by finally absorbing into jobs the last of the employable unemployed – black women.

On the other hand the government of the United States also contrived to pass into law as vindictive a statute against labour as even that country could show. When the Kaiser shipyards signed an agreement recognizing the American Federation of Labor, which had practically no members there, and thus created a closed shop against the more militant Congress of Industrial

56. J. Seidman, *American Labor from Defense to Reconversion*, University of Chicago Press, 1953, p. 177 ff.

Organization the National Labor Relations Board enforced the laws on fair employment against them. This led only to a fatal weakening of its own position and to a breach of the Wagner Act by Congress. The War Labor Disputes Act of 1943 (The Smith–Connally Act) was a wholesale attack on collective bargaining and union organization. In the circumstances it was a futile piece of spiteful bravado by Congress but it remained waiting on the statute book for a time when the economic situation was less favourable to labour. In 1947 the Taft–Hartley Act took up its themes and the statutory position of trade unions became considerably worse than it had been in 1937.

These acts did not prevent an increase in union membership from 10·5 million to 14·7 million during the war and the virtual establishment of the collective bargaining process everywhere. In Britain membership of trade unions increased from 6·3 million in 1939 to 8·8 million in 1946. This increase of membership coincided with a more militant policy on matters of pay. There were more strikes in the United Kingdom and the United States during the war than in the 1930s. The response of government was to create mediation and arbitration machinery which involved it intimately in the collective bargaining process. When the Union of Automobile Workers closed down the River Rouge plant of the Ford company in spring 1941 they achieved their aims of recognition there partly through the military intervention of the government on the advice of the National Defense Mediation Board. In June the strikes at the North American Aviation plant at Inglewood, California, also resulted in the plant being directly taken over, but this time the striking workers, who were actually classified as essential, were drafted into the army. In practice, the National Defense Mediation Board came very close to compulsory arbitration. Their decision in the case of the North American Aviation Company, for example, was responsible for raising wage rates in all aircraft plants throughout the industry. The most dramatic example of government enforcement of this kind came with the takeover of the Federal Shipbuilding and Dry Dock Company, a subsidiary of United States Steel, for refusing to accept decisions arrived at in mediation. Union leaders were able to shelter in the lee of such eminently practical decisions from the wind of persecution which blew in their direction from Congress.

In such circumstances the temporary abandonment of 'the

right to strike' in both the United States and Britain could only be a conciliatory and tactical gesture which had little impact on the shop-floor members. When the Combined War Labor Board in the United States could not accept the principle that wages should always rise with the cost of living, on the grounds that labour should also make sacrifices, the machinery for settling wage disputes could be seen to be an instrument of the government's anti-inflation policy, a situation that was to become all too familiar and embarrassing in the post-war years. In the 'Little Steel' decision, accepted as the basis for future settlements, the Board turned down a pay increase while at the same time stating that the companies concerned were quite capable of paying what was demanded. At this point the labour members broke from the Board on the grounds that its decisions were against collective bargaining. In April 1943 the Board was obliged by executive order to apply the 'Little Steel' formula in all cases, thus practically removing its flexibility as a mediating agent. Neither in Britain nor the United States did the wartime administrative machinery ever provide, as far as most ordinary union members were concerned, an effective and unbiased substitute for the collective bargaining process. To use its new advantages the labour force had no alternative but to strike.

There were 3,000 strikes in the United States in 1942. In 1943 the number of man days lost through strikes increased threefold, to 13·5 million. In 1944 the actual number of strikes increased still further but involved far fewer workers; 8·7 million man days were lost. By mid August 9·6 million man days had been lost in 1945.[57] In Britain 1·5 million man days were lost in 1942, 1·8 million in 1943. Given the respective sizes of the two labour forces involved the figures are basically similar. They do not suggest that the labour force in either country felt that the war could be left to its own devices to remove economic and social distinctions.

The restrictions on freedom of action so bitterly debated in the Allied economies were not of course discussed on the Axis side. The years 1939 and 1940 saw the final disintegration of the Japanese labour movement. In its place emerged the Great Japan Patriotic Industrial Association sponsored by the government. It organized nationalist lectures in factories and interested itself in

57. Seidman, pp. 275–6.

welfare only in the most paternalistic way. Like the German Labour Front it was a reversal of the aims of the original trade unions it took over. In Germany, allowing for the success of price controls and the high level of labour imports the fall in real earnings was basically due to the hopeless political position of workers in the face of so brutal a rule. The history of labour movements in Germany in the National Socialist period leaves no loopholes for optimism. Economic circumstances were in their favour but they were stamped comprehensively out of existence.

Nevertheless the basic economic circumstances of a high and increasing demand for labour did change the conditions which had long prevailed for most employees in most industrial countries. These changes were effected more through the altered aspirations of labour than through substantial increases in real earnings. And these aspirations were recognized by governments both in Britain and the United States by declarations in 1944 that they would give the highest economic priority after the war to sustaining full employment. All economies were able to satisfy their labour requirements during the war, but the way in which they did so had profound consequences for the post-war world. The history of labour during the war was not simply the history of a factor of production, it was the history of most human beings involved in the war. The big changes in their economic circumstances which took place inevitably expressed themselves in important shifts in social aspirations and political opinions. And these went far towards making the post-war economic world a very different one from that of the 1930s.

8

War, Agriculture and Food

Ce n'est pas assez d'avoir des citoyens et de les protéger, il faut encore songer à leur subsistance; et pourvoir aux besoins publics, est une suite évidente de la volonté générale, et le troisième devoir essentiel du gouvernement. Le devoir n'est pas, comme on doit le sentir, de remplir les greniers des particuliers, et les dispenser du travail, mais de maintenir l'abondance tellement à leur portée, que pour l'acquérir le travail soit toujours nécessaire, et ne soit jamais inutile.

[It is not enough to have citizens and to protect them, it is also necessary to think about their sustenance; and to provide for the public needs follows obviously from the general will and is the third essential duty of government. It must be understood that this duty is not to fill the storehouses of private individuals and to exempt them from work, but to keep abundance just within their reach, such that, to acquire it, work is always necessary and never useless.]

Jean-Jacques Rousseau,
'Économie', in *L'Encyclopédie*, 1751

The economics of world food supply in war

Most economic theorists of war seem to have agreed on the fact that food is a good of unique strategic significance. Agriculture has always been considered as a sector of the economy having a special importance in wartime, and food is seldom treated as a commodity like any other commodity. Ultimately the reason for this seems to be that although it is possible to devise a correct strategy which economizes on, for example, steel or coal, by exploiting more fully some other commodity in more plentiful supply, food does not fall into this category to quite the same degree. The population must be fed and the troops fed better, otherwise the will to win will quickly disappear. And without food even resistance is impossible. It is frequently argued that for these reasons agricultural tariffs are justifiable even in the most liberal of peacetime economies because a country heavily dependent on foreign trade for its food supply is in an especially weak strategic position. Seventy per cent of the cash value of the food consumed in Britain in 1938 was imported, equivalent to twenty-three million tons of shipping space for food, fodder and fertilizer. Between 15 and 20 per cent of the calorific value of the annual pre-war food consumption of Japan was also imported. The danger that food might be impossible to obtain in a prolonged war did not threaten only combatants; it applied equally to a neutral country such as Switzerland. There, domestic food production was responsible for 55 per cent of annual food consumption between 1934 and 1938 on a calorific basis.[1] Switzerland has no direct access to the sea and was surrounded by combatants.

Even countries with a large agricultural sector are seldom self-sufficient in food in peacetime conditions. In the earliest stages of economic development human diet becomes differentiated enough to produce international trade in agricultural produce and households living on a staple food and little else begin to consume sugar or tea or coffee or other commodities whose production is very localized on the earth's surface. War produces disturbances in the normal channels of international trade in agricultural produce which affect the whole world. This is as true of a highly developed economy such as Switzerland, dependent on a high proportion of imported food, as of those less-developed economies whose export trade consists to a large degree of agricultural produce. In the first place attempts by the combatant powers to adjust domestic food production to the dictates of strategy produce immediate

1. J. Rosen, *Wartime Food Developments in Switzerland*, Stanford Food Research Institute, Paper no. 9, Stanford, 1946.

changes in the pattern of international trade in food. In the second place many kinds of strategy disrupt the lines of international commerce, by physically preventing trade to other combatant or even neutral powers, by causing a sudden increase in the demand for shipping space, or, as happened in both world wars, by sinking a substantial proportion of the world's merchant shipping. Thus a country with a highly efficient agriculture producing an enormous quantity and variety of food, like the United States, still found itself in a position where the restriction of food supply to consumers was unavoidable and countries like Australia or Argentina with substantial surpluses of food found themselves, in a period of rising world demand for food, having to restrict agricultural exports and occasionally having to destroy food. Britain had drastic meat rationing when large meat surpluses existed in Australia and Argentina and the United States introduced sugar rationing when there were sugar surpluses in the West Indies. Corn production was being increased in the United States when it was being burnt as fuel in Argentina. The shipping space available, when allocated to food, had to be allocated to foodstuffs less substitutable than meat and corn, and voyages had also to be decided on the availability of strategically valuable return cargoes.

It seems to have been assumed widely in 1939 that consumption of food would shrink to adjust to the inevitable restrictions on supply. What was not clearly foreseen was the increase in demand. The growing demand resulted from the higher level of employment, longer hours of work, higher earnings, the fact that the numerous members of the armed forces were usually better fed than they had been as civilians, and, in some cases, the severe restrictions on the availability of most other forms of consumption. These effects were not restricted to combatants; in neutral countries and in countries which were only nominally combatant, higher incomes arising from an increased world demand for goods had the same effect of increasing the demand for food. This increase in the demand for food occurred in 1939 in an international economy where agricultural prices had been at very low levels for a decade and where most primary producing countries had been unable to maintain a satisfactory level of capitalization in their agriculture. World agriculture was not well placed to respond to the sudden change in conditions. And these were exacerbated by changes in consumption brought about by the war. Most of the world's population was fed so meagrely in 1938 that even small increases in demand caused significant shifts in the consumption of particular foodstuffs; this tendency was further reinforced by the physical obstructions to foreign trade. The general history of food during the war was therefore one of growing demand, acute local food shortages and finally a severe shortage of food which cast a sombre shadow over the post-war years.

There were numerous devices by which this increased demand for food was prevented from having too disruptive an effect on the economic strategy of the combatant powers apart from the unavoidable physical controls imposed by shipping shortages. The one most commonly resorted to was rationing. But the term rationing covered several methods of food control whose basic principles were rather different, as no doubt was only to be expected in the wide variety of societies in which it was introduced. The effectiveness of food rationing does in fact depend very much on the nature of the society to which it is applied. Even in the society best constituted for an effective rationing system the problem of food supply in a strategic context remains an extremely complicated one. Biologically, only two questions matter. Is there enough food and is the diet adequately balanced? Within these requirements the possibilities of substitution are very large. But people's diets are in reality rigidly formed matters of custom. To what extent are foods in fact substitutable? The experience of the Second World War would suggest that given an efficient and coherent system of food control there is no special mystique adhering to food, and for the purposes of strategic analysis it may in fact be considered in most ways like any other commodity.

But a reservation is still necessary because the consumption of food cannot be deferred as can the consumption of most other goods. It is not necessary that food consumption should resemble its peacetime pattern but supply must be regular. Regularity of supply, efficiency of control, and the willingness of the population to accept substantial changes or reductions, or both, in its daily diet are all necessary; they imply a certain degree of social homogeneity, together with support for the government and its cause. The more society and government move away from these desiderata the more complicated do the strategic issues of food supply become. In the Second World War the two countries with seemingly the most impossible task with regard to organizing a regular food supply to their population, the United Kingdom and Switzerland, achieved the most remarkable success. By contrast, countries where the problems seemed far less ran into severe difficulties. In Bengal, although this was by no means solely the fault of the Indian government, a famine recalling in its horrors the famine conditions of the nineteenth century killed one and a half million people. In such a society the same economic rules did not govern the supply of food as governed it in Britain; not only were systems of food control and rationing essential but they had also to reflect the reality of the society they were applied to.

A fundamental consideration was the possibility of drastic alterations in the final composition of agricultural output, permitting a much greater level of food output, in terms of calories, from the same amount of production and imports. The most striking of these was the sharp increase in human food per unit of land obtained by growing it directly in the form of grain or vegetables instead of rearing livestock. The average pre-war diet in Britain derived about 37 per cent of its energy from livestock products, at the end of the war only 30 per cent. This represented a saving of as much as 20 per cent of the acreage needed to provide the civilian diet.[2] Beef cattle produce about 7 per cent of the energy and 10 per cent of the protein contained in the fodder which nourishes them. The percentages for sheep are comparable and for dairy cattle, pigs and fowl a little higher.[3] The use of the equivalent land unit for human rather than animal food therefore produces an enormous economy in land at the expense of a change of diet. Economies in land use can also be effected by changing the pattern of crops. The calorific yield per acre of potatoes, for example, is over twice that of wheat. But livestock can have advantages in the variety of food which they produce. Furthermore some cattle and many sheep graze on land which cannot be tilled. The problem of maximizing the calorific output of the available land was therefore a complex one involving adjustments in the balance of crops as well as conversion from livestock to arable farming.

2. K. A. H. Murray, *Agriculture*, H.M.S.O., London, 1955, p. 241.

3. M. Olson, jr, *The Economics of the Wartime Shortage. A History of British Food Supplies in the Napoleonic War and in World Wars I and II*, Duke University Press, Durham, N.C., 1963, p. 24.

Land was, of course, not always the scarcest factor. In the economies of some of the major combatants labour was at least as scarce. Where labour was the scarce factor the comparative advantages of various crops were different. For instance in the United Kingdom wheat provided two and a half times more food value per man hour of labour than potatoes. Dairy cows required roughly five times the amount of labour that pigs required to produce a comparable food value. A case could be made out for the argument that for the United Kingdom the scarcest factor was the available shipping space for imports, and that the maximum economy in the cubic capacity of the necessary imports was the major influence on the balance and pattern of domestic agricultural production. Although sugar beet, for example, gave an even higher calorific yield per acre than potatoes, to do so it required five times the volume of fertilizer that a grain crop grown for fodder required. One thousand cubic feet of shipping space devoted to sugar would have yielded 83,000 calories, to fats over 100,000 calories, to wheat 56,000 calories and to eggs in shell only 12,000 calories.[4]

Economic policy and its effects

The great regional diversity of agriculture makes it even more difficult to decide the weight which should be attached to all these considerations in formulating a strategy for agriculture in wartime. In some areas the aims may be achieved by encouraging conversion to arable farming but it may still be bad economics in other regions, even under wartime scarcity conditions. For this reason the control of agricultural policy in most countries during the war was in fact exercised on a regional and even a local level. But planning was always conceived on a national level, based on national needs and national statistics. Local organizations usually had national policy guidelines or even definite requirements to work towards as a goal and everywhere this proved to be a weakness. Regional policies were not built up into a national policy; a national policy was imposed on the regions. The overriding reason for this was the sense of national emergency in which such plans were formulated and the fact that they were conceived as an

4. ibid., p. 26.

aspect of national defence rather than of agricultural planning and policy *per se*. Agricultural policy was usually pragmatic, and was designed, sometimes at the last moment, to meet desperate circumstances and to try to solve immediate problems caused by the disruption of trade. Even so, in spite of its pragmatic nature, it revealed everywhere the closeness and the complexity of the connections between agriculture and wartime strategy. The British government planned to make 1943 the peak harvest of its agricultural plan because it was thought that in that year the Second Front would be opened and the demand for shipping be at its greatest.

But the experience of the war showed that the flexibility needed to overcome disruptions by greater flexibility of output and consumption existed only in the most developed economies with the most efficient agriculture. The United Kingdom, which appeared to have the most insuperable strategic problems in feeding its population was able to overcome them so triumphantly that the success of its agricultural policy during the war has become the yardstick by which other countries' efforts must be measured. The high level of development of the economy and the high level of agricultural productivity allowed shifts in production and consumption of foodstuffs. By contrast, economies like India or Egypt, which were practically self-sufficient in foodstuffs, had so low a level of consumption and agricultural efficiency that they were unable to cope with rising prices and shortages of imports such as fertilizers, and there the response to increasing world demand was falling production. Food was a substitutable commodity and the restructuring of agriculture a strategic possibility only where the agricultural sector of the economy was sufficiently capitalized and had a high enough level of productivity. Over most of the world agricultural economies were unable to cope with the difficulties caused by interruptions of supply and changes in markets, while the major combatants, who were responsible for these disruptions, were able to avoid the worst problems.

The effort to adjust in many countries led to long-term changes in agricultural policy; in Britain, for example, the economic situation of farmers and of the agricultural sector was completely altered by the war. But these long-term changes in national agricultural policy were no more striking than the way in which the war brought a full awareness of the international extent of the problem and the need for international food and agricultural policies. The Allied powers were forced at an early stage into a close collaboration in the use of shipping space, which effectively meant a certain amount of cooperation in their domestic agricultural policies; at times international considerations had necessarily to override the interests of national producers and consumers. The active military intervention of the Allied powers in other areas forced them to formulate international food policies in the Middle East and in India also. Such control and manipulation of the available food over so wide an area also forced them to take into close account the wishes of neutrals who might have great difficulties in obtaining supplies. Food supply therefore became an international issue from the start of the war. The food shortages at the end of the war made it even more so and a thin thread of international collaboration and cooperation survived unbroken from the Second World War through the Marshall Plan and the United Nations Food and Agriculture Organisation. The first administrative begetter of the international conferences in permanent session, such as O.E.E.C. and Nato, which developed after 1947, was the Anglo-American-Canadian Combined Food Board which sat in permanent session during the war.[5]

The foundation of agricultural policy in Britain was to make the country as independent of international supply as possible by ploughing up more land and sowing it with wheat, potatoes and animal fodder. The total area of tilled land increased by 66 per cent between 1939 and 1944 and only in 1945 was there any obvious slackening in this extraordinary transformation of agriculture. In 1943 meat output had fallen to 69 per cent of its 1938 level and wheat production had risen to 200 per cent above that of 1940. The success was not merely one of extending the tilled area, the yield per acre of most of the principal crops increased as the area over which they were cultivated was extended. The regular male labour force declined by a little over 5 per cent but the actual amount of labour employed in the agricultural sector may well have increased thanks to the use of a large force of specially recruited female labour and the more extensive use of schoolchildren and other types of casual labour. But even with the use of a less experienced labour force labour productivity per person increased.

5. E. Roll, *The Combined Food Board*, Food Research Institute Publications, Stanford University Press, 1956.

The total net output of calories from British agriculture rose from 14,700 million in 1938–9 to 28,100 million in 1943–4.[6] If the calculation is made on a gross rather than a net basis the success is perhaps more striking, because about 4,000 million of the annual pre-war calories depended on imported feeding stuffs, seeds and livestock whereas in 1943–4 only 1,000 million did. Not only was there an increase of over 40 per cent in that part of the annual British calorie consumption which was domestically produced but immense economies in shipping space were also made. The higher output of calories per unit of land or labour occasioned by the conversion from livestock to arable farming was mainly responsible for these results. The policy of ploughing more land became so central that every year the ploughing targets were revised upwards beyond the original plan. In fact the earlier plans were much less influential in dictating policy than the changes in the shipping position. The Import Programme of the Ministry of Food was originally 22·5 million tons annually. In the first year of the war it was cut to 20·5 million tons, in the second year to 14·5 million tons, and by early 1943 was running at a monthly level equivalent to 6 million tons a year.

In this sense agricultural policy was a successful response to an emergency situation and at the same time a demonstration that the agricultural sector of a highly developed economy is very flexible. There is no avoiding the time-limits which nature imposes on changes in agricultural output. An annual programme to plough an extra two million acres will only show results in a harvest eighteen months later. But in fact this is quite comparable to the time needed for basic capital investment in a new armaments or synthetic rubber factory to bear fruit. Indeed the comparison is slightly to the advantage of agriculture. But to measure the success of such a policy in terms of calorific output is to use the most favourable measure although also the most accurate one. Calories are not all a human being needs or desires even in wartime and the extent to which the response to the shipping emergency was always to maximize the calorific output will easily be seen from the drastic changes in total crop composition during the wartime period. The difficulties of estimating output by value are very great and are aggravated by wartime price policy. Nevertheless the net output by value of British agriculture at constant

6. Murray, p. 242.

1945–6 prices appears to have been 25 per cent above its 1936–7 level. If the value of the extra productive resources transferred to the agricultural sector is valued at 1945–6 prices there is still a net increase in output of 15 per cent by value.[7] What had to be sacrificed was, of course, variety.

The actual changes in the pattern of food production can be seen in Table 26. The increase in temporary grassland partly indicates the decision to switch the emphasis in livestock farming

TABLE 26
CHANGES IN THE AREA DEVOTED TO CROPS IN BRITAIN, 1939–44
(in thousands of acres)

	1939	1944
Wheat	1,766	3,220
Barley	1,013	1,973
Oats	2,427	3,656
Potatoes	704	1,417
Sugar beet	345	431
Total tilled area	8,813	14,548
Temporary grass	4,093	4,725
Total arable area	12,906	19,273
Permanent grass	18,773	11,735

SOURCE: E. Whetham, *British Farming, 1939–49*, Nelson, London, 1952, p. 141.

from the production of meat to the production of milk. The number of dairy cattle increased whereas the number of pigs was cut by 50 per cent and of chickens by 33 per cent. Until the close of the 1943 harvest the decline in grassland was continuous and rapid but by 1945 land was being laid down to temporary grass at the same rate as 'permanent' grassland was being ploughed up. The area of grassland per unit of livestock fell from 2·1 acres to 1·5 acres in spite of the drastic reductions in other animal feedstuffs caused by the shipping shortage and this in itself was one of the greatest gains in productivity. But set against that must be the fact that in spite of the increased numbers of dairy cattle milk production declined for the first three years of the war and the average milk yield per cow fell.

The area of crops other than grass grew by four million acres between 1939 and 1941, twice the increase for the whole of the

7. Olson, p. 126.

First World War. The plans for the specific use of this new land were altered drastically by the shipping shortage. Theoretically wheat was the most economical crop if it was desired to economize both on land and labour. But the sharp fall in imports at the start of the war took the Ministry of Agriculture by almost total surprise and the emphasis in the 1940 harvest had to be hurriedly switched to fodder crops. In fact, although the total acreage of barley and oats compared well with what it had been before the great decline in British grain farming began after 1873, when there was far more agricultural land available, and the total acreage of potatoes was greater than it had ever been, the total acreage of wheat only reached that level in 1943 and then declined to less than two thirds of it in 1945.

Policy and practice in countries in the same strategic situation as Britain had to be equally drastic and far-reaching. In Switzerland the Wahlen Plan actually aimed at self-sufficiency in agriculture for a country where agriculture was responsible for only 9 per cent of the national income, three quarters of the value of whose agricultural output was animal products, and which had almost as little pre-war arable land *per capita* as Britain. There had to be an active policy of changing the final composition of agricultural output. The domestic production of calories in 1944 was 17 per cent above its 1937 level, whereas imports of calories were only one quarter of that level.[8] The increase in domestic food production was thus far less than in Britain but the reduction in imports a drastic one. The total calorific consumption fell by 28 per cent between 1934-6 and the end of 1944, in spite of the increase in domestic output. The pre-war level of consumption in Switzerland had been amongst the highest in the world and obviously the pinch was not felt acutely enough for the Wahlen Plan to serve as more than a set of objectives to be partly attained. Nevertheless, by 1944 the country had made itself effectively self-sufficient in potatoes and eggs, supplied three quarters of its bread grains and one half of its consumption of vegetable fats and oils (a commodity which it had not produced at all before the war).

In the case of both Britain and Switzerland adjustments of this kind were possible because of the high level of agricultural efficiency, and because the population consumed a wide range of

8. Rosen, *Wartime Food Developments in Switzerland*, p. 60.

different foodstuffs before the war and acute or even absolute shortages of some of them could be and were accepted. In the case of the other major combatant dependent on food imports, Japan, the problem had a different dimension because the relative poverty of the population made it much more dependent on one staple foodstuff, rice. Almost fourteen million workers were employed in direct crop production, with rice overwhelmingly the most important crop. To make this fundamental difference more complete there was very little possibility of extending the cultivable area, which was already intensively exploited by small peasant farms. This intensive exploitation, furthermore, depended on one of the highest levels of fertilizer consumption in the world, approximately comparable to that of Germany in terms of fertilizer used per unit of arable land.[9] The raw materials from which this fertilizer was manufactured were almost all imported. Not only was the Japanese population dependent for its narrow range of staple foods on imported food, but domestic food production also depended on a high level of imports and there was very little scope for improving the efficiency of agriculture or for changing the composition of output.

Furthermore the same problems facing other combatants were present in even greater force in the Japanese situation. Her shipping losses, for example, were more severe than those of any other combatant. Of the total merchant shipping capacity available during the war, 88 per cent was sunk and losses soon exceeded building capacity. Because strategic planning had scouted all idea of a long war, stockpiles were smaller than in Britain or Switzerland. Everything depended on the success with which food imports could be obtained from the Co-Prosperity Sphere, and the catastrophic shipping losses, mostly inflicted by United States submarines, were a mortal blow to Japanese strategic planning.

Although rice was so important compared to all other foods, wheat, barley, potatoes and sweet potatoes could also be considered as staple crops and the output of these five items of consumption accounted for 90 per cent of domestic food production. Agricultural policy after 1932 was designed to produce self-sufficiency in wheat, but for the other staples, particularly rice, the answer was sought in the development of a 'colonial'

9. B. F. Johnston and others, *Japanese Food Management in World War II*, Food Research Institute Publications, Stanford University Press, 1953, p. 8.

empire. Both Korea and Formosa were developed by Japanese capital in the 1930s into large-scale rice producers for the Japanese market. The annual average production of rice in Japan between 1935 and 1938 was 9·5 million metric tons, the annual average level of imports two million metric tons. Korea was the largest supplier, usually providing slightly over one million metric tons. But in fact the effects of the war had already brought problems. The increasing level of Japanese military involvement in China from 1937 led to an expansion of Korean industrial production and an increase in farm incomes there. Since rice exports to Japan had been squeezed out of the Korean economy by the desperate need to export a cash crop, the result of increasing incomes there was to increase the domestic consumption of rice and by 1939 exports were beginning to fall. The level of Formosan rice exports had always been much lower and one purpose of Japanese strategy was to secure a regular and sufficient supply of rice from South-East Asia. As Table 27 indicates this aim no longer was achieved after 1942 when imports of South-East Asian rice fell steeply.

TABLE 27
DOMESTIC PRODUCTION AND IMPORTS OF RICE IN JAPAN, 1939–45
(in thousands of metric tons)

Rice year (Nov.–Oct.)	Domestic harvest	Total net imports	Net imports from South-East Asia	Imports from Korea	Imports from Formosa
1939–40	10,324	1,533	1,131	59	418
1940–41	9,108	2,115	1,457	496	295
1941–2	8,245	2,247	1,312	785	255
1942–3	9,999	990	720	0	246
1943–4	9,422	652	154	525	195
1944–5	8,784	201	0	213	23

SOURCE: Johnston, p. 136.

In the end, therefore, the general failure of Japanese strategy bore heavily on the food supply of the population, although in the short run the total available quantity of rice was considerably increased by the extension of military control in the Pacific. The short-term success is more noticeable when the size of Japanese armies in the occupied territories is considered. Military rations were about twice as high as civilian rations and the drop in exports from Formosa and Korea was partly due to the need to feed the soldiers. But the determination to solve the question of food supply within the terms of the initial strategy meant that the agricultural sector was ill-prepared for any change at all when that strategy failed. In 1941 a programme to extend the rice-growing area by 6,000 hectares and to reclaim a further 5,000 hectares of land was initiated and in August 1943 a more immediate programme along similar lines but designed to concentrate on more short-term results replaced it. One obvious policy, the only one to show real success, was to follow the European example and emphasize potato farming. The area devoted to rice cultivation fell from 3·15 million hectares in 1939 to 2·9 million hectares in 1945. The total area cultivated remained relatively unchanged so that rice was replaced by the other staples, barley and sweet and white potatoes. The area devoted to sweet potatoes rose from 245,000 hectares to 400,000 and to white potatoes from 164,000 hectares to 213,000.

The potato had the advantage in Japan in wartime, as elsewhere, of giving a very high calorific output per unit of land. But in addition its cultivation suffered less from the acute fertilizer shortages which developed. The yield per hectare of the other staple crops fell during the war, that of wheat and barley by as much as 20 per cent, but the potato was better able to cope with the situation. However, the energetic programme to change the composition of total food supply ran up against the growing labour shortage in agriculture. With so high a proportion of the population engaged in agriculture it was inevitable that the armed forces would draw heavily on that labour force. But the relatively high yields obtained in Japanese agriculture were a function of labour-intensive farming methods. And the heavy concentration on rice cultivation made this problem worse because of the great seasonal demand for labour when the rice plants are transplanted from seed beds. The total loss of labour to the agricultural sector through military service, including those killed, was about 1·9 million. To that should be added the 1·9 million men and women who had left agricultural for industrial employment by February 1944.[10] The increased use of temporary and female labour could

10. Johnston, p. 94 ff.

not compensate for such a drain, although by 1944 58·4 per cent of the agricultural labour force was female. This decline in labour spread its effects throughout the whole food economy. In the fishing industry, the shortage of fishermen was just as critical as naval warfare and the decline in the number of larger fishing boats, leading to a reduction in the total fish supply by 60 per cent. The labour shortage cannot be solely attributed to the adherence to the initial strategy of conquest, because the greatest period of expansion in the size of the armed forces came after 1943. The problems which would be posed by dependence on food imports had never been thoroughly considered because it had been too glibly assumed that they would be solved by conquest.

Agriculture under occupation

Before discussing the general questions which these contrasts raise it is necessary to compare the Japanese experience with that of Germany, whose agricultural sector was more akin in levels of development to that of Britain or Switzerland but whose strategy of conquest was fundamentally similar to that of Japan. The National Socialist party had inherited a situation in which German agriculture, which still employed 26 per cent of the labour force in 1939, closely approached the desired goal of self-sufficiency. But the strategy of territorial expansion meant that this goal had to be achieved for a larger area of Europe. Planning was not on a national but on a continental scale and where agricultural production did not suffice to meet the future needs of Greater Germany the solution was sought in a restructuring not of Germany's but of Europe's agriculture.

Within this continental setting the demands of German consumption itself were mainly for fruit, vegetables, eggs and fats. About half of the leguminous vegetables consumed were imported, one third of the eggs and one quarter of the fruit. The foundations of a continental policy which might provide a permanent basis, guaranteeing strategic safety, for German food supply were laid in the 1930s by the bilateral trading treaties and clearing agreements with the underdeveloped states of south-eastern Europe. By offering these countries a guaranteed long-term market for their agricultural exports at prices well above the prevailing international level Germany was offering them a chance to save themselves from the wreckage of the international economy, a chance which, despite all the dangers involved, they could not refuse, for exporting was their only source of capital for development. On the whole the agricultural exports of these countries coincided well with Germany's needs and the growing domination of their export trade by the German market was sustained throughout the war. But the foundations of the *Grossraumwirtschaft* were to be built in Russia. A study by the Institut für Konjunkturforschung in 1941 indicated that even with the complete use of all 'surpluses' from the Soviet Union, the remainder of Continental Europe would still only be self-sufficient if it could count on the same level of imports from north Africa as before the war.[11] What was meant by 'surplus' is an interesting question; on present evidence it appears that the German intention was to reduce the standard of food consumption in European Russia to a level scarcely sufficient to sustain human life and to leave the population of Siberia to fend for itself. The occupation of food deficiency countries like Belgium and Norway implied the most ruthless policy in a food-surplus country like the Soviet Union if the agriculture of German-controlled Europe was to be self-sufficient.

The potential of the Ukraine seems to have had an almost mystical significance and 'the black-soil area' to have been seen as the answer to all economic problems. The reality was far different. The early planning by the Reichs Ministry for the Occupied Eastern Territories counted on getting seven million metric tons of grain a year from the area. This target was not intended to be reached by wholly confiscatory methods. Germany's contribution was made up of steel ploughs, electric generators, tractors, livestock for breeding and agricultural 'advisers'.[12] Nevertheless the intention was to reduce drastically the standard of living of the inhabitants. The grain delivery quotas fixed by the German administration were about two thirds of the gross crop. The actual amount of grain obtained is difficult to estimate because so much of it went to feed the German army of occupation. The contribution of the amount coming into foreign

11. Milward, *The New Order*, p. 26.
12. K. Brandt and others, *The Management of Agriculture and Food in the German-occupied and other Areas of Fortress Europe*, Food Research Institute Publications, Stanford University Press, 1953, p. 142.

trade, rather than consumed on the spot by the German forces, fell far short of what had been planned. Net imports of wheat from Russia in 1941 and 1942 were 464·5 thousand tons, of rye 232·1 thousand tons, of barley 329·7 thousand tons and of oats 194·8 thousand tons.[13] The total net value of all food imports in the period from Russia was 197·9 million RM in 1940, 139·5 million RM in 1941, 281·2 million RM in 1942, and 132·4 million RM in 1943. Russia's total contribution to the agricultural economy of the *Grossraumwirtschaft* was less in these years than that of France or Denmark and less than the value of Italian food exports to Germany.

Dreams of agricultural exploitation in eastern Europe were dispelled by the decline in productivity of land and labour which was greater in eastern Europe than in the west. German food imports between 1936 and 1940 had come increasingly from south-eastern Europe. Food imports from France fell after 1933, from the Netherlands after 1934, and imports from Denmark no longer increased after 1936. This trend was reversed in 1940, as Table 28 shows, when food imports from Denmark and Italy rose to record heights. In the following year they were joined by food imports from France. Economic realities made western Europe the substitute for the dreams of agrarian empire in the east As far as Germany proper was concerned food imports were sufficient to avoid all serious problems until 1944–5. Only in that harvest year did the German grain harvest fall significantly below its pre-war level, while the total volume of imports of grain, plus grain supplied to German soldiers outside Germany, in 1942–3 and 1943–4 approached twice the level of a normal pre-war year. This still meant a drop in consumption because of the enormous number of foreign workers and prisoners of war in Germany but until the last year of the war the drop was not very marked. The more acute problems were experienced in meat supply where, because Germany had been practically self-sufficient in meat before the war, they had not been anticipated. But the same pressures which operated everywhere to reduce the number of livestock operated with equal force on Germany. The domestic output of meat fell from 3·4 million metric tons in 1938–9 to

13. K. Hunscha, Eidesstaatliches Gutachten, 'Die wirtschaftlichen und finanziellen Beziehungen Deutschlands zu den von ihm besetzten Ländern Kontinentaleuropas 1940–1944' (unpublished document).

TABLE 28
NET IMPORTS OF FOODSTUFFS INTO GERMANY, 1936–44, AND THE PART OF MAJOR SUPPLIERS BY VALUE (in millions of Reichsmarks)

Year	U.S.S.R.‖	south-eastern Europe*	Belgium-Luxemb'g†	Czecho-slovakia‡	Denmark	France	Italy	Nether-lands	Norway	Poland§	Spain	Sweden	Total imports current prices	Total imports constant 1925 prices
1936	4·0	285·9	11·6	4·6	134·2	0·5	114·8	83·1	43·7	21·8	54·7	21·7	1411·8	3034
1937	1·2	437·3	14·7	19·2	137·0	9·0	119·5	112·6	43·1	28·9	43·4	25·7	1956·3	3978
1938¶	1·9	451·1	15·4	14·9	143·4	19·6	135·2	97·6	39·3	43·9	33·6	31·8	2050·2	4367
1939	6·2	621·8	15·1	21·1	144·7	20·7	155·6	100·8	40·5	56·6	31·9	32·1	2326·6	4897
1940	6·3	598·1	11·3	19·0	157·4	6·2	158·0	86·6	26·3	32·5	61·7	26·6	1917·2	3966
1941	197·9	728·3	18·4	29·6	466·0	29·2	268·9	247·1	43·4	−30·4	9·0	16·6	2243·5	3679
1942	139·5	640·9	−60·2	25·5	376·1	141·6	467·1	297·0	49·2	−10·4	89·1	7·2	2407·5	3063
1943	281·2	866·7	4·1	16·9	232·4	321·6	455·4	228·1	50·4	86·0	81·5	2·1	2713·1	2662
1943	132·4	1034·3	−14·3	29·3	350·0	483·4	301·9	237·3	−74·8	103·0	119·1	−4·6	2720·5	2010
1944	0	n.a.	−33·2	44·9	458·0	328·5	215·6	109·6	39·7	15·2	n.a.	−3·0	2131·0	n.a.

SOURCE:
Sondernachweis der Aussenhandel Deutschlands; K. Hunscha, Eidesstaatliches Gutachten, 'Die wirtschaftlichen und finanziellen Beziehungen Deutschlands zu den von ihm besetzten Ländern Kontinentaleuropas, 1940–44' (unpublished document). Foodstuffs are defined according to the classification Ernährungswirtschaft in the new German trade classification of 1936. This includes all kinds of food and drink for human consumption, animal fodder, livestock and tobacco.
The author would like to thank Kim Sweeney for his statistical help with this table.
* Bulgaria, Greece, Hungary, Romania, Turkey, Yugoslavia.
† After 15 August 1940 Belgium only.
‡ After March 1939 Slovakia only.
§ From 1940 the 'General-Government of Poland'.
‖ In 1940 includes Estonia, Latvia, Lithuania. From 1942 to June 1943 is the Reichskommissariat Ostland plus Reichskommissariat Ukraine plus other occupied eastern territories.
¶ The top line includes the Sudetenland in Germany after October but excluds Austria. The bottom line includes Austria after April. The Protectorate of Bohemia and Moravia is counted as Germany from the start of October 1940.

1·8 million in 1942–3 and the rise in imports was far short of compensating for this. Outside the German frontiers, however, acute problems developed.

Unfortunately there is as yet no satisfactory study of Russian agriculture under the German occupation. One cause of Germany's failure there was the inability of an under-capitalized agricultural sector to respond in such drastic conditions to the demands made on it. But it is clear that to this must be added the total administrative confusion of the occupying power. And it is at this point that the interesting questions are left unanswered. In the 1930s the Communist state had radically reconstructed the agricultural sector on collectivist lines. The stage was already set for a profound clash of political ideas about the nature of human society to be fought out in terms of agricultural policy as collective agriculture came into collision with the National Socialist idea of a society of peasant freeholders.

There was, however, no attempt to break down the system of collective farming in the Soviet Union in the earlier periods of the occupation. Rather the occupiers seem to have wished to maintain the *kolkhoz* as an efficiently manageable farming unit. A mixed governmental and private corporation, Landbewirtschaftungs-Gesellschaft Ukraine, was set up, comparable to the Ostland corporation which managed land in Poland and France, but only a small amount of land was managed by it. A similar organization, Zentralhandelsgesellschaft Ost, bought and processed the produce of the *kolkhozy* but this was no more than a practical measure since with the collapse of Soviet control no satisfactory private trading mechanism existed to fill the gap. When some fundamental changes were finally introduced into the system it seems to have been only under the pressure of Russian military successes, and the changes planned were in fact part of a wider scheme of a gradual return to a wholly agrarian economy in Russia. The so-called 'New Agrarian Order', promulgated on 15 February 1942, constituted the *kolkhozy* as farms temporarily held in common cultivation but the individual dwelling house and the area around it as full private property, exempt from taxation. The *sovkhozy* and the tractor stations were transferred to the direct ownership of the German administration. All farms held in common which fulfilled their delivery obligations to the German authorities could apply to be divided into privately owned farms but if this change of status was granted they would have to join an agricultural society, Landbau Genossenschaft, under whose auspices they would still use the tractors and other farm machinery in common. This legislation was applied mainly in the Ukraine. Outside that region, in the northern Caucasus for example, the transition was sometimes made more abruptly, but such cases almost always involved livestock farming rather than grain farming areas. In the great grain region of the Ukraine all that happened was that the small private plots of the *kolkhozniki* were increased in size, the families were given strips of land in the fields to be sown privately and the meadow and pasture land were still effectively common property in spite of the change of legal status. About two thousand *kolkhozy* with about 380,000 families had their status changed in this way.

Setting aside all questions of social organization, the new arrangements did nothing to increase the efficiency of farming operations and much to reduce it. They were curiously reminiscent of the period after the abolition of serfdom in Russia and before the agricultural reforms associated with Stolypin. They fell far short of the institution of the peasant proprietary agriculture so much admired in National Socialist literature. The *kolkhoz* seemed to be under attack as much for its role as an instrument for the industrialization of Russian society as for any political or agricultural shortcomings it may have had. This was possibly no more than an expression of the powerful racial prejudices on which German policy was based. The occupying authorities required every *kolkhoz* to deliver in full all produce that was not actually required for food or animal fodder and thus left less scope for private initiative than had the Soviet administration. Ultimately, on 3 June 1943, the occupiers decreed the introduction of fully privately owned family farms, but by that time it was meaningless, for the German power in the east was in full retreat.

The longer-term plans which Germany had for Russian agriculture were, as elsewhere, expressed more in terms of trying to adapt the final composition of output to the needs of the new Europe. Hitler himself had had great hopes that Germany's reliance on expensive synthetic rubber might be ended by producing rubber on a large scale in Russia from the Russian dandelion (*kok-sagyz*) and a special factory was erected at Uman in the Ukraine for this purpose under the direct control of the SS.

It was permanently short of the necessary raw material. There were also plans to introduce food-processing plant more extensively. But the existing plant was so badly damaged in the initial Russian retreat that it was never fully restored during German rule. The annual supply of Russian grain for all German purposes. including consumption by the German forces in Russia, was equivalent to 14 per cent of Germany's own crop in the two harvest years of organized occupation. The cultivation of oil seeds in the southern Ukraine and elsewhere supplied in the same period about 6 per cent of Germany's total fat supply.

In eastern European areas where there was no fighting the output of most crops also fell so that the increased proportion of agricultural exports going to Germany was less useful to German food supply than pre-war planning had assumed. Shortage of capital, fertilizer and labour brought down the total output of grain in Hungary between 1940 and 1942 by 19·5 per cent, in Bulgaria by 24·8 per cent and in Romania by 31 per cent.[14] The specialized crops which German agricultural policy tried to encourage continued to develop until 1943. But after that date Bulgarian output of oil seeds and soya beans no longer increased and this was also true of fruit and tobacco. The area sown with industrial crops in Romania increased by about 50 per cent between 1940 and 1943 but not after that year. For most other crops, such as grain, the sown area was probably shrinking after 1941 and it is estimated that total output in agriculture in the smaller eastern European countries fell by about a quarter in the first four years of the war. It was here and in the Soviet Union that Europe's biggest proportionate losses of livestock took place. The number of cattle in Hungary, Poland, Romania and the territory which became East Germany fell from 19·4 million to 12 million over the course of the war and the number of pigs fell from 21·6 million to 9·5 million. Exports of meat and dairy produce to Germany from Romania and Bulgaria were lower than before the war.

In the western European economies, where agriculture proved better able to withstand the economic shocks of occupation, long-term planning was more decisive than in eastern Europe. In some

14. Calculated from the figures of S. Zagoroff, J. Vegh and A. Bilimovich, *The Agricultural Economy of the Danubian Countries, 1935–1945*, Food Research Institute Publications, Stanford University Press, Stanford, 1955.

ways the lines of policy were already defined by the economic facts of the situation. Over the continent as a whole the number of livestock had to be reduced and the area devoted to grain and potatoes increased. Such a policy meant a noticeable protein deficiency in many areas of the continent. But because of occupation and poor administration, livestock numbers in fact declined far more than was ever intended. Fodder was in shorter supply than foreseen and the widespread black market encouraged illicit slaughtering at good prices. By December 1941 the Danish pig herd was only 57 per cent its average size between 1934 and 1938.[15] The consumption of bread and potatoes on the continent had increased by about 10 per cent.[16] The cultivation of oil seeds also extended rapidly to fill the obvious gap in the continent's supply.

The way in which these long-term plans and changes operated in each occupied economy was not uniform. For example, the reduction in livestock in Norway was to be compensated by an increase in the number of sheep because they could be grazed on the natural terrain. There was also to be a long-term programme to extend the area of heathland which could be used for hill pasture.[17] Even so the agricultural planning for Norway was based on increasing the quantity of bread grain grown, a solution which had been rejected in pre-war Norwegian strategic planning on the grounds that not enough could be done in that direction to make an effective change in the situation.[18] The total area under the plough in Norway increased from an average of 280,000 hectares between 1934 and 1938 to 490,000 hectares in 1942. In almost every Norwegian county there was an extension of wheat and potato farming. After 1942 this trend stopped, so that for the period of the occupation as a whole the overall annual average growth in the area of arable land was less than in the 1930s. After 1941 the area devoted to bread grain was only sustained by a drastic fall in the area devoted to fodder grains. The 1944 agricultural plan proved utterly unrealizable, and this was

15. H. C. Farnsworth, *Livestock in Continental Europe during World War Two* (Food Research Institute Papers, no. 6), Stanford University Press, 1945.

16. E. Woermann, *Die europäische Ernährungswirtschaft in Zahlen*, Nova Acta Leopoldina, no. 14, Berlin, 1944.

17. Milward, *The Fascist Economy*, p. 77.

18. K. Evang, *Norway's Nutrition Problem*, London, 1942 (mimeographed).

an experience common to all the occupied countries. By autumn 1944 there were severe food shortages in Norway. These were exaggerated by the failure of the other parts of the agricultural programme. The number of pigs was reduced by about 30 per cent and of poultry by about 60 per cent, but the corresponding increase in the number of sheep did not materialize and the total sheep population stayed at about the same level during the war. The supply of feed was restricted to the extent foreseen, but the plans to convert heathland to pasture remained on paper after 1941.

In Denmark there was overt resistance to the policy of slaughtering livestock in order to increase the output of grain and vegetables and the German administration had to abandon all idea of coercion and fall back on price policy to achieve its ends. Although Danish food production increased during the war there was no significant increase in the area devoted to grain production. Total crop land was increased slightly at the expense of grassland and fallow but the only crops to show noticeable increases in cultivation were vegetables and oil seeds.[19] The shortage of animal feed led to the stock of poultry being halved and that of pigs reduced by 30 per cent. But after 1942 the dairy-cow population, which the Germans had reduced and hoped to reduce further, climbed back to its pre-war level.

In Belgium a similar attempt to increase grain and potato cultivation at the expense of fodder was also a failure. The acreage devoted to wheat and rye remained about the same level throughout the war and that utilized for potatoes had by 1944 fallen one third below its 1935 level. The area devoted to animal feed did fall greatly but the only significant increase in crop area, a small one, was in oil seeds. Bread-grain production was about 92 per cent of the pre-war level, potato production about 65 per cent of that level.

In France, the major supplier, the story was the same. The area of ploughed land may actually have fallen during the war and the area utilized for grain farming by 1943 was 1·4 million hectares below the average of 1935 to 1938.[20] In that year the wheat

19. Brandt, *Management*, p. 307.
20. M. Weinmann, *Die Landwirtschaft in Frankreich während des zweiten Weltkrieges unter dem Einfluss der deutschen Besatzungsmacht*, Veröffentlichungen des Instituts für Besatzungsfragen, no. 20, Tübingen, 1961, p. 79.

harvest was over one million metric tons below the annual average of 1935 to 1938 and the oats harvest showed an even greater decline. The potato harvest showed no significant increase over the inter-war years. The number of livestock fell very drastically; even the stock of sheep had fallen by one third by October 1943. Animal foodstuffs declined even more than grain. Almost alone in Europe the area of pasture increased, perhaps in an attempt to counterbalance the severe fodder shortages.[21] On almost every count German agricultural policy in France was a failure. That Germany was able to feed her armed forces there and at the same time secure such large food imports from France was a reflection of the extent to which food supply to the French population was restricted. The 1944 wheat harvest was 21 per cent below the average of the 1930s; the potato harvest never regained its 1940 level; the production of wine fell. Meat production fell by 8 per cent by 1943 and then was only maintained by slaughtering more animals and running down the stock; milk output had fallen by 30 per cent by the end of 1944.[22] The only success to be attributed to German policy was the increased area planted with oil seeds; it rose from 19,000 hectares in 1941 to 287,000 hectares in 1944.

Although western European agriculture was able to meet Germany's new demands, the legacy of the occupations was a sad one. And in the world food shortage after the war the damage done to European agriculture in the war years played an important part. The occupations left European agriculture in no state to meet the new demands after 1945. Only in the Netherlands and in Denmark did the output of food increase in the war years.

Behind the sweeping changes in Britain lay the implicit assumption that the new guaranteed support prices and firm markets would in some way be continued after the war in government policy. European farmers, on the other hand, realized after 1942 that the new marketing and price structures were only temporary because Germany would lose the war. The investment climate for European farmers was very poor. They were being asked to change their operations to meet what they perceived as only a temporary situation and patriotism combined with commercial wisdom to make them resist German pressures. Their reluctance

21. M. Cépède, *Agriculture et alimentation en France durant la IIe guerre mondiale*, Génin, Paris, 1961, p. 294.
22. ibid., *passim*.

to invest was greatly reinforced by the immediate economic difficulties which European agriculture experienced throughout the war.

Labour shortages in agriculture were acute. About one million French prisoners of war remained in Germany during the war and a large proportion of their number had been employed in agriculture before the war. Far more agricultural work was done by women, by the old and by the young. The subsequent labour draft by the occupying forces probably meant that by the end of 1944 the pre-war French agricultural labour force had decreased by about 400,000, most of them from the best age groups. Added to the shortage of labour were the shortages of fertilizers, machinery and horses. In France the quantity of both phosphoric and nitrogenous fertilizer used fell by more than half during the war. Phosphoric fertilizers had come from north Africa and it was impossible to find adequate shipping space for them after 1940; nitrogenous fertilizers were scarcer everywhere because nitrogen had other military uses in wartime. Norway, which manufactured nitrogenous fertilizer, was able to maintain her consumption but the import of phosphate products came to an almost complete halt. Everywhere there was less animal manure available and this accentuated these shortages. Farm machinery of all kinds fell into disrepair and because tractors were made in plant which could be switched fairly easily to tank production their supply was strictly rationed. Furthermore the acute fuel shortages meant that all petrol- and oil-driven machinery had to be used very sparingly. The Wehrmacht's demand for draught horses often prevented the use of this alternative source of power. In Norway the amount of wood provided for construction purposes in autumn 1944 fell directly as a result of Wehrmacht horse purchases. In France almost half a million horses were requisitioned for military purposes during the war. When it is borne in mind that there were only 35,000 tractors in service in the whole of France in 1939 the effect of these requisitions can easily be understood. Two firms in France were actually switched to tractor production in 1943 but their output was small and by 1944 only 28,000 tractors were in service there.[23]

The effect of fighting on agriculture needs no stress. Three

23. Cépède, p. 215.

European countries, the Soviet Union, Italy and Poland, suffered particularly from long-drawn-out military campaigns over large areas of agricultural land. In the Soviet Union the total sown area fell from 150·6 million hectares in 1940 to 113·8 million hectares in 1945. Since the shortages of all inputs meant that grain yields fell by half over the whole period this was too much to support; in the area under German control the population had to scavenge for food on the outskirts of cities. An index of livestock holdings shows a drop of 36 per cent over the war years. The burden of this destruction set severe difficulties for the Russian economy after the war. It was not until 1955 that gross agricultural production decisively passed its immediate pre-war level. Polish estimates indicate that 60 per cent of the livestock was lost, 25 per cent of the forests and 15 per cent of the agricultural buildings.

Equally severe was the loss of agricultural land to occupation forces, particularly for airfields. A survey carried out by the Reichskommissariat in Norway in 1943 revealed that the Wehrmacht had already confiscated 11,400 hectares of land, over half of it good agricultural land, in a country where only about 2 per cent of the land surface came into that category.[24] A long frontier zone of north-eastern France was taken over completely and the inhabitants forced to leave for varying periods. Between 5 and 7 per cent of the pre-war area in France was lost to cultivation by 1944.[25]

The attempts to extend the area of arable cultivation generally took place on marginal land and this, combined with the shortages, with the labour difficulties and with the reluctance to invest in a tottering system, meant reduced yields, at least in all those countries for which such figures exist. The average size of the remaining livestock also appears to have declined. The contrast with what happened in Britain is the more striking because there great quantities of marginal land were taken into cultivation with improved yields. The lower yields on the continent were the symptom of many problems. Shortages of labour, capital, and machinery meant that the land was no longer so well maintained. Drains were not cleared, ditches not dug, weeds not cleared. Shortages of materials led to a gradual deterioration of the land, particularly where specialized crops such as vegetables and vines were grown.

24. Milward, *The Fascist Economy*, p. 214.
25. Cépède, p. 293.

Farming techniques themselves virtually stagnated. The recovery was very slow. Beef, mutton and pork production in 1947 in France was still well below the 1939 level and this was also true of most other European countries. Similarly in France grain harvests in 1947 were on average still 5 per cent below the normal pre-war level allowing for climatic fluctuations.[26]

The food exporting countries

The European picture was repeated on a world scale for essentially the same reasons. The world's total food production in 1947-8 was 7 per cent below pre-war levels.[27] The disruptions meant that the areas with the least efficient agriculture suffered the biggest losses of output and they were usually the areas where people were hungriest. The increased demand for food in the wealthier countries led to a diminution in their food exports. In 1942, before the introduction of consumer rationing, *per capita* food consumption in the United States was 8 per cent above its average level of 1938-9 and this persisted after the war.[28] In other areas of the globe it had fallen by up to 30 per cent. Higher incomes not only stimulated greater demand for food, they also stimulated an upward movement in people's expectations, and this was encouraged in some countries by the improvement which equitable food-rationing systems brought to lower-income diets. But in a world of rising population and rising expectations the output of bread grains and rice per person was reduced by the war below the already inadequate level of the 1930s. The problems of strategic planning and agricultural cooperation during the war and of the world shortage of food after the war fell on those countries with an export trade in agricultural produce. They were economically and psychologically quite unprepared.

In the United States and Australia it was assumed that the coming of a world war would only intensify the severe agricultural problems of the 1930s. It was thought that exporting would be even more difficult because of armed combat and the attempts of

26. Cépède, p. 311.
27. United Nations, Dept. of Economic Affairs, *Salient Features of the World Economic Situation 1945-47*, New York, 1948.
28. L. H. Bean, 'Agricultural Capacity', in J. F. Dewhurst and others, *America's Needs and Resources*, Twentieth Century Fund, New York, 1947.

countries to grow their own food, that capital and labour would be diverted to industrial production and that those producers depending on foreign markets for their income would have difficulty in surviving. Far from preparing to increase production farmers were preparing for mere survival and beseeching government help. The main economic concern of the Australian government at the start of the war was to try to persuade the United Kingdom to guarantee long-term purchases of fruit, wool and other agricultural produce in advance at pre-war prices. Thus emerged one of the war's greatest ironies, that countries which in 1939 were trying to restrict agricultural production were by 1942 introducing food rationing.

It was not only pessimism that was inherited from the 1930s but institutional arrangements designed for a period of stagnating production. Most of the food exporting countries had evolved complicated links between government and agriculture, one of whose main purposes was to keep up agricultural incomes. In the United States the agricultural programme of the New Deal had preserved the balance of the different crops, sometimes for political reasons, and had been based on the idea that returns to farmers should be distributed in proportion to production costs. It had also concentrated on restricting output as a means of increasing farm incomes. The advent of a world war, far from changing this atmosphere of restriction, strengthened it. In fact the events of 1940 tended to justify this pessimism. The export of grain, fruit and tobacco was 30 per cent below the level of the previous year and large surpluses of cotton, wheat, maize and tobacco accumulated. Rural poverty and unemployment worsened and as far as agriculture was concerned the world war seemed a serious threat to the New Deal. Agricultural pricing policy for the year 1941 was aimed at further restrictions in output although employment in the defence industries was rising rapidly in 1941. By the 1941 harvest this was reflected in a noticeable increase in the domestic demand for food. The export outlook, however, was still thought of as unfavourable for the whole war, in spite of the signing of the Lend-Lease Acts in spring 1941. Only at the end of 1941 was the 'Food for Freedom' drive translated into increased production goals for 1942.

Even at this stage apprehension about the post-war situation when lend-lease would have terminated meant firm opposition to going beyond immediate demands on production. The armed forces added to this demand in America by their concentration on the immediate accumulation of stockpiles of food at all strategic points where they might be needed. Added to this came the quite unexpected increase in demand from abroad to which the Lend-Lease Acts permitted full expression without financial impediment. By 1943 food exports were about 14 per cent of the total farm output, the highest level since the years 1916 to 1920. The main constituents of this demand were the food shortages of three allied powers. That in Britain has already been discussed. Within the constraints imposed by shipping space it could be eased after summer 1941 by the import of American food. In the Soviet Union two thirds of pre-war food production had come from the area controlled by the Germans at the maximum extent of German occupation. Even basic bread and potato rations could sometimes not be met and in the allocation of shipping space to Russia food received the same priority as tanks and planes. In China about 40 per cent of the food-producing area had been overrun by Japan. The breakdown of administration and normal marketing arrangements made farmers within the unoccupied area concentrate increasingly on producing merely for their own needs and the volume of production there fell. These considerations led directly to the assimilation of American agriculture into an overall strategic plan, which at first served purely the national interest and eventually came to serve the interests of a general Allied strategic plan. Specialization of function within this international plan made American agriculture into a vital strategic strength of all the Allied powers and inexorably involved the United States in the world's food problems, a situation from which she was unable to withdraw after 1945.

When all these demands were put together, as they were in planning for the harvest year 1943–4, American agricultural production no longer had the problem of disposing of its surpluses. Instead it had significant deficits in important areas: milk and other dairy products, potatoes, fruits and fruit juice and sugar.[29] The United States did not escape the difficulties in importing which all other combatants experienced; indeed absolute economy and precision in the use of shipping space were unavoidable. It

29. B. Gold, *Wartime Economic Planning in Agriculture. A Study in the Allocation of Resources*, Columbia University Press, 1949, p. 49 ff.

was finally, but reluctantly, accepted that military strategy demanded that the high level of food consumption in America be cut back and controlled. Not only did the climate change to one of emphasis on increasing rather than restricting production but the international involvements of American strategy also meant that, just as in countries faced with food shortages, there should be considerable changes in what was actually produced.

In the first place import deficiencies were particularly in two fields, fats and sugar. Japan now controlled areas which had been the source of about one third of the fats and oils entering international trade. Sugar was available, but only at the cost of diverting shipping from more immediate priority purposes. The demand from abroad was expressed in terms of particular items: meats, dairy products, eggs, and processed fruit and vegetables. To some extent the demand for particular foods was determined by the attempts to economize on shipping capacity. Without loss of calorific value fruit and vegetables could be dried, eggs could be dried and powdered, meat could be canned and milk condensed and canned. All these processes represented enormous savings in shipping space, but by no means all of them had been part of America's pre-war export trade. How successfully did American agriculture cope with this quite new situation?

The index of gross farm production compiled by Barton and Cooper shows an increase from 100 in 1940 to 116 in 1944 and that of farm output for human use a slightly larger increase.[30] The increase in animals and animal products is greater than that of crop and pasture production, indicating that there was a response to the demand for particular products coming from abroad. On the other hand almost the whole of the gain in gross farm production had been achieved by 1942 when the index stood at 114. After that year the upward trend is barely noticeable. Total agricultural production in fact fell short of the requirements of Allied strategy. It has usually been considered that it also fell short of what would have been feasible. The total increase by 1944 was about half of what had been thought practical and urgent by the Department of Agriculture. One reason was the survival of pre-war attitudes in the farming community. Another was the difficulty of asserting some universally effective control over crop

30. G. T. Barton and M. R. Cooper, *Farm Production in War and Peace*, United States, Dept. of Agriculture, G.P.O., Washington, D.C., 1947.

planning. Before a purposeful administrative machinery, with sufficient powers to do more than advise, had been evolved in the Department of Agriculture, farmers responded to changes in price levels occasioned by internal demand or to the short-term needs of the lend-lease programmes. The result was that by the end of 1943 the value of total livestock products had increased by more than twice that of crop and pasture production. Because of the eighteen-month delay before any agricultural planning matures it proved very difficult to right this imbalance in the last two years of the war. From 1941 to 1943 production of some badly needed commodities, such as sugar and fruits, actually declined, as did grain crops for food. The clearest aspect of this failure was that the total acreage devoted to the crops it was desired to encourage scarcely increased. Indeed by 1945 it had actually shrunk for thirteen out of fifteen of them, compared to 1940.

What was at fault was the planning machinery for directing agriculture into new opportunities. The area cultivated and the productivity per acre both shot upwards. On the other hand the area planted to crops under the war food programme for 1942-3, 364 million acres, was still ten million acres less than in the previous record year of 1932, when restrictions had first been implemented. The yield per harvested acre of the major crops rose by 13 per cent between 1940 and 1942 and by the same amount again by 1945. Record maize yields per acre were obtained in 1941, 1942 and 1944, and the average yield of fruit crops persistently rose to new high levels. As in Britain renewed government interest and buoyant markets stimulated investment in a sector which before the war had been sadly neglected. Combined with this change the effects of the labour draft led to a rapid increase in mechanization, of which the consequence was a sharp rise in productivity. Between 1940 and 1943 the number of tractors on farms increased from 1·5 to 1·9 million; the increase alone was about ten times the total number of tractors at work in France. Although the planning mechanism was so defective many of the serious consequences of this were avoided because of the great reserves available, which in many cases could be brought to bear without government intervention.

The same attitudes prevailed in Australia at the beginning of the war as in the United States, except that the situation in

Australia required some international consideration as early as 1937 because of Australia's dependence on the British market for her food and wool exports. Wool exports were guaranteed, within the limitations of shipping, by a British government contract to purchase the whole clip for the duration of the war. It was the aim of the government to come as near as possible to this ideal arrangement for the other agricultural exports: meat, butter, cheese, eggs, fruit and sugar.[31] The emphasis was wholly on safeguarding the export trade in primary produce; there was no conception that increases in food production might be necessary. It was even later than in the United States, not in fact until 1942, that the reversal of attitudes came. In the harvest year 1940–41 half the crop of apples and pears was allowed to rot on the trees and compensation paid to the growers. In April 1942 the Australian Food Council surveyed the position comprehensively for the first time and by July it became clear that production must be increased and, as in America, definite production goals established.

The reasons were fundamentally the same: an increased level of industrial employment at higher incomes, military demand, including that of the 100,000 United States troops in Australia and New Guinea by the end of 1942, and the realization that the Allied strategy had to be an international one in which Australian agriculture, like that of the United States, had a specialized function. In 1943 agriculture could no longer meet demand – including the still increasing demand from American forces in the Pacific – and it was recognized that food production and munitions production were equally important in the economy. In October 1943 the Australian armed forces were, by general consent, reduced in size in order to free labour for the agricultural sector. The Australian government was not prepared to extend this international cooperation beyond the end of the war – in common with the other powers – and would not increase the acreage sown to wheat in 1943 in order to provide for post-war relief. But within the terms of Allied strategy it accepted that the pattern of Australian agriculture must change.

These new policies had very little success and it is instructive to compare the results obtained in Australia with those in the United States. The acreage of priority crops increased, that of

31. S. J. Butlin, *War Economy 1939–42*, Australian War Memorial, Canberra, 1955, p. 30 ff.

potatoes by over 150 per cent between 1942 and 1945. But the yield of many crops fell drastically. The average wheat yield of 16·8 bushels per acre in the harvest year 1942–3 was only 6·2 bushels per acre in 1944–5. Production increases over the whole period were therefore the exception rather than the rule. Sugar production declined from 800,000 tons annually before the war to 524,000 tons in 1943–4. The stock of dairy cattle and the output of milk both fell, contrary to the intentions of government policy. Manpower was seriously short because in the early stages of the war it had been assumed that agricultural labour would be the most dispensable in wartime. Between July 1939 and July 1941 the rural labour force fell by 30 per cent. This drop was too great to be compensated for by an increase in other inputs, given the nature of the Australian economy. The proviso is important for, theoretically, the agricultural labour force could have been greatly reduced in wartime. Australia depended for its tractors on imports from the United States and the average level of imports, 7,000 annually in the years before the war, had fallen to only 2,700 by 1943–4. Whereas the total number of tractors employed in the United States between 1939 and 1946 rose by 11 per cent in Australia it rose by only 6 per cent. Japan controlled the Pacific areas from which most Australian fertilizer had come. An index of fertilizer use in the United States which showed an average of 100 for the period 1937–9 stood at 173 for 1945. In Australia an index with a similar base would have fallen to 48 by 1944.[32] The reserves of a richer and more complex economy were lacking and it was more difficult than in the United States to remedy the mistakes of the early period of the war.

Many of Australia's problems came from being an active combatant in the war rather than from shipping shortages. Other food exporters like Argentina, on the other hand, were affected principally by the lack of shipping; the registered tonnage entering her ports in 1942 was only 70 per cent of the average level of the years 1934–8. Since practically the whole of her exports were agricultural produce considerable changes were necessary to sustain them. Bulky cargoes like wheat and maize were no longer carried and meat was increasingly dehydrated, boned or canned

32. J. G. Crawford and others, *Wartime Agriculture in Australia and New Zealand 1939–1950*, Food Research Institute Publications, Stanford University Press, 1954, p. 104.

as corned beef. As in Australia a range of food-processing industries was developed by the rationing of shipping space.[33] Oil seeds
were increasingly exported as vegetable oil. Maize fell from 21 per
cent of exports to one per cent by 1941. It was used instead for
feeding pigs for meat processing and the number of pigs in the
country doubled between 1937 and 1945. By shifts of this kind
Argentina was able to maintain the value if not the volume of her
export trade and remained an important supplier to the United
Kingdom and the United States.

The Allied powers were prepared to adopt an internationalist
stance in this case because it was in their own post-war interests
and, in spite of the disruption, the circumstances did promote
some development in the Argentinian economy. In the case of
primary producers with nothing to offer as cargo, dependence on
Allied shipping controls was absolute.

Allied troops in Egypt and Iran consumed substantially more
than the inhabitants and their arrival strained the food resources
of these countries to the utmost. Where diets were in any case
seldom much above starvation level the disruption of the international foodstuffs trade was in itself a dire threat to human
existence, without the arrival of soldiers from elsewhere. Nor did
such countries have their own shipping resources for food
imports. Their imports had been carried in the ships of the fighting
powers, which were now fully deployed for other purposes. The
Australian government sought a solution by initiating its own
shipbuilding programmes, but this was far beyond Middle
Eastern economies. International shipping control thus became
international food control. Its origins lay in the Anglo-American
Food Committee, which had been formed because of the British
demand for American food, at a time when the American demand
was also rising. Canada became a member of the same Committee because it was in the dollar area and because the Canadian
Mutual Aid Act, being complementary to the Lend-Lease Acts,
tied Canadian production policy closely to that of the United
States. The Combined Food Board of the three powers became a
planning body whose ultimate responsibilities soon stretched well
beyond the Atlantic. It was not merely a method by which Britain
obtained influence over the allocation of American food; it was a

33. P. P. Egoroff, *Argentina's Agricultural Exports During World War II*,
Food Research Institute Papers no. 8, Stanford University Press, 1949.

permanent body in which problems common to all its members could be solved. Both Britain and the United States for example had a high demand for canned meat from South America and for fats and oils from elsewhere. Military events brought Australia, and also New Zealand, into a similar planning framework. When the Italian army invaded Greece in October 1940 the British government guaranteed economic aid to the Greeks. Greece imported annually about 500,000 tons of wheat and in all demands for aid foodstuffs figured prominently. They could only be supplied by diverting foodstuffs intended for Palestine, Egypt and Turkey. The consequence was a committee to coordinate food supply between these countries, which eventually became the Middle East Supply Centre. After the American entry into the war this committee also became in many ways a joint enterprise because of the American military interests in the area. It had a general, although sometimes vague, responsibility for supply to Egypt, the Sudan, Cyprus, Palestine, Syria, Lebanon, Iraq, Iran, Libya, Transjordan, and Saudi Arabia. But even with boundaries so widely drawn it could not solve its problems without extensive reference to events in India, Ethiopia and Somaliland as well.[34]

The links between the Centre and Anglo-American planning were very strong. As early as June 1941 it was decided that many essential supplies for the area would be shipped directly from the United States because American ships, being neutral, could still sail to Red Sea ports. Eventually the Centre became a regional branch of the Combined Boards, its main function being to restrict and control American exports to the area. These exports fetched an increasingly high price as incomes there rose. Although there was such diversity between the countries with which the Centre dealt, the centralization of supply and the attempt to persuade all the countries involved to adopt at least some elements of a common food policy were implicit in the situation. Sugar was rationed over almost the whole area and several other commodities were rationed by national governments with varying degrees of success, in response to pressure from the Allies or other neighbouring states.

But very little progress was made in changing the agriculture of the area. It was too poorly equipped to respond to rising prices

34. E. M. H. Lloyd, *Food and Inflation in the Middle East 1940–45*, Food Research Institute Publications, Stanford University Press, 1956, p. 15 ff.

or to planning of a kind which necessarily had to be very general. The level of consumption was so low that rising incomes on peasant farms often resulted in a greater level of consumption on the farm itself and a smaller total quantity of food reaching the market. The shortages of consumer goods of all kinds increased this tendency because in normal times basic foodstuffs were marketed in order to obtain such goods. In order to mop up increasing income and also to provide peasants with a motive for selling their grain the British government shipped out gold sovereigns and ingots to the Middle East as well as to India and sold them on the open market. There must, of course, have been very few commodities whose value in terms of size better suited the stringent restrictions on shipping space! In order to counter the rice shortage in Ceylon the prices offered for rice in Egypt were raised relative to those offered for cotton. The output of rice increased by 35 per cent. But the volume of exports rose only by 5 per cent; the rest of the increased output went towards improving *per capita* consumption in Egypt itself.[35]

It was precisely this problem that lay at the root of the worst food disaster of the war. It was all too likely that this complicated re-ordering of the international trade in foodstuffs and the changes taking place so rapidly in national economies, in upsetting the delicate mechanism of the world's food economy, would strike at its most vulnerable spot, India. Of the seventy million tons of food grains grown annually in India only twenty-one million found their way to market. The lives of the urban population depended on their doing so. About one million tons of rice were imported annually from Burma. When the Japanese occupation of Burma cut off this supply it was more than ever necessary to make certain that the domestic supply reached the markets. In spite of the disruption of domestic trade caused by the widespread fears of Japanese invasion, the British administration in India seems to have remained faithful to the *laissez-faire* attitudes which the British government had adhered to in Ireland in similar circumstances a century earlier. The consequences of such administrative callousness were equally brutal. From March 1943 famine prices were paid for rice in Calcutta. Other Indian provinces refused to provide food in short supply to relieve the

35. ibid., p. 250.

approaching famine and the British government allowed 'unrestricted free trade' in rice throughout the Eastern Region. In this way higher prices spread to other provinces which had tried to contain the famine without doing anything to alleviate distress in the seat of the disaster, Bengal.[36] The requisitioning of boats to combat the threatened invasion impeded relief food distribution. The local government was no better able to cope than the British administration. Unhappy droves of refugees came into the area fleeing from the front. Local resistance had already been sapped by a severe cyclone in October 1942. It has been estimated that the Bengal famine was responsible for the death of one and a half million people in 1943.

An event of that kind throws into a sober reality the successes of the great powers in adapting their food production to their strategic requirements. In Bengal, miserably poor and wretchedly overcrowded, might be seen the proof that these strategic successes in the economies of the greater powers were not won without cost elsewhere. The daily calorific intake of a Bengali before the famine was less than one quarter that of an American soldier. Whatever could have been done to stave off the famine, such cruel disparities in well-being presented almost insuperable problems in food control and raised many questions which had been more easily ignored in peacetime.

Food controls and rationing

In such circumstances allocation and distribution of food became all-important. But once again the evidence is that in a more developed country, with a more homogeneous level of food consumption, this problem was more easily solved. The food rations in Britain represented a considerable drop in diet for some, but they maintained the population *as a whole* at a slightly more satisfactory level of health than before the war. The social difficulties of implementing a comprehensive rationing scheme were overcome with relative ease because to standardize consumption at a level well below the average pre-war level of consumption was neither economically nor medically unrealistic. In Palestine, on the other hand, where rationing of some commodities was

36. H. F. Knight, *Food Administration in India 1939–1947*, Food Research Institute Publications, Stanford University Press, 1954, p. 63.

introduced, the calorific consumption of the Jewish population was much higher than that of the Arabs, the consumption of all urban dwellers much higher than that of all rural inhabitants, and the types of foodstuffs eaten by the Jewish and Arab communities showed great differences. In such a society the rationing of food was an economic problem of different scope. What differences in the level of food consumption existed during the war? How effective were rationing systems in removing the inequalities which must otherwise be felt so much more keenly in wartime?

The first point to be made is that the 'official' ration of foodstuffs in countries where food rationing prevailed cannot be compared between countries. In some countries it represented a guaranteed minimum of food to be provided by the authorities, in others a target to be aimed at but often missed. In some countries little food was available outside the official ration, in others most food was still sold on the open market to the highest bidder. In many occupied countries – Belgium was the most flagrant example – the black market was as active as the official food markets. Access to the black market is restricted according to income and also according to locality. It was a common experience in occupied countries in Europe that those living in rural areas had better access to food than those living in towns. In several countries there was a measurable movement of population back to rural areas in the early years of the occupation. Employment was usually at a low ebb and to live in the countryside usually meant being safer and better fed. The high prices paid on the black market were an expression of the very high risks involved; the black market was one aspect of resistance to the will of the occupier. Illegal slaughtering of animals was common; in France the difference between the official figures for delivery of carcasses and the actual number of beasts slaughtered may have been as high as 350,000 a year. Transport difficulties meant that daily milk collections could not be made and dairy farmers were forced on to the black market to defend themselves. As the black market developed into a network almost as comprehensive as the official market, rural inhabitants came to live more and more outside the framework of the official economic system. The peasant consumed more of his own food, sold at prices higher than the official ones to his acquaintances, and on the black market at prices which had no connection at all with official price policy. In France the official butter price rose from 66 francs a kilo in December 1942 to 80 francs in June 1944; over the same period the black market price rose from 175 francs to 445 francs. In summer 1944 potato prices were about double the official price, eggs four times the official price.[37] By summer 1942 the German administration had decided to come to terms with these facts of life and in those countries where black markets were most developed large sums of money were allocated from the occupation costs to secret black-market purchasing organizations whose operations became more extensive as the occupations continued. The armed forces themselves often supplemented their rations by illegal local black-market operations. In Belgium two parallel markets existed, and the official market served only the less fortunate.

There were few countries where black markets did not exist as an established method of allocation of supply. In most countries the machinery of allocation was a mixture of price controls, rationing by physical quantity and uncontrolled black market prices. The extent to which any of these three methods prevailed determined the social experience of the war for most people. The black market seems to have played the smallest role in Britain. Physical controls were much easier to enforce in an island where so high a proportion of the food was imported in government-controlled shipping. The rationing schemes covered so many foodstuffs that they amounted to a comprehensive system of food control. In many other areas, such as the United States, only foodstuffs in short supply were rationed. In some areas allocation was left almost entirely to the working of the market. In Palestine, a complicated food rationing system was applied to retailers in towns and no attempt was made to control the sale of food in the countryside.

In a general sense black markets are socially unjust in the most flagrant way; rationing, by contrast, is often a device for reducing inequalities. The ethics of rationing tend towards the idea of a just reward, at least in terms of calories, for a day's work done.

37. H. Kistenmacher, *Die Auswirkungen der deutschen Besetzung auf die Ernährungswirtschaft Frankreichs während des zweiten Weltkrieges*, Veröffentlichungen des Instituts für Besatzungsfragen, no. 16, Tübingen, 1959, pp. 98–9.

Wartime governments strove hard to avoid these implications, often guaranteeing only minimum rations and leaving all extra quantities to the market. But the more comprehensive rationing becomes the more it requires strict price controls to operate efficiently. It thus becomes a strict control on expenditure in a period of rising incomes and rising demand. The tendency is to pitch the prices of rationed goods at a low level because the basic element of a ration is a universally guaranteed minimum supply. Thus rationing, as it spreads, has a direct influence on the financial and taxation policies of the state. The state is required to decide what level of expenditure on food is desirable and even what diet is desirable. At this point, government decisions pass from what is technically feasible in the present to what is socially desirable. And where controls were as extensive as they were in the United Kingdom this involvement of government in what society *should* be like in wartime was inevitable. Military and economic strategy depend on the social coherence of the country, and rationing in Britain produced coherence and a sense of fairness which stood out all the more sharply against the savage inequities of German administration on the mainland.

The United Kingdom rations covered every basic item of daily diet except bread and potatoes. It took the inflexible form of a fixed weekly minimum quantity of each food for every consumer. Rationing schemes offering the consumer a range of choice might have been more economically satisfactory and such a scheme, the 'points' scheme, was used for some 'non-essential' items such as sweets, and also for household consumer goods and clothing, permitting the consumer to choose between one product and another. But the opposition to such schemes came from the fear that demand would be much more difficult to estimate and hesitations about the state's ability to replace the private distribution of food without an extreme simplification of the pattern of consumer demand.[38] The only comparable previous example of rationing of such scope was that of the Soviet Union, which was hardly appropriate, since in Britain prices were still the main prop of agricultural policy.

Under the 'points' system the weighting of each item of

38. W. B. Reddaway, 'Rationing', in D. N. Chester, ed., *Lessons of the British War Economy*, National Institute of Economic and Social Research, Cambridge University Press, 1951.

consumption in terms of points spent by the consumer could be quickly and easily varied, which had the same effect as raising or lowering its price. But the quantities of food produced from year to year were determined by the money prices set by the state and in time of scarcity there was no avoiding the fact that these prices had to rise steeply. The cost of imported fodder and grain rose in the early part of 1940 partly because of higher world prices and partly because of the higher shipping and insurance charges in war. To this increased cost of domestic production was added the cost of increasing the miserable wages of agricultural workers, who were now vitally important to Britain. At the first general review of agricultural prices in June 1940 current prices, which had risen rapidly since the start of the war, had to be acknowledged as the *de facto* price level. It was also agreed to allow farmers a further profit, equal in total to four fifths of the increase in profits which the price rise was already estimated to have brought them, which was in itself already far above the increased costs of production caused by dearer labour.[39] The rate of return to food producers was thus revised sharply upwards; indeed their whole status in the economy was revised upwards. Either the consumer or the state had to foot the bill for what proved on the whole a successful use of incentives and the price mechanism. Social coherence demanded that it be the state; in April 1941 the government committed itself to a comprehensive policy of subsidizing the price of most basic foods. Thus while farm incomes rose, food prices rose much more slowly, and the government entered on an anti-inflationary policy designed to preserve social harmony. The last remnants of this policy were not swept away until Britain's entry into the European Economic Community. Rationing was only one aspect of a significant realignment of economic relationships.

Between 1938 and 1949 the increase in value of the *per capita* income of farmers after the deduction of tax was much higher than that of any other group. It was three times the increase in value of *per capita* incomes of wage earners.[40] The system of guaranteed prices and annual price reviews tempering almost all

39. E. F. Nash, 'Wartime Control of Food and Agricultural Prices', in Chester, *Lessons*, p. 208.
40. D. Seers, *Changes in the Cost of Living and the Distribution of Income since 1938* Clarendon Press. Oxford. 1949.

the winds of competition to farmers became virtually permanent. The increased income was not fairly distributed – it benefited particularly farmers in arable areas whose capital costs in ploughing new land were less – but it could still be said that farmers benefited more than any other comparable group from the war economy in Britain. The general index of agricultural prices rose from 100 for the period from 1936–7 to 1938–9 to 195 in 1944–5, over half the rise coming before the stabilization programme in 1941. But the subsidies and the strict rationing controls meant that the index of food prices rose by only 42 per cent between 1938 and 1946. Personal disposable income after direct taxation rose by 68 per cent in that period, personal expenditure on food by only 36 per cent, and the percentage of personal income spent on food fell from 29 per cent to 23·4 per cent.[41] The other aspect of this was that tobacco and alcohol were left unrationed and highly taxed as a means of mopping up the increased unspent income. (In the United States, in contrast, where food prices were not subsidized, food costs as a proportion of total expenditure moved in the opposite direction, rising from 24·3 per cent in 1940 to 30·6 per cent in 1943.)[42] The best testimony to the success of Britain's comprehensive policy is the health of the population. The mean annual death rates for children were better than in any previous year. In large cities infant mortality rates showed a progressive decline. Deaths from a large number of diseases were lower than in the pre-war years.[43] Regular employment and a guaranteed diet which, however monotonous, was medically better than before led to an improvement in the health of the population as a whole. In France, where the circumstances of the occupation prevented such policies, infant mortality increased and the average weight and fitness of the population at all ages declined.[44]

41. E. F. Nash, 'Wartime Control of Food and Agricultural Prices', in D. N. Chester, ed., *Lessons of the British War Economy*, N.I.E.S.R., Cambridge University Press, 1951, p. 201.

42. J. D. Black and C. A. Gibbons, 'The War and American Agriculture', in *The Review of Economic Statistics*, no. 26, 1944.

43. United Kingdom, Ministry of Health, *On the State of the Public Health during Six Years of War*, H.M.S.O., London, 1946.

44. A. Chevalier and J. Trémolières, 'Enquête sur l'état de nutrition des populations pendant la guerre', in *Annales de la Nutrition et de l'Alimentation*, no. 9, 1947.

In spite of the gross differences in income and standard of living the United Kingdom was a suitable subject for the control of food, prices, incomes and expenditure. Where the differences in income were even more flagrant rationing served a different purpose. The logical opposite of the United Kingdom rationing system was 'social standard rationing' in Egypt. Rations of kerosene and sugar were allocated according to the size and social standing of the house. Many other rationing schemes which were based on standard quantities for all consumers had so many different categories of consumer that they approached the Egyptian model more nearly than the British.

A comprehensive system like that in Britain forced a lot of thinking on the desirable medical composition of the official ration. In continental Europe or the United States where official rations were eked out by purchases of unrationed commodities at market prices or by black-market buying these matters were left to adjust themselves according to income. In fact, the 'official' rations in almost every European country were critically low in vitamins A and D and in protein.[45] They reveal the very wide discrepancies that existed in standards of consumption. Shortage of food was a relative consideration; the basic minimum ration, varying widely from country to country, reflected the divergence of views on what a man could live on. The imputed average daily intake of calories within the possibilities of the official ration in the Netherlands in November 1943 was 1,705. In France it was less than 1,300. Official German rations over the same period including the regular supplementary allowances were 2,008 calories a day. In Sweden the official ration plus the supplement in April 1944 amounted to 2,491 calories a day and a far wider choice of foodstuffs was available off the ration. For comparison, the average daily *per capita* consumption of food in Japan between 1937 and 1939 was only 2,102 calories and the wartime food ration, which applied only to the staple foods, was 1,160 calories daily.

A better framework in which comparisons may be made is that of military rations. Only rarely does the soldier have access to non-rationed food in significant quantities and in his case

45. J. Rosen, 'Die Entwicklung der Kriegsernährung in sieben europäischen Ländern 1939–1944. Der Verbrauch an Nährstoffen und Vitaminen', in *Schweizerische Medizinische Wochenschrift*, no. 31, 1945.

maximum personal efficiency must be maintained as far as possible at all times. For many groups of civilians of course, that is not strategically necessary. Japanese military rations of staple foods were about twice the level of the civilian ration. When the army in the Home Islands was increased at the end of the war from one million to 3·5 million it placed an intolerable burden on food supply. Australian military rations, at 3,944 calories a day, were almost twice those of a Japanese soldier. American military rations in the Pacific and Australia, which were provided out of Australian supply by Australian food control, however, reached 4,758 calories a day.

TABLE 29
CALORIFIC VALUE OF NORMAL CONSUMERS' RATIONS
ABOUT JANUARY OF EACH YEAR 1941–4

Country	1941	1942	1943	1944
Germany	(1,990)*	(1,750)*	1,980	1,930
Italy	(1,010)†	950	990	1,065‡
Belgium	1,360	1,365	1,320	1,555
Bohemia and Moravia	(1,690)§	1,785	1,920	1,740
Finland	(1,940)‖	(1,495)‖	1,630	1,780
France	(1,365)¶	(1,115)¶	(1,080)¶	1,115
Netherlands	(2,050)**	1,825	1,765	1,580
Norway	(1,620)††	1,385	1,430	1,480
Government-General	845	1,070	855	1,200

* Including 400 calories of potatoes.
† Including 390 calories of bread, 55 of potatoes and 45 of cheese.
‡ Northern Italy.
§ Including 165 calories of milk and 230 of potatoes.
‖ Including 430 calories of potatoes.
¶ Including 100 calories of potatoes.
** Including 340 calories of potatoes.
†† Including 340 calories of potatoes, 20 of cheese and 40 of milk.

SOURCE: League of Nations, *World Economic Survey 1942/44*, Geneva, 1945, p. 125.

The legacy of the war

The more developed the agricultural sector of the economy is, the more nearly is it possible in practice to achieve the flexibility which is theoretically possible in strategic planning for the agricultural sector. The ability to substitute one product for another, to expand the area of cultivated land, to begin the cultivation of new crops, is more present in an agriculture where the levels of productivity are high, where technical knowledge is widespread, and where there is enough machinery and fixed capital to allow adjustments to be made. The less efficient the agricultural sector the more it imposes limitations of economic choice on strategy. In a highly developed economy with a relatively homogeneous society, on the other hand, food control and rationing schemes are more easily devised and more workable, so that the limitations imposed by economic choice are extended even further.

The general effect of war on agriculture ought theoretically to be an increase in mechanization and productivity; war should lessen the obstacles to strategic planning imposed by lack of development in agriculture. The greatly increased demand for labour in the armed forces and in the industrial economy will lead to large movements of labour out of agriculture, which will no longer be able to compete with industrial wages. In consequence, capital should be substituted for labour to increase the level of agricultural productivity; the classic case of this is the mechanization of American farming during the Civil War where the cost of certain forms of agricultural machinery (relative to the cost of labour) was decisively reduced. In the Second World War the cost of labour increased, and the gap between industrial and agricultural wages grew wider in almost all countries. Except where agriculture was a particular strategic problem, as it was in Britain, the armed forces made rapid inroads into the agricultural labour force, while recruitment from many types of skilled industrial employment was often forbidden. In Australia, the rural labour force fell by 30 per cent between July 1939 and July 1941 and the temporary male labour force by 10 per cent. In 1942 soldiers and prisoners of war had to be used as agricultural labour. But the loss of labour in Australian agriculture led to relatively little technical progress. Most agricultural machinery was not made in Australia and had to come from the United States. It was made easily available only in those cases where its deployment could relieve pressure on shipping space. The plant for dehydrating and concentrating foodstuffs such as fruit and eggs also came to Australia from the United States, and for the same purpose. There was some mechanization of vegetable production and the use of milking machines continued to increase but these effects were very slight and were nullified by the drop in tractor imports. The loss of labour was in fact the main cause of the poor performance of Australian agriculture during the war. In the more developed United Kingdom economy tractor manufacture could be deliberately stimulated by government orders. The Ministry of Agriculture built up its own stockpile of 3,000 tractors in the first year of the war to make available to farmers in those areas where, because there had hitherto been little arable farming, there was likely to be a shortage of tractors. Stockpiles of binders and threshers were also built up. The Fordson tractor company, which sold 4,000 tractors in 1938, sold 17,000 in 1940. Domestic production of almost every kind of agricultural machine increased in Britain during the war.[46]

These were the two extreme examples, but the history of wartime agriculture elsewhere indicates that it was only to the rich that success was given. In Japan the shortage of agricultural labour was as serious as in Australia. There was very little technology available which could have made a significant difference on the small units of landholding. The fact that no substitute was discovered for labour in the most labour-intensive period of the rice-farming cycle should have imposed limits on the size of the armed forces, but in a war which became a struggle for survival such limits were far exceeded. The People's Mobilization Ordinance of July 1939 established a labour programme in which rural communities were chiefly regarded as a source of industrial labour. The underlying assumption was that food supply would come from the occupied territories and no attempt was made in the earlier stages of the war to stop the rural exodus which had gathered speed with the campaigns in China. It was not until 1942 that measures were taken to combat the effect of the draft. Students, schoolchildren and organized teams of townspeople performed temporary rural labour at the busiest periods. As the crisis developed the government actively intervened to promote mechanization, by setting cultivation norms for each locality in the production of the staple foods. Those norms covered changes in seeding methods, in manuring and fertilizing. There were significant increases in the use of agricultural machinery up to 1942; after that date the needs of the armaments industries became over-

46. Murray, p. 378.

riding. But these machines did nothing to alleviate the situation when the need for labour was at its greatest.

The country with the highest productivity per unit of labour in agriculture was New Zealand. Agricultural policy there was activated by much the same fears as in Australia, as well it might have been, for 71 per cent of all New Zealand's agricultural and pastoral produce was exported. Here also it was only with the

TABLE 30
AGRICULTURAL MACHINERY IN JAPAN, 1937–45
(in thousands of units)

	1937	1939	1942	1945
Electrical motors	67	91	145	152
Internal combustion engines	121	202	317	262
Pumping machines	44	83	73	88
Powered threshers	129	211	357	352
Powered hulling machines	108	133	180	177

SOURCE: Johnston, p. 103.

impact of demand from the United States services that the economic emphasis switched to increasing agricultural output. There were 155,000 men in the New Zealand armed forces in July 1942 out of a population of about half a million fully employed males. The army was used as agricultural labour in peak periods in 1942 and 1943 and conscription in 1943 was more for agricultural labour than for the armed forces. Although it might have been thought that there was practically no spare labour in the agricultural sector, the number employed in agriculture fell from 150,813 in 1936 to 118,541 in 1945. The performance of the agricultural sector of the economy, however, was quite unlike that of Australia. One reason seems to have been a much easier access to machinery, almost all of which came from the United States in exchange for food supplied directly to the American armed forces. The number of tractors doubled during the war and their average horsepower increased. Combined harvesters were very few in 1939; in 1946 80 per cent of the wheat crop was harvested by them. The use of milking machines also increased at a more rapid rate than in Australia.

The developed economies seldom provided technological help except where, as in the case of New Zealand, it could be justified on a comparative cost basis against military expenditure. At the maximum extent of German occupation in eastern Europe there were 14,000 agricultural specialists employed, including small numbers from other west European countries. Large quantities of agricultural machinery were shipped eastwards, together with better quality livestock and processing plant. Most of this equipment was deliberately destroyed in the retreat, some of it subsequently found its way to France. The deliberate damage done by the retreating German armies in the east left the land in a worse state than before their arrival. Large sums were spent by

TABLE 31
AGRICULTURAL MACHINERY IN NEW ZEALAND, 1939–46

	1939	1940	1941	1942	1946
Electric motors	51,344	56,511	61,826	65,699	76,946
Farm tractors	9,639	11,278	12,516	13,967	18,940
Milking machines	28,970	29,564	30,878	31,487	31,805
Shearing machines	10,064	10,634	10,916	11,555	13,544
Power threshers	740	873	967	1,129	1,520

SOURCE: Crawford, p. 291.

Americans and Russians in building roads and railways along their supply lines in Iran but little or no direct help was provided for Iranian agriculture. Indeed its labour force was seriously depleted by the alternative employment created. When the problems of food control in Iran became too difficult to solve because of the local habit of buying fresh bread daily from a multiplicity of corrupt bakers who mixed their product with straw and dirt the United States provided a large modern American bakery for Teheran. But investment was needed in a lower-level technology; the Iranians found American bread even worse than a mixture of bread and straw, and rioted.[47] On another occasion, one thousand British and Egyptian troops were spared for a highly successful expedition to the breeding grounds of the locust in central Saudi Arabia. No severe crop losses were incurred that year in the period which, it had been feared, would be the peak of the locust cycle. But even in this case, the motive was a potential saving of shipping space by increasing food production in the Middle East. In general, except where such considerations ap-

47. T. H. Vail Motter, *The Persian Corridor, and Aid to Russia*, The United States Army in World War II, G.P.O., Washington, D.C., 1952, p. 163.

plied, there was little effort at improving productivity in most of the underdeveloped countries.

In spite, therefore, of the inherent tendency of war to raise both the output and the productivity of agriculture, the complicated realities of the war reduced both. One result of the Second World War was to reduce the world's total available food supply and make it difficult for world agriculture to regain its former output levels. Of the main products of agriculture only grains were still produced in quantities close to the pre-war levels. The devastation of battles, the deterioration of capital equipment, the loss of labour (for large numbers of former agricultural workers were either unable or did not choose to return to their previous employment), the loss of draught animals and the delays in retooling factories to produce agricultural machinery all played their part. And even in countries where output had gone up, a certain percentage of this rise had been due to a concentration on short-term gains which, because of soil exhaustion, could not be sustained in peacetime.

As incomes improved and people's expectations rose it became clear that the war had been the turning point between the apparent food surpluses of the 1930s and a new situation in which, in terms of human expectations, food shortage was to become a permanent feature of the post-war world.

9

Economic Warfare

Of late years a feeling of false humanity has attempted to make
the rights of private property respected in war. Life may be
sacrificed with as much prodigality as ever. The foremost
mechanical genius of this mechanical age is devoted to the
production of weapons of death; but civilization, it is said,
demands that there should be no wanton destruction of property. No such attempt to palliate the material disaster of war
ought to be encouraged; war will be rendered less frequent, if
a whole nation is made to feel its horrible consequences,
instead of concentrating all the horrors in the sacrifice of
thousands of helpless victims who may be marshalled at the
caprice of a despot.

H. Fawcett, *Manual of
Political Economy*, 7th ed., 1888

Armed intervention in the economy

The phrase 'economic warfare', with its curious implication that
there is some kind of warfare which is not economic, does not
seem to have become established usage until the 1930s. The
extraordinarily high hopes which were attached to it as a strategic
concept may be assessed from the fact that the phrase had barely
entered into use before there appeared in Britain a fully fledged
Ministry of Economic Warfare. Its purpose was to conduct
operations directly against the enemy's economy 'so as', in its

own phrase, 'to prevent h
developments did not pass
the period of neutrality th
what was to become, at th
Warfare, subsequently
Administration. Its pur
with those of its British
was hardly used and
strategy. The German
blockade measures by
shipping supplying
from the general pa'
strategic action and it was ...
of supporting actions against Allied coc.

The reasons for this are not hard to find. First a...
is the fact that the immediate strategic strength of the United
Kingdom and the United States lay in their sea power. They were
the two greatest naval powers. Neither country seriously envisaged
a favourable chance for its arms in land warfare on the European
continent except at some years' distance. In both countries therefore the army at first had the lowest priority among the armed
forces in the period of rearmament. For if direct pressure were to
be brought to bear upon a possible European or Japanese enemy
at an early stage of the war it seemed obvious that it could only
be by naval power or, in certain geographical and political circumstances, by air power. It was not likely that German or Japanese
fleets would seek battle against such enormous navies and the
question therefore arose as to how naval power could strategically
be brought to bear. For Britain the history of all European wars
since the late seventeenth century pointed to the answer: by the
establishment of a blockade of the trade of a European enemy.
In the First World War the United States had quickly arrived at
the same answer. There was a long history of such successful
deployment of sea power and in the Napoleonic Wars it had been
evolved into a combination of naval, diplomatic and economic
pressure sufficient to exert a stranglehold on French expansion.
In 1914 the strategy had been resurrected with only such alterations as a hundred years of technological change in naval weapons

1. W. N. Medlicott, *The Economic Blockade*, H.M.S.O., London, 1952,
vol. 1, p. 1.

1917 the United States had added its
British blockade without modifying the
.² No wonder that with the approach of war
gain to the same strategy. But the even greater
pinned on it were a reflection not so much of its
ss as of two other factors, the supposed weakness of
terial base of the German economy and the develop-
ir power in the inter-war period.

only was Germany a smaller country with less raw material
urces than in 1914, but the increased material demands of
arfare would make this weakness a more serious one. Such
thinking was further encouraged by the obvious importance which
the German government, in its trade negotiations in the 1930s,
attached to acquiring strategic supplies; the change in the geographical pattern of German trade after 1933 was often interpreted
as being primarily an attempt to provide a stronger economic base
for rearmament. German literature on the topic of *Wehrwirtschaft*
paid enormous attention to the same problems of supply; from
this literature in turn was distilled a smaller number of works
published outside Germany which, by analysing these weaknesses,
encouraged the belief that Germany's war potential could be
nullified by a thoroughgoing campaign against her supply.³

As for Japan her strategic weakness in this respect was obvious
to all the world. In fact it had been long considered in the State
Department that economic action was a prime weapon in anti-
Japanese diplomacy. When, in July 1941, the Japanese army
moved southwards from its recently acquired bases in north
Indo-China and occupied positions in the Saigon area the United
States government froze all Japanese assets and imposed an
economic embargo with the intention of cutting off supplies of oil
and machines to the Japanese economy. The effect on Japan was
to compel a decision either to withdraw and come to terms with
the United States, or to continue with her strategy and break the
economic stranglehold by territorial expansion. Seizure of the
Dutch Indonesian colonies would, for example, nullify the

2. D. T. Jack, *Studies in Economic Warfare*, P. S. King & Son, London,
1940.

3. See, for example, F. Sternberg, *Die deutsche Kriegsstärke*, Sebastian
Brant, Paris, 1938; translated into English as *Germany and a Lightning War*,
Faber & Faber, London, 1938.

American embargo on oil supplies. The long Cabinet struggle in Japan led ultimately to the decision for war. The strength of the economic weapon had been properly judged by the State Department, and, although its use brought a result opposite to the one they had hoped for, the alarmed reaction in Japan to the economic measures only added strength to the conviction that here was a new and valuable dimension in which a modern war could be fought.

The development of aircraft which could bomb the enemy's economic installations clinched the matter, although there were no bombers in 1939 capable of carrying out such operations against the Japanese Home Islands from the nearest American territory. Even from Britain towns in central and eastern Germany were dubious targets because of the distance. But the great industrial areas of western Germany could be reached. It is not surprising that it should have been the two great sea-powers which evolved air forces which had a strategic independence and significance of their own rather than merely functioning as tactical aids in land warfare. The bomber was understood in Britain even in the First World War as a means of carrying the offensive to the enemy while avoiding large land battles.[4] Warships had always been used to shell the shore; anywhere in western Germany could now be reached by bombs. As early as 1935 the British government concentrated the weight of its rearmament drive on the construction of a fleet of long-range bombers. They were built for use against 'civilian' targets. That is what they were mainly used for and, had they been as effective as it was hoped they would be, they would have been used even more against such targets. Their existence eliminated the last frail distinctions surviving from the First World War between combatant and non-combatant personnel and placed, for example, workers in aircraft factories in as much mortal danger as infantry men.

There are inherent problems in trying to shut off supply by means of naval blockade from a power which dominates a whole continent militarily and diplomatically, problems which had also been made very clear in the war against France between 1803 and 1811. Even if naval blockade were to be linked to all the other possibilities of economic warfare which the Ministry of Economic

4. N. Frankland, *The Bombing Offensive Against Germany*, Faber & Faber, London, 1965, p. 25 ff.

Warfare envisaged, such as sabotage, psychological warfare, and diplomatic threats, there would still be a big geographical area where Germany would have the advantage in all these tactics. But the existence of a fleet of bombers offered the theoretical possibility that when weak links in the German economy were identified, instead of applying gradual pressure to that point, the link might actually be destroyed there and then. Although the bombers remained under the command of the Royal Air Force the Ministry of Economic Warfare had an important role in selecting targets they might bomb; from the outset the strategic air offensive was conceived as an essential part of the strategy of economic warfare.

But what sort of targets, whose destruction might cause it to cease functioning, does an economy actually offer either to naval and diplomatic blockade or to the bomber? The Ministry of Economic Warfare, Bomber Command, the United States Eighth Army Air Force, and their respective governments all tended to believe what they wanted to believe in this regard. Their knowledge of the German economy itself was, it should be remembered, a very inaccurate one, for they believed the economic chain to be stretched tautly awaiting only pressure in the right spot from the Allies for it to snap. As we now know, the opposite was the case and there was more slack in the German economy than in the Allied war effort. The Allies turned the small rays of hope which their not very accurate intelligence offered into brightly shining rainbows. And for this no doubt the underlying reason was the apparent impossibility of devising any other strategy in the circumstances. It was in fact widely believed that no possible defence existed against the bomber, other than the threat of violent counter-attack by the same means. In this sense Allied strategy had also a strong defensive element.

Economic warfare did have its tactical successes and played its role in the Allied victory. But it fell far short of the extravagant hopes placed on it and a study of its effects is more a study of failure. German and Japanese production continued to rise steeply until summer 1944 and by the time they began to fall many other causes than Allied economic intervention were also at work. One of them was the time-honoured strategic concept of invasion of the enemy's territory. Furthermore, the strategic air offensive only became fully effective after the German air defences had been sought out in battle and destroyed; the aeroplane proved itself in that respect subject to the same strategic laws that governed land warfare.

One cause of the failure of economic warfare was that its tools were not as efficient as had been supposed. The idea that there was no adequate defence against the bomber proved quite false. Systems of air defence improved with the improvement in bombers, and fighter planes in particular inflicted heavy losses on the best-designed and most heavily armed bombers. Naval blockade still was not efficient enough to prevent large quantities of supplies reaching Germany. Another cause was the lack of consistency with which economic warfare, in the face of these discouragements, was carried on by the Allies. Although weak links in the German and Japanese economies were in fact discovered they were never attacked for long enough or frequently enough, because forces were diverted either to other tempting but less useful targets or to other forms of warfare altogether. Thirdly, the Axis powers were well aware both of their own weaknesses and of the tactics that would be used against them. The strategy of conquest was coupled with the accumulation of large stockpiles of strategic materials and with the ruthless acquisition of such materials by seizure and by forced exports from all occupied territories. Finally, both individual national economies and the international economy proved to be systems more complex than was allowed for in most plans of economic warfare. In retrospect these plans can be seen as drastically inaccurate simplifications of economic existence. By substituting factors and by altering priorities the Axis economies proved capable of avoiding seemingly unavoidable perils; the Allies persisted throughout the war, for example, in their false assumption that the shortage of precision bearings in Germany would impose serious handicaps on the economy. Furthermore, neutral states managed to sustain the vestiges of the pre-war pattern of trade; even under the hammer blows rained on it by the greatest powers, international trade continued to exist outside the rival economies of the two armed camps and in so doing to provide a small but very important supply to Germany.

The selection of economic targets

It was easy to draw up lists of those goods important for war in which Germany and Japan were dependent on foreign supply. A list of those in which they were self-sufficient would have been shorter. But to proceed from there to the point of selecting a target for attack which would make a vital difference to the enemy war effort was a tortuous economic journey through unmapped country. Practically no aluminium, for example, was made in Germany out of domestic raw materials but the supply of foreign bauxite could not be cut off by economic warfare after the occupation of France. Aluminium smelters, on the other hand, made bad targets. Because of these difficulties the strategic bomber offensive was subsequently launched directly against aircraft factories. But to attack the finished product in this way proved to be an error. Component parts were stored away from the factories, machines were protected against blast in such a way that they could only be seriously damaged by a direct hit, factories themselves were moved underground, stocks of raw and semi-finished material were not easily damaged by bombs.

There were, however, raw materials and components which were indispensable and which could be attacked. The blockade identified certain non-ferrous metals as such targets. Their quantities were small, their source of supply on the whole well known and their importance in armaments production a vital one. But in most cases the stockpile which Germany had, combined with stockpiles captured in occupied countries, was adequate; the blockade merely served as a constant reminder of the need for economy in the use of raw materials. Furthermore once a raw material became so scarce that its whole supply could be cornered its wartime price became such as to reward smuggling on the most ambitious scale. In many of the targets selected by the Ministry of Economic Warfare, such as wolfram or industrial diamonds, private and government-aided smuggling developed to such an extent that it became impossible to know exactly what stocks were where.

A third type of target might be neither raw material nor finished product but vital component parts of armaments or particular industrial processes. High-quality bearings, indispensable for precision armaments, were made in 1939 by only a few engineering firms, of which the most important was the Swedish firm SKF. The blockade concentrated all available diplomatic weapons on preventing Swedish bearings from reaching the German war economy; subsequently the strategic bombers were launched in one of the most costly operations of the war against the town of Schweinfurt, where most German precision bearings were made. But Germany was able to develop her own bearings industries during the war, and, in certain cases, by adapting the final armament, to use lower quality bearings. The ball-bearing factories themselves were hard to hit and when hit the damage done to the machines was not such as to disturb production seriously.

As for industrial processes, the most obvious was that of synthetic oil manufacture. Germany was highly dependent on it and the industrial plant was both very large and easily identifiable from the air. The capacity to bomb such factories seemed to circumvent the fact that by producing synthetic oil Germany had avoided the most obvious of the possible dangers of blockade. In this case the target selected proved a very good one, but it would have been virtually impossible even by the most penetrating economic analysis to have discovered its superiority over other targets in 1939. Domestic economic circumstances changed so rapidly that a good target in 1944 might well have been a bad one in 1939. And the intelligence obtained in wartime about the workings of enemy economies is poor. Although there are excellent studies of the effects of economic warfare, there are still no good studies of how the targets were selected. They seem to have emerged from the interplay of intelligence information, economic knowledge of pre-war Germany and Japan, decisions by the navies, air forces, and diplomatic services about what was actually feasible, political pressures and the changing strategic situation. Amongst these influences the question of feasibility undoubtedly played a bigger part than economic theory. Economic justification was often found for what was in fact a decision dictated by the capacity of the weapons available.

Of this the most striking example is the use of bombers for so-called 'area bombing'. In the early stages of the strategic bombing offensive it became clear that defences against aerial bombardment were much more effective than earlier strategic thinking had supposed. The development of radar and of fast fighter planes meant that daytime bombing was soon seen as too costly. And at night it was an altogether more difficult business to find the target. The United States bombers were at first constructed for daylight bombing, in spite of the evidence against its feasibility already collected by the German and British air forces, because only in daylight could bombers be launched against targets as small as a factory. The first experiences of night bombing, indeed, showed that the smallest target that could reliably be hit was a city. With the gradual evolution of better navigational systems, and more particularly with the development and production of long-range fighter escort planes which could engage the German fighters in battle, more accurate night bombing and, later, safer daylight bombing became practical. Out of the initial failure, however, was born the idea of area bombing. It rested on two assumptions. One was that certain areas, in particular industrial towns, had so high a concentration of economically valuable plant that if an attempt were made at a target of known high economic value in such an area the bombs that missed would still be damaging to the enemy's economy. The second assumption was that it was also damaging to the enemy's economy to have to employ resources in clearing up rubble, mending gas and water mains and restoring urban services generally. At times air force generals were prepared to claim that this was more economically damaging than the destruction of what Sir Arthur Harris, Chief of Bomber Command, called 'panacea targets'.[5] Few believed, after the experience of the German bomber raids on British cities, that bombing caused any worthwhile damage to civilian morale. Area bombing of this kind, which was directed both against specific economic targets and against *any* economic target, was in itself an admission of failure, although that does not mean that it was necessarily less effective than attacks on specific economic targets. That it did, however, also have a certain attraction beyond more selective methods because of its quality of retribution appears from the works of Churchill and of Harris. It appears even more clearly from the economically pointless destruction of Dresden in the last stage of the offensive.

5. Sir A. Harris, *Bomber Offensive*, Collins, London, 1947, p. 87 ff.

Imperfections of the weapons

The relative failure of area bombing was the best example of the weakness of the weapons available for economic warfare. But it must be admitted that the economic difficulties in actually measuring the effect of such bombing tactics are almost insuperable, and such a judgement can only be based on the relative performance of the German economy. No accurate expression can be made of the effect of so many disrupted public utilities, of so many buildings destroyed, railways and roads cut, of the disturbance of the normal working routine of daily life, of the diversion of labour towards running repairs to bomb damage and even of the loss of life. Let it be firmly stated that such estimates as do exist, including those made by the United States and British Strategic Bombing Surveys, are just guesses, and due to the impossibility of getting reliable information no more likely to be accurate because they are the guesses of expert economists.

It is not known how many casualties were caused through bombing. In Berlin alone by the close of April 1945 50,000 residents in the city had been killed by air raids.[6] In two instances, the first largely accidental and the second planned, Allied bombers were able to start a storm of uncontrollable fire which completely destroyed a large part of a city and incinerated many of its inhabitants. This happened in Hamburg in July 1943 and again in Dresden at the end of the war. About 9,000 tons of bombs were dropped in Hamburg in less than nine days and killed most of the 30,482 victims of air raids in the city that year.[7] The numbers killed in Dresden are not known. They were probably at least on a par with those killed by the explosive effect of the atomic bombs on Japan. The bomb on Hiroshima killed 64,000 people within four months and that on Nagasaki 39,000. German casualties from bombing all told may be put between 200,000 and 600,000.

In return for the 74,172 tons of bombs, including the V weapons, dropped by the German forces on Britain the Allies dropped a total of 1,350,000 tons of bombs on Germany, excluding Austria. Including German-occupied territory and the territory of German

6. H. Rumpf, *Das war der Bombenkrieg*, Gerhard Stalling, Oldenburg, 1961; translated into English as *The Bombing of Germany*, Frederick Muller, London, 1963, p. 126.

7. ibid., p. 82.

allies 1,996,036 tons were dropped.[8] Until 1944 most of these bombs were used in area bombing because more precise tactics were not possible. Afterwards, when a genuine choice existed, it still sometimes fell on area bombing. Estimates made by the United States Strategic Bombing Survey of the loss of total annual production due to area bombing put the figure at 2·5 per cent in 1942, 9 per cent in 1943, 17 per cent in 1944 and 6·5 per cent in January – April 1945.[9] The equivalent British report has not been published but the estimates which it makes of loss of overall production seem to be lower. Its conclusion is that:

> area attacks against German cities could not have been responsible for more than a very small part of the fall which actually had occurred in German production by the spring of 1945, and . . . in terms of bombing effort, they were also a very costly way of achieving the results which they did achieve.[10]

The British report, however, also tried to estimate the effects of raids on particular industries and concluded that in the second half of 1943 31·9 per cent of overall production in the iron and steel industry was lost and 46·5 per cent of that part of the production of the iron and steel industry which could be called war production. The comparable figures for the second half of 1944 are 26·4 per cent and 39 per cent. Whatever they mean, these figures are startlingly high. We shall have to wait to discover what they mean, as the report is still, for practical purposes, secret. What information we have contradicts the figures. It indicates that area bombing had little effect on the enemy economy for the resources expended on it.[11]

The targets selected for the economic blockade had perforce to be imported goods and were thus largely made up of raw materials. Lists of goods which were considered of strategic value to the Axis powers were published and proclaimed as contraband. The principle of contraband, long established in international law, had a double value, for not only did it offer a naval power

8. Lord Tedder, *Air Power in War*, Hodder & Stoughton, London, 1948, p. 106.

9. U.S.S.B.S., *Area Studies Division Report, No. 31*, p. 18.

10. Sir C. Webster and N. Frankland, *The Strategic Air Offensive against Germany, 1939–1945*, H.M.S.O., London, 1961, vol. 4, p. 49.

11. U.S.S.B.S., *Effects of Strategic Bombing on Germany, Effects of Strategic Bombing on Japan.*

such as Britain the opportunity to forbid the import of these goods into an enemy harbour but it also permitted their seizure on the high seas. The list of contraband was an extremely wide one and embraced practically every commodity that could be considered of any economic value in wartime, even goods such as leather or drugs. The circumstances of the blockade, once the United States had entered the war, were such that it was practically impossible for any European power, Axis or neutral, to import any commodity on a large scale from outside Europe without Allied knowledge or permission. But this did not cover the trade of neutral European powers with the Axis and in trying to control this trade by diplomatic and economic pressure it was necessary to establish certain priorities in the targets and abandon a complete control over all supply. Thus enormous efforts were made to dam or restrict the export trades in iron ore and bearings from Sweden to Germany, in machinery from Switzerland to Germany and Italy, in chrome ore from Turkey to Germany and Italy, and in other ores, particularly wolfram, from Portugal and Spain. Of these targets bearings appeared also as a target for the bombers and were included on the list of primary targets drawn up jointly on 18 May 1943 by the British and Americans for the Combined Bomber Offensive.

The Allied powers were by no means always in agreement over what means could and should be used and these disagreements were more prominent in the blockade than in the strategic air offensive. There was a stronger conviction in the United States that bombing raids should be confined to specific economic targets and more moral hesitation about the value of raids launched in a less discriminate fashion, but such sentiments made little headway once it was discovered that the possibilities of bombing raids were circumscribed by what could be done without too great a cost. In the conduct of the other aspects of economic warfare, however, the United States Board of Economic Warfare was often a lively critic of its British partner and after 1942 led the way in introducing new tactics which the British government was reluctant to consider, partly out of respect for neutral powers but more out of a sentiment that permanent damage might be done to international economic relations by such tactics. It was perhaps never wholly out of the minds of British officials that the United Kingdom was the most vulnerable of all powers to blockade tactics because its dependence on imports was the greatest.

Between the late eighteenth century and 1917, the United States had shown itself the most ardent of all champions of neutrality and had played the leading part in establishing neutral 'rights' to trade with belligerent powers in periods of war. In 1917 she had completely abandoned this stance and the Neutrality Acts in force in 1939 were isolationist in intent, seeking to prevent any contact between the United States and a belligerent power which might again embroil the country in a war on another continent. The Roosevelt administration's gradual whittling away of these Acts after 1939 was based not on any desire to involve the United States in war, but on the realization that in a major war such an isolationist stance was against the real interests of the United States and also ultimately impossible in an economic sense. When the war involved all the major trading economies and when a major naval power had classed as contraband a large proportion of the commodities in international trade the Neutrality Acts could only be ultimately meaningful if the United States withdrew almost entirely from her position as a major international trader. To revert to her traditional historical stance was meaningless, because the existence of British sea power was her best defence against the powers which most threatened her, and to insist on her neutral 'rights' would only weaken her own defences. Thus the administration, while working to modify the Neutrality Acts, covertly aided many of the British blockade measures; the first breaches of those Acts were specifically designed to provide military and economic aid to Britain. By the time of the official declarations of war between Germany and the United States a state of open economic war had existed between them for several months quite comparable to that which existed between the United States and Japan. After 1942 the world's two greatest naval powers combined their actions. International law respecting neutral 'rights' to trade during wars, which had been recognized in international treaties over one hundred and fifty years since the success of the League of Armed Neutrality, was destroyed in three years; the power which had most sustained the international law of neutrality in the past now became its most virulent enemy. After so long a struggle the neutral powers lost the 'rights' so painfully acquired and were blatantly prevented by the threat of force from conducting a free and unlimited commerce with both belligerent camps. In 1945 the United States government was still urging a reluctant partner into devising further methods of pressure on neutral powers.

But this pressure did not make the various measures completely efficient; to the last they had serious limitations. The blockade was enforced virtually without the use of ships, although it rested on the firm foundation of the existence of naval power. Developments in long-range shore guns and the laying of extensive minefields meant that the earlier techniques of close-cordon blockade of an enemy port were no longer possible. Other methods of control, which had been evolved in the First World War and were first used in 1939, formed the basis of the blockade. They depended, in principle, on the seizure of contraband wherever it was found. But in practice it was easier to force shipping companies and neutral powers to ensure that there was no contraband among the cargoes carried. This was done by the issuance of certificates of clearing, so-called 'navicerts' and 'ship's warrants'. Without a ship's warrant a vessel could not get supplies or repairs at any port under Allied control, which meant after 1942 almost any port outside Europe. Behind these powers still lay the right of arrest and search on the high seas but as paper control of cargoes at the port of departure became more effective the need for such searches diminished. There was in any case only a small part of the world's merchant shipping, apart from the German and Japanese merchant navies, which was not under Allied control or very susceptible to financial and commercial pressure from the Allies, and the profits to be gained from blockade running were negligible compared to the commercial discrimination which it would bring. The Norwegian merchant fleet, one of the world's largest, had for the most part not returned to Norway after the occupation of the country. It was managed from London by Nortraship, an organization working in harmony with the Norwegian government in exile, on behalf of the Allies. The earnings from these charterings all accumulated to the credit of the exiled government.[12] On a smaller scale other merchant ships were at the disposal of the Allies in a similar way. Navicerts and ship's warrants were backed up by black-listing, by which firms or

12. B. Askelund, 'Nortraships hemmelige fond', in *Norge og den 2 verdenskrig: mellom nøytrale og allierte*, Universitetsforlaget, Oslo, 1968.

persons were subsequently excluded from all business with Allied countries. In November 1943 the important Swiss engineering firm, Sulzer, was so black-listed, in order to force the firm and the Swiss government to reduce machine exports to Germany; the black-listing led almost immediately to a new trade agreement more favourable to the Allies.[13]

It was in matters such as black-listing that the United States took the lead in extending the scope of economic warfare. The Board of Economic Warfare believed that blockade should take less and less the aspect of naval warfare and become more and more what it called 'control at source'. It was this which led to the use of techniques such as 'pre-emption', the purchase of the whole available future supply of a commodity which was of strategic value to the enemy. This was the tactic pursued in trying to corner the supply of chrome ore from Turkey. Where a country such as Portugal continued to assert its right to sell metal ores, wolfram in this case, in equal shares to each side, at huge prices, and where naval blockade was useless, 'pre-emption' became a private activity conducted by paid intelligence agents. But the use of such methods led naturally to attempts to coerce neutral governments by official diplomatic means. All these methods had definite limits to their effectiveness and it was not until Germany could be clearly seen to be defeated that the gap in the Allied blockade caused by the existence of neutral European states could satisfactorily be plugged.

One example is worth analysing in greater detail to demonstrate the greatly exaggerated ideas held of the value of economic warfare against so complex an economy as the German. Among the targets to get highest priority in Allied strategy was the supposedly irremediable dependence of Germany on imports of iron ore, a dependence which it was supposed would place the German steel industry in severe peril in a sustained war. In 1938 Germany imported 10·4 million metric tons (Fe content) of iron ore. The main supplier was Sweden, providing 5·4 million tons, followed by France with 1·4 million. The assumption was that German steel production was ultimately dependent on Swedish supply. At the time of the Russo-Finnish war the Allies considered securing control of the iron ore mines in Arctic Sweden by a relief column sent to fight with the Finns. But less drastic strategic

13. Medlicott, vol. 2, p. 498 ff.

moves seemed as though they might serve the same purpose. Swedish ore was exported by two routes, one from the Baltic ports Luleå, Oxelösund and Gävle, which were icebound from mid-December to mid-April, and the other by an all-year route from Narvik in northern Norway. The second route involved a long sea voyage, exposed to the possibility of Allied attack, down the Norwegian coast; because it was open all the year round, and because the land journey in Sweden was shorter, it had been the preferred route in the 1930s. In the winter of 1939–40 the Allies seriously considered invading Norway to prevent this traffic, so convinced was the British Ministry of Economic Warfare that the trade was a main artery of the German economy, and they did eventually mine the sea passages from Narvik. Germany formulated her plans to occupy Norway on strategic grounds, among which the possibility of securing this traffic by the establishment of naval bases certainly played some part. Intense interest in the Narvik route was provoked by the outbreak of war, which meant the cessation of French ore exports to Germany, leaving Sweden the sole important supplier. It has been argued in fact that if the supply from Sweden in that period had been cut off immediately after the declarations of war German blast furnaces would have had to cease production before the invasion of France.[14]

Such an argument is quite false. It echoes the unwise optimism of the early years of the Ministry of Economic Warfare. In the first place Swedish supply was not as significant in this crucial period as in other periods. In the first three months of 1940 it was only 25·2 per cent of total German consumption and in the second three months 33·8 per cent, the lowest proportions for any period of the war except the last year.[15] One reason for this was that ore exports from Narvik to Germany throughout this crucial period were much lower in every month than in the corresponding month of the previous year, presumably because of the greater dangers now attendant on any route west of the Sound.[16] In the second place the size of German stockpiles was

14. R. Karlbom, 'Sweden's Iron Ore Exports to Germany, 1933–1944', in *Scandinavian Economic History Review*, no. 13, 1965.

15. A. Milward, 'Could Sweden have Stopped the Second World War?', in *Scandinavian Economic History Review*, no. 15, 1967.

16. P. Brøyn, 'Den svenske malmeksport fram til okkupasjonen av Narvik i april 1940 – med saerlig tanke på utførselen til Tyskland', in *Norge og den 2 verdenskrig: mellom nøytrale og allierte*, p. 101.

ample to cover the period. The iron content of the ore imported from Sweden between September 1939 and June 1940 was less than half the total weight of stocks of iron by iron content and of pig iron and scrap still available in Germany on the latter date.[17] Although these stocks were very heavily reduced in this period they were obviously sufficient, especially when the ore production of Austria, the Protectorate and Poland is added to the available German supply, to have made the German steel industry in the short run independent of Swedish ore supplies. In the third place, given the kind of economy which prevailed in Germany, there were large reserves of steel available that could still have been diverted to armaments purposes. Between the outbreak of war and the end of September 1940 over 40 per cent of German steel production in every quarter was allocated to civilian consumption, not including constructional purposes or exports.[18] Had Swedish supply been cut off it would have done nothing to prevent the invasion of France and the German steel industry would have continued to function unaffected in the interim.

But if Allied strategy was quite mistaken in 1939–40 that does not imply that the German steel industry was not in the long run, even with a limited level of armaments production, dependent on Swedish supply. Whether this was so or not was a problem that never had to be squarely faced. With the occupation of Denmark and Norway, Sweden was in no position to attempt any reduction in the level of iron ore exports to Germany which she had provided in the 1930s. Imports, as Table 32 shows, were always more than a quarter of Germany's iron ore supplies after 1940 and they came overwhelmingly from Sweden. The British market was virtually closed and the ore trade to Germany became more crucial to the Swedish economy. Indeed the quantities exported only fell below the 10 million tons stipulated in the annual German–Swedish trade agreements for the most part because Germany could not provide the shipping to carry such quantities away.

In spite of this, when in November 1943 the Ministry of War Production in Berlin considered the possibility of a total cessation of ore supply from Sweden they concluded that once the process

17. J.-J. Jäger, 'Sweden's Iron Ore Exports to Germany, 1933–1944', in *Scandinavian Economic History Review*, no. 15, 1967.

18. Milward, *The German Economy*, p. 30.

TABLE 32
GERMANY'S SUPPLY OF IRON ORE, 1940–44

	Domestic production								Imports						Total
	Pre-1938 boundaries		End-1940 boundaries*		Occupied areas		Total		From Sweden		From other countries		Total		
Year	000 metric tons	%	000 metric tons	%	000 metric tons	%	000 metric tons	%	000 metric tons	%	000 metric tons	%	000 metric tons	%	000 metric tons
1940	5,019	37·5	2,354	17·6	—	—	7,373	55·1	5,339	39·5	666	5·4	6,005	44·9	13,378
1941	4,755	25·4	5,960	31·9	2,664	14·2	13,379	71·5	5,027	26·9	298	1·6	5,325	28·5	18,704
1942	4,137	22·8	5,979	32·9	3,026	16·7	13,142	72·4	4,205	23·2	806	4·4	5,011	27·6	18,153
1943	4,080	20·1	6,702	33·1	3,636	18·0	14,418	71·2	5,568	27·5	264	1·3	5,832	28·8	20,250
1944	2,636	24·0	4,403	40·1	1,230	11·2	8,269	75·3	2,628	23·9	83	0·8	2,711	24·7	10,980

* Including Austria, Bohemia and Moravia, annexed Poland and Alsace-Lorraine.

SOURCE: M. Fritz, *German Steel and Swedish Iron Ore 1939–1945*, Kungsbacka, Gothenburg, 1974.

of conversion to different processes of production had taken place total steel output would fall by only 10 per cent. When, after August 1944, Swedish supply did fall away steeply as allied pressures first stopped the ore traffic in Swedish ships and then, from the end of September, in German ships, the coincidental fall in steel production was more to be attributed to acute transport difficulties, which created coal shortages and to the recapture of the Lorraine ore fields by Allied forces. But this hardly clinches the matter either; rather it shows how complicated the functioning of a war economy is. War production required a higher proportion of open-hearth and electro-steel in Germany than that prevailing in peacetime, and that in its turn required a higher proportion of inputs of iron ore with a low phosphorus content. The percentage of low-phosphorus ore in Swedish exports to Germany rose from 18 per cent in 1936 to 27 per cent between 1940 and 1943, serving to meet the greater demand in Germany for armour plate and other special steels. And this did not come about merely because Germany now was able to import the greater quantity of low-phosphorus ores which had previously gone to the British steel industry; the output of low-phosphorus grades in Sweden increased. More low-phosphorus ore for German blast furnaces reduced the amount of coke and labour needed for each ton of steel. Iron ore was never in itself a bottleneck for the German steel industry, but labour on several occasions was, and coke was in short supply throughout the war. The Ministry of War Production's estimates may well therefore have been too optimistic and Swedish deliveries less easily replaceable than it seemed. This impression is furthered by the readiness of Germany even in 1944 to sustain coal exports to Sweden in very difficult circumstances, in return for iron ore.

But the conquest of territory was a highly effective riposte to economic blockade. The increase in domestic production of iron ore in Germany was an increase within the boundaries as they existed at the end of 1940, including, that is, Austria, the Protectorate and, most important of all, a large part of the French *minette* ore field. Output within the boundaries as they existed before 1938 shrank. It was in fact run down deliberately because the additional resources brought by conquest could be mined more cheaply. That part of the *minette* ore field in France annexed to Germany produced 14·9 million metric tons of ore (Fe content) in 1943, which was treated entirely as German domestic supply. Germany was also able to exert control over that part of the ore field which remained in France, whose output was roughly the same, and in most years over 50 per cent of its production was also exported to Germany. Furthermore it was the conquest of such large areas that gave Germany so powerful a bargaining position in the annual negotiations with Sweden. Only late in 1943 as the fortunes of war were seen to have turned decisively did the Swedish government begin to try by small administrative hindrances to slow down the supply of ore to Germany.[19] Whatever difficulties the German steel industry encountered in five and a half years of warfare, Allied trade pressures on Sweden had a very small part in their making, especially when compared to the effort involved.

It was not only on the deficiencies in iron ore that Allied hopes were pinned but also on the lack of non-ferrous ores for alloying high-grade armament steels. Four metals in particular were indispensable for such production, manganese, nickel, chrome and tungsten – the first three as constituents of armour plate and the fourth as a constituent of high-speed cutting tools to shape it. German domestic production of the ores for these metals was too small to be significant and yet by the end of the war finished steel production had not suffered in any way from their shortage, apart from the occasional reductions and changes in quality of high-grade steel due to substitutions of one alloy for another or economies in particular non-ferrous metals. The reasons were the large stockpiles of many of these metals which existed in Germany before the war, the extension of German territorial control in Europe which both ensured imports and also permitted the capture of stockpiles of these metals in other countries, and the fact that the Allies were never completely able to cut off supply from neutral countries to Germany.

At the outbreak of war Germany had a stockpile of manganese ore sufficient for fifteen to twenty months' consumption and of nickel for six months. The German–Soviet trade agreement then gave Germany access to the exports of the world's biggest manganese producer, exports which could in no way be intercepted by the Allies. The manganese looted from the Soviet Union during

19. M. Fritz, *German Steel and Swedish Iron Ore 1939–1945*, Kungsbacka, Gothenburg, 1974, p. 120.

the retreat, 360,000 metric tons, was sufficient, together with the small supply from Slovakia and Hungary, to keep German stockpiles at such a level in September 1944 that at the current rate of consumption they would have sufficed until June 1946.[20] Nickel was in much shorter supply and the small amounts available from Norway and Greece would not have maintained stockpiles without the growing imports from the Petsamo mines in northern Finland which began in 1941, delayed only by the British refusal to supply the mines with the necessary plant. Seizure of stockpiles in other countries was also a rich source of supply. Shortages of chrome ore could have been more serious as there were few special steels made without a chromium admixture. Turkey had committed herself to selling her whole export to the Allies until 8 January 1943, but with absolute control over the smaller available quantities in Yugoslavia, Greece and Bulgaria Germany was still able to stave off shortages until Turkish supply again revived for a brief period. After summer 1941 88 per cent of German consumption came from the Balkans.[21] These supplies, together with loot seized there, were adequate to maintain German stocks in September 1944 at a level adequate for a further ten months' consumption. Tungsten was manufactured out of wolfram imported from Portugal and Spain whose exports were responsible for 63 per cent of German consumption between 1941 and 1944. The Allies probably devoted a greater and more diversified effort to cutting off wolfram supplies than to any other metal but at the end of 1944 Germany had stockpiles adequate for two more years' consumption.

Imperfections of strategy

Allowing for the fact that the weapons of economic warfare were less effective in the reality of war than in the hopes of pre-war strategists it still remains true that a more consistent application against certain targets could have brought more success. In the circumstances of comparative failure the restless hunt for a better target was understandable but the original theoretical conception

20. J.-J. Jäger, *Die wirtschaftliche Abhängigkeit des Dritten Reiches vom Ausland dargestellt am Beispiel der Stahlindustrie*, Berlin Verlag, Berlin, 1969, p. 205; Petzina, *Autarkiepolitik*, p. 144.
21. Jäger, *Die wirtschaftliche Abhängigkeit*, p. 255.

of economic warfare was not without economic validity and with a more precise evaluation of targets and results it could have been more successful. This can be seen from two examples, the air attack on German synthetic oil production and the naval blockade of Japan.

The strategic air offensive against Germany's oil supply was relegated to the background after its early failures due to the inaccuracy of bombing and was not resumed in full force until May 1944. The German oil industry presented about a hundred separate targets amongst which the crude oil producers and refiners were easy to hide. But out of the hundred targets there was a small number of very visible ones which were of extreme importance. One third of the synthetic output by the hydrogenation process was concentrated in the two large works at Leuna and Pölitz. But the Allies did not fully appreciate the extent to which the output of aviation fuel depended on the hydrogenation process. Apart from the 10 per cent produced from imported crude oil from Romania it was all produced in the most visible and destructible targets. Had the air attacks been concentrated more against hydrogenation plant lack of aviation fuel for the German air force would have paralysed its activities even sooner than it did. What was also not realized, however, was the speed with which damaged plant could be restored to production if special measures were taken immediately after the raid. By providing a pool of building labour and materials and by allocating the highest priority to rebuilding synthetic oil plant the Ministry of War Production was able to restore a hydrogenation plant to a high level of working capacity within six to eight weeks after a direct air strike.[22] Since the Allies counted on a longer interval, by the time the follow-up attack was delivered, even if all went according to plan, output equivalent to two weeks' full production would already have been obtained. Within the latitude offered by the intervals between air attacks and by the dispersal of the attacks against less valuable targets, and with the aid of occasional patches of bad weather, Germany was just able to sustain a sufficient level of oil production. But production of aviation fuel fell below any reasonable safety mark and it could certainly have been driven below that mark at an earlier date.

22. Milward, *The German Economy*, p. 119.

The development of the oil shortage in Germany has also of course to be seen against the diminution in importance of foreign supply; it was not solely due to the air offensive. March 1944 was the last month in which imports made a substantial contribution to German oil supply, between a quarter and a fifth of the total.[23] By May they accounted for barely more than 10 per cent. But in May the Allied air offensive first pushed monthly aviation fuel production below the level of consumption, a situation from which it never again clearly emerged in spite of the enormous drop in consumption from 195,000 tons in May 1944 to 44,000 tons in December.[24] Total stocks of aviation fuel in May were 574,000 tons; by December four fifths of the stock had been consumed. The disaster seemed to be approaching with greater speed after mid July when output sometimes fell below 500 tons a day. The production of other oils such as diesel fuel and carburettor fuel was also in decline and this reduced possibilities of substitutions or shifts in output. In any case all production of synthetic fuel depended on keeping the air force supplied with aviation fuel.

By July 1944 it seemed as though September and October would be the decisive months for fuel supply. A large-scale programme of undergound dispersal was estimated to be capable of producing by December about 90,000 tons of aviation fuel. Breweries and other installations with similar plant were converted into primitive fuel-producing works to remedy the drop in other types of fuel, but, as Speer reported to Hitler, if the attacks continued a planned use of the air force would become impossible in September or October. In early September bad weather and the diversion of the bombers to other targets brought a great improvement in the situation and by 10 September the forecast production figures had been reached. Between 11 and 19 September, however, the Allies succeeded in stopping all aviation fuel production in Germany.[25] Output of aviation fuel in September was a mere 10,000 tons, one sixth of consumption. It was at this point that reprieve came, partly through the onset of winter weather and partly through Allied vacillation. In November 49,000 tons of aviation fuel were produced. Pölitz was attacked

23. Birkenfeld, p. 224.
24. Birkenfeld, p. 228.
25. Webster and Frankland, vol. 4, p. 133.

very little in the winter and substantial production took place there, although the level of output was ultimately still too low for an effective air defence to be maintained. The army also suffered from fuel shortages in its failure to press home the Ardennes counter-offensive and in its inability to prevent the Russian advance into Silesia. In September 1944 the Allies had been very close to reducing one branch of the German armed forces to complete immobility by economic warfare alone.

The campaign against Japan was of a different character from that against Germany. There were no important neutral powers involved and although there was no state of war between Japan and the Soviet Union until 1945 there was practically no trade between them. By contrast there was an active and acknowledged trade between unoccupied China and Japan which was too vital to the Chinese interests for the Allies to intervene. In spite of this complication, however, the character of the campaign was more military and naval. The large size of the Japanese merchant fleet and the fact that Japanese imports were necessarily sea-borne put a premium on sinking merchant vessels. Although this policy was pursued with great consistency, in retrospect it appears not only that the Allies were closer to bringing the war to a successful conclusion than they realized before the atomic bomb was dropped but that with a more accurate and consistent application of the techniques of economic warfare the Japanese economy might have been brought earlier to the stage of dangerous weakness. It was therefore in the Pacific that, almost unnoticed, economic warfare achieved its greatest success.

Japan entered the war with about 6·5 million registered tons of merchant shipping. From an early stage losses exceeded building capacity and by the end of the war 88 per cent of the total merchant shipping available during the war had been sunk, over half of it by United States submarines. By the end of the war the merchant fleet consisted of only 1·5 million registered tons of inferior vessels. This, combined with the forced withdrawal of Japanese troops from their strongholds in South-East Asia and the Pacific islands, gradually produced shortages of materials more acute than in Germany and severely limited the types of military action which were now open to Japan. The shortages were crucial in steel, oil and coal.

The restrictions imposed by the United States on imports of

pig-iron and scrap iron into Japan in 1941 had had the effect of increasing Japan's dependence on imported iron ore. These imports reached their peak in the last quarter of 1942 and thereafter followed a declining trend. Steel production, however, continued to expand through the utilization of stockpiles. In this, as in so many cases, the Allies were misled, through their own false assumptions about the nature of the Japanese economy, into supposing their economic warfare measures to be having no effect. Because in 1943 the level of utilizable reserves was much higher than the Allies thought the real effects which economic warfare was having were not apparent outside Japan, and the natural result in the United States was one of disillusionment with such tactics.

But so long as the Yangtze river was kept virtually closed to navigation by Allied action Japanese iron ore imports from north China could not be increased. In spite of the great increases in armaments output the total quarterly production of finished steel showed no increase in the first three quarters of 1943 and only a very small upward movement in the last quarter. After the first quarter of 1944 it began to decline steeply. In fact in 1944 iron ore imports depended as much on Korean supply as Chinese. Total imports declined from 5 million metric tons in 1941 to 1·7 million metric tons in 1944. Imports of scrap metal fell from 1·4 million metric tons in 1940 to 74,000 tons in 1944 and stockpiles of scrap fell from 5·7 million metric tons to 449,000 metric tons over the same four-year period.[26] In the first quarter of 1945 total finished steel production was only 492,000 metric tons. The level of production of ingot steel in the next quarter was the equivalent of only 18 per cent of the wartime peak. Nor does it seem likely that this could have been turned into the same amount of finished steel. Naval bombardment of steel plant and attacks on the transport system between Hokkaido and Honshu imposed on the Honshu railway system the insupportable burden of moving 700,000 additional metric tons of iron ore and 1·2 million metric tons of Hokkaido coal to under-utilized blast furnaces in central Honshu and northern Kyushu. Shortages would have been even greater in special armaments steels which were being produced in the first quarter of 1945 at less than one tenth the average quar-

26. U.S.S.B.S., *The Effects of Strategic Bombing on the Japanese War Economy*, p. 114.

terly output of the previous year. The small number of air raids on steel works themselves made little difference but a greater concentration of attacks on the inter-island transport systems would have greatly intensified the steel production crisis.

This is equally applicable to the crises in oil and coal supply. Synthetic oil production in Japan compared to that in Germany was negligible. The main safeguard against the vulnerability of the Japanese economy to its oil supplies being cut off had been the accumulation of enormous oil stockpiles, about 5·7 million tons in December 1941.[27] Oil imports in fact continued to rise until the end of 1943, and in spite of the Allied successes in sinking merchant vessels the tanker capacity available to Japan also increased substantially in that time. What had not been foreseen was the high level of oil consumption of the armed forces, so high as to preserve an element of danger in what would otherwise have been a safe situation. Stocks of crude oil declined from 1941 onwards, of aviation fuel from 1942, and of diesel oil from the beginning of 1943. The sustained attack on shipping, especially on the long oil-run from Borneo, was bound to cause a deterioration in the situation. Oil imports fell sharply in 1944 and in the last quarter were one third below their level of the previous year. By February 1945 they had come to a complete stop. In early 1945 100,000 registered tons of oil-burning shipping was laid up in spite of the desperate shipping shortage, aircraft pilot training was drastically reduced, and battleships had to stay in port while the United States forces invaded Okinawa. Only by June when stocks of crude oil were practically exhausted and refineries no longer working did American bombers from the Marianas begin the first methodical attacks on the oil refineries.

Imports of coal into Japan declined from 1940 onwards. In that year they stood at 10·1 million metric tons, in 1943 they were only 6 million metric tons and in 1944 3·1 million.[28] Until the end of 1943 this fall was mainly due to the competing claims of other goods on scarce shipping space. In 1944 the influence of the blockade became the main factor. Imports from China were reduced by half and although their total weight was not great this was the most significant blow economically because there was no

27. Medlicott, vol. 2, p. 407.
28. U.S.S.B.S., *The Effects of Strategic Bombing on the Japanese War Economy*, pp. 128–9.

other accessible source of good coking coal. The shortfall in imports was accompanied by a drop of six million metric tons in domestic production in 1944, mostly concentrated in the last six months of the year. The effects of this drop in domestic production were exaggerated by the increasing difficulties of inter-island transport. The level of domestic output in August, if sustained, would have been sufficient for an annual output in 1945 of less than twenty million metric tons compared to the 57·3 million metric tons of 1940. The effect of this shortfall was felt most directly by the steel industry. Economies in the use of Chinese coking coals reduced the quality of finished steel. They also meant that iron ore had increasingly to be moved about over the damaged transport system; some Hokkaido ores could now only be used by moving them to Tokyo. Though not so grave as the shortages of oil and steel, the coal shortage was accelerating rapidly to the same position in 1945, and, combined with the other difficulties, threw great doubt on the ability of Japan to sustain military operations for much longer.

An island power which consists of several separate islands is of course an excellent target for economic warfare. The firm strategic decision by the Allies to give the war against Germany first priority meant that the potential weaknesses of Japan's economic position were less exploited than those of Germany until 1944. But subsequent events suggest that economic warfare applied with greater consistency and precision is in certain circumstances a strategic concept of great power; the state of the Japanese economy in early 1945 in many ways justified the high hopes which economists had pinned on such methods of warfare before 1939. The lack of consistency with which they had been applied to Germany had produced a certain disillusionment before the attacks on Japan. The primary German targets included in the joint list of 18 May 1943 were oil supply (provided that raids on the Romanian oil-fields and refineries at Ploesti would be possible), aircraft production, submarine repair yards and bases, and bearings. Oil, which ultimately proved the most successful, was the first choice and had been the subject of special but unsuccessful attention for four months in the summer of 1941. From July to December 1941 raids were concentrated on communications in the hope that this would prove more feasible and equally harmful. Later, before the invasion of the continent, the bombing offensive was again diverted to attacks against the enemy's communications, this time with a more obviously tactical military purpose. In spring 1944 oil supply again became the top priority target. Outside the bounds of these periods, when priorities were fairly clearly defined, there was a generalized attack on a number of targets of equal priority which was also part and parcel of area bombing. On the whole therefore out of the very large number of potential material deficiencies of the German economy none was consistently attacked. And of the primary targets of 1943 one, bearings, was a mistake.

Economic warfare depends for its success on the ability to restrict an enemy economy to a small and known stock of basic resources. Economic warfare was so successful against Japan because Japan was driven back from her imperial outposts to the limited economic base of the Home Islands and Korea. The extent of German conquests was such as to offer the control of the resources and trade of virtually a whole continent, and that in itself thwarted Allied strategy more effectively than the deficiencies of economic warfare as an idea or the inability to enforce it or the lack of consistency with which it was enforced.

Neutrals and the survival of international trade

Allowing for the possibilities of substitution of materials and for changes in priority which prevented bottlenecks from having a permanently harmful effect on the economy – policies which had certainly not been used to their maximum in the German steel industry – it can be said that economic warfare was still in 1945 a long way from making any marked difference to that industry's performance. This is equally true for other industries with an inadequate raw material base, such as aluminium. Only the case already considered, that of oil and in particular aviation fuel, was an exception. The history of the German steel and coal industries during the war makes it clear that although international trade was greatly distorted and reduced to low levels it survived as a system sufficiently complex to prevent the Allies from completely achieving the aims of their economic warfare. Important elements in the supply of the Axis powers were still obtained by the 'normal' channels of import. Even in a world where all the greatest powers were at war and the neutrals a relatively small and helpless group it proved impossible completely to prevent them from carrying on their 'normal' trade. If the American Board of Economic Warfare had had its own way entirely it would have liked to remove these last vestiges of the pre-1939 international economy. Had it done so it might well have acted against its own best interests. Neutral trade survived because it was in the interests of both camps, and in surviving it thwarted effective economic warfare against Germany.

The British government, which perhaps more clearly than the United States saw itself as an inextricable part of a complex mesh of trading connections, sought to regulate the problem in a reasonably equitable way by negotiating War Trade Agreements with the neutral states, and these agreements still held sway when the United States entered the war. The general principle involved was that the neutral powers agreed to quotas being imposed on their imports through the British blockade in accordance with the level of their pre-war import trade in order that the British and French governments might have some guarantee that goods were not being imported for re-export to the Axis powers. Neutral states also bound themselves not to export to Germany 'similar products' to those covered by the quotas. Such agreements were inevitably whittled away by German military victories which left Switzerland surrounded by German-occupied territory and German allies, and gave the German naval forces complete control over Sweden's seaborne commerce. The clearing agreements signed between Switzerland and Germany in July and August 1940 acknowledged these new realities and opened bigger credits for Swiss exports in Germany. The agreement of July 1941 was even more favourable to Germany.[29]

A similar trend in Swedish–German commercial relations and a secret protocol between the German and Turkish governments guaranteeing a resumption of Turkish chrome ore exports to Germany once the agreements with the Allies expired in 1943 had nullified the expected benefits of the War Trade Agreements by late 1941. The German–Turkish agreement bound the Turkish government to export 90,000 tons of chrome ore annually in 1943 and 1944 in return for German armaments. After the Swiss–German agreement of July 1941 the British government took the

29. H. Homberger, *Schweizerische Handelspolitik im zweiten Weltkrieg*, Eugen Rentsch, Erlenbach-Zürich, 1970, p. 24.

more drastic step of cutting off all supplies of raw materials to Switzerland as far as was in its power. At this point the necessity for preserving neutral trade became clear to both camps. With one exception the main railway connections between Germany and Italy ran through Switzerland and the safety of this transit trade was vital to the Axis war effort. Nor could the British entirely dispense with Swiss exports. Jewel precision bearings manufactured there were for the first two years of the war indispensable for aircraft instrument panels. A type of silk bolting cloth made only in Switzerland was used throughout the world in flour and grain mills. Together with Germany Switzerland was the only source of good-quality glass eyes, much in demand after 1939. All the Allies also used a patent of the Swiss armament firm Oerlikon to manufacture the most effective anti-aircraft gun for mounting on merchant ships. Nor did the Allies wish to be the agent through which Switzerland finally lost its long neutrality. By playing off these needs and attitudes the Swiss government was able to negotiate the so-called 'Compensation Agreement' in Berlin in September 1942. The agreement allowed Switzerland to import certain materials from the Allies in return for exports to them, including war equipment. The concession on the German side was greater because the Allies could still threaten Swiss supplies at any time, but it removed some of the onus on the Axis powers to keep Switzerland supplied with raw materials and food. In December 1943 the Allies increased the amount of foodstuffs they allowed through the blockade to Switzerland.

If Switzerland was still able to play some part in the real interests of the belligerent parties this was even more the case with Sweden, not only because of her position as an iron-ore exporter but because of her key position in the world's ball-bearing industry and in other specialized engineering fields. The total value of Swedish trade with Germany in 1941 was twice its level of 1938, but the reprisals of the Allies were less than against Switzerland. It was only as a result of United States pressure on the British that Sweden was forced into a new agreement with the Allies in September 1943 by which she agreed to reduce her total exports to Axis countries by 14 per cent in value and by a greater percentage in volume. This agreement was only successfully concluded because it appeared that the Allies would win the war in 1944.[30] When it later appeared they would not, Swedish exporters were not always too scrupulous in observing its terms. This was particularly the case with the SKF ball-bearings firm. The Allies were able by continuing pressure and complaints nominally to stop the export of certain types of bearings to Germany altogether and reduce the overall volume of ball- and roller-bearings exports by 30 per cent.[31] It was too late to make any difference to the German position and also, it might be added, to that of SKF whose gross profits in 1943 were three times their 1939 level.[32]

It cannot be said in any sense that these two countries ever abandoned genuine principles of commercial neutrality except when forced to do so by the belligerent nations. But because the belligerent nations had so much power and were prepared to use it the neutrality exercised by countries such as Switzerland and Sweden was far from any traditional concept of that word. The real situation was made clear when the Allies blockaded Sweden on 9 April 1940. One half of Swedish merchant tonnage was trapped inside the Baltic, which in the period of the Soviet Union's 'neutrality' put it entirely under the control of German guns. The quantities of iron ore shipped from Sweden to Germany throughout the war would have fallen still further below the amounts which were agreed on in the trade negotiations had not a greater proportion of Swedish merchant shipping been used for their carriage than originally stipulated. Swedish shipping seeking employment partly remedied the growing losses of German shipping through Allied actions. The situation in spring 1940, diplomatically complicated, was economically simple for Sweden. She was better able to survive without imports from Britain than was Britain without imports of special steel and charcoal iron from Sweden. She was able to use this bargaining power to acquire the right to certain imports of oil and rubber from the Allies. But it required a carefully carried out long-term policy of fuel economy in the domestic economy before Sweden

30. G. Hägglöf, *Svensk krigshandelspolitik under andra världskriget*, Stockholm, 1958, chapter XV.

31. B. Steckzén, *Svenska kullagerfabrikens historia*, Göteborg, 1957, pp. 563–8.

32. D. L. Gordon and R. J. Dangerfield, *The Hidden Weapon*, Harper & Brothers, New York, 1947, p. 216.

could be independent of fuel imports from Germany. Increasingly in the inter-war period Swedish coal imports had come from Poland and with the capture of the Polish coal mines Germany's bargaining position was too strong to permit any but the most technical commercial neutrality on Sweden's part. The total value of Swedish exports fell from an average of 1,786 million kronor between 1936 and 1938 to an average of 1,172 million between 1941 and 1944; but exports to Germany rose from an average of 301 million to 492 million over the same periods, or from 17 per cent of all exports to 42 per cent. By the end of 1943, however, studies in the German Ministry of War Production now suggested that Sweden would be able to survive for one year from that date without German supply and the policy of threatening Sweden with a suspension of exports had now to be modified to a policy of making every effort to provide coal, even in late 1944 when there were severe coal shortages in the domestic economy, in return for iron-ore and ball-bearing imports.[33] But by this time Allied diplomatic pressures were as strong in Stockholm as those of Germany had been earlier. Sweden's foreign trade was governed at every turn by political intervention of the most pressing kind.

Whether such neutrality was justified in the face of a political and social system so threatening and opposed as that of National Socialist Germany is another question and not an economic one. Some neutrals, like the United States, actively and purposely discriminated against Axis trade from 1939, and others, like the Soviet Union, became trading partners of great importance to Germany. In fact the signing of the German–Russian trade agreements after August 1939 was a mortal blow to the blockade against Germany.

From the German point of view the re-opening of trade with the Soviet Union was seen as an extremely important economic safeguard against the Allied blockade which was bound to be imposed on the first day of any attack on the western powers. It opened not only a rich Russian source of raw materials and food but also a door to the east for supply from Manchuria and China. It provided also a land-transport link with a friendly power, Japan. As long as this eastern breach existed the blockade was but half a blockade. The importance of the trade to Germany

33. S.-O. Olsson, *German Coal and Swedish Fuel 1939–1945*, Kungsbacka, Gothenburg, 1975, p. 135 ff.

was such that the agreements when signed were substantially different from what Germany had originally planned and the difference represented serious concessions of real interest to the Soviet Union, made with considerable reluctance.

After 1933 Germany's trading links with the Soviet Union had virtually withered away. Exports to and imports from the Soviet Union by value in 1938 were both less than 1 per cent of the total value of German exports and imports in that year and the growing concentration of German trade on south-eastern Europe was accompanied by a long decline of trade with the Soviet Union. In 1940 imports from the Soviet Union rose to 7·9 per cent of German imports by value, making it fifth in importance among German suppliers, including those countries which had been occupied. As an export market for Germany it was less important but it still took 4·5 per cent of all German exports. The composition of this virtually completely new trade was as important as its size. The original German intention was to offer long-term investment goods, such as industrial installations, in return for raw materials of immediate relevance to the war effort. But from the outset the Soviet government made it abundantly clear that its main interest was in securing armaments and armaments technology from Germany.[34] Within the first year of the agreement, in return for goods including one million metric tons of fodder grains, 900,000 metric tons of crude oil, 500,000 metric tons of manganese ore and 100,000 metric tons of chrome ore, Germany agreed to provide plans for the battleship *Bismarck* and for as the yet undeveloped Messerschmidt 209, and a plant for manufacturing titanium alloy.

Deliveries did not get properly under way on either side until December 1939 and at the end of March 1940 they were suddenly and temporarily halted on the Russian side because the Soviet Union had already delivered goods more than twelve times the value of those she had received. The delays had not been accidental, for Hitler had issued instructions to delay as long as possible the delivery of all important strategic goods and armaments plans. At the end of the first half year Russian deliveries were still twice the value of Germany's and from spring 1941 Germany had no interest in fulfilling the agreements honestly other than to obtain

34. W. Birkenfeld, 'Stalin als Wirtschaftspartner Hitlers (1939 bis 1941)', in *Vierteljahrschrift für Sozial- und Wirtschaftsgeschichte,* no. 53, 1966.

the more vital supplies from Russia. These supplies of raw materials continued to roll to the interchange stations until the very eve of the war and on balance the agreements were very profitable to Germany, the more so as by haggling over prices and contriving bureaucratic delays she was able to prevent the more dangerous technology from reaching the Soviet Union. In 1940 692,000 metric tons of barley, over 90 per cent of the total quantity imported, came from the Soviet Union and virtually the whole of German imports of oats. In the more vital strategic materials Soviet deliveries were equally important. In 1940 and the first six months of 1941 they amounted to 140,000 metric tons of manganese ore, 26,000 metric tons of chrome ore and 863,000 metric tons of crude oil. German exports to the Soviet Union in the same period consisted of roughly equal shares of metal manufactures and machinery and electrical products.[35]

After the entry into war of the United States, the Soviet Union and Japan the remaining neutral states appeared in the eyes of the belligerent powers mainly as a nuisance. Their economic neutrality had already had inroads made upon it by the naval blockades of the First World War; it was now threatened still further. Sweden was forced to permit the transit of German troops and military supplies and then forced to stop the traffic later. Switzerland was also forced to restrict some transit traffic. The Spanish and Portuguese governments were forced into controlling and restricting the supply of wolfram although it was an indigenous product. As compensation for these infringements they all prospered greatly. Spain was able to turn an important deficit into an export surplus and repatriate part of her foreign debt. The price of wolfram, whose output increased to 4,500 tons a year, rose on the Portuguese open market from $1,144 a ton in August 1940 to $20,000 a ton in October 1941. After the catastrophe of the civil war began a hesitant economic recovery. The output of coal, steel and iron ore increased and by 1946 total production again briefly touched the level it had reached in 1929.[36] An increase in industrial output *per capita* was attained during the war in spite of the restricted trading opportunities.

35. F. Friedensburg, 'Die sowietischen Kriegslieferungen an das Hitlerreich', *Vierteljahrschrift zur Wirtschaftsforschung*, Duncker und Humblot, Berlin, 1962.

36. H. Paris Eguilaz, *Diez años de politica economica en España, 1939-1949*, J. Sanchez Ocaña, Madrid, 1949.

This experience was the common lot of the other neutrals. Two of them, Sweden and Switzerland, were better placed to take advantage of the situation because of their less desperate circumstances in the previous decade, their high levels of *per capita* income, and their sophisticated industrial structure. These two states emerged in 1945 with their basic economic structure unscathed as the two richest European nations and with their industry in a perfect position immediately to supply the demands of reconstruction. This was so in spite of the fall in the volume of their trade after 1939. The strong bargaining position of Germany meant that she could often dictate trade prices; the price index of Swedish imports rose almost twice as rapidly as that of exports between 1938 and 1943. Many Swedish firms were less fortunate than SKF and made a loss in these years. Real wages declined. Swiss foreign trade declined even more severely than that of Sweden, especially in 1944, but the export of machinery, including armaments, rose. It accounted for half the value of Swiss exports to Axis territory in 1943. The wealth and rapid economic growth of these states in the immediate post-war period was in many ways a reflection of the absence from their economies of the problems which war brought to the economies of the combatants.

Economic warfare did no real harm to neutral states even if it virtually destroyed existing international law on neutrality. It did only limited damage to the German economy. It might well have crippled the Japanese economy if it had not been overtaken by other tactics. It might have been more successful both against Germany and Japan if better understood and more consistently and accurately pursued. As a strategic conception it has by no means been proved worthless by the Second World War. But unless the odds are so overwhelmingly in favour of one side that it probably would have no need of such a slow-working strategy its effectiveness depends on a very exact knowledge of the functioning of a highly complex economic system. That knowledge was insufficient in the Second World War, and there is no real reason to suppose that in the majority of wars between major industrial powers it ever could be sufficient for sole reliance to be placed on such a strategy.

10

Reconstruction of the International Economy

Die Theorie fordert also, dass bei jedem Kriege zuerst sein Charakter und seine grosen Umrisse nach der Wahrscheinlichkeit aufgefasst werden, die die politischen Grössen und Verhältnisse ergeben. Je mehr nach dieser Wahrscheinlichkeit sein Charakter sich dem absoluten Kriege nähert, je mehr die Umrisse die Masse der kriegführenden Staaten umfassen und in den Strudel hineinziehen, um so leichter wird der Zusammenhang seiner Begebenheiten, um so notwendiger, nicht den ersten Schritt zu tun, ohne an den letzten zu denken.

[Theory demands, therefore, that at the commencement of every war its character and main outline shall be defined according to what the political considerations and relationships lead us to anticipate as probable. The more nearly its character according to this probability appears to approach absolute war – the more its outline embraces the mass of the belligerent states and draws them into the vortex – the more loosely related will its events be and the more necessary will it be not to take the first step without thinking what may be the last.]

Carl von Clausewitz,
Vom Kriege, 1821

'Loss' and 'gain'

As Germany moved into chaos and the forces marshalled against Japan became invincible, the victors were faced with the fact that the future economic world was theirs to make. In the Soviet Union these decisions could not have been too difficult. The political system there was hardly conducive to change. In any case the war was interpreted as a triumph of the Soviet system over a mortal enemy. A weakened country set about recouping its losses from the great territorial gains which the war brought. For the Western powers the situation was more ambiguous. The war had placed in sharp relief certain weaknesses and deficiencies in society before 1939, especially exemplified in France,. which had collapsed so quickly. At the same time it brought also a new sense of social cohesion in a common purpose which offered the hope of healing some of the pre-war social divisions. This hope seemed more attainable because of the new prosperity which the war brought to some states.

The military and economic outcome of the war left one country, the United States, in an overwhelmingly dominant situation, and it was inevitable that economic policy there would be the chief factor in determining the post-war international economy. That this would be so had already been understood by the more far-sighted members of the Roosevelt administration as early as 1941. As the American industrial economy expanded vigorously to meet the demand of domestic rearmament the economic problem for the United States changed completely. The question was no longer how to share out an inadequate level of income and employment by the cautious regulation of output but rather how to sustain the economy after the war at the new levels of output and income which it had attained.

By 1941 the National Resources Planning Board was already writing of maintaining the national income at a level of at least $100,000 million a year, and it was soon to climb well beyond that figure.[1] Such an objective appeared to demand that after the war there would be foreign markets capable of absorbing at least the same level of exports as the United States had maintained during the war with lend-lease financing. The weak and dangerous situation of Britain in 1941 and its ultimate dependence on the United States offered a diplomatic opportunity to the American government to pursue these new economic aims. In the discussions between Roosevelt and Churchill in Placentia Bay which

1. United States, National Resources Planning Board, *After Defense – What?*. G.P.O., Washington, D.C., 1941.

led to that rhetorically obscure document, the Atlantic Charter, the United States administration brought great pressure to bear on Britain to end 'discrimination' in international trade. The immediate target was the tariff and quota preferences which Britain gave to Commonwealth countries under the terms of the Ottawa agreements. But the government in Washington, in spite of the opposition of the older New Dealers, was developing wider ambitions. It wanted to create after the war a viable system of multilateral trading which would permit as consistent an expansion of international trade as the gold standard had done before 1914. This aim was not without its own idealism; the events of the 1930s had appeared to support the view that protectionist, autarkic, national economies led to war. And certainly the devices of bilateral trading agreements, exchange and currency controls, import and export controls and trading blocs had done little to expand international trade by 1939 above the very low level of 1933. Multilateralism in trade was seen in the United States as a concomitant of democratic government, as well as the only way to preserve the economic gain which the war had brought.

In other countries the situation was less clear cut. In Chapters 1 and 3 the argument was briefly made that war has been far too frequently condemned as an economic loss; the example of the United States economy between 1938 and 1945 adds powerful support to the argument. It is estimated that, at 1929 prices, the *per capita* national product increased from $794 in 1938 to $1,293 in 1945. But except in Canada, where the rate of increase of national income was even greater, no other country for which we have figures fared so well. The fluctuations of prices and, in some countries, the steep inflation during the war period make such calculations even more difficult to interpret for comparative purposes than they usually are. And for the major combatant powers increases in Gross Domestic Product until mid 1944, very marked in Japan, Germany and Britain, were in any case achieved by policies which could not long be sustained. Most of the neutral countries, however, showed a growth of total output between 1939 and 1945 even when allowance is made for inflation and so did some of the other combatant countries, such as Australia, whose economy was less dominated by investment for the purely short-term purposes of winning the war.

In spite of this, attempts at assessing the impact of the war on the economy often concentrate on calculating the 'loss' to the various national economies caused by the war. This 'loss' is often seen as the immediate problem for the post-war economic world. Old habits of thought died hard and they were preserved by countries attempting to calculate the extent of their national economic loss with a view to claiming reparations from the defeated states. The purpose of such calculations inevitably gave the figures an upward bias. But there are other reasons also for regarding them with some scepticism. Most contain an allowance for capital stock depreciation, and the question has to be put as to how far such depreciation was due entirely to the war. The answer can only be obtained by comparison with a so-called 'normal' period. But there is no normal period; war is merely one of the forces which change the criteria by which investment decisions are made. So does peacetime rearmament, something which bears with particular force on all comparisons made with the late 1930s. After the end of 1941, of course, investment decisions were often made in a situation of extreme bias towards one purpose only. But the point has already been made that even in a situation of that kind, approximating to the familiar cliché 'total war', the period of time over which investment decisions were dictated by such relatively simple considerations was quite short. Considerations applying to the period after the war were already weighing importantly in early 1944. In these circumstances it seems quite misleading to pretend to identify accurately the amount of replacement of capital stock deferred because the economy was at war. Furthermore, it must also be asked whether the capital stock was actually used before the war. In 1938 industrial production in Italy and France was lower than in 1929. In most, if not all, combatant countries the rate of replacement of fixed capital was surely higher during the war period than in the preceding decade. In addition there are the well-known problems of the valuation of capital, made no easier by the way in which the production function of many economies was altered by warfare.

There is, however, the separate problem of the actual destruction of capital, a much bigger item in establishing the 'loss' caused by the war. Bombers, submarines and invading armies all had the destruction of fixed capital as a main objective. How far did they succeed? Maddison has estimated from other sources the extent of the loss of capital assets in some European countries over the period 1939–45.[2] His estimates put the loss of domestic pre-war capital stock at about 25 per cent in the Soviet Union by the end of 1945, at 13 per cent for the territory of the future Federal Republic of Germany, at 8 per cent for France, 7 per cent for Italy and 3 per cent for Britain. The conceptual difficulties of such estimates and the different ways in which they are compiled suggest they should be regarded with caution. War was also responsible for the creation of much new fixed capital, some of it more useful in the period after 1939 than the capital stock it replaced. If war is considered as a normal force in capital replacement the period would more accurately be seen as one in which under its influence the composition of the capital stock in many countries underwent a rapid change.

It has been suggested that the level of investment in capital-goods industries in Germany during the war was so high that in spite of the great physical destruction of 1945 the basic productive capacity of the economy in this area was still at the end of that year as high as it had been in 1940.[3] The damage done by armies and armaments to capital goods was certainly less everywhere than the damage they did to capital in general. Only about 6½ per cent of the German machine-tool stock was damaged in 1944 in the heaviest period of bombing suffered by any country and most had been repaired by the end of the year.[4] The damage was in fact insignificant compared to the growth of capacity and at the end of the war the machine-tool inventory was bigger than at the beginning. At the height of the German raids on Britain, from August 1940 to December 1941, only 1·7 per cent of the British stock of machine tools was damaged. Obviously the experience of occupied countries was different in the sense that conditions were much less favourable to investment there. But in some occupied countries the capacity of installed motive power in manufacturing industry increased during the war. It did so in Norway, for example, from 2·16 million horse-power in 1938 to 2·37 million horse-power in 1945. Part of this increase came from the German investment programmes in power stations and

2. A. Maddison, *Economic Policy and Performance in Europe 1913–1970*, The Fontana Economic History of Europe, vol. V, chapter 10, London, 1973.
3. Krengel, p. 94.
4. U.S.S.B.S., *The Effects*, p. 45.

electrolytic smelting there. In Denmark it increased from 0·55 million horse-power to 0·71 million over the same period. The isolation of the European continent from world trade and the ideological conceptions of National Socialism meant that the effects of import substitution were not confined to Germany alone. Investment in synthetic fuel and synthetic rubber production took place in Bohemia and in aluminium manufacture and oil drilling

TABLE 33
MACHINE-TOOL INVENTORY OF SOME COMBATANT COUNTRIES, 1938–45 (in thousands of units)

	1938	1940	1945
Germany			
metal-cutting	900	1,178	1,737–1,233*
metal-cutting and metal-forming	1,281	1,577	2,316–1776*,
all metal-working	1,614	n.a.	2,594–2,143*
United Kingdom			
metal-cutting and metal-forming	n.a.	700	800
France			
all metal-working	550	n.a.	600
Italy			
all metal-working	207†	n.a.	290
United States			
metal-cutting	n.a.	942	1,883

* Maximum and minimum estimates respectively.
† 1939.

SOURCE: United Nations, Department of Economic Affairs, *Economic Survey of Europe since the War. A Reappraisal of Problems and Prospects*, Geneva, 1953, p. 3.

in Austria. The extensive industrial investments in Norway have already been discussed. In Belgium the capacity of the synthetic fibre industry was expanded.

As capital investment in these areas of production increased, destruction and depreciation particularly affected housing (a very high proportion of the capital stock), transport, merchant shipping and the land. But the effect of these losses was seen much less in the difficulties they created in reaching and maintaining high levels of output in the national domestic economies than in those they created in the reconstruction of the international economy. For most countries not on high levels of output and employment at the end of the war recovery to such levels was very rapid after 1945 and where it was slowed down it was, except in eastern Europe, mainly slowed down because of the international rather than the domestic economic problems which the war had created.

Indeed this seems to have been recognized by the very short space of time over which most of the victorious powers claimed 'reparations' from the defeated. This did not apply to the Soviet Union. It was evident from the outset that there was little possibility that that country would be able to take any part in the type of new international economic arrangements advocated by the United States. It would remain an isolated economy, whose international trade played only a very restricted role, adhering firmly to its pre-war domestic economic policies. Nothing could eradicate the idea that the 'loss' caused to the Soviet economy by Germany could be recouped by transferring the equivalent sum from Germany to Russia in goods and cash. This led to many ludicrous examples of factories and equipment being transferred in this way immediately after the war which were in fact virtually useless in Russian production conditions.

The western Allies at first thought in the same terms. But having reduced large parts of Germany to kilometres of rubble through which the population searched for the wherewithal to survive, the victorious powers also decided to restrict severely the future levels of German production, an absurd contradiction in policy. They saw the temporary economic vacuum which they had suddenly created in the centre of Europe as an advantage to themselves, believing that their problem was one of recovery of output and that this would be achieved by supplying the markets which Germany could be prevented from supplying. In the Quebec Conference of September 1944 Roosevelt and Churchill agreed on the future level of industrial output in Germany. Steel output was not to exceed 5·8 million tons and the output of most other industries was similarly to be between one quarter and one half of its 1936 level. Although the Level of Industry Plan was never properly applied, German industrial output in 1946 did in fact remain at about one third the level of 1936. This was far too low to meet the specified sum of reparations, even to the Soviet Union alone, $10,000 million.

But a policy aimed at impoverishing in perpetuity almost seventy million people in the centre of Europe could not long survive if the United States was to succeed in maintaining the levels of employment and *per capita* income which the war had brought. East Germany continued to pay reparations to the Soviet Union but in the western zones the seizure of assets, apart from merchant shipping and the small amount of foreign assets, was on a very small scale compared to the immense demands made after 1918. The currency reform of 1947 created very quickly the conditions in which the productive capacity of the economy of the western zones could begin the same rapid recovery to high levels of production that had begun two years earlier in other European countries.

It is quite unrealistic to argue that the economic 'loss' caused by the war, the 'cost' of the war, was a serious matter for the post-war world. The most serious legacy came rather from the fact that the outcome of the war was a decided economic 'gain' to some countries and an economic 'loss' to others. It was the redistributive effects of the war, not its 'cost', which made the problems of reconstructing the post-war economy so difficult to solve in spite of the rapid recovery of output in the separate national economies.

Major difficulties were put in the way of reconstructing a multilateral trading and payments system by the economic changes brought by the war. Firstly, these changes were reflected in abrupt shifts of military and diplomatic power which made political agreement between the victors, the first essential of any lasting settlement, more difficult to achieve. Secondly, popular aspirations had changed in western Europe as well as the United States; the changed aspirations there entailed the introduction of post-war domestic economic policies which made a smoothly working multilateral payments system more difficult to operate. Thirdly, and most importantly, the war produced structural alterations in the pattern of world trade and payments which presented unforeseen obstacles to the construction of a more smoothly functioning international economy. It brought about shifts in the direction of foreign trade and alterations in the pattern of foreign investment and invisible earnings which proved to be long-term changes. Although it was in this third area, in its immediate impact on the flow of world trade and payments, that the war's consequences were most serious, their seriousness may only be measured by first considering the other two areas.

Difficulties of international agreement

The first may be quickly disposed of. When the United States government first began to press in 1941 for changes in the post-war economy the attitude in Britain to these new developments was cautiously favourable. The system of imperial preference had not worked well, and the Commonwealth countries were even less likely after the war, and after the changes in their economic structure which the war was already bringing about, to be content with their position as a protected market for British industry. But the British government objected strongly to the separation between 'discrimination' and tariffs; it was hardly prepared to end imperial preference without a reduction in the United States tariffs. The seventh clause of the lend-lease agreements, however, bound the United Kingdom to end discrimination in international trade after the war and to help in setting up a multilateral trading system. What this actually meant in practice was left to subsequent discussion throughout the war.[5] The British government's economic position was so weak that it had in any case no alternative but to sign and no doubt it was at that time preoccupied with more immediate threats. But by late 1943 Britain was also a major and ambitious military power. Furthermore, the successful experience of economic controls, together with a clear perception of the great difficulties of reconverting to peaceful purposes an economy so concentrated on warfare, had developed a strong body of opinion in favour of retaining trade controls as one method of circumventing these difficulties. Opposition to fulfilling the implications of clause seven now came from a section of right-wing opinion which saw imperial preferences as one way of retaining great power status, and equally strongly from a section of left-wing opinion which wanted to reinforce the greater prosperity and greater social justice and equality of the war years by means of a planned and controlled economy after the war.

The arguments which raged about the maintenance of economic controls show the extent to which the debate on future economic priorities in Britain was concerned with the purely domestic context. Where employment had been high in the inter-war period it had been mostly in economies which had cut themselves off

5. R. N. Gardner, *Sterling-Dollar Diplomacy*, Clarendon Press, Oxford, 1956, p. 54 ff.

from the movements of the international economy. The issue was whether economic objectives such as a high level of employment could be attained without far-reaching controls over foreign trade, and without controls of capital movements, interest rates and the balance of payments. By the end of the war the real economic and military power had effectively shifted once more. The extent of the change was shown by the American decision to end the lend-lease arrangements immediately on the end of the war with Japan. This applied even to orders being produced at that moment which would henceforward have to be paid for in dollars. This left Britain with no alternative to seeking a large interest-bearing loan in the United States, something that had been avoided during the war. The American government used the occasion to insist that under the terms of the loan sterling was to be made a convertible currency in July 1947. Some concessions were made in the lend-lease accounting but their price was a firm commitment to multilateralism and free convertibility by the United Kingdom. The British decision to do everything to preserve sterling as a convertible international currency within this new framework was unavoidable. There was in 1945 no means of repaying lend-lease supply other than by reparations from Germany, of which the historical experience was not a happy one, or a great and rapid increase in exports, which in any case suggested alignment with American economic policy. But the decision looked at the time a shaky and faltering step and has looked so since. The free convertibility of sterling when introduced under the terms of the dollar loan in fact lasted only one month. By the end of 1947 Britain was again operating controlled exchanges and restrictive trade agreements. In the intervening period before the introduction of the convertibility of sterling the shortage of dollars meant that countries in the sterling area continued to pool their dollars as a way of confining imports from the United States to necessities and it needed little formal management by London to keep in existence a set of trading practices which discriminated against United States trade, because it was in everyone's short-term interest to do so.

These political disagreements accompanied the more fundamental disagreement between the western Allies and the Soviet Union over the future economic system. The outcome of this was that in 1947 Germany itself began to be divided into two separate economies and that eastern European countries became mere instruments of Soviet policy passing definitively out of consideration in any new international economic arrangements. The pattern of intra-European trade was consequently very different from that before 1939. The complete failure to agree over the economic future of Germany made the attempts to reconstruct a viable international economic system more difficult and complicated. And these complications were only enhanced by the hostility between the two most powerful of the victorious powers which prevailed only two years after the German surrender. The creation of a multilateral trading system had already by that date acquired obvious connections with United States foreign policy and this was to make some of the international economic institutions designed to operate it less than neutral in their composition and operations.

Changes in domestic economic policy

Ultimately, however, the international economic interests of western Europe and north America were one because agreement on an international payments system seemed the only way of realizing the aims of domestic economic policy. The low levels of production and employment in the inter-war period were now seen as a needless waste of resources and one which by knowledgeable management of the economy could be averted. The ultimate problem was, as in the United States, to sustain and sell a greater volume of production. It was in Britain that these changes in economic and social aspirations had become most institutionalized. This expressed itself throughout the negotiations with the United States in the fear that any future multilateral system might result in the United Kingdom's domestic economic policies being at the mercy of any deflationary policy in the United States. In fact the tide of political and social opinion in the United States was flowing in the same direction as in Britain under the same influences. In January 1943 the President's message to Congress identified full employment after the war as the official aim of the administration. The British government only made a public acceptance of the same aim in a White Paper in 1944.[6] But underlying the acceptance of full employment in Britain was the idea

6. United Kingdom, Parliamentary Papers, VIII, 1943–4, Cmd 6257, *Employment Policy*, H.M.S.O., 1944.

that this was the essential, rather than merely desirable, basis of support for continuing the institutional changes which had come to be accepted during the war. The social aspirations which led to these institutional changes were just as prominent in the United States. The threatened march of black trade unionists on Washington in January 1941 had been the direct cause of the Fair Employment Practices Committee whose task was to eliminate racial discrimination on the shop floor. Nowhere more than amongst the black population of the United States was the demand for a better place in post-war society more aroused. But these desires remained to be translated into effective political action after the war whereas in Britain even during the war important changes had been made and there was a natural anxiety lest they should be undone by subsequent international agreements.

Pre-war social policy in Britain had been concerned to ease the lot of particular unfortunate groups, such as orphans, widows or old people. But 'total war' was a danger involving everybody, a point driven home savagely by the use of aircraft to bomb civilians. In such a situation it was absurd to provide free medicine and hospitals only to patch up the fighting forces to send them back to battle, when the restoration of damaged civilians was of equal value. In Britain, the Emergency Hospitals Service and other changes in health services were an important step towards the post-war creation of a comprehensive National Health Service related to a comprehensive system of national insurance. Numerous other welfare measures were introduced while the war was at its height.[7] The semi-official Beveridge Report, proposing a comprehensive and compulsory social insurance scheme for all citizens after the war, became extraordinarily popular and political sentiment in favour of such a scheme mounted rapidly.[8] In the United States also the seventh report of the National Resources Planning Board, published in November 1942, advocated a Bill of Rights which, like the Beveridge Report, proposed 'freedom from fear of old age, want, dependency, sickness, unemployment and accident'.[9]

7. R. H. Titmuss, *Problems of Social Policy*, H.M.S.O., London, 1950.

8. Sir W. Beveridge, *Social Insurance and Allied Services* (Parliamentary Papers, VI, 1942–3), H.M.S.O., London, 1942.

9. United States, National Resources Planning Board, *Post-war Agenda: Full Employment Security, Building America*, G.P.O., Washington, D.C., 1942.

It is tempting to argue that the consequence of 'total war' must always be to produce a significant volume of social change because the state must retain the allegiance of its citizens, and the greater the demands it makes on them the more they will seize the opportunity to make demands on it. But this process depends on the governmental arrangements and it would be nearer the truth merely to say that the economic, social and psychological experience of war produces a change in the climate of social consciousness.[10] Lest the reality of this changed climate be doubted it needs only to be considered that in Britain at the height of the war Parliament began a reform of the education system and passed the Town and Country Planning Act. The administration of welfare provision lost some of the petty cruelty which had been its hallmark and was interpreted in a rather more generous spirit. A government which began by planning to fight the anticipated fearful reactions of its own subjects under bombing and combat was brought to realize that the enterprise of war demanded a greater amount of trust and cooperation between government and all its subjects. However vaguely conceived, the aims of reconstruction had to take the form of a job, an income and basic social security for everyone.

Five years of full employment had produced in themselves a certain amount of measurable economic change in the position of the poorer members of the community. Only in the United States did increased real earnings play a big part in this change. In Britain it was more directly related to the wartime incidence of government financial policy. The establishment in Britain of a more progressive income tax was in itself a cause of income redistribution. The stabilization of the old-fashioned Board of Trade cost-of-living index, while it did not represent a genuine stabilization of the expenditures of the lower income groups, nevertheless kept the cost of certain basic items of consumption at a low level. This combination of price controls and progressive taxation was the prime cause of a more rapid and consistent redistribution of income than in previous periods. The part of wage earners, including servicemen and their dependants, in the national income in Britain increased by about £900 million at 1947 prices between 1938 and 1947. This gain was mainly made

10. A. Marwick, *Britain in the Century of Total War. War, Peace and Social Change 1900–1967*, The Bodley Head, London, 1968.

up of a drop in the income of salary earners and of unearned income. In 1947 working-class income, as measured by Seers, was 59 per cent of private income. In 1938 it had been 55 per cent. The total real net income of the same working-class group rose by more than 9 per cent, of the 'middle-class' category it fell by more than 7 per cent. These calculations are made on a post-tax basis; if they were made on a pre-tax basis the element of income redistribution would be scarcely perceptible. By 1948 price controls and progressive taxation had been mainly responsible for transferring about £500 million at 1938 prices from the most highly paid one sixth of the population to the rest, increasing their purchasing power by about 25 per cent.[11]

If, however, we ask the question to what extent war redistributed wealth rather than income, the answer is hardly at all. Since it was the gross inequalities of wealth which were the foundation of social inequality in capitalist economies it cannot be said that the war went very far to removing these inequalities. The percentage of the national capital stock in Britain belonging to those owning between £1,000 and £5,000 was about 17·5 per cent in 1936–8 and about 21·5 per cent in 1946–7. The proportion in the hands of those holding over £100,000 fell markedly, but the proportion belonging to those holding under £1,000 scarcely changed.[12] The evidence suggests that the redistribution of capital in Britain accelerated during the Second World War but it also points to the fact that this hardly touched the poorest groups. In 1946–7 1 per cent of the persons aged over 25 owned half of the total capital holdings in England and Wales. The bottom 52 per cent of a sample of working-class families in 1944–5 owned a mere 9 per cent of the aggregate savings of the whole group, the top 12 per cent of the sample owned 50 per cent of the total savings. In general, in spite of full employment, long hours, and the lack of consumer goods the level of working-class savings in 1945 was very low.[13]

In the United States the picture was slightly more favourable.

11. Seers, *Changes*.

12. K. Langley, 'The Distribution of Capital in Private Hands in 1936–8 and 1946–7', in *Bulletin of the Oxford University Institute of Statistics*, no. 13, 1951.

13. H. Durant and J. Goldman, 'The Distribution of Working-Class Savings', in *Bulletin of the Oxford University Institute of Statistics*, no. 7, 1945.

The average share of the top 5 per cent of income earners varied little over the two interwar decades. Between 1939 and 1944 it dropped five percentage points.[14] The reasons were similar to those applying in Britain: an increase in employment and wage earnings, changes in the savings and investment habits of the rich forced on them by wartime economic policy, lower interest rates and, most important, steeper rates of personal taxation on the higher incomes. Studies of the lower income groups show that the Second World War was a period of considerable reductions in the level of personal debt. The general level of savings was higher than in any previous period.[15]

People's new aspirations were built on nothing more than a job and more money, because for most people in both economies these had been the real economic changes in the war. Yet in spite of the very limited degree of economic change, the war also brought a change of social climate: social equality was now more widely accepted as a desirable end. The less conspicuous consumption of the wealthy, the curbs on individuals' property rights, the general antipathy to profiteering, the existence of rationing, the expectation that everyone should work, all tended to influence thought in this direction. These social aspirations were more readily accepted because bombs did not make class distinctions, because death and sacrifice were common to all, because it was not psychologically possible to go through such danger and discomfort without aspiring to better things, and because, in such a holocaust, humanity, even in the shape of the enemy, could be sometimes understood to have a common fate.

But there is all the difference in the world between hoping for and making statements about the maintenance of full employment as the basic priority of economic policy and actually putting such a policy into successful operation. Those who wished to build permanently into the system the social change which had been produced during the war advocated the retention of wartime economic controls for an unspecified period after the war. Businessmen generally were in favour of scrapping them at once.

14. S. Kuznets, *Shares of Upper Income Groups in Income and Savings*, National Bureau of Economic Research, publication no. 55, Princeton University Press, 1953.

15. R. W. Goldsmith, *A Study of Saving in the United States*, 3 vols., Princeton University Press, 1955.

In the United States internal quarrels on this issue developed as early as 1943. There had been much political agitation over the fact that bigger firms, because they had greater economies of scale and lower production costs, and also because they had the technological adaptability, got the lion's share of war contracts. Congress legislated for a certain proportion of contracts to be allocated to smaller businesses. These pressures in favour of bigger firms applied everywhere. Studies of the production committees in the German economy will almost certainly show that they were not dominated by the most efficient manufacturers, as they were officially supposed to be, but by the largest manufacturers; however, one reason for this was that, under wartime conditions, the largest manufacturers in many cases actually were the most efficient. One branch of opinion in the War Production Board hoped to stabilize this situation in the United States after the war by dismantling economic controls as quickly as possible.[16] In that way the bigger firms would be able to exploit their greater purchasing power in a period when raw materials would still be scarce and would thus corner the markets at the expense of their smaller competitors. The Office of Production Administration on the other hand was concerned to prolong controls precisely to avoid this situation.

This was in fact a central question in post-war reconstruction, just as it also was in many ways in the impact of the war on society as a whole. Because of this the proper and full consideration of such issues belongs to the next volume in this series. In the United States economic controls were relaxed extremely quickly, and their relaxation led to a scramble for goods and services in which victory went to the strongest and richest. In the United Kingdom controls were maintained longer than anywhere, virtually for a decade after the end of the war. The accumulated savings and other claims of the American labour force were liberated when goods were still in short supply and expensive. In Britain they were more gradually liberated while rationing and subsidized prices were maintained.

But these differences in post-war policy did not affect the underlying harmony of economic intention in the two countries:

16. B. J. Bernstein, 'Industrial Reconversion: The Protection of Oligopoly and Military Control of the Wartime Economy', in *American Journal of Economics and Sociology*, no. 26, 1967.

to make national policies of full employment compatible with an international economic system which would increase the level of world trade. The self-adjusting mechanisms of the pre-1914 gold standard had operated through creating periodic deflation and unemployment. They had also operated at the expense of under-developed countries who were rarely able to gain access to the flow of short-term capital lending which cushioned these effects on the more developed economies. What was needed was a system of multilateral payments which operated less stringently on the underdeveloped economies and a set of international financial institutions which might act as intermediaries in payments adjustments and create an adjustment mechanism less harsh than that which had operated semi-automatically through the domestic money supply before 1914. This was what was proposed, in different forms, on all sides. But these proposals never took adequate account of the structural changes in the international economy which the war had produced.

International economic consequences of the war

The war had produced great changes in the invisible receipts of western European countries. At the same time it had altered the pattern of world commodity prices in such a way as to produce a decisive shift in the terms of trade against developed economies which were importers on a large scale, like those of western Europe. These difficulties were made much worse by alterations in the direction of world trade during the war which turned out also to be long-term changes.

The total receipts of western European countries from overseas earnings in the immediate pre-war period had been almost one third of the earnings from exports; in 1950–51 they were only about 9 per cent of the value of 1938 exports. The marine and commercial insurance business of other areas of the world had had perforce to develop during the war. And the destruction of merchant shipping bore particularly heavily on western Europe and Japan. Although the war had seen an increase in the gross tonnage of the world's merchant fleet the permanent increase had taken place predominantly in the United States' mercantile marine. The United States' merchant navy, which comprised less than 17 per cent of the world's merchant tonnage in 1939, was

52 per cent by 1947, including the tonnage held in reserve. The share of the British merchant navy had dropped considerably. The large merchant fleets of Germany, Italy and Japan were practically destroyed. The United States was the only effective carrier of goods on the scale that was required in the immediate post-war years.

TABLE 34
SIZE OF THE WORLD'S MERCHANT FLEETS, 1939–47
(in thousands of gross tons)

	1939	1947
United States	9,000	27,000
(except Great Lakes fleet)		
in reserve	0	11,000
British Empire	21,000	17,500
Japan	5,600	1,100
Norway	4,800	3,400
Germany	4,500	700
Italy	3,400	700
Netherlands	3,000	1,900
France	2,900	1,700
Greece	1,800	700
U.S.S.R.	1,300	1,200
Denmark	1,200	700

SOURCE: United Nations, Dept. of Economic Affairs, *Salient Features of the World Economic Situation, 1945–47*, 1948, p. 224.

A further factor in the loss of invisible earnings was the sale of foreign investments to pay for the war. The actual extent of the diminution of overseas investments by the two countries principally concerned, Britain and France, is very difficult to estimate with any sort of precision. For Britain it meant the reversal of her financial situation in respect of some important suppliers of war material such as India and Canada. South Africa practically extinguished its pre-war foreign debt. The process did not affect Britain and France only. The United States also used its foreign assets to pay for supplies. In fact the financial impact of the war on former debtor countries was most striking, not merely because their exports grew, for often they did not, but also because of the sale of supplies to armed forces in the country or region. This combination of factors could completely reverse the international financial position of a debtor country providing, of course, that the demand from the more powerful economy could be properly managed.

There were few underdeveloped areas of the globe on which the relatively well-fed and well-paid armed men of the combatant powers did not descend with their technology and their money. The annual expenditure of the United States forces in Iceland was roughly the equivalent of Iceland's annual earnings from exports. Although her positive trade balance was a very small one Iceland's foreign credits in 1944 were almost as big as her national income for 1943.[17] In this case the institutional arrangements were such as to prevent the country being completely swamped by inflation. The United States paid for Iceland's exports of fish to the United Kingdom in a dollar balance in New York and the sums were charged as lend-lease to the United Kingdom. Price and wage levels still rose steeply and left Iceland, like all other countries in the same position, with a very difficult task in adjusting to world prices – a task which was nevertheless unavoidable because so small an economy depended absolutely on foreign trade. The happy result was, of course, that from being a chronically insolvent international debtor she became a creditor. But what was Tonga to do when the irruption of United States soldiers caused the production of copra to fall by 80 per cent because most of the population made more money renting bicycles to soldiers for black-market dollars?

These are extreme examples of tiny countries but they are deliberately chosen to show the forces at work in the under-developed world in wartime. British military expenditure in India rose from £3 million in the financial year 1939–40 to £287 million in 1944–5, and over the same period the Indian budget passed from balance to a deficit, mainly due to defence expenditure, of £168 million.[18] In most Middle-Eastern countries there was a fairly close correspondence between the increases in money supply and the amount of Allied military expenditure during the war. The increase in Iraq was eightfold, in Syria and the Lebanon sevenfold, in Palestine, Iran and Cyprus fivefold.[19] Controls and

17. W. C. Chamberlin, *Economic Development of Iceland through World War II*, Columbia University Press, New York, 1947, p. 99.

18. A. R. Prest, *War Economics of Primary Producing Countries*, Cambridge University Press, 1948, p. 58.

19. Lloyd, p. 190.

rationing could not disguise the fact that in these areas suppressed inflation was even greater than in the major combatant countries. In Palestine the armed forces consumed about a third of the total goods and services in 1943. Production had increased by about 20 per cent since 1939. The net result was that the level of consumption of the population had been reduced in real terms by almost 20 per cent. Such reductions were much harder to bear and to remedy in an underdeveloped economy than in a rich land; the sad proof of that came in Bengal.

To control inflation was much more difficult in such economies. Consumption was so low that its reduction could do little to reduce inflation. Rationing of foodstuffs had little meaning in an economy where three quarters of the population drew its livelihood from producing or trading in food. The civil service was seldom adequate to operate the battery of controls that existed in Britain or Germany. Where foreign troops were stationed the control of inflation also depended on another government which might have other interests at stake. The example of the Norwegian forestry workers and fishermen who left these vital sectors of employment to work for higher wages for the German armed forces on construction sites was repeated all over the world. Trinidad, a country of endemic unemployment, actually developed a labour shortage in 1943, so great were the numbers employed in construction in the United States bases there. They were attracted from the sugar industry, which provided one of Trinidad's main exports. As inflation caused the exchange rate of local currencies to depreciate in terms of the currency in which friendly or occupying soldiers were paid, the black-market operations of troops gave a further boost to inflation. The device of issuing a special occupation currency like the German *Reichskreditkassenschein* or the 'yellow-seal' dollars with which American troops in north Africa were paid did not stop this pressure because the occupation currencies themselves became a currency in general use with a higher black-market value than the official currency.[20] But in many cases the United States did not even bother with this device and allowed servicemen to change dollars into local currency at depreciated rates and then buy dollars at official rates with very few restrictions. About $530 million were 'lost' in

20. Munz, p. 21.

this way during the war.[21] It can only be assumed that this was in fact a method of providing extra pay for soldiers serving abroad, a more sophisticated form of loot.

Controlling inflation was indeed almost impossible when soldiers arrived. But there was a further element in the situation. Until the situation became too difficult governments of primary producing countries did not want to control inflation because it brought one important international benefit. Most governments did not have a budget deficit and their currencies remained fully covered without an immediate fall of their exchange values. They were accumulating large claims on foreign goods after the war and they wanted to continue to accumulate them. The transformation of Iceland from an international debtor to an international creditor was of no great moment except for 130,000 Icelanders. But the same phenomenon repeated in India and in Egypt as well as in debtor counᵣries elsewhere was of fundamental importance for the international economy after the war.

United Kingdom exports to India fell from £34 million in 1938 to £18 million in 1943, while military orders and expenditure in India shot upwards. India's real trade balance with the United Kingdom became a favourable one, and the rapid inflation there increased the cost of exports and of military supplies to the United Kingdom, exaggerating this swing in the trade balance. Not only was India dependent on British arms but, like many other primary producers who had been in the sterling area in the 1930s, she was ultimately dependent on the British market also. Therefore it was possible for Britain to pay for supply by piling up post-war claims against balances kept in London for use after the war. The Indian government insisted on using these sterling balances to buy out British investments in India. But in spite of the systematic sale of these investments the sterling balance of the Indian government still rose from £259 million in the middle of 1942 to £1,321 million at the end of 1945. By substantially the same process Egypt and the Sudan piled up sterling balances of over £500 million, while buying out British assets there. Such was the history of sterling as an international currency, and such the dangerous dependence of underdeveloped economies on an international market now entirely controlled by the Allies, that

21. W. Rundell, jr, *Black Market Money*, Louisiana University Press, Baton Rouge, 1964.

it even proved possible to persuade countries outside the sterling area such as Argentina and Portugal to hold similar sterling balances. The total value of sterling debts in this form at the end of the war was £3,000 million, of which about 40 per cent was owed to India.[22]

The repatriation of British capital holdings also took place in Canada and the United States. In the United States it had been a condition of the lend-lease agreements. It was estimated in 1945, for the Washington negotiations on reconstruction, that British receipts from the liquidation of foreign investments amounted to $4,500 million out of an estimated investment total of $22,905 million in 1938.[23] The reduction in income from overseas investments was not, however, the most serious cause of disequilibrium in the British balance of payments. In 1946, for example, the gross receipts from interest were only about £50 million less than before the war.

The extent of the drop in French earnings from foreign investment is not known. There were two areas where disinvestment was heavy: in the United States where investments were used to purchase supplies in 1939 and in central and eastern Europe where for a brief period they were used to pay the occupation costs demanded by Germany. In 1947 the interest on capital appearing in the balance of payments was 2,750 million current francs, about 1,250 million 1938 francs.[24] This would represent, at 1938 interest rates, an investment of about 40,000 million 1928 francs. The total foreign investment in 1937–8 was somewhere between 80,000 million and 130,000 million 1928 francs.[25] This circumstantial evidence suggests that the loss of returns on foreign investment was proportionately greater for France than for the United Kingdom.

But for Britain there was also the question of paying back the

22. H. A. Shannon, 'The Sterling Balances of the Sterling Area', in *Economic Journal*, no. 60, 1950.

23. United Kingdom, *Statistical Material Presented during the Washington Negotiations*, Cmd 6707, H.M.S.O., London, 1945; C. Lewis, *Debtor and Creditor Countries 1938, 1944*, The Brookings Institution, Washington, D.C., 1945.

24. R. Jolivot, 'La balance des paiements', in *Revue d'économie politique*, no. 58, 1948. Conversion at the rate of 1:2·2.

25. L. Rist and P. Schwob, 'La balance des paiements', in *Revue d'économie politique*, no. 53, 1939.

wartime borrowings. Much depended on the way in which the inter-Allied war debts would be cleared up. The methods of lend-lease accounting were not very convincing economically. It could surely be argued, for example, that in those cases where British tank crews had used American tanks it would make at least as much sense to charge the United States for the crew as the United Kingdom for the tank. But this was not the view taken in the United States which at first displayed no more enlightenment on this issue than it had on the question of war debts after 1918. The British for their part matched the nationalism of American public opinion with an absurd complacency that the question of these debts would be amicably resolved within the framework of the proposed new international arrangements. The position of the pound sterling and the ability of Britain and the world to accept and put into practice the proposals for multilateralism obviously depended on a concerted resolution of this problem.

For Britain in fact the problem concerned three countries because Canada had played a minor but important role in the lend-lease arrangements. When the Lend-Lease Acts were passed in March 1941 the British gold and dollar reserves had been almost exhausted. In the same month Canada, which was not a member of the sterling area, began to provide supply in return for sterling balances. Since about one third of the materials in Canadian supplies to Britain was imported from the United States Canada maintained an adverse trade balance with her southern neighbour. She was inextricably a part of the lend-lease network and this was recognized by the reconstitution of Anglo-Canadian financial relationships in terms of 'Mutual Aid'. Supplies to Canada from the United States for ultimate export to Britain were covered by lend-lease. The total value of United States lend-lease aid to Britain was about $30,000 million of which only a small part was cancelled out by 'reciprocal aid' from Britain to the United States.[26] The value of United Kingdom liabilities to Canada was $1,200 million Canadian, together with about $3,000 million Canadian designated as Mutual Aid. When the negotiations for the dollar loan in Britain were concluded that part of the lend-lease account which represented the value of goods transferred in wartime, $20,000 million, was covered by

26. D. F. McCurrach, 'Britain's U.S. Dollar Problem, 1939–1945', in *Economic Journal*, no. 58, 1948.

the loan repayments. About $6,000 million of lend-lease goods and military surplus property in Britain was sold to Britain at a low price and for the goods still on order Britain had to pay $650 million on the same terms as the loan repayments. The lend-lease obligations of the United States' other allies were subsequently covered on rather less favourable terms by Export–Import Bank credits. The winding-up of the British war debts to Canada was conducted on the Canadian side with generosity. The sums due from Britain as Mutual Aid were written off as a gift together with a further $1,000 million Canadian already written off as a gift during the war. Ultimately the Canadian attitude was to prove far-sighted. Faced with large payments to make in dollars, with her invisible earnings reduced, with her industries still not geared to exporting, Britain hardly looked strong enough for one of the two pillars of the new international financial system. With the United States the obvious, indeed the only, source of supply of goods to satisfy the immediate demand from Britain and Europe, dollars were at a premium. The changes in the pattern of international trade, it was soon clear, had made them much harder to earn.

In the 1930s western Europe had had on average a deficit on current account with the United States and its American and Caribbean neighbours, the 'dollar area' as the area came to be called after 1945, of about $2,000 million. It had been easier to export elsewhere because of the high level of protection of the American economy. These deficits had been settled by trading surpluses earned elsewhere. The impact of the war was to make it much more difficult for European exporters to earn dollar surpluses to compensate for their even greater demand for United States commodities.

Partly this was because the war stimulated manufacturing capacity in some underdeveloped economies which had imported European manufactured goods before 1939. But the extent to which this occurred has usually been exaggerated. The impact of the war on the underdeveloped countries was very complex and did not produce import substitution on the same scale as the war of 1914–18 had done. The stimulus which the First World War had given to the process of economic development in the underdeveloped countries had been largely because the events of the war had provided their economies with an artificial barrier of protection. Behind this protection many of them had made sufficiently decisive advances in the output of textiles to be able to retain the new volume of output after 1918. The Second World War, however, was to show that for the development of most manufacturing industries something more than protection was required. The leap from textile production in small domestic units to mass production in factories was easier to make than the transition to mass production in most other technologies. Side by side with artificial protection came also acute shortages of raw materials and all the other necessary inputs of manufacturing industry. Not least, underdeveloped countries suffered from a lack of technological help and this was often crucial. The industries which did develop in such countries, except where direct technological help was provided by the belligerent powers, were confined to the simpler technologies. At the same time the developed powers were moving rapidly towards more advanced technologies and widening the gap between themselves and the underdeveloped world.

As argued in Chapter 5, even in those countries with high *per capita* incomes but with engineering industries of only limited capacity, even when the demands of war were most directly and urgently felt and even when technological help was provided on a large scale, the level of technology fell behind that attained in the major belligerent powers. Two such countries, Australia and Canada, did make significant strides in industrialization during the war, but in a country with lower levels of income, India, where the same forces were operating, the consequences were different. There were some important industrial and technological developments there which were directly attributable to the war. Whereas in 1939 there were only 600 workshops capable of supplying engineering components, in 1945 there were 1,500 supplying government contracts alone. Machine tools had been produced there before the war at a rate of less than 100 a year; in 1945 they were being made at the rate of about 350 a month. For the first time high speed and stainless steels were manufactured there. A shipbuilding industry employing 50,000 grew up during the war.[27] But only in munitions, shipbuilding and engineering did India, in spite of its large-scale participation in the war, show any indications of industrialization. The production of coal, pig iron and

27. Prest, p. 30 ff.

steel fell after 1940 and in other industries increases in output were very slight. Cotton cloth production, averaging 3,800 million metres annually in the years 1937–9 rose to a peak of 4,450 million in 1943 but by 1946 it was below the pre-war average.

This was a common experience for underdeveloped economies. The experience of the war was that only certain industries, in particular textiles, cement, and processed foods, were successfully started or developed in most of the poorer countries of the world. The demand for textiles came from the fact that this was above all the industry whose output and sales were reduced in the combatant countries; the demand for cement was frequently boosted by military construction in the country in question. The demand for processed foods came from the soldiers themselves and from the fact that they were more economical of shipping space than unprocessed food. None of these industries required much technological expertise nor capital to get going; the main thing was that demand should increase and foreign competition should stop. By providing temporary protection and an increased demand the war promoted some rudimentary economic development along these lines in many countries. But where development needed imported materials or a higher level of technology the war impeded it.

The production of cotton yarn in Syria and the Lebanon increased by about 80 per cent between 1939 and 1943 and that of cotton piece-goods in Egypt more than doubled in the same period, as did the output of cement. In Argentina the two industries to show the biggest increases in output were also textiles and cement. The output of canned food in Egypt rose from 400 tons a year before the war to about 20,000 tons in 1943, that of beer in Syria from 2·4 million litres to 7 million litres. In most of these cases the demand was coming from allied armies either in the country itself or in the region. Where the demand for such goods came directly from one of the belligerent economies the extent to which it could be met depended on allied shipping controls. Here the severe shipping shortage militated against economic development. Imports were hard to obtain and exports depended on the whole range of factors which determined the allocation of Allied shipping space. A greater number of countries than in the First World War were active belligerents and in certain cases the destruction which this caused to their economies was a severe setback. In

China, for example, the output of yarn and cotton cloth declined throughout the war so that by 1947 only about three million cotton spindles were operating compared to the five million before the war. Coal output fell from 41 million tons in 1937 to 18·5 million tons in 1946 and the output of electric power from 4,000 million kilowatt hours to 1,500 million.[28]

Only in Canada and Australia was there a large and decisive shift towards industrialization. The volume of manufacturing in Canada at the end of the war had increased two and a half times over its level in 1935–9.[29] After 1940, for the first time, the net volume of manufacturing production exceeded that of primary production; by 1943 it was over 50 per cent higher. In Australia the output of metals and machines increased by 120 per cent during the war, that of chemicals, dyes, explosives and paint by 66 per cent, of clothing by 59 per cent and of processed food and drink by 38 per cent. Employment in the aircraft industry increased by 250 per cent between 1939 and 1946, in shipbuilding by 150 per cent and in the manufacture of surgical, optical and scientific instruments by 260 per cent.[30] Coal production by 1947 was 30 per cent above its pre-war levels.

Elsewhere the effect of the war was, by widening the gap with the developed lands, and also by its psychological and political impact, to stimulate the desire for economic development rather than development itself. But one favourable circumstance, the possibility of exporting primary products in greater quantities during the war, sometimes made this desire more realizable after 1945. Once again this depended on the circumstances of war and on the application of Allied shipping controls. In most Asian countries mineral production fell below pre-war levels and exports fell even further. In Indonesia oil production at the end of the war was only 5 per cent of pre-war output and in Burma it had virtually come to a standstill. The output of tin in Malaya was only 14 per cent of its pre-war level and Chinese mineral exports gradually disappeared during the war. In Latin America the great reduction in exports to the United Kingdom and continental

28. United Nations, Statistical Office, *Monthly Bulletin of Statistics*.

29. Canada, Dept. of Trade and Commerce, *Monthly Review of Business Statistics*, July 1945.

30. United Nations, Dept. of Economic Affairs, *Salient Features of the World Economic Situation 1945–47*, Lake Success, 1948, p. 61.

Europe, 45 per cent of the continent's pre-war export trade, left that area dependent on the United States. Although by the end of the war a satisfactory adjustment had taken place so that 50 per cent of Latin America's exports now went to North America the difficulties of this transition period restricted the growth of primary exports. Many of the African countries which had depended on single European markets for their primary exports suffered severely. The total weight of the exports of French West Africa, Togoland, the Cameroons and French Equatorial Africa fell from 1,539,400 metric tons in 1938 to 588,400 metric tons in 1945.[31] Here the war interrupted an expansion in the exports of ground nuts and palm oil. In the same area cotton production fell by two thirds and cacao production by almost one half.

But in more favourable circumstances the war could provide sudden opportunities for capital accumulation. Before 1939 the Belgian Congo had exported 90 per cent of its exports to Belgium and continental Europe. Cut off from these markets and from Belgian control it fell under the general economic domination of the Allies. New markets for copper, its main export, were readily found in Britain and the United States and new commercial links with South African capital were forged. Metal refining capacity increased and exports of copper, tin, cobalt, tungsten, zinc and uranium ores all increased. Exports more than doubled in value by 1943.[32] South Africa and British East Africa, which likewise exported materials of great strategic importance, also benefited. Sisal, 29 per cent of Tanganyika's exports in 1939, had increased to 44 per cent of the total in 1946, and the total volume of exports had also grown. In Nigeria earnings from exports of timber and tin increased.

These changes in circumstances combined with changes in political outlook to produce in underdeveloped economies plans to use their domestic raw materials in a controlled way for national economic development. They too were anticipating a world where greater knowledge of methods of economic control and planning would stand them in good stead. The difficulties which European exporters had in earning greater dollar surpluses there came from this post-war change of attitudes as much as or

31. France, *Bulletin mensuel de statistiques d'outre-mer.*
32. United Nations, Dept. of Economic Affairs, *Salient Features*, p. 108.

more than from the real economic changes which the war produced in the underdeveloped economies. These difficulties were in any case only a limited part of the obstacles to developing a multilateral system for the dollar shortage had other components more immediately attributable to the war.

One was the shift in the origin of United States imports towards Latin America and the Caribbean, the 'dollar area'. The dangers to shipping and the great comparative advantages of short hauls when shipping was at a premium, together with the falling away in European trade with those areas, all diverted United States foreign trade so that a larger proportion of it was with its American neighbours. The great increase in *per capita* incomes in the United States stimulated an increase in the consumption after 1945 of eight categories of imports in particular: coffee, cocoa, non-ferrous metals, petroleum products, wool, timber and paper products, sugar and rubber. Of four of these categories the proportion of total imports coming from the 'dollar area' was much higher after the war than in the 1930s. Coffee imports grew mainly because of increased imports from Colombia and the Caribbean, oil imports through increased imports from Venezuela and the Netherlands Antilles, non-ferrous metals through imports from Canada, Bolivia and Chile, and timber and paper products now came overwhelmingly from Canada. Sugar had always come mainly from this area. This relocation of United States foreign trade meant a lower proportion of dollar earnings after 1945 for such countries as Malaya and the Dutch East Indies, which had been important purchasers of European exports before 1939. After 1945 it was harder for European countries to earn dollars there.

The difficulties which underdeveloped countries outside the 'dollar area' had in exporting to the 'dollar area' were increased by two other factors which have been so far considered separately: the expansion in the war of food production in the dollar zone and the extensive damage done to land and livestock in Asia. In those countries occupied by Japan the effect on agriculture was severe. As in occupied Europe fertilizer was never available in anything approaching pre-war quantities. The land was ill-treated, and the quantity of livestock reduced. The world food shortage of 1947 had already been foreshadowed in the war years. But it had the additional consequence of weakening the capacity to export to the dollar zone while United States export balances with other parts of the world grew rapidly.

In the two years before the German surrender the United States had a surplus of $16,700 million on its balance of payments on account of goods and services, of which the main component was a rapidly expanding surplus of exports to Europe. The damage done to European agriculture increased the demand for American food and the releasing of pent-up demand for other goods in the primary producing countries meant that at first this demand also tended to be satisfied from United States exports, even though their exports of primary produce to the United States were lower, because American manufactured goods were more available. The background to the negotiations for a post-war multilateral payments system appears in a somewhat ironical light in Table 35.

TABLE 35
SIZE AND GEOGRAPHICAL DISTRIBUTION OF UNITED STATES
EXPORT (+) AND IMPORT (−) BALANCES, 1938 AND 1946
(in millions of dollars, half-yearly averages)

	1938	1946
Europe	+380	+1,653
Latin America	+39	+201
North America	+104	+273
Asia	−26	+218
Africa	+32	+91
Oceania	+39	−33

SOURCE: United Nations, *Economic Report*, January 1948.

Although the exports of the other developed economies recovered quickly the United States had firmly captured many new markets during the war, especially in Latin America. At the same time the great increases in production there had taken place when few imports were available and had led to a greater utilization of domestic raw materials. The quantum of United States imports in 1947, in spite of the increase in manufactured goods production, was lower than in 1937. And in the first half of 1947 United States exports represented one third of world exports. The consequence of the disequilibrium which the war had bequeathed to the international economy was an ineradicable shortage of dollars in the world trading system.

To these structural shifts in world trade was also related a sharp alteration in the terms of trade against developed economies which obviously affected the European economies more because of their high level of imports. The war raised the prices of their imports relative to those of their exports by about 25 per cent as compared to the levels of 1938. The biggest items of western European imports were raw materials and foodstuffs, areas in which demand grew very rapidly between 1945 and 1947. The countries which had been occupied had a particularly high level of food imports in 1945 and 1946 before their own agriculture had recovered to its former capacity. And it was no longer possible, as it had been for France and Britain before the war, to acquire such a high proportion of food imports from cheaper sources. The proportion of total French food imports in 1946 originating in French overseas territories was much lower than in 1938.[33]

One important area of European food supply was virtually eliminated by political divisions and by national economic development plans. The eastern European countries rapidly cut themselves off from the international trade of the continent, and behind their efforts at economic reconstruction already appeared the shape of plans for the industrialization of their economies. This increased Europe's reliance on extra-European food and raw materials. South-eastern Europe had played an important and growing part in Germany's imports of primary produce during the German recovery after 1933. The economic recovery in western Germany had to depend on other sources. This break in the pattern of intra-European trade did not begin in 1945 but in 1940, when the domination of the trade of the whole continent by Germany had brought about a clear break with the trends of the 1930s. Until 1940 German trade had increasingly gone to the underdeveloped countries of south-eastern Europe. After that date, in spite of the creation of the eastern empire, trade swung back to western Europe. Table 36 shows the extent to which Germany's import surpluses from occupied western Europe came to balance her export surpluses to her weaker allies. There was no longer any need for the German trading bloc as a device for saving hard currencies, and, in spite of the more ruthless methods of control exercised in eastern Europe, the basic economic fact

33. Institut National de la Statistique et des Études Économiques, *Le Mouvement économique en France de 1938 à 1948*, Paris, 1950, p. 255.

that the trade of developed economies will tend to flow towards other developed economies asserted itself even under the occupation régimes. The events of the war foreshadowed the pattern of intra-European trade which would be built up after 1945, except that in the war years it was all directed through the central clearing in Berlin. But after 1945 the eastern primary producers were absorbed into the Soviet bloc, whose capacity to absorb their primary exports was much lower and the pattern of trade on which they had completely depended could not be recreated in the future. Western Europe, as a consequence, needed more food from outside the continent.

TABLE 36

GERMAN TRADING BALANCES BY GROUPS OF COUNTRIES, 1936–44
(in millions of Reichsmarks; + = export surplus, − = import surplus)

	1936	1940	1941	1942	1943	1944
Occupied western countries*	+487	−409	−387	−1,413	−1,399	−1,409
Neutral countries†	+97	+129	−71	−122	+119	+279
Allied or friendly countries‡	+59	+235	+586	+811	+1,376	+917
Other countries	−93	−99	−212	−408	+234	+153
Overall balance	+550	−144	−84	−1,132	+330	−60

* France, Belgium, Netherlands, Norway, Denmark.
† Sweden, Switzerland, Spain, Portugal, Turkey.
‡ Italy, Finland, Slovakia, Hungary, Romania, Bulgaria, Croatia.

SOURCES: *Sondernachweis der Aussenhandel Deutschlands;* K. Hunscha, Eidesstaatliches Gutachten, 'Die wirtschaftlichen und finanziellen Beziehungen Deutschlands zu den von ihm besetzten Ländern Kontinentaleuropas 1940–1944' (unpublished document).

As it was more dependent than before the war on imports, western Europe was in a position of having to import a greater proportion of them from the 'dollar area' and was now less able, because of the structural changes which the war had produced in world trade, to earn the dollars to pay for its deficit on current account in dollars. That this was not due to any temporary deficiency in post-war economic policies in western Europe or to an insufficient output there was indicated by the fact that Canada and Latin America in the immediate post-war years only maintained their wartime level of exports to the United States whereas

European exports began slowly to increase from the low levels they had reached. In fact with the rapid recovery of output in Europe exports generally recovered very rapidly, more rapidly than the most favourable prognostications. The assumption of the British government in 1945 was that to maintain post-war imports at their pre-war level exports would have to increase by 50 per cent above their pre-war level, and that to repay the debts incurred during the war they would have to increase by yet another 25 per cent. Except in 1947, however, the deficit on commercial account was always less in the immediate post-war years than it had been in 1938 when the United Kingdom had been faced with such a heavy rearmament programme. Even by 1946 the volume of exports had virtually attained its pre-war level. And yet the balance of payments did in fact bear out the gloomiest assumptions of the closing stage of the war. To solve the problem by an increase in exports to the 'dollar area' would have meant increasing the pre-war volume of exports by more than three times to an area which was more self-sufficient than before.

The failure of multilateralism

The intermediary institutions proposed by both the United States and Britain as an essential part of any new multilateral payments system were not of a scope able to deal with such a massive disequilibrium. The ideas of both countries centred on a Stabilization Fund, a pool of foreign exchange available to all countries and to which all countries would contribute. Every country finding its reserves endangered by imbalances in its foreign accounts would be able to draw on the Fund in order to obtain time to take corrective action. The assumption was that such corrective action would still consist of alterations in domestic economic policy rather than changes in the specified exchange rates and certainly not exchange controls. Supporting the Fund would be an International Clearing Union to facilitate multilateral settlements. The existence of the sterling balances itself suggested that these measures were far too limited. The assumption that international exchange rates could be stabilized on such a basis would only work if there was a long-term economic equilibrium between the countries concerned. It was assumed that one cause of disequilibrium would be the situation of the primary producers, and in the wartime discussions one institution which might be used to deal with this, an international development bank which would make development capital available on purely financial and economic considerations without any political strings, had also been proposed. But it is all too evident from these proposals that the essential difference between reconstruction and the institutional arrangements necessary to operate a system already in equilibrium had not been clearly grasped.

The United Nations Monetary and Financial Conference held at Bretton Woods in 1944 drafted two agreements which were subsequently accepted. One was for the constitution of an International Monetary Fund, the other for an International Bank for Reconstruction and Development. The I.M.F., which began operations in 1947, was designed to promote international monetary cooperation, to facilitate the expansion of international trade, to promote exchange stability, and to provide backing for a multilateral system of payments by allowing members to correct 'maladjustments' in their balance of payments while preserving the multilateral network. It was intended to maintain the same stability of exchange rates as the pre-1914 gold standard while alleviating some of the disadvantages which the operations of the gold standard had brought in terms of recession and unemployment. The member states all contributed a fixed quota to the resources of the fund. At the point when, under the gold standard, there would have been a tendency for gold to leave the country, or, in a system of floating exchange rates, for a fall in the exchange rate to occur, member countries would be able within certain definite limits to buy the currencies they needed from the Fund in return for their own currency. In the case of a chronic deficit the Fund would also eschew the violent deflationary methods of earlier multilateral payments systems and provide for an 'orderly' reduction in the exchange value of the member's currency. The only exchange restrictions envisaged were on large capital movements, in order to enable members to protect themselves against such movements.

The purposes of the International Bank were to assist in economic reconstruction and development by promoting foreign investment and by supplementing private investment with its own funds. The capital of the Bank was subscribed by all member countries and the Bank was designed to act in a strictly commercial way by using its capital as a reserve for borrowing and re-lending. But the amount of credit which the Bank could initially provide, $10,000 million, was relatively insignificant in terms of the world's needs. Nor did the Bank have any power to make creditors buy the increased exports out of which it was assumed, wrongly for the most part, that underdeveloped countries would pay the cost of the loans.

By themselves these two institutions were only very small and insecure blocks on which to build and the conditions to which all their members were bound by acceptance were set about by so many exceptions, each already recognizing the harsh economic realities of the situation, that from the outset they were more honoured in the breach than the observance, in spite of the general agreement on the laudability of their aims. The attempts to reduce trade discrimination resulted in even more complicated compromises. Unless the United States had the political option and the will to reduce tariffs the dollar shortages would continue to force trade controls like those of the 1930s on the other trading powers. This had already happened in Britain but the abrupt cessation of lend-lease placed the United States in a much stronger bargaining position. A set of commercial proposals negotiated at the same time as the dollar loan was agreed between the United States and Britain in December 1945 and subsequently submitted to the International Conference on Trade and Employment. The terms of the loan excluded the further use of bilateral trade treaties and related trade controls by the United Kingdom.

When the International Conference met at Geneva in 1947 the realities of the economic situation had already dissipated much of the euphoria of victory. The underdeveloped countries burst on the scene with a united voice taking exception to the proposed tariff policies as preventing their plans for economic development. Their response to the attempt by the United States to create easier conditions for international capital lending was to insist on the right to impose restrictions on the inflows of capital and under certain conditions to appropriate foreign investments. The developed economies showed little sympathy, but they were unable to agree amongst themselves. The American tariff was reduced to its lowest level since 1913 but the United Kingdom refused to make more than slight reductions in its apparatus of Commonwealth preferences. What emerged from the disagreements was a framework for future discussion and negotiations, the General Agreement on Tariffs and Trade. It was not ratified until 1948 and its terms were vague. In the first six months of 1947 the United States trade surplus with the rest of the world grew to even greater proportions than in 1946. As it did so the failure to agree on the more important matters, the terms of a peace settlement, became blatant. The Soviet Union did not ratify the Bretton Woods agreements. The eastern European countries began to be transformed into satellite states and some Asian countries found themselves in virtually the same relationship to the United States. Instead of an epoch of universally expanding trade what emerged in 1947 was an epoch dominated by the two greatest military powers facing each other with an implacable economic and political hostility. In the same year the International Bank and the I.M.F. became subordinated to United States control and operated no longer in the universal interest but as instruments of United States policy.

The wartime plans and the agreements signed at Bretton Woods came therefore to failure only two years after the end of the war. American capital was subsequently made available under the Marshall Plan for reconstruction in order to defend Europe and Asia from the threat of Soviet arms and ideology within the framework of the defences of the United States itself. The Marshall Plan in fact tackled those very international consequences of the war whose previous neglect had caused the stillbirth of the new international economy. But by 1949 the dependence of world trade on controls, exchange restrictions and bilateralism was still at least as great as in the 1930s.

The international institutions and agreements which survived the collapse of those high hopes in 1947 were protoplasmic rather than rigid. Essentially the post-war world could form what it wanted from them. But the prospects for a successful implementation of new domestic economic policies were now more complicated and less hopeful than public and political opinion had assumed in 1945. The hopes for a better world, which had after all been the purpose of the long struggle against the Axis powers, were replaced with the prospect of a long uphill struggle. Nowhere was this sadder than in the United Kingdom, where the Labour government, voted into power by a massive majority to fulfil those hopes, struggled manfully to realize its own policies in the midst of the climate of 'austerity' now forced on it. Seen in retrospect there is a certain air of unrealistic missionary simplicity about both the domestic and international aspirations of the powers at the end of the war. In the event, in the next quarter of a century in the developed economies the number of unemployed was to be much lower and the general level of income and welfare higher than in the inter-war years. But over the whole world the number of poor, hungry and downtrodden has remained very high. The defeat of so cruel a society coloured the last cataclysmic years of the war with bright hues of social and economic idealism. They did not long survive the so-called peace.

Bibliography

List of Abbreviations

G.P.O.   Government Printing Office
H.M.S.O.   Her (His) Majesty's Stationery Office
J.R.S.S.   *Journal of the Royal Statistical Society*
N.B.E.R.   National Bureau of Economic Research
N.I.E.S.R.   National Institute of Economic and Social Research
P.U.F.   Presses Universitaires de France
R.d.g.m.   *Revue de la deuxième guerre mondiale*
R.I.I.A.   Royal Institute of International Affairs
U.S.S.B.S.   United States Strategic Bombing Survey
Vj.f.Z.   *Vierteljahrshefte für Zeitgeschichte*
W.P.B.   War Production Board

Statistical

The usual rich sources of statistical information for modern economic history become more fragmentary for the war years and many valuable statistical series were discontinued or the data simply lost. After 1943, for example, there are very few economic statistics for Italy. Soviet statistics became even less meaningful after 1939. In many ways the most useful are those scattered throughout the volumes of Institut Marksizma-Leninizma,

Istoriya velikoy otechestvennoy voyny Sovietskogo Soyuza 1941–45, Moscow, 1960– . These volumes are now also available in German as *Geschichte des Grossen Vaterländischen Krieges der Sowjetunion*. These gaps are the two most serious. But in many occupied countries the collection of economic information became a haphazard and sporadic affair. In France some attempt was made to remedy this after the war in a publication of the Institut National de la Statistique et des Études Économiques, *Le Mouvement économique en France de 1938 à 1948*, Paris, 1950. But many of its more important tables are speckled with blanks. In complete contrast, in Norway Statistisk Sentralbyrå continued the publication throughout the period of its excellent series *Norges Offisielle Statistikk* and supplemented it later with *Statistisk-økonomisk utsyn over krigsårene*, Oslo, 1945. Post-war summaries of wartime statistical information also exist for other countries but usually as part of an official narrative. An exception is Britain with Central Statistical Office, *Statistical Digest of the War*, H.M.S.O., London, 1951, which is a purely statistical account. But it is a poor volume and much information still has to be sought in parliamentary papers and in Central Statistical Office, *Annual Abstract of Statistics, No. 86, 1938–1948*, H.M.S.O., London, 1949. The normal annual statistical publications, together with these occasional post-war revisions, are the first statistical source. The best of them continued to be throughout the war, Statistisches Reichsamt, *Statistisches Jahrbuch für das Deutsche Reich*. The volumes after 1939 were only issued confidentially to ministries. Even among the debris of 1945 economic data was still collected assiduously in Germany, but some important information is lacking.

These annual publications have to be supplemented by certain other official publications undertaken for specific purposes. Of these the most important are the publications of the United States Strategic Bombing Survey. There are 208 separate publications dealing with specific aspects of the German economy under attack and a smaller number of lower quality volumes dealing with Japan. Of special interest is the volume, *The Effects of Strategic Bombing on the German War Economy*, G.P.O., Washington, 1945. Another important source is the volumes of the Commission Consultative des Dommages et des Réparations, *Dommages subis par la France du fait de la guerre et de l'occupation ennemie* (*1939–45*), Imprimerie Nationale, Paris, 1950. United States wartime statistics were made readily available in published documents by the various presidential agencies. The published 'documents' of the War Production Board are a particularly valuable amplification of the normal series. Attention should also be drawn to the Office of Foreign Liquidation, *Lend-Lease Export Summaries*. The League of Nations and the International Labour Office also continued to collect statistical information during the war. The Economic, Financial and Transit Department of the League of Nations published the *World Economic Survey* for 1939–41, 1941–2, and 1942–4, but it has obvious limitations. Where normal statistical series were continued throughout the war I have referred to them by the normal references rather than include them in the bibliography of secondary works.

I have therefore freely used the statistical information which has emerged from my own and other scholars' documentary research to overcome these problems. As far as Germany is concerned the enormous efforts of so many scholars have provided an almost complete coverage of the necessary information apart from the last three months of the war. It can only be hoped that the same effort will now take place for Italy and, when the materials become more available, for the United Kingdom. For the latter country it is still impossible to make accurate comparisons with the type of detailed information now available for Germany or the United States. This is the more unfortunate as so much information about Britain is enshrined in *The Official History of the Second World War*, Civil Series, where it appears without footnote references. And although many volumes in this splendid enterprise are fully worthy of it they remain, nonetheless, official. As things stand, therefore, the period 1939–45 remains exceptional in the twentieth century in its paucity of much essential information.

Other Publications

ALLEN, R. G. D., 'Mutual Aid between the U.S. and the British Empire, 1941–5', in *J.R.S.S.*, no. 109, 1946.

ANDEXEL, R., *Imperialismus, Staatsfinanzen, Rüstung, Krieg. Probleme der Rüstungsfinanzierung des deutschen Imperialismus*

(Schriften des Instituts für Wirtschaftswissenschaften, no. 25), Akademie-Verlag, Berlin, 1968.

ANSBACHER, H. L., 'Testing, Management and Reactions of Foreign Workers in Germany during World War II', in *American Psychologist*, no. 5, 1950.

ARNOULT, P., *Les Finances de la France et l'occupation allemande* (*1940/44*), P.U.F., Paris, 1951.

ASKELUND, B., 'Nortraships hemmelige fond', in *Norge og den 2 verdenskrig: mellom nøytrale og allierte*, Universitetsforlaget, Oslo, 1968.

AUKRUST, O., and BJERVE, P., *Hva krigen kostet Norge*, Dreyers Forlag, Oslo, 1945.

BACKE, H., *Um die Nährungsfreiheit Europas*, Wilhelm Goldmann, Leipzig, 1942.

BARTON, G. T., and COOPER, M. R., *Farm Production in War and Peace* (United States, Dept of Agriculture), G.P.O., Washington, D.C., 1947.

BASCH, A., *The New Economic Warfare*, Routledge, London, 1942.

BASCH, A., *The Danube Basin and the German Economic Sphere*, Columbia University Press, New York, 1943.

BATES, S., 'The Price System and the War Economy' in *Canadian Journal of Economics and Political Science*, no. 7, 1941.

BAUDHUIN, F., *L'Économie belge sous l'occupation 1940–44*, E. Bruylant, Brussels, 1945.

BAUDIN, L., *Esquisse de l'économie française sous l'occupation allemande*, Librairie de Médicis, Paris, 1945.

BEHRENS, C. B. A., *Merchant Shipping and the Demands of War*, H.M.S.O., London, 1955.

BELIKOV, A. M., 'Transfert de l'industrie soviétique vers l'est', in *R.d.g.m.*, no. 41, 1961.

BENTHAM, J., *Principles of International Law*, in J. Bowring (ed.) *The Works of J. Bentham*, Edinburgh, 1843.

BEREND, I., and RÁNKI, G., 'Die deutsche wirtschaftliche Expansion und das ungarische Wirtschaftsleben zur Zeit des zweiten Weltkrieges', in *Acta Historica*, no. 5, 1958.

BERNARD, H., *Guerre totale et guerre révolutionnaire*, 3 vols., Brepols, Brussels, 1965.

BERNHARDT, W., *Die deutsche Aufrüstung 1934–39, Militärische und politische Konzeptionen und ihre Einschätzung durch die Allierten*, Bernard und Graefe, Frankfurt am Main, 1969.

BERNSTEIN, B. J., 'Industrial Reconversion: The Protection of Oligopoly and Military Control of the Wartime Economy', in *American Journal of Economics and Sociology*, no. 26, 1967.

BERSTEIN, S., and MILZA, P., *L'Italie fasciste*, Armand Colin, Paris, 1970.

BEVERIDGE, Sir W., *Social Insurance and Allied Services* (Parliamentary Papers, VI), H.M.S.O., London, 1942.

BILLIG, J., 'Le rôle des prisonniers de guerre dans l'économie du IIIᵉ Reich', in *R.d.g.m.*, no. 37, 1960.

BILLIG, J., *Les Camps de concentration dans l'économie du Reich Hitlérien*, P.U.F., Paris, 1973.

BIRKENFELD, W., *Der synthetische Treibstoff 1933–1945, Ein Beitrag zur nationalsozialistischen Wirtschafts- und Rüstungspolitik* (Studien und Dokumente zur Geschichte des Zweiten Weltkrieges, no. 8), Musterschmidt-Verlag, Göttingen, 1964.

BIRKENFELD, W., 'Stalin als Wirtschaftspartner Hitlers (1939 bis 1941)', in *Vierteljahrschrift für Sozial- und Wirtschaftsgeschichte*, no. 53, 1966.

BISSON, T. A., *Japan's War Economy*, International Secretariat, Institute of Pacific Relations, New York, 1945.

BISSON, T. A., *Zaibatsu Control and Dissolution in Japan*, University of California Press, Berkeley, 1954.

BLACK, J. D., and GIBBONS, C. A., 'The War and American Agriculture', in *The Review of Economic Statistics*, no. 26, 1944.

BLUM, A. A., and GROSSMAN, J., 'La lutte pour une armée nombreuse et les problèmes de main-d'oeuvre industrielle' in *R.d.g.m.*, no. 66, 1967.

BOELCKE, W. A., ed., *Deutschlands Rüstung im zweiten Weltkrieg: Hitlers Konferenzen mit Albert Speer 1942–1945*, Akademische Verlag, Frankfurt am Main, 1969.

BOUDOT, F., 'Aspects économiques de l'occupation allemande en France', in *R.d.g.m.*, no. 53, 1964.

BOUTHILLIER, Y., *Le Drame de Vichy*, 2 vols., Plon, Paris, 1950–51.

BRACHER, K. D., SAUER, W., and SCHULTZ, G., *Die nationalsozialistische Machtergreifung, Studien zur Errichtung des totalitären Herrschafts-systems in Deutschland 1933/34*, Westdeutscher Verlag, Cologne, 1960.

BRACHER, K. D., 'Die Speer-Legende', in *Neue Politische Literatur*, vol. 4, 1970.

BRANDT, K., *The German Fat Plan and its Economic Setting* (Food Research Institute Publications, Fats and Oils Studies no. 6), Stanford University Press, 1938.

BRANDT, K., and others, *The Management of Agriculture and Food in the German-occupied and other Areas of Fortress Europe* (Food Research Institute Publications), Stanford University Press, 1953.

BRÄUTIGAM, O., *Überblick über die besetzten Ostgebiete während des zweiten Weltkrieges*, Veröffentlichungen des Instituts für Besatzungsfragen, no. 3, Tübingen, 1954.

BROSZAT, M., *Nationalsozialistische Polenpolitik 1939–1945* (Schriftenreihe der *Vj.f.Z.*, no. 2), Deutsche Verlags-Anstalt, Stuttgart, 1961.

BROSZAT, M., *Der Staat Hitlers*, Deutscher Taschenbuch Verlag, Munich, 1969.

BROWN, A. J., *Applied Economics. Aspects of the World Economy in War and Peace*, Allen & Unwin, London, 1947.

BRY, G., *Wages in Germany 1871–1945*, N.B.E.R., Princeton University Press, 1960.

BRØYN, P., 'Den svenske malmeksport fram til okkupasjonen av Narvik in april 1940 – med saerlig tanke på utførselen til Tyskland', in *Norge og den 2 verdenskrig: mellom nøytrale og allierte*, Universitetsforlaget, Oslo, 1968.

BUTLIN, S. J., *War Economy, 1939–42*, Australian War Memorial, Canberra, 1955.

CARR, W., *Arms, Autarky and Aggression. A Study in German Foreign Policy 1933–1939*, Edward Arnold, London, 1972.

CARROLL, B. A., *Design for Total War. Arms and Economics in the Third Reich*, Mouton, The Hague, 1968.

CATALANO, F., *L'economia italiana di guerra. La politica economico-finanziaria del fascismo della guerra d'Etiopia alla caduta del regime 1935–1943*, Istituto Nazionale per la Storia del Movimento di Liberazione, Milan, 1969.

CATALANO, F., 'Les ambitions mussoliniennes et la réalité économique de l'Italie', in *R.d.g.m.*, no. 76, 1969.

CÉPÈDE, M., *Agriculture et alimentation en France durant la IIe guerre mondiale*, Génin, Paris, 1961.

CHADAEV, I. E., *Ekonomika SSSR v Period Velikoy Otechestvennoy Voyny*, Mysl', Moscow, 1965.

CHAMBERLIN, W. C., *Economic Development of Iceland through*

World War II, Columbia University Press, New York, 1947.

CHARDONNET, J., *Les Conséquences économiques de la guerre, 1939–1946*, Hachette, Paris, 1947.

CHESTER, D. N., ed., *Lessons of the British War Economy*, N.I.E.S.R., Cambridge University Press, 1951.

CHEVALIER, A. and TRÉMOLIÈRES, J., 'Enquête sur l'état de nutrition des populations pendant la guerre', in *Annales de la nutrition et de l'alimentation*, no. 9, 1947.

CLARK, R. W., *The Birth of the Bomb*, Phoenix House, London, 1961.

CLARKE, I. F., *Voices Prophesying War 1763–1984*, Oxford University Press, London, 1966.

CLARKE, R. A., *Soviet Economic Facts 1917–1970*, Macmillan, London, 1972.

COHEN, J. R., *Japan's Economy in War and Reconstruction*, University of Minnesota Press, Minneapolis, 1949.

CONNERY, R. H., *The Navy and the Industrial Mobilization in World War II*, Princeton University Press, 1951.

COPELAND, M. A., and others, *The Impact of the War on Civilian Consumption in the United Kingdom, the United States and Canada. A Report to the Combined Production and Resources Board from a Special Combined Committee on Non-food Consumption Levels*, G.P.O.,Washington, D.C., 1945.

COURT, W. H. B., *Coal*, H.M.S.O., London, 1951.

CRAF, J. R., *A Survey of the American Economy, 1940–1946*, New River Press, New York, 1947.

CRAWFORD, J. G., and others, *Wartime Agriculture in Australia and New Zealand 1939–1950* (Food Research Institute Publications), Stanford University Press, 1954.

DAIRE, E., ed., *Économistes-financiers du XVIIIe siècle*, Paris, 1893.

DAITZ, W., *Der Weg zur völkischen Wirtschaft und zur europäischen Grossraumwirtschaft*, Meinhold, Dresden, 1938.

DALLIN, A., *German Rule in Russia, 1941–1945*, Oxford University Press, New York, 1957.

DEJONGHE, E., 'Problèmes sociaux dans les houillères du Nord et du Pas-de-Calais pendant la seconde guerre mondiale', in *Revue d'histoire moderne et contemporaine*, no. 18, 1971.

DENZEL, R., *Die chemische Industrie Frankreichs unter der*

deutschen Besetzung im zweiten Weltkrieg, Veröffentlichungen des Instituts für Besatzungsfragen, no. 18, Tübingen, 1959.

DESPRES, E., 'The Effects of Strategic Bombing on the German War Economy', in *Review of Economic Statistics*, no. 28, 1946.

Deutsche Institut für Wirtschaftsforschung, *Die deutsche Industrie im Kriege 1939–1945*, Duncker und Humblot, Berlin, 1954.

DEVONS, E., *Planning in Practice, Essays in Aircraft Planning in Wartime*, Cambridge University Press, 1950.

DEWHURST, J. F., and others, *America's Needs and Resources*, Twentieth Century Fund, New York, 1947.

DOMKE, M., *Trading with the Enemy in World War II*, Central Book Co., New York, 1943.

DURANT, H., and GOLDMANN, J., 'The Distribution of Working-class Savings', in *Bulletin of the Oxford University Institute of Statistics*, no. 7, 1945.

EGOROFF, P. P., *Argentina's Agricultural Exports during World War II* (Food Research Institute Papers no. 8), Stanford University Press, 1949.

EICHHOLTZ, D., *Geschichte der deutschen Kriegswirtschaft, 1939–1945*, vol. 1, 1939–1941, Akademie-Verlag, Berlin, 1969.

EICHHOLTZ, D., 'Zur Lage der deutschen Werktätigen im ersten Kriegsjahr 1939/40. Eine Studie über die staatsmonopolistische Kriegswirtschaft des deutschen Faschismus', in *Jahrbuch für Wirtschaftsgeschichte*, no. 44, 1967.

EICHHOLTZ, D., and GOSSWEILER, K., 'Noch einmal: Politik und Wirtschaft 1933–1945', in *Das Argument*, no. 47, 1968.

EICHHOLTZ, D., and SCHUMANN, W., *Anatomie des Krieges: neue Dokumente über die Rolle des deutschen Monopolkapitals bei der Vorbereitung und Durchführung des zweiten Weltkrieges*, Deutscher Verlag der Wissenschaften, Berlin, 1969.

EINZIG, P., *Hitler's "New Order" in Europe*, Macmillan, 1941.

EINZIG, P., 'Hitler's "New Order" in Theory and Practice', in *Economic Journal*, no. 51, 1941.

EMMENDÖRFER, A., *Geld- und Kreditaufsicht in den von Deutschland während des zweiten Weltkrieges besetzten Gebieten*, Veröffentlichungen des Instituts für Besatzungsfragen, no. 12, Düsseldorf, 1957.

ERBE, R., *Die nationalsozialistische Wirtschaftspolitik 1933–39 im Lichte der modernen Theorie*, Polygraphischer Verlag, Zürich, 1958.

ERICKSON, J., *The Road to Stalingrad. Stalin's War with Germany*, vol. 1, Weidenfeld & Nicolson, London, 1975.

ESENWEIN-ROTHE, I., *Die Wirtschaftsverbände von 1933 bis 1945* (Schriften des Vereins für Sozialpolitik-Gesellschaft für Wirtschafts- und Sozialwissenschaften, Neue Folge, no. 37), Duncker und Humblot, Berlin, 1965.

FAIRCHILD, B., and GROSSMAN, J., *The Army and Industrial Manpower* (United States Army in World War II, Office of the Chief of Military History), G.P.O., Washington, D.C., 1959.

FARNSWORTH, H. C., *Livestock in Continental Europe during World War Two* (Food Research Institute Papers, no. 6), Stanford University Press, 1945.

FEDERAU, F., *Der zweite Weltkrieg. Seine Finanzierung in Deutschland*, Rainer Wunderlich Verlag, Tübingen, 1962.

DE FELICE, R., *Le interpretazioni del fascismo*, Laterza, Bari, 1970.

DE FELICE, R., *Mussolini*, Einaudi, Turin, 1965, 1968.

    vol. I, *Il revoluzionario 1883–1920*;
    vol. II, *Il fascista*   *1921–1925*;
    vol. III, *Il fascista*   *1925–1929.*

FÖRSTER, G., *Totaler Krieg und Blitzkrieg. Die Theorie des totalen Krieges und des Blitzkrieges in der Militärdoktrin des faschistischen Deutschlands am Vorabend des zweiten Weltkrieges* (Militärhistorische Studien, no. 10, N.F.), Deutscher Militärverlag, Berlin, 1967.

FORSTMEIER, F., and VOLKMANN, H. E., eds., *Wirtschaft und Rüstung am Vorabend des zweiten Weltkrieges*, Droste, Düsseldorf, 1975.

FOURASTIÉ, J., 'La population active française', in *R.d.g.m.*, no. 57, 1965.

France, Institut National de la Statistique et des Études Économiques, *Le Mouvement économique en France de 1938 à 1948*, P.U.F., Paris, 1950.

FRANKLAND, N., *The Bombing Offensive Against Germany*, Faber & Faber, London, 1965.

FREYMOND, J., *Le IIIᵉ Reich et la réorganisation économique de l'Europe 1940–1942: Origines et projets*, Institut Universitaire de Hautes Etudes, Geneva, Collection de relations internationales, 3, Sithoff, Leiden, 1974.

FRIED, F., *Die Zukunft des Welthandels*, Knorr und Hirth, Munich, 1941.

FRIED, J. H. E., *The Exploitation of Foreign Labour by Germany*, International Labour Office, Montreal, 1945.

FRIEDENSBURG, F., *Die Rohstoffe und Energiequellen im neuen Europa*, Stalling, Oldenburg, 1943.

FRIEDENSBURG, F., 'Die sowietischen Kriegslieferungen an das Hitlerreich', in *Vierteljahrschrift zur Wirtschaftsforschung*, Duncker und Humblot, Berlin, 1962.

FRITZ, M., *German Steel and Swedish Iron Ore 1939–1945* (Publications of the Institute of Economic History of Gothenburg University, 29), Kungsbacka, Gothenburg, 1974.

FRUMKIN, G., *Population Changes in Europe since 1939*, Allen & Unwin, London, 1951.

FUÀ, G., *Notes on Italian Economic Growth 1861–1964*, Giuffrè, Milano, 1965.

FUNK, W., 'Wirtschaftliche Neuordnung Europas' in *Südost-Echo*, 26 July 1940.

GARDNER, R. N., *Sterling – Dollar Diplomacy*, Clarendon Press, Oxford, 1956.

GEER, J. S., *Der Markt der geschlossenen Nachfrage, eine morphologische Studie über die Eisenkontingentierung in Deutschland 1937–1945* (Nürnberger Abhandlungen zu den Wirtschafts- und Sozialwissenschaften, no. 14), Duncker und Humblot, Berlin, 1961.

GENSCHEL, H., *Die Verdrängung der Juden aus der Wirtschaft im Dritten Reich*, Musterschmidt, Göttingen, 1966.

GEORG, E., *Die wirtschaftlichen Unternehmungen der SS.* (Schriftenreihe der *Vj. f.Z.*, no. 7), Deutsche Verlags-Anstalt, Stuttgart, 1962.

GERBER, B., *Staatliche Wirtschaftslenkung in den besetzten und annektierten Ostgebieten während des zweiten Weltkrieges unter besonderer Berücksichtigung der treuhänderischen Verwaltung von Unternehmungen und der Ostgesellschaften*, Veröffentlichungen des Instituts für Besatzungsfragen, no. 17, Tübingen, 1959.

Germany, Statistisches Reichsamt, *Statistische Jahrbücher für das Deutsche Reich*.

GOLD, B., *Wartime Economic Planning in Agriculture. A Study in the Allocation of Resources*, Columbia University Press, 1949.

GOLDSMITH, R. W., *A Study of Saving in the United States*, 3 vols., Princeton University Press, 1955.

GORDON, D. L., and DANGERFIELD, R. J., *The Hidden Weapon*, Harper and Brothers, New York, 1947.

GOWING, M. M., *Britain and Atomic Energy, 1939–1945*, Macmillan, London, 1964.

GRAND-JEAN, P., *Guerres, fluctuations et croissance*, Société d'Édition d'Enseignement Supérieur, Paris, 1967.

GREEN, C. M., THOMSON, H. C., and ROOTS, P. C., *The Ordnance Department: Planning Munitions for War* (United States Army in World War II), G.P.O., Washington, D.C., 1962.

GUARNERI, F., *Autarkie und Aussenhandel* (Kieler Vorträge no. 65), Fischer, Jena, 1941.

GUARNERI, F., *Battaglie economiche tra la due grandi guerre*, 2 vols., Garzanti, Milan, 1956.

GUILLEBAUD, C. W., 'Hitler's New Economic Order for Europe', in *Economic Journal*, no. 50, 1940.

HÄGGLÖF, G., *Svensk krigshandelspolitik under andra världskriget*, Stockholm, 1958.

HALL, H. D., *North American Supply*, H.M.S.O., London, 1955.

HALL, H. D., and WRIGLEY, C. C., *Studies of Overseas Supply*, H.M.S.O., London, 1956.

HAMMOND, R. J., *Food*, H.M.S.O., London, 1951.

HANCOCK, W. K., and GOWING, M. M., *The British War Economy*, H.M.S.O., London, 1949.

HARRIS, Sir A., *Bomber Offensive*, Collins, London, 1947.

HARTMANN, S., and VOGT, J., *Aktstykker om den tyske finanspolitikk i Norge 1940–1945*, Dreyers Forlag, Oslo, 1958.

HEILBRONNER, A., 'Le ravitaillement en France', in *Revue d'économie politique*, no. 57, 1947.

HEWLETT, R. G., and ANDERSON, O. E., *The New World 1939–1946*, vol. 1 of *A History of the U.S.A.E.C.*, Pennsylvania State University Press, Philadelphia, 1962.

HILLGRUBER, A., *Hitlers Strategie: Politik und Kriegsführung 1940–41*, Bernard und Graefe, Frankfurt am Main, 1965.

HILLMANN, H. C., 'The Comparative Strengths of the Great Powers', in R.I.I.A., *The Economic Structure of Hitler's Europe* (Survey of International Affairs, 1939–46, Oxford University Press, London, 1954.

HINRICHS, A. F., 'The Defense Program and Labor Supply in the United States', in *Canadian Journal of Economics and Political Science*, no. 7, 1941.

HOMBERGER, H., *Schweizerische Handelspolitik im zweiten Weltkrieg*, Eugen Rentsch, Erlenbach-Zürich, 1970.

HOMZE, E. L., *Foreign Labor in Nazi Germany*, Princeton University Press, 1967.

HORNBY, A. N., *Factories and Plant*, H.M.S.O., London, 1958.

HOUSE, F. H., *Timber at War*, Ernest Benn, London, 1965.

HOWARD, F. A., *Buna Rubber. The Birth of an Industry*, Van Nostrand, New York, 1947.

HUBATSCH, W., ed., *Hitlers Weisungen für die Kriegführung 1939–45, Dokumente des Oberkommandos der Wehrmacht*, Bernard und Graefe Verlag, Frankfurt am Main, 1962; trans. H. R. Trevor-Roper, ed., *Hitler's War Directives 1939–1945*, Sidgwick & Jackson, London, 1964.

HURSTFIELD, J., *The Control of Raw Materials*, H.M.S.O., London, 1953.

INCE, Sir G., 'The Mobilisation of Manpower in Great Britain in the Second World War', in *The Manchester School of Economic and Social Studies*, no. 14, 1946.

INMAN, P., *Labour in the Munitions Industries*, H.M.S.O., London, 1957.

Institut Marksizma-Leninizma Pri Tsk KPSS, *Istoriya velikoy otechestvennoy voyny Sovetskogo Soyuza 1941–1945*, Moscow, 1960.

JACK, D. T., *Studies in Economic Warfare*, P. S. King & Son, London, 1940.

JÄCKEL, E., *Hitlers Weltanschauung. Entwurf einer Herrschaft*, Rainer Wunderlich Verlag Hermann Leins, Tübingen, 1969; trans. *Hitler's Weltanschauung. A Blueprint for Power*, Wesleyan University Press, Middletown, 1972.

JACOBSON, P., 'Le financement de la guerre en Allemagne', in *Kyklos*, no. 1, 1947.

JACQUEMYNS, G., *La Société belge sous l'occupation allemande*, 3 vols., Nicholson et Watson, Brussels, 1950.

JACQUEMYNS, G., 'Réactions des travailleurs belges sous l'occupation', in *R.d.g.m.*, no. 31, 1958.

JÄGER, J. J., 'Sweden's Iron Ore Exports to Germany, 1933–1944', in *Scandinavian Economic History Review*, no. 15, 1967.

JÄGER, J. J., *Die wirtschaftliche Abhängigkeit des Dritten Reiches vom Ausland dargestellt am Beispiel der Stahlindustrie*, Berlin Verlag, Berlin, 1969.

JANSENS, G., *Das Ministerium Speer. Deutschlands Rüstung im Krieg*, Ullstein, Berlin, 1968.

JENSEN, W. G., 'The Importance of Energy in the First and Second World Wars' in *Historical Journal*, no. 11, 1968.

JOHNSTON, B. F., and others, *Japanese Food Management in World War II* (Food Research Institute Publications), Stanford University Press, 1953.

JOLIVOT, R., 'La balance des paiements', in *Revue d'économie politique*, no. 58, 1948.

JONES, F. C., *Japan's New Order in East Asia: Its Rise and Fall, 1937–45*, Oxford University Press, London, 1954.

JONES, R. H., *The Roads to Russia*, University of Oklahoma Press, Norman, 1969.

KALDOR, N., 'The German War Economy', in *Review of Economic Studies*, no. 13, 1945–6.

KANNAPIN, H. E., *Wirtschaft unter Zwang: Anmerkungen und Analysen zur rechtlichen und politischen Verantwortung der deutschen Wirtschaft unter der Herrschaft des Nationalsozialismus im Zweiten Weltkrieg*, Deutsche Industrieverlag, Cologne, 1966.

KARLBOM, R., 'Sweden's Iron Ore Exports to Germany 1933–44', in *Scandinavian Economic History Review*, no. 13, 1965.

KASTEN, H., *Die Neuordnung der Währung in den besetzten Gebieten und die Tätigkeit der Reichskreditkassen während des Krieges 1939/40*, Bank-Verlag, Berlin, 1941.

KEYNES, J. M., *How to Pay for the War*, Macmillan, London, 1940.

KISSEL, H., *Der Deutsche Volkssturm 1944/45. Eine territoriale Miliz im Rahmen der Landesverteidigung* (Beiheft 16/17 der Wehrwissenschaftlichen Rundschau), E. S. Mittler und Sohn, Berlin, 1962.

KISTENMACHER, H., *Die Auswirkungen der deutschen Besetzung auf die Ernährungswirtschaft Frankreichs während des zweiten Weltkrieges*, Veröffentlichungen des Instituts für Besatzungsfragen, no. 16, Tübingen, 1959.

KLEIN, B. H., *Germany's Economic Preparations for War* (Harvard Economic Studies, no. 109), Harvard University Press, Cambridge, Mass., 1959.

KLUKE, P., 'Nationalsozialistische Europaideologie', in *Vj.f.Z*, no. 3, 1955.

KNIGHT, H. F., *Food Administration in India 1939–1947* (Food

Research Institute Publications), Stanford University Press, 1954.

KNORR, K., *The War Potential of Nations*, Princeton University Press, 1956.

KOEHL, R. L., *RKFDV: German Resettlement and Population Policy 1939–45*, Harvard University Press, Cambridge, Mass., 1957.

KOLKO, G., *The Politics of War*, Weidenfeld and Nicolson, London, 1969.

KOLNAI, A., *The War against the West*, Victor Gollancz, London, 1938.

Kommission der Historiker der DDR und der UdSSR, *Der deutsche Imperialismus und der zweite Weltkrieg* (Materialien der wissenschaftlichen Konferenz von 14 bis 19 Dezember 1959 in Berlin), 5 vols., Berlin, 1960.

KRÁL, V., *Otázky hospodářského a socialniho vyvoje v Céských zemich 1938–1945*, Nakl. Československé akademie věd., 3 vols., Prague, 1957–9.

KRAVCHENKO, G. S., *Voennaya ekonomika SSSR 19⁄1–1945*, Voen. ied-vo, Moscow, 1963; 2nd ed., 1970.

KRENGEL, R., *Anlagevermögen, Produktion und Beschäftigung der Industrie im Gebiet der Bundesrepublik von 1924 bis 1956*, Duncker und Humblot, Berlin, 1958.

KRUGMANN, R. W., *Südosteuropa und Grossdeutschland. Entwicklung und Zukunftsmöglichkeiten der Wirtschaftsbeziehungen*, Breslauer Verlag, Breslau, 1939.

KULISCHER, E. M., *Europe on the Move: War and Population Changes 1917–1947*, Columbia University Press, New York, 1948.

KUZNETS, S., *National Product in Wartime* (N.B.E.R.), Princeton University Press, 1945.

KUZNETS, S., *Shares of Upper Income Groups in Income and Savings* (N.B.E.R., publication no. 55), Princeton University Press, 1953.

LANGLEY, K., 'The Distribution of Capital in Private Hands in 1936–8 and 1946–7', in *Bulletin of the Oxford University Institute of Statistics*, no. 13, 1951.

LAUFENBURGER, H., *Les Finances de 1939 à 1945*, Librairie de Médicis, Paris, 1948.

LEIGHTON, R. M., 'Les armes ou les armées? Origines de la

politique d' "Arsenal de la Démocratie" ', in *R.d.g.m.*, no. 65, 1967.

LEWIS, C., *Debtor and Creditor Countries 1938, 1944*, The Brookings Institution, Washington, D.C., 1945.

LIBAL, M., *Japans Weg in den Krieg. Die Aussenpolitik der Kabinette Konoye 1940/41*, Droste-Verlag, Düsseldorf, 1971.

LINDEMAN, J., 'The Armaments Program and National Income', in *American Economic Review*, no. 31, 1941.

LLOYD, E. M. H., *Food and Inflation in the Middle East 1940–45* (Food Research Institute Publications), Stanford University Press, 1956.

LONG, C. D., *The Labor Force in Wartime America*, N.B.E.R. (Occasional Papers, no. 14), 1944.

LONG, C. D., *The Labor Force in War and Transition – Four Countries*, N.B.E.R. (Occasional Papers no. 36), New York, 1952.

MCCURRACH, D. F., 'Britain's U.S. Dollar Problem, 1939–45', in *Economic Journal*, no. 58, 1948.

MARLIO, L., *A Short War through American Industrial Superiority*, The Brookings Institution, Washington, D.C., 1941.

DE MARSANICH, A., 'Unità economica dell'Europa', in *Economia fascista*, no. 17, 1940.

MARSCHNER, H., ed., *Deutschland in der Wirtschaft der Welt*, Deutscher Verlag für Politik und Wirtschaft, Berlin, 1937.

MARWICK, A., *Britain in the Century of Total War. War, Peace and Social Change 1900–1967*, Bodley Head, London, 1968.

MASAO, M., *Thought and Behaviour in Modern Japanese Politics*, Oxford University Press, London, 1963.

MASON, T. W., 'Innere Krise und Angriffskrieg 1938/1939', in F. Forstmeier und H. E. Volkmann, eds., *Wirtschaft und Rüstung am Vorabend des zweiten Weltkrieges*, Droste, Düsseldorf, 1975.

MEADE, J. E., *The Economic Basis of a Durable Peace*, Oxford University Press, London, 1940.

MEDICI, G., and others, *Die italienische Landwirtschaft* (Reichs- und Preussisches Ministerium für Ernährung- und Landwirtschaft, – Berichte über Landwirtschaft, no. 149), Berlin, 1940.

MEDLICOTT, W. N., *The Economic Blockade*, 2 vols., H.M.S.O., London, 1952, 1959.

MELLOR, D. F., *The Role of Science and Industry*, Australian War Memorial, Canberra, 1958.

MILWARD, A. S., 'Fritz Todt als Minister für Bewaffnung und Munition', in *Vj.f.Z.*, no. 14, 1966.

MILWARD, A. S., 'The End of the Blitzkrieg', in *Economic History Review*, no. 16, 1964.

MILWARD, A. S., *The German Economy at War*, Athlone Press, London, 1965; translated into German as *Die deutsche Kriegswirtschaft 1939–1945* (Schriftenreihe der *Vj.f.Z.*, no. 12), Deutsche Verlage-Anstalt, 1966.

MILWARD, A. S., 'Could Sweden have Stopped the Second World War?', in *Scandinavian Economic History Review*, no. 15, 1967.

MILWARD, A. S., 'German Economic Policy towards France 1942–1944', in K. Bourne and D. C. Watt, *Studies in International History*, Longmans, London, 1967.

MILWARD, A. S., 'French Labour and the German Economy, 1942–45: An Essay on the Nature of the Fascist New Order', in *Economic History Review*, no. 23, 1970.

MILWARD, A. S., *The New Order and the French Economy*, Oxford University Press, London, 1970.

MILWARD, A. S., *The Fascist Economy in Norway*, Clarendon Press, Oxford, 1972.

MITZAKIS, M., *Principaux Aspects de l'évolution financière de la France 1936–44*, Les Publications Techniques, Paris, 1945.

DE MOLINARI, M. G., *Comment se résoudra la question sociale,?* Guillaumin, Paris, 1896.

DE MOLINARI, M. G., *Grandeur et décadence de la guerre*, Guillaumin, Paris, 1898.

DE MOLINARI, M. G., *Esquisse de l'organisation politique et économique de la société future*, Guillaumin, Paris, 1899.

MOORE, G. H., *Production of Industrial Materials in World War I and II*, N.B.E.R. (Occasional Paper, no. 18), New York, 1944.

MORSOMME, A., *Anatomie de la guerre totale*, Pierre de Meyère, Brussels, 1971.

MUNZ, A., *Die Auswirkungen der deutschen Besetzung auf Währung und Finanzen Frankreichs*, Veröffentlichungen des Instituts für Besatzungsfragen, no. 9, Tübingen, 1957.

MURRAY, K. A. H., *Agriculture*, H.M.S.O., London, 1955.

NELSON, D. M., *The Arsenal of Democracy*, Harcourt Brace, New York, 1946.

NICHOLSON, J. L., 'Employment and National Income during the War', in *Bulletin of the Oxford University Institute of Statistics*, no. 7, 1945.

NOVE, A., *An Economic History of the U.S.S.R.*, Penguin Books, Harmondsworth, 1969.

NOVICK, D., ANSHEN, M., and TRUPPNER, W. C., *Wartime Production Controls*, Columbia University Press, New York, 1949.

OLSON, M., jr, *The Economics of the Wartime Shortage. A History of British Food Supplies in the Napoleonic War and in World Wars I and II*, Duke University Press, Durham, N.C., 1963.

OLSSON, S.-O., *German Coal and Swedish Fuel 1939–1945* (Publications of the Institute of Economic History of Gothenburg University, 36), Kungsbacka, Gothenburg, 1975.

OLSSON, U., *Upprustning och verkstadsindustri i Sverige under det andra världskriget* (Publications of the Institute of Economic History of Gothenburg University, 28), Kungsbacka, Gothenburg, 1973.

PARIS EGUILAZ, H., *Diez años de politica economica en España 1939–1949*, J. Sanchez Ocaña, Madrid, 1949.

PARKER, H. M. D., *Manpower*, H.M.S.O., London, 1957.

PARKINSON, J. F., ed., *Canadian War Economics*, University of Toronto Press, Toronto, 1941.

PETZINA, D., *Autarkiepolitik im Dritten Reich. Der nationalsozialistische Vierjahresplan* (Schriftenreihe der *Vj.f.Z.*, no. 16), Deutsche Verlags-Anstalt, Stuttgart, 1968.

PETZINA, D., 'Grundriss der deutschen Wirtschaftsgeschichte 1918 bis 1945' in Institut für Zeitgeschichte, *Deutsche Geschichte seit dem ersten Weltkrieg*, vol. 2, Deutsche Verlags-Anstalt, Stuttgart, 1973.

PETZINA, D., 'La politique financière et fiscale de l'Allemagne', in *R.d.g.m.*, no 76, 1969.

PFAHLMANN, H., *Fremdarbeiter und Kriegsgefangene in der deutschen Kriegswirtschaft 1939–1945* (Beiträge zur Wehrforschung, vol. XVI/XVII), Wehr und Wissen Verlagsgesellschaft, Darmstadt, 1968.

PHELPS, R. H., 'Hitler als Parteiredner im Jahre 1920', in *Vj.f.Z.*, no. 11, 1963.

PIATIER, A., 'La vie économique de la France sous l'occupation', in *La France sous l'occupation* (Esprit de la Résistance), P.U.F., Paris, 1959.

Political and Economic Planning, *Britain and World Trade*, P.E.P., London, 1947.

POSTAN, M. M., *British War Production*, H.M.S.O., London, 1952.

POSTAN, M. M., HAY, D., and SCOTT, J. D., *Design and Development of Weapons*, H.M.S.O., London, 1964.

PREST, A. R., *War Economics of Primary Producing Countries*, Cambridge University Press, 1948.

PROKOPOVITCH, S., *Histoire économique de l'U.R.S.S.*, Flammarion, Paris, 1952.

RADANDT, H., *Kriegsverbrecherkonzern Mansfeld. Die Rolle des Mansfeld-Konzerns bei der Vorbereitung und während des zweiten Weltkrieges* (Geschichte der Fabriken und Werke, vol. 3), Akademie-Verlag, Berlin, 1957.

RADANDT, H., 'Die IG Farbenindustrie und Südosteuropa 1938 bis zum Ende des zweiten Weltkrieges', in *Jahrbuch für Wirtschaftsgeschichte*, no. 1, 1967.

RAUSCHNING, H., *The Beast from the Abyss*, Heinemann, London, 1941.

REITLINGER, G., *The Final Solution*, Valentine, Mitchell, London, 1953.

RENTROP, W., and KAYSER, H., *Preispolitik und Preisüberwachung in Europa*, C. H. Beck, Munich, 1941.

Revue d'économie politique, 'La France économique de 1939 à 1946', numéros spéciaux, 2 vols., 1947.

RIEDEL, M., *Eisen und Kohle für das Dritte Reich: Paul Pleigers Stellung in der NS-Wirtschaft*, Musterschmidt, Göttingen, 1973.

RIEDEL, M., 'Die Eisenerzversorgung der deutschen Hüttenindustrie zu Beginn des Zweiten Weltkrieges, in *Vierteljahrschrift für Sozial- und Wirtschaftsgeschichte*, no. 58, 1971.

RIEDEL, M., 'Bergbau und Eisenhüttenindustrie in der Ukraine unter deutscher Besatzung (1941-1944)', in *Vj.f.Z.*, no. 21, 1973.

R.I.I.A., *The Economic Structure of Hitler's Europe* (Survey of International Affairs, 1939-1946), Oxford University Press, London, 1954.

RINGEL, K., *Frankreichs Wirtschaft im Umbruch*, Goldmann, Leipzig, 1942.

RIST, L., and SCHWOB, P., 'La balance des paiements', in *Revue d'économie politique*, no. 53, 1939.

ROLL, E., *The Combined Food Board* (Food Research Institute Publications), Stanford University Press, 1956.

ROSEN, J., *Wartime Food Developments in Switzerland* (Stanford Food Research Institute, Paper no. 9), Stanford University Press, 1946.

ROSEN, J., 'Die Entwicklung der Kriegsernährung in sieben europäischen Ländern 1939–1944. Der Verbrauch an Nährstoffen und Vitaminen', in *Schweizerische Medizinische Wochenschrift*, no. 31, 1945.

ROSENSTOCK-FRANCK, L., *Les Étapes de l'économie fasciste italienne: du corporatisme à l'économie de guerre*, Librairie Sociale et Économique, Paris, 1939.

RUMPF, H., *Das war der Bombenkrieg; deutsche Städte im Feuersturm ein Dokumentarbericht*, Gerhard Stalling, Oldenburg, 1961; trans. *The Bombing of Germany*, Frederick Muller, London, 1963.

RUNDELL, W., jr, *Black Market Money*, Louisiana University Press, Baton Rouge, 1964.

SARTI, R., *Fascism and the Industrial Leadership in Italy, 1919-1940. A Study in the Expansion of Private Power under Fascism*, University of California Press, Berkeley, 1971.

SAUNDERS, C. T., 'Manpower Distribution 1939–1945', in *The Manchester School of Economic and Social Studies*, no. 14, 1946.

SAUVY, A., 'Heurs et malheurs de la statistique', in *R.d.g.m.*, no. 57, 1965.

SAYERS, R. S., *Financial Policy*, H.M.S.O., London, 1956.

SCHECHTMAN, J. B., *European Population Transfers 1939-1945*, Oxford University Press, New York, 1946.

SCHOENBAUM, D., *Hitler's Social Revolution: Class and Status in Nazi Germany 1933-1939*, Weidenfeld & Nicolson, London, 1966.

SCHUMANN, W., 'Das Kriegsprogramm des Zeiss-Konzerns', in *Zeitschrift für Geschichtswissenschaft*, no. 11, 1963.

SCHWARZ, U., *Die schweizerische Kriegsfinanzierung 1939-1945 und ihre Ausstrahlungen in der Nachkriegszeit*, Keller, Wintherthur, 1953.

SCHWEITZER, A., 'The Role of Foreign Trade in the Nazi War Economy', in *Journal of Political Economy*, no. 51, 1943.

SEEBER, E., *Zwangsarbeiter in der faschistischen Kriegswirtschaft* (Schriftenreihe des Instituts für Geschichte der europäischen

Volksdemokratien, no. 3), Deutscher Verlag der Wissenschaften, Berlin, 1964.

SEERS, D., *Changes in the Cost of Living and the Distribution of Income since 1938*, Clarendon Press, Oxford, 1949.

SEIDMAN, J., *American Labor from Defense to Reconversion*, University of Chicago Press, 1953.

SHANNON, H. A., 'The Sterling Balances of the Sterling Area', in *Economic Journal*, no. 60, 1950.

SHILS, E. A., 'Social and Psychological Aspects of Displacement and Repatriation', in *Journal of Social Issues*, no. 2, 1946.

SINGER, J. D., and SMALL, M., *The Wages of War 1816–1965, A Statistical Handbook*, Wiley, New York, 1972.

SMITH, R. E., *The Army and Economic Mobilization* (United States Army in World War II, Office of the Chief of Military History), G.P.O., Washington, D.C., 1959.

SMITH, R. E., 'La mobilisation économique', in *R.d.g.m.*, no. 66, 1967.

SÖLTER, A., *Das Grossraumkartell. Ein Instrument der industriellen Marktordnung im neuen Europa*, Meinhold, Dresden, 1941.

SOMERS, H. M., *Presidential Agency: The Office of War Mobilization and Reconversion*, Harvard University Press, Cambridge, Mass., 1950.

SORLIN, P., *La Société soviétique, 1917–1964*, Armand Colin, Paris, 1964.

SPEER, A., *Erinnerungen*, Ullstein, Berlin, 1969.

SPEIER, H., 'Class Structure and "Total War" ', in *American Sociological Review*, no. 4, 1939.

SPEIER, H., 'Effect of War on the Social Order', in *Annals of the American Academy of Political Science*, no. 218, 1941.

SPLETTSTOESSER, J., *Der deutsche Wirtschaftsraum im Osten*, Limpert, Berlin, 1939.

STEINWEG, G., *Die deutsche Handelsflotte im Zweiten Weltkrieg*, O. Schwartz, Göttingen, 1954.

STERN, F., *The Politics of Cultural Despair*, University of California Press, Berkeley, 1961.

STERNBERG, F., *Die deutsche Kriegsstärke*, Sebastian Brant, Paris, 1938; trans. *Germany and a Lightning War*, Faber & Faber, London, 1938.

STETTINIUS, E. R., jr, *Lend-Lease, Weapon for Victory*, Macmillan, London, 1944.

STIMSON, H. L., 'The Decision to Use the Atomic Bomb', in *Harper's Magazine*, February, 1947.

STRASSER, O., *The Gangsters around Hitler*, W. H. Allen, London, 1940.

STRENG, H. VON, *Die Landwirtschaft im Generalgouvernement*, Veröffentlichungen des Instituts für Besatzungsfragen, no. 6, Tübingen, 1955.

Switzerland, Département fédéral de l'économie publique, *l'Économie de guerre en Suisse 1939/48*, Bern, 1951.

TAEUBER, I. B., *The Population of Japan*, Princeton University Press, 1958.

TEDDER, Lord, *Air Power in War* (The Lees-Knowles Lectures), Hodder & Stoughton, London, 1948.

THOMAS, G., *Geschichte der deutschen Wehr- und Rüstungswirtschaft (1918-1943/45)* (Schriften des Bundesarchivs, no. 14), Boppard am Rhein, 1966.

THOMSON, H. C., and MAYO, L., *The Ordnance Dept.: Procurement and Supply*, United States Army in World War Two, G.P.O., Washington, D. C., 1950.

TITMUSS, R. H., *Problems of Social Policy*, H.M.S.O., London, 1950.

TRUELLE, J., 'La production aéronautique militaire française jusqu'en juin 1940', in *R.d.g.m.*, no 73, 1969.

ULSHÖFER, O., *Einflussnahme auf Wirtschaftsunternehmungen in den besetzten nord-, west-, und südosteuropäischen Ländern während des Zweiten Weltkrieges insbesondere der Erwerb von Beteiligungen (Verflechtung)*, Veröffentlichungen des Instituts für Besatzungsfragen, no. 15, Tübingen, 1958.

United Kingdom, Ministry of Health, *On the State of the Public Health during Six Years of War*, H.M.S.O., London, 1946.

United Nations, Department of Economic Affairs, *Salient Features of the World Economic Situation 1945-47*, Lake Success, 1948.

United States, Bureau of the Budget, *The United States at War. Development and Administration of the War Program by the Federal Government*, G.P.O., Washington, D.C., 1946.

United States, Civilian Production Administration, *Industrial Mobilization for War. History of the War Production Board and Predecessor Agencies 1940-45*, G.P.O., Washington, D.C., 1947.

United States, National Resources Planning Board, *After Defense – What?*, G.P.O., Washington, D.C., 1941.

United States, National Resources Planning Board, *Post-War Agenda: Full Employment, Security, Building America*, G.P.O., Washington, D.C., 1942.

United States, Office of Air Force History, *The Army Air Forces in World War II*, University of Chicago Press, Chicago, 1948.

VAIL MOTTER, T. H., *The Persian Corridor and Aid to Russia* (The United States Army in World War Two), G.P.O., Washington, D.C., 1952.

VANDERLINT, J., *Money Answers All Things, or an Essay . . . shewing the Absurdity of going to War about Trade . . .* ed. J. H. Hollander, Baltimore, 1910 (first published London, 1734).

VIDALENC, J., *L'Exode de mai–juin 1940*, P.U.F., Paris, 1957.

VINCENT, J., 'Conséquences de six années de guerre sur la population française', in *Population*, no. 3, 1946.

VOZNESENSKII, N. A., *The Economy of the USSR during World War II*, Public Affairs Press, Washington, D.C., 1948.

WAGENFÜHR, R., *Die Flugzeugindustrie der Anderen* (Schriften des Instituts für Konjunkturforschung, Sonderheft 46), Hanseatische Verlagsanstalt, Hamburg and Berlin, 1939.

WALKER, E. R., *The Australian Economy in War and Reconstruction*, Oxford University Press, New York, 1947.

WEBER, E., *Varieties of Fascism. Doctrines of Revolution in the Twentieth Century*. Van Nostrand, Princeton, 1964.

WEBSTER, Sir C., and FRANKLAND, N., *The Strategic Air Offensive against Germany, 1939–1945*, 4 vols., H.M.S.O., London, 1961.

WEINMANN, M., *Die Landwirtschaft in Frankreich während des zweiten Weltkrieges unter dem Einfluss der deutschen Besatzungsmacht*, Veröffentlichungen des Instituts für Besatzungsfragen, no. 20, Tübingen, 1961.

WELK, W. G., *Fascist Economic Policy. An Analysis of Italy's Economic Experiment* (Harvard Economic Studies, no. 62), Harvard University Press, Cambridge, Mass., 1938.

WELTER, E., *Falsch und richtig Planen. Eine kritische Studie über die deutsche Wirtschaftslenkung im zweiten Weltkrieg*, Veröffentlichung des Forschungsinstituts für Wirtschaftspolitik an der Universität Mainz, no. 1, Heidelberg, 1954.

WHETHAM, E., *British Farming 1939–49*, Nelson, London, 1952.

WILCOX, W. W., *The Farmer in the Second World War*, Iowa State College Press, Ames, 1947.

WILSON, G. M., 'A New Look at the Problem of "Japanese Fascism" ', in *Comparative Studies in Society and History*, no. 10, Cambridge University Press, 1968.

WIPPERMANN, W., *Faschismustheorien. Zum Stand der gegenwärtigen Diskussion*, Wissenschaftliche Buchgesellschaft, Darmstadt, 1972.

WOERMANN, E., *Die europäische Ernährungswirtschaft in Zahlen*, Nova Acta Leopoldina, no. 14, Berlin, 1944.

WORSLEY, T. B., 'La stabilisation économique', in *R.d.g.m.*, no. 66, 1967.

WRIGHT, G., *The Ordeal of Total War 1939–1945* (The Rise of Modern Europe Series), Harper & Row, New York, 1968.

ZAGOROFF, S., VEGH, J., and BILIMOVICH, A., *The Agricultural Economy of the Danubian Countries, 1935–1945* (Food Research Institute Publications), Stanford University Press, Stanford, 1955.

ZECK, H. F., *Die deutsche Wirtschaft und Südosteuropa*, Teubner, Leipzig, 1939.

Index